...ogramming

Your visual blueprint™ ... interactive spreadsheets, 3rd Edition

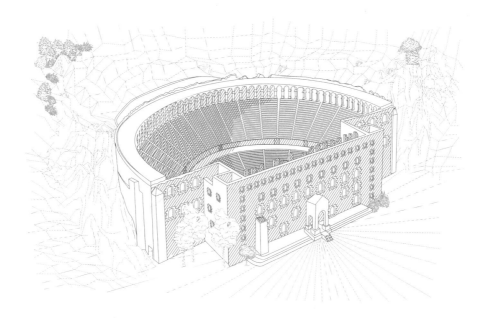

by Denise Etheridge

WILEY

Wiley Publishing, Inc.

Excel® Programming: Your visual blueprint™ for creating interactive spreadsheets, 3rd Edition

Published by
Wiley Publishing, Inc.
10475 Crosspoint Boulevard
Indianapolis, IN 46256

www.wiley.com

Published simultaneously in Canada

Library of Congress Control Number: 2010929410

ISBN: 978-0-470-59159-8

Manufactured in the United States of America

10 9 8 7 6 5 4 3 2 1

Trademark Acknowledgments

Contact Us

For general information on our other products and services please contact our Customer Care Department within the U.S. at 877-762-2974, outside the U.S. at 317-572-3993 or fax 317-572-4002.

For technical support please visit www.wiley.com/techsupport.

The Roman Theater of Aspendos

Built when Marcus Aurelius was Emperor of Rome (161–180 A.D.), this magnificent theater, faithful to the Greek tradition, nestles into the side of a hill. It is among the best preserved of its era, and concerts and operas are still performed upon its stage today. Its acoustics are quite literally legendary. A favorite story tells how the architect, Zeno, won the king's daughter by creating this masterpiece in which a word murmured from the stage could be heard throughout the arena.

Learn more about Aspendos and its artifacts in *Frommer's Turkey, 6th Edition* (ISBN 978-0-470-59366-0), available wherever books are sold or at www.Frommers.com.

Disclaimer

In order to get this information to you in a timely manner, this book was based on a pre-release version of Microsoft Office 2010. There may be some minor changes between the screenshots in this book and what you see on your desktop. As always, Microsoft has the final word on how programs look and function; if you have any questions or see any discrepancies, consult the online help for further information about the software.

WILEY

Sales

Contact Wiley
at (877) 762-2974
or (317) 572-4002.

Credits

Executive Editor
Jody Lefevere

Sr. Project Editor
Sarah Hellert

Technical Editor
Namir Shammas

Copy Editor
Scott Tullis

Editorial Director
Robyn Siesky

Editorial Manager
Rosemarie Graham

Business Manager
Amy Knies

Sr. Marketing Manager
Sandy Smith

Vice President and Executive Group Publisher
Richard Swadley

Vice President and Executive Publisher
Barry Pruett

Sr. Project Coordinator
Kristie Rees

Graphics and Production Specialists
Andrea Hornberger
Jennifer Mayberry
Heather Pope

Quality Control Technician
Jessica Kramer

Proofreader
Sossity R. Smith

Indexer
Slivoskey Indexing Services

Media Development Project Manager
Laura Moss

Media Development Assistant Project Manager
Jenny Swisher

Media Development Associate Producer
Marilyn Hummel

Screen Artists
Ana Carrillo
Jill A. Proll
Ron Terry

Illustrator
Cheryl Grubbs

About the Author

Denise Etheridge is a certified public accountant as well as the president and founder of Baycon Group, Inc. She publishes Web sites and authors computer related books. You can visit www.baycongroup.com to view her online tutorials.

Author's Acknowledgments

Writing this book was a pleasure. I would like to thank all of the people who assisted me. I give special thanks to Jody Lefevere, for allowing me this privilege; Sarah Hellert, for keeping things on track; Namir Shammas, for his technical review; and Scott Tullis, for his copy review.

Dedication

This book is dedicated to Raquel Etheridge.

How to Use This Visual Blueprint Book

Who This Book Is For

This book is for advanced computer users who want to take their knowledge of this particular technology or software application to the next level.

The Conventions in This Book

❶ Steps

This book uses a step-by-step format to guide you easily through each task. Numbered steps are actions you must do; bulleted steps clarify a point, step, or optional feature; and indented steps give you the result.

❷ Notes

Notes give additional information — special conditions that may occur during an operation, a situation that you want to avoid, or a cross reference to a related area of the book.

❸ Icons and Buttons

Icons and buttons show you exactly what you need to click to perform a step.

❹ Extra or Apply It

An Extra section provides additional information about the preceding task — insider information and tips for ease and efficiency. An Apply It section takes the code from the preceding task one step further and allows you to take full advantage of it.

❺ Bold

Bold type shows text or numbers you must type.

❻ Italics

Italic type introduces and defines a new term.

❼ Courier Font

`Courier font` indicates the use of scripting language code such as statements, operators, or functions, and code such as objects, methods, or properties.

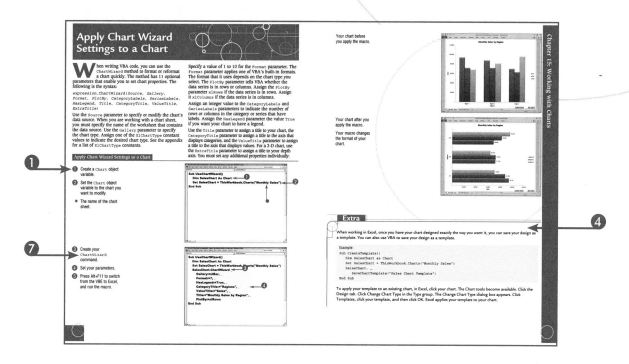

TABLE OF CONTENTS

TABLE OF CONTENTS

TABLE OF CONTENTS

Introducing Excel Programming

A s you probably know, Microsoft Excel is an electronic worksheet you can use for a variety of purposes, including the following: maintain lists; perform mathematical, financial, and statistical calculations; create charts; analyze your data with PivotTables; locate data; find trends in your data; and present your data to others.

This book is about automating the tasks you perform in Excel by using Visual Basic for Applications (VBA). You can use VBA to automate those repetitive tasks you perform frequently. For example, if the layout of your monthly report rarely changes, you can use VBA to set up your report each month.

VBA is a programming language; however, you do not have to be a programmer to automate the tasks you perform in Excel. You can also automate a task by using the macro recorder to create a macro. A macro is a

recording of the steps you want to automate. You just click a button to turn on the macro recorder and begin performing the steps as you normally would. Excel records each step and creates the VBA code. When you finish, you click the Stop Record button. When you select your macro in the Macro dialog box and then click the Run button, Excel plays back the steps you recorded. For example, if you record the steps necessary to set up your monthly report, all you have to do each month thereafter is click a button and Excel automatically sets up your report.

With VBA, you can do more than just create macros. You can use VBA to edit macros, create new functions, create custom applications, and create add-ins. For these tasks, you must learn the VBA programming language. This book teaches VBA. It is based on Office 2010. Code you write for Office 2010 may not be compatible with earlier versions of Excel.

Introducing Excel Programming

1 Click the Developer tab.

Note: See the section "Introducing Macros" to learn how to display the Developer tab.

    Use the options in the Code group to automate your tasks.

2 Click either of these Record Macro buttons to record a macro.

Note: See the section "Record a Macro" for more details.

3 Click Macros to run a macro.

Note: See the section "Run a Macro" for more details.

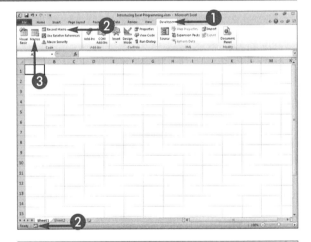

- Use the options in the Controls group to add check boxes, fields, and other form controls to your worksheet.

- Use the options in the XML group to work with XML.

4 Click Visual Basic or press Alt+F11.

    Excel moves to the Visual Basic for Applications Editor (VBE).

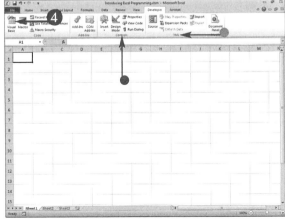

Use the VBE to write and edit code.

Note: *See Chapter 2 to learn more about the VBE.*

5 Click the proper module to access your macros or the VBA code you have written.

6 Type or edit your code here.

7 Press Alt+F11 to return to Excel.

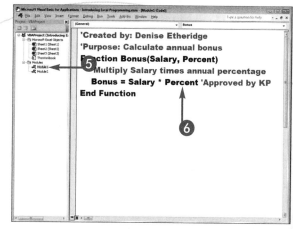

The VBE returns you to Excel.

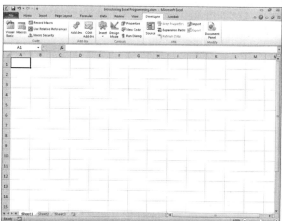

Extra

You can also use Microsoft Visual Studio Tools for the Microsoft Office System (Visual Studio) to develop programs for Microsoft Office products. With Visual Studio, you can write in languages such as Visual Basic .NET, Visual C#, and Managed Extensions for C++. Visual Studio is not part of Microsoft Office; you must purchase it. Microsoft supports both VBA and Visual Studio.

Visual Studio is more difficult to learn than VBA, and setting up and using Visual Studio is much more difficult than setting up and using VBA. However, Visual Studio offers better security, a more sophisticated development environment, and built-in Web services.

Introducing Macros

You can use macros to automate many of the tasks you perform in Excel. For example, if you frequently format your data in a particular way, you can use Excel's macro recorder to record the steps you use to format your data. You can then play back the recorded steps whenever you want to apply your format. Most of the commands you can execute in Excel, you can also record and play back.

The commands you use to create and execute macros are located on the Developer tab. By default, the Developer tab does not display in Excel. To display it, you must select Developer in the Customize the Ribbon pane in the Excel Options dialog box.

You begin recording macros by clicking Record Macro on the Developer tab or by clicking the Record Macro button

on the status bar. Both options open the Record Macro dialog box. For detailed instructions on how to use the Record Macro dialog box, see the section "Record a Macro."

When you record a macro, you can record it using an absolute reference or a relative reference. If you record using an absolute reference, when Excel plays back your macro, it plays back the exact cells you clicked when you recorded the macro. If you record using a relative reference, Excel plays back the relative location of the cells you used when you recorded your macro. Click Use Relative References on the Developer tab to record using a relative reference. To learn more about absolute and relative references, see the section "Record a Macro."

When you save a workbook that has macros, you must save it as a macro-enabled workbook. Excel gives macro-enabled workbooks an .xlsm extension.

Introducing Macros

① Click the File tab.

A menu appears.

② Click Options.

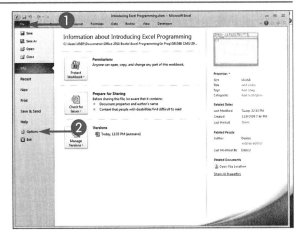

The Excel Options dialog box appears.

③ Click Customize Ribbon.

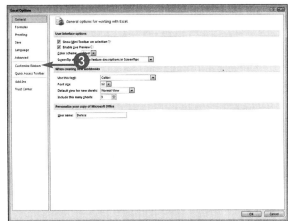

The Customize the Ribbon pane appears.

④ Click the down arrow and then select Main Tabs.

⑤ Click Developer (☐ changes to ☑).

⑥ Click OK.

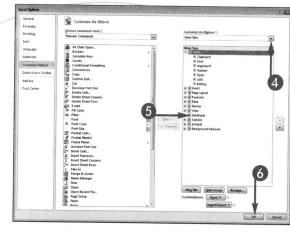

● The Developer tab appears on the Ribbon.

● Click Record Macro to record a macro.

● Click Use Relative References to record with a relative reference.

● Click Macro Security to change macro security.

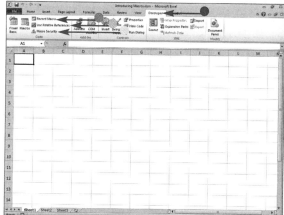

Extra

Because of problems with macro viruses, by default Excel disables all macros when you open a workbook. You can read the file, but you cannot execute the macros. You can click Macro Security on the Developer tab to change the default setting, or you can click the Enable Content button that appears when you open the workbook to enable the macros. To learn more about macro security, see the sections "Set Macro Security," "Create a Digital Signature," and "Assign a Digital Signature to a Macro" in this chapter.

To save a workbook that has macros, click the File tab. A menu appears. Click Save As. The Save As dialog box appears. Locate the proper folder. Type a filename in the File Name field. Select Excel Macro-Enabled Workbook (*.xlsm) in the Save As Type field. Click Save. Excel saves your workbook as a macro-enabled workbook and gives the workbook an .xlsm extension.

Set Macro Security

Because of increasing problems with computer viruses, specifically macro viruses, the default Excel macro security setting disables all macros when you open a workbook and enables you to decide on a case-by-case basis whether you want to enable them. This is true whether you created the macros or someone else created them. You can change the Excel macro security by choosing one of four options.

The Disable All Macros without Notification option disables all macros. This option does not provide you with any security alerts to let you know macros exist.

The Disable All Macros with Notification option is the default setting. It notifies you if macros are present so you can enable them on a case-by-case basis.

The Disable All Macros except Digitally Signed Macros option disables all macros except those digitally signed by a trusted publisher. If the publisher has digitally signed

the macro but you have not opted to trust the publisher, you can enable the macro or trust the publisher. See the Extra section of "Assign a Digital Signature to a Macro" in this chapter to learn how to trust a publisher.

The Enable All Macros (Not Recommended; Potentially Dangerous Code Can Run) option enables you to run all macros. Because potentially dangerous code can run, Microsoft does not recommend this option.

Changes you make to macro security in Excel do not change the macro security in other Office programs.

Macro creators use digital signatures to verify the safety of the macros they create. You can create a digital signature by using the Digital Certificate for VBA Projects tool, or you can obtain a digital certificate from a commercial certification authority. For more information on the Digital Certificate for VBA Projects tool, see the next section, "Create a Digital Signature."

Set Macro Security

1 Click the Developer tab.

Note: See the section "Introducing Macros" to learn how to display the Developer tab.

2 Click Macro Security.

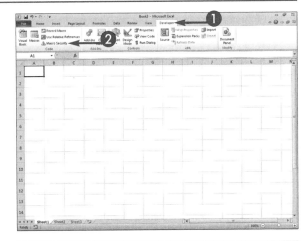

The Trust Center dialog box appears.

3 Click a macro security setting (○ changes to ◉).

4 Click OK.

Excel changes your macro security setting.

Create a Digital Signature

I f you create a workbook that contains macros, you should consider using a digital signature. A digital signature provides assurance that no one has altered the macro. You can create a personal digital signature by using the Digital Certificate for VBA Projects tool. Digital signatures created with the Digital Certificate for VBA Projects tool work only on the computer on which the digital signature was created.

If you plan to distribute your workbook to others, you should consider acquiring a commercial digital signature. When you use a commercial digital signature, the digital ID attaches to the macro and

remains with it; if anyone alters the macro, Excel notifies the user that the macro should not be trusted. The most common provider of commercial digital certification is VeriSign, Inc. To obtain a commercial certification, you must submit an application and pay a fee. You can find out more at www.verisign.com.

To view the certificates in your Personal Certificate store, open Windows Internet Explorer. On the Internet Explorer menu, click Tools and then click Internet Options. The Internet Options dialog box appears. Click the Content tab. Click the Certificates button. The Certificates dialog box appears. Click the Personal tab. All of your personal certificates appear.

Create a Digital Signature

1. Click the Start button.

2. Click All Programs.

3. Click Microsoft Office.

4. Click Microsoft Office Tools.

5. Click Digital Certificate for VBA Projects.

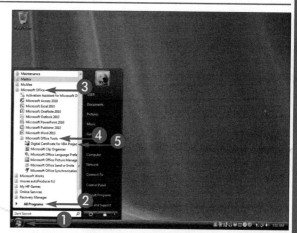

The Create Digital Certificate dialog box appears.

6. Type the name you want to give your certificate.

7. Click OK.

Excel creates a Personal Digital Certificate.

Record a Macro

A macro enables you to automate common tasks. You can use a macro to record most of the series of commands you can execute in Excel. For example, if you frequently apply a certain format to your worksheet, you can record the steps for creating the format and then play them back each time you want to apply the format.

Clicking the Macro Recorder button opens the Record Macro dialog box. You can use the Record Macro dialog box to name your macro, assign your macro to a shortcut key, and tell Excel where you want to store your macro. You can name your macro anything you want; however, the name must start with a letter; only contain letters, numbers, and underscores; and not contain any spaces.

You can assign any upper- or lowercase letter to act as the shortcut key.

In the Record Macro dialog box, the Store Macro In field tells Excel where to store your macro. You can choose to store your macro in the Personal Macro Workbook, a New Workbook, or This Workbook. Use the Personal Macro Workbook option if you want to make your macro available to all Excel files. After you have stored at least one macro in the Personal Macro Workbook, the workbook opens whenever you open an Excel file. Use the New Workbook option if you have specialized macros that you want to use with multiple files. If you store your macro in a New Workbook, you can use the macros whenever that workbook is open. Use the This Workbook option if you want to store your macro in the workbook in which you are currently working.

Record a Macro

1. Click the Developer tab.

   Note: See the section "Introducing Macros" to learn how to display the Developer tab.

   - Alternatively, click the Record Macro button on the status bar and skip Step 2.

2. Click Record Macro.

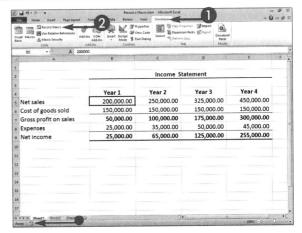

   The Record Macro dialog box appears.

3. Type the name you want to give your macro.

4. Type the shortcut key you want to assign to your macro.

   Press Shift as you type to assign an uppercase key.

5. Click the down arrow and then select the workbook in which you want to store your macro.

6. Type a description of your macro.

7. Click OK.

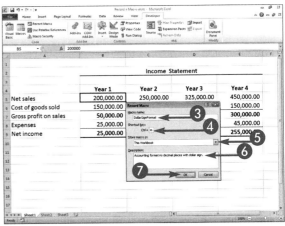

8 Perform the steps you want to record.

Note: This example changes the number format using the following steps. Click the Home tab. Click the Number Group launcher. Click Accounting. Set Decimal Place to 0. Select $ as Symbol. Click OK.

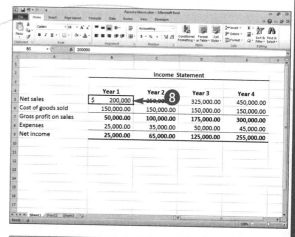

9 Click the Developer tab.

● Alternatively, click the Stop Recording button on the status bar and skip Step 10.

10 Click Stop Recording.

Excel stops recording your macro.

Your macro is ready for you to use.

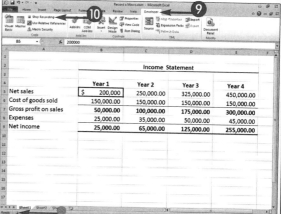

Extra

A macro you create in Excel can have a relative, an absolute, or a mixed reference. If you use a relative reference, Excel performs the macro based on a relative location. For example, suppose you move up two cells from cell A3 to cell A1 when creating your macro. When you run your macro, if you are in cell C3, Excel moves up two cells from cell C3 to cell C1. If you use an absolute reference, however, Excel performs the macro based on the exact cell addresses. For example, suppose again that you move up two cells from cell A3 to A1. When you run your macro, if you are in cell C3, Excel moves from there to the cells you used when you recorded your macro. That is, Excel moves from cell A3 to cell A1.

By default, Excel creates macros with an absolute reference. To create a macro with a relative reference, click Use Relative References in the Code group on the Developer tab to toggle the relative reference option on. To create a macro with both a relative and an absolute reference — a mixed reference — toggle the Use Relative References button on and off as needed as you create your macro.

Assign a Digital Signature to a Macro

A digital signature provides assurance that a workbook file that contains macros is valid and no one has altered the macros. There are two types of digital signatures: personal digital signatures and commercial digital signatures. You can create a personal digital signature by using the Digital Certificate for VBA Projects tool, or you can purchase a digital signature. Refer to the section "Create a Digital Signature" to learn how to create a personal digital signature. After you create a digital signature, you must attach it to your workbook. Attaching a digital signature is similar to sealing an envelope. If an envelope arrives sealed, you have some level of assurance that no one has tampered with its contents.

Use the Digital Signature dialog box to attach a digital signature. The Visual Basic Editor (VBE) is a separate Excel module that you can use to edit your macros.

Access the Digital Signature dialog box by opening the VBE. The Digital Signature dialog box lists valid certificates. You can use the Digital Signature dialog box to view certificates and to select the one you want to use.

Unless you have on your computer a valid digital signature certificate for the signature used to sign a macro, Excel removes the digital signature when you modify a macro and you must reattach it. If you are not sure if a workbook has a digital signature, you can check the signature by reviewing the Digital Signature dialog box. If a workbook has a digital signature, the name of the signature appears in the Certificate Name field. If you click the Remove button in the Digital Signature dialog box, Excel removes the digital signature.

Assign a Digital Signature to a Macro

1 Click the Developer tab.

Note: See the section "Introducing Macros" to learn how to display the Developer tab.

2 Click Visual Basic in the Code group.

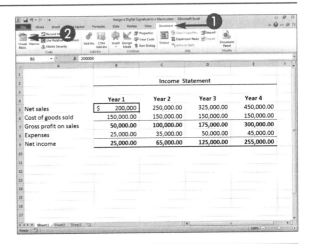

The Visual Basic Editor appears.

3 Click Tools → Digital Signature.

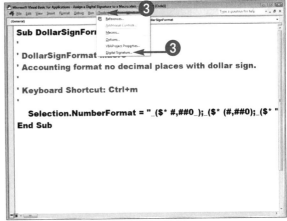

The Digital Signature dialog box appears.

④ Click Choose.

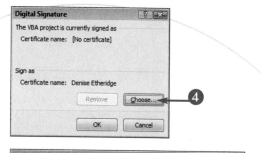

The Select Certificate dialog box appears.

Note: *See the section "Create a Digital Signature" to learn how to create a digital signature.*

⑤ Click the signature you want to apply.

⑥ Click OK to close the Select Certificate dialog box.

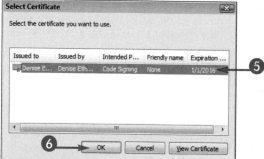

⑦ Click OK to close the Digital Signature dialog box.

Excel attaches the digital signature to your workbook.

Note: *To return to Excel, press Alt+Q.*

Extra

If you have Macro Security enabled, Excel displays the Trust Bar below the Ribbon when you open a workbook containing a signed macro. You can modify the workbook, but you cannot use the macros. If you trust that the document is safe, you can click the Enable Content button on the Trust Bar to enable the macros in the workbook. The workbook then becomes a trusted document and you will not need to enable the workbook again.

You can use the Microsoft Office Security Options dialog box to select the security option you want. On the Trust Bar, click Macros Have Been Disabled. Security warning options appear. Click the Enable Content button. A menu appears. Click Advanced Options. The Microsoft Office Security Options dialog box appears. Click Help Protect Me from Unknown Content (Recommended) to disable the macros; click Enable the Content for This Session to enable the macros for one session; or click Trust All Documents from This Publisher to add the macro publisher to the Trusted Publisher list. Excel does not display a warning when you open workbooks with macros if the publisher is on the Trusted Publisher list.

Run a Macro

Macros enable you to quickly perform tasks that would normally take multiple steps. When you run a macro, Excel replays the steps you recorded when you created the macro. You can run any macro located in any workbook as long as the workbook in which the macro is located is open. To run a macro, you can press the shortcut key you assigned when you created the macro, or you can select the macro from the Macro dialog box.

When you create a macro, you can choose to store it in one of three locations: the current workbook, a new workbook, or the Personal Macro Workbook. By default, the Macro dialog box lists all the macros in open workbooks. If a macro is stored in the Personal Macro Workbook, the macro opens as a hidden file each time

you open a file. By default, the files in the Personal Macro Workbook always appear in the Macro dialog box.

You can use the Macros In field to limit the number of macros listed in the Macro dialog box. To see the macros in any open workbook, including the Personal Macro Workbook, select All Open Workbooks from the Macros In drop-down list. To see the macros from a specific workbook, select the name of the workbook from the Macros In drop-down list. To see global macros stored in the Personal Macro Workbook, select PERSONAL.XLSB from the Macros In drop-down list.

To run macros from another workbook, the macro must be from a signed source or you must enable the macros. You can set the security setting for macros. See the section "Set Macro Security" to learn more about macro security.

Run a Macro

① Select the cells where you want to apply your macro.

② Click the Developer tab.

Note: *See the task "Introducing Macros" to learn how to display the Developer tab.*

③ Click Macros.

Alternatively, press Alt+F8.

The Macro dialog box appears.

④ If your macro does not appear in the Macro dialog box, click the down arrow and then select the workbook that contains your macro.

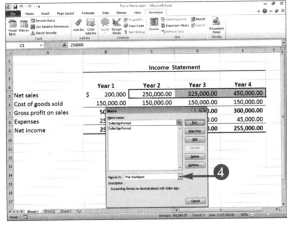

5 Click the name of the macro you want to run.

6 Click Run.

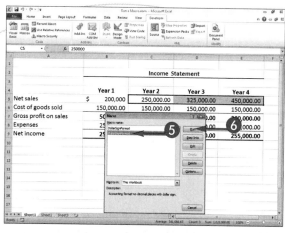

● Excel runs the macro.

You can also run your macro by pressing the shortcut key you assigned when you created the macro.

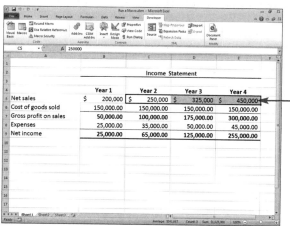

Extra

Excel differentiates between macros listed in the Macro dialog box by placing the name of the workbook that contains the macros in front of the macro name. For example, Excel lists a macro named Sum_Expenses in the Personal Macro Workbook as PERSONAL. XLSB!Sum_Expenses. If the macro Sum_Cells exists in both the Budget.xlsm and Expenses.xlsm workbooks, Excel treats them as two different macros. The Macro dialog box lists them as Budget.xlsm!Sum_Cells and Expenses.xlsm!Sum_Cells.

Unless you have your macro settings set to enable all macros, Excel checks all documents you open for macros. See the section "Set Macro Security" for more information. If you have files that you do not want Excel to check, you can store them in a trusted location. Click the Developer tab. Click Macro Security in the Code group. The Trust Center appears. Click Trusted Locations. The Trust Location pane appears. Click Add New Location. The Microsoft Office Trusted Location dialog box appears. Enter the path to the trusted location. Click OK.

Create and Launch a Keyboard Shortcut

A keyboard shortcut is a combination of keys you press to execute a command. You can use a keyboard shortcut to launch an Excel macro command. You can assign an upper- or lowercase key to a macro when you create it or assign one later by using the Macro Options dialog box. You execute a macro keyboard shortcut by pressing the Ctrl key along with the assigned upper- or lowercase key. Refer to the section "Record a Macro" to learn how to create a macro.

Keyboard shortcuts are case sensitive. For example, Excel interprets a lowercase *m* and an uppercase *M* as two different keys. To execute a macro you have assigned to a lowercase letter, press Ctrl plus the letter; for example, Ctrl+m. To execute a macro you have assigned to an uppercase letter, press Ctrl and Shift plus the letter; for example, Ctrl+Shift+M.

If you give the same keyboard shortcut to macros in two different workbooks, you may execute the wrong macro if you use the shortcut while you have both workbooks open. Excel cannot discern from which workbook you want the macro. You can use the Macro Options dialog box to reassign one of the conflicting macros to a new key.

You should also be careful not to assign the macro to a keyboard shortcut that Excel uses. If you do, Excel executes your macro instead of the command it created. For example, by default, Ctrl+o opens the Open dialog box. If you assign *o* to a macro, your macro overrides Excel's assignment.

Create and Launch a Keyboard Shortcut

Create a Keyboard Shortcut

1. Press Alt+F8.

   The Macro dialog box appears.

2. Click the desired macro.

3. Click the Options button.

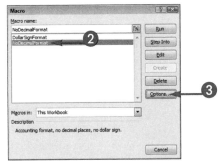

   The Macro Options dialog box appears.

4. Type the desired shortcut key.

   Press Shift as you type to assign an uppercase key.

5. Type a description.

6. Click OK to close the Macro Options dialog box.

7. Click Close to close the Macro dialog box.

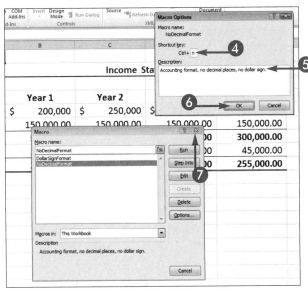

Launch a Keyboard Shortcut

1 Select the cells where you want the macro to execute.

2 Press Ctrl and the shortcut key.

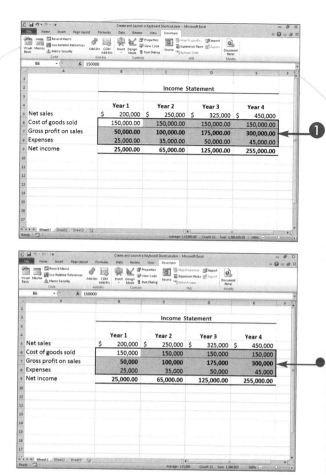

● The macro executes.

3 Repeat Steps 1 and 2 to execute the macro again.

Note: In this example, the macro removes the decimal places.

Extra

If you do not use a macro shortcut frequently, it is easy to forget the keyboard shortcut you assigned to your macro. If you forget your keyboard shortcut, you can view it in the Macro Options dialog box.

You can execute a macro by assigning the macro to a picture, clip art, a shape, or smart art. For example, if you want to assign a macro to a picture, you start by inserting the picture into your worksheet by clicking the Insert tab and then clicking Picture. The Insert Picture dialog box appears. In the Look In field, select the folder in which you stored the picture you want to insert. The pictures in that folder appear. Click the picture you want to insert and then click the Insert button. The picture appears in the worksheet. Click and drag the picture to place it where you want it and then double right-click the picture. A menu appears. Click Assign Macro. The Assign Macro dialog box appears. Click the macro you want to assign to the picture and then click OK. Excel assigns the macro to the picture. Click the picture when you want to execute the macro.

Assign a Macro to the Quick Access Toolbar

You can assign a macro to the Excel Quick Access toolbar. You can execute macros assigned to the Quick Access toolbar using a shortcut key or the Macro dialog box; however, using the Quick Access toolbar means you can access the macros by simply clicking the appropriate button.

When you add a button to the Quick Access toolbar, you can specify whether it should appear on the toolbar of all Excel workbooks or only on the Quick Access toolbar in the workbook you specify. By default, the button appears in all workbooks. If you have placed your macro in the Personal Macro Workbook, you probably want your macro button to appear in all workbooks because the macro is available to all workbooks. If your macro will be available only to a single workbook, your macro button should appear only on the Quick Access toolbar for that workbook.

You use the Customize the Quick Access Toolbar page of the Excel Options dialog box to add a macro button to the Quick Access toolbar. You can use the Modify button to specify the button you want to use to represent your macro. You can specify where on the Quick Access toolbar your button appears and whether the Quick Access toolbar appears above or below the Ribbon. You can click the Reset button to return the Quick Access toolbar to its default state.

Deleting a macro does not remove the macro button from the Quick Access toolbar. When you press the button for a deleted macro, you receive an error message. Use the Remove button on the Customize the Quick Access Toolbar page of the Excel Options dialog box to remove a macro button.

Assign a Macro to the Quick Access Toolbar

① Click the Customize Quick Access Toolbar button and then select More Commands.

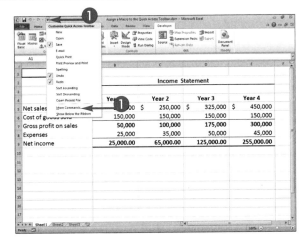

The Excel Options dialog box appears.

② Click the down arrow and then select Macros.

③ Click the down arrow and then select the workbook in which the button should appear.

④ Click the macro you want to assign to the Quick Access toolbar.

⑤ Click Add.

● The macro appears in the box on the right.

⑥ Click Modify.

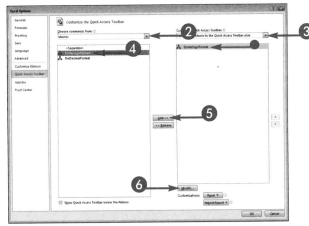

The Modify Button dialog box appears.

7 Click the button you want to use to represent your macro.

8 Click OK to close the Modify Button dialog box.

9 Click OK to close the Excel Options dialog box.

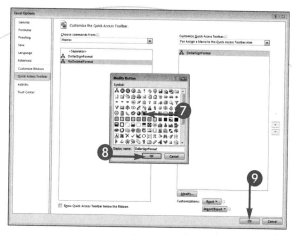

● The button appears on the Quick Access toolbar.

10 Click the button to execute your macro.

Excel executes the macro.

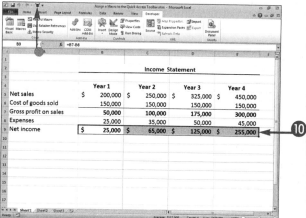

Extra

You can also assign a macro to a custom Ribbon tab. Right-click the Microsoft Office Ribbon. A menu appears. Click Customize the Ribbon. The Excel Options dialog box appears with the Customize the Ribbon pane selected. Click the down arrow (▼) next to the Choose Commands From field and then select Macros. Click the down arrow (▼) next to the Customize the Ribbon field and then select Main Tabs. Click the New Tab button. Excel creates a new tab and a new group. Click New Tab (Custom) and then click Rename. The Rename dialog box appears. Type the name you want to give the tab and then click OK. Click New Group (Custom) and then click Rename. The Rename dialog box appears. Type the name you want to give the group and then click OK. Click the macro you want to add to the custom Tab and then click the Add button. Excel places the macro in the Main Tabs box. Click Rename. The Rename dialog box appears. Click the symbol you want to use to represent the macro. Click OK to close the Rename dialog box. Click OK to close the Excel Options dialog box. The macro appears on the new tab you created.

Delete a Macro

Y ou can delete macros you no longer need by clicking the Delete button in the Macro dialog box. Because the Macro dialog box only displays macros in open workbooks, the workbook that contains the macro must be open before you can delete the macro.

The Personal Macro Workbook stores macros you want to make available to all workbooks. Excel creates the Personal Macro Workbook when you choose to store your first macro in it. After Excel creates the Personal Macro Workbook, the workbook opens as a hidden file every time you open Excel. To learn more about storing macros in the Personal Macro Workbook, see the section "Record a Macro."

If your macro is in a hidden workbook such as the Personal Macro Workbook, you must unhide the workbook before you can delete the macro. If you try to

delete a macro from the Personal Macro Workbook prior to unhiding it, Excel displays the following message: "Cannot edit a macro on a hidden workbook. Unhide the workbook using the Unhide command." You unhide the Personal Macro Workbook and other hidden workbooks by executing the Unhide command on the View tab.

If you unhide the Personal Macro Workbook, make sure you hide it again using the Hide command on the View tab after you delete the macros. Hiding the workbook prevents you from making inadvertent changes to it.

You cannot undo the deletion process. If you delete a macro by mistake, you can close the workbook without saving. Of course, if you close without saving, you will lose all the work you have done since saving. Your only other alternative is to re-create the macro.

Delete a Macro

Unhide a Workbook

① Click the View tab.

② Click Unhide.

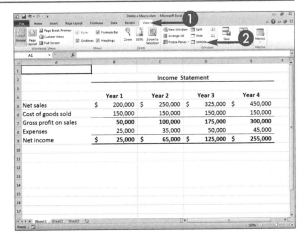

The Unhide dialog box appears.

③ Click the workbook you want to unhide.

④ Click OK.

Excel unhides the workbook.

You are now in the workbook you selected to unhide.

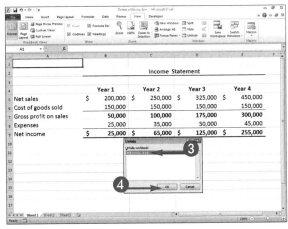

Delete a Macro

1 Press Alt+F8

The Macro dialog box appears.

2 Click the macro you want to delete.

3 Click Delete.

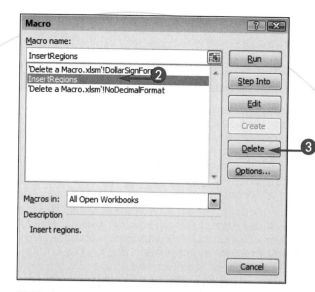

A message box appears, asking you to confirm you want to delete the macro.

4 Click Yes.

Excel deletes the macro.

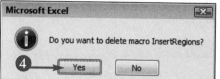

Extra

There are two ways to create a macro. One way is to use the macro recorder to record the steps needed to perform the action. The other way is to create the steps by typing the Visual Basic for Applications (VBA) code into the Code window of the Visual Basic Editor (VBE). When you use the macro recorder, Excel automatically creates the VBA code for you. You can use the VBE to edit macros you have created with the macro recorder. Often, it is convenient to use a combination of the two methods to create your VBA code: You record part of the VBA code, and then you use the VBE to augment or modify your code.

To activate the VBE, you can press Alt+F11 while in Excel or click the Visual Basic button on the Developer tab. If you create your macros using the macro recorder, Excel defines each macro you create as a procedure and stores each procedure in a module. The VBE lists modules in the Project Explorer under the workbook in which they are located.

Add a Form Control to a Worksheet

You can add controls to a worksheet to make it easier to enter data. Form controls can aid users who are not familiar with Excel and can increase the accuracy of data entry by limiting the options a user has. For example, you can add check boxes to your worksheet so your worksheet looks like a paper form. You can also add a combo box from which users can select an entry.

Excel provides nine controls you can add to a worksheet. You add controls by selecting the control you want from the Form Controls menu. After you add a control, you can adjust its size by dragging the side or corner handles. When you add a control or when you right-click a control twice and then click the control, you are in Design mode.

In Design mode, you can modify the properties and size of the control, but you cannot test its functionality.

When you place a control on a worksheet, it sits on top of the worksheet. You can size it so it appears to be located in a cell, but controls are separate from cells. You can place controls anywhere on the worksheet. A control can cover any portion of a cell or range of cells.

After you add a control to a worksheet, you can assign it values. See the next section, "Assign Values to a Form Control," to learn how. Form control options are located on the Developer tab. See the section "Introducing Macros" in this chapter to learn how to display the Developer tab.

Add a Form Control to a Worksheet

1 Click the Developer tab.

2 Click Insert.

The Form Controls menu appears.

3 Click to select the control you want.

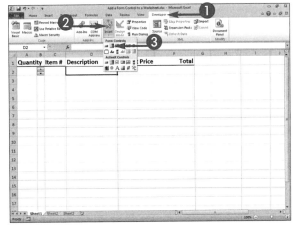

4 Click and drag the mouse pointer to create the control.

5 Click and drag the handles on the sides and corners to adjust the size.

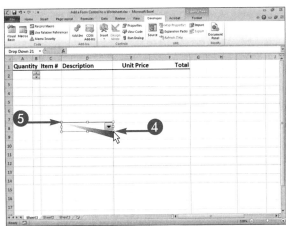

6 Place your mouse pointer on the control and when the mouse pointer turns into a four-sided arrow drag the control to change the location.

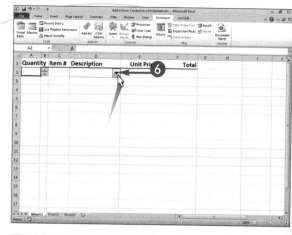

7 Right-click the control twice and then click it to place it in Design mode.

To cancel Design mode, click any cell in the worksheet.

To remove a control, place it in Design mode and then press Delete.

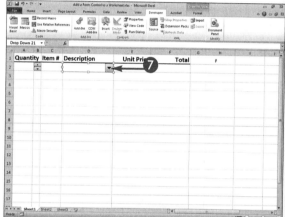

Extra

You can add the controls listed in the following table to your worksheets.

CONTROL	CONTROL NAME	DESCRIPTION
	Button	Runs an associated macro when clicked
	Combo box	A menu that displays a list of items
	Check box	Selects or deselects an option
	List box	Displays a list of items for selection
	Radio button	Selects one of a group of items
	Group box	Groups related controls, such as radio buttons, together
	Label	Provides information about an associated control
	Scroll bar	Increases or decreases a value when the user clicks the arrows or drags the bar
	Spinner	Scrolls up and down through a list of numeric values

Assign Values to a Form Control

After you add a control to a form, you can assign values to it. For example, if your worksheet contains a combo box, you can assign the list of values that appear when users access the combo box. Some controls enable you to define a range of valid numeric values for the control. For example, if you use a spinner, you can define the starting value and the maximum value for the control. For combo boxes and list boxes, you can place the options associated with the control in a range of cells. For example, if you use a combo box, you tell Excel the list of values used by the control by entering the range of cells containing the values. The values can be located on another worksheet or even in another workbook, as long as Excel can access the workbook when users view the worksheet that contains the control.

You can link a cell to a control. If you link a cell to a control, whatever value users select when utilizing the control becomes the value in the linked cell. If you use a combo box control or list box control, the value in the linked cell is a number that represents the user's selection. Excel assigns the number based on the position of the selected value in your list. If the list is Computer, Monitor, Keyboard, and the user selects Monitor, the linked cell receives the value 2, because Monitor is second in the list.

With a control, such as a check box, you can tell Excel whether you want the option initially selected or unselected. Both options — selected and unselected — have an associated value.

Assign Values to a Form Control

1 Right-click the control twice.

A menu appears.

2 Click Format Control.

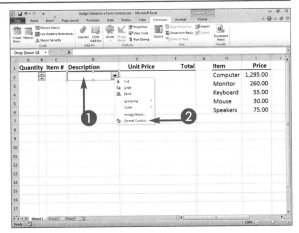

The Format Object dialog box appears.

3 Click the Control tab.

The available fields depend on the control type. This example uses a combo box.

4 Enter the range that lists the valid values.

5 Enter a cell to assign a linked cell.

6 Enter the number of items in your drop-down list.

The value associated with your selection appears in the linked cell.

7 Click OK.

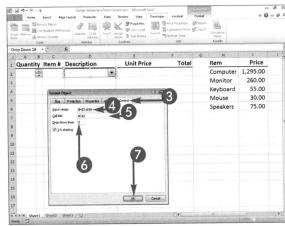

8 Click the down arrow and then select the desired control value.

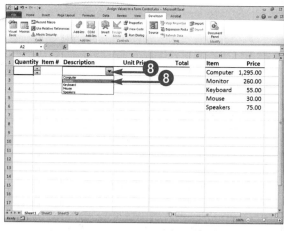

● Excel selects the value and places a numeric value representing the control selection in the linked cell.

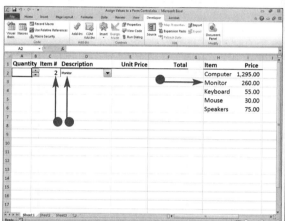

Apply It

When working with a value selected from a list box or combo box control, you may want to use the value in the linked cell to set the value of another cell. For example, assume you have the following Excel list in cells H2:I4:

Example:

Computer	$1295
Monitor	$995
Keyboard	$55

You can use the INDEX function to determine the price based on the equipment selection. For example, if the user selects Monitor from the control, Excel places a value of 2 in the linked cell. If you want users to find the cost of the selection, you type a formula similar to the following, assuming that C2 is the linked cell:

Example:
```
=INDEX($H$2:$I$4,C2,2)
```

When the user selects Monitor, the INDEX function returns $995. The INDEX function actually creates an array of the Excel list and uses the control selection to determine which element in the array to return. The function uses three arguments: Array, Row_num, and Column_num. See the file Form Control Example.xlsm, which you can download from the Web site for this book to see an example.

Add a Macro to a Form Control

Y ou can use macros to automate the tasks you perform in Excel. You can assign a macro to any form control on a worksheet. For example, if a user clicks a button control, you can have Excel execute a macro.

You can create one macro for each control on a worksheet. You create a macro either by recording a series of keystrokes or by writing a Visual Basic for Applications (VBA) procedure. When you select the Assign Macro menu option, Excel automatically creates a new macro name by using the name of the control followed by an underscore and an event name, such as _Click. Excel assigns the control name to the control when you add it to a worksheet. For example, the first OptionButton control that you add to a worksheet is named OptionButton1. If

you create a macro for the option button, Excel gives the macro the name OptionButton1_Click. Every time you add a new control, Excel gives the control a unique name by adding a sequential number to OptionButton; for example, OptionButton2_Click, Option Button3_ Click, and so on.

The portion of the macro name following the underscore character corresponds to an action, commonly referred to as an *event*. For example, with an OptionButton control, the user clicks the radio button to select the option, so the event is Click. If you create a macro for a combo box control, Excel assigns Change to the name of the event because you want to execute the macro when the value of the control changes. The event extension tells Excel to monitor the control and execute the macro whenever a user clicks the control.

Add a Macro to a Form Control

① Right-click your control twice.

   A menu appears.

② Click Assign Macro.

   The Assign Macro dialog box appears.

● Excel assigns a default macro name for the selected control.

③ Click Record.

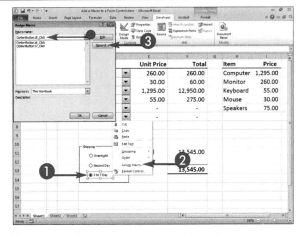

   The Record Macro dialog box appears.

④ Click OK.

⑤ Record your macro.

Note: *See section "Record a Macro" to learn how to record a macro.*

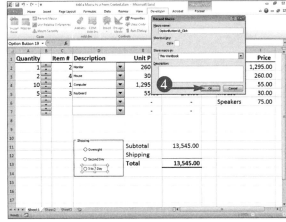

6 Click the control with the assigned macro.

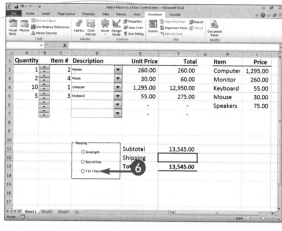

Excel executes the associated macro.

● In the example, Excel assigns postage to the invoice.

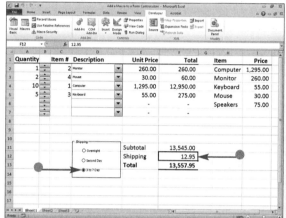

Extra

To assign a macro to a button, create the macro, and then click the Developer tab. Click Insert in the Controls group. A menu appears. Select the button control and then click and drag to create a button. The Assign Macro dialog box appears. Click the macro you want to assign and then click OK. Right-click the button twice and then click Edit Text on the menu that appears. Type the name you want to give the button. You can now click the button to execute the macro.

If you no longer want a macro to be assigned to a control, you can right-click the control twice and then click the Assign Macro option. In the Assign Macro dialog box, delete the macro name from the Macro Name field and then click OK. Excel removes the macro assignment from the control, but the macro remains as part of the workbook. To remove the macro from the workbook, click the View tab. Click Macros in the Macros group. Click View Macros. The Macro dialog box appears. Select the macro you want and then click Delete.

Introducing the
Visual Basic Editor

View of the Visual Basic Editor

Ⓐ Project Explorer

The Project Explorer lists all projects. The VBE considers each open workbook and each add-in a project. Microsoft Office arranges projects in the Project Explorer in a tree-like structure. Click plus (+) to show more information. Click minus (−) to show less information. To display the Project Explorer, click View → Project Explorer.

Ⓑ Code Window

Use the Code window to write, edit, and display VBA code. Every VBA object has a Code window that stores the code associated with the object. In the Project Explorer, double-click an object's name to see the associated code. To display the Code window, click View → Code.

Ⓒ Object List Box

The Object list box lists the objects associated with a form.

Ⓓ Procedure List Box

The Procedure list box lists the procedures associated with the selected object.

Ⓔ Properties Window

To select an object, click the object name in Project Explorer. To display the Properties window, click View → Properties Window. Use the Properties window to set the properties associated with the selected object.

Ⓕ Locals Window

Use the Locals window to monitor declared variables. To open the Locals window, click View → Locals Window.

Ⓖ Watches Window

Use the Watches window to monitor properties and variables. To display the Watches window, click View → Watch Window.

Ⓗ Immediate Window

The Immediate window returns the results of statements you type into the Immediate window. To display the Immediate window, click View → Immediate Window.

The Visual Basic Editor

Excel provides two ways to create a macro: You can record a macro or you can type Visual Basic for Applications (VBA) code into the Visual Basic Editor (VBE). The VBE is a separate application you use to write VBA code. You can access the VBE through most Microsoft Office Applications, including Excel.

You access the VBE by clicking the Visual Basic button on the Developer tab in the Code group, or by pressing Alt+F11. Inside the VBE, you can reposition windows to create the development environment you prefer. You can use the View menu to tell Excel which windows and toolbars you want visible.

The Project Explorer

The Project Explorer resembles the treelike structure used by the Windows Explorer folders pane. When you open the VBE, the VBE opens a VBA project for each open Excel workbook. The VBE names each project VBAProject (*workbook name*). Under the project name, the VBE lists the workbook and each worksheet in the workbook.

When you record a macro, you can choose to store it in the Personal Macro Workbook. Once you have stored a macro in the Personal Macro Workbook, the Personal Macro Workbook opens as a hidden file whenever you run Excel. If the Personal Macro Workbook is open, you can see it listed as a project in the Project Explorer window as VBA Project (PERSONAL.XLSB).

Modules

VBA executes procedures in response to a system action or a user action. A module is a set of procedures that Excel can execute. The VBE stores each macro you create or record as a procedure in a module. The Project Explorer lists each module a project contains. You can add modules by using the steps outlined later in this chapter. When you double-click a module name in the Project Explorer, the contents of the module appear in the Code window. Use the Procedure list box to select the procedure you want to view.

Properties Window

You use VBA code to manipulate objects. Workbooks and worksheets are examples of objects. A property is an attribute of an object. VBA uses attributes to define such things as the name, color, location, or size of an object. The Properties window displays the properties associated with the selected object. To select an object, you click the object name in the Project Explorer window. A module has only one property: its name. Hence, if you select a module, the only property that you see in the Properties window is the module name. Sheets have many properties, and if you select a sheet, you can view and modify the many sheet properties.

To change the properties associated with an object, you simply click the field beside the property and make the desired changes. Some property fields, such as Name, require you to type a value. Other fields have drop-down lists from which you can select the appropriate value. Some properties are read-only. You cannot change read-only properties.

Activate the Visual Basic Editor

here are two ways to create a macro. One way is to use the macro recorder to record the steps needed to perform the action. The other way is to create the steps by typing the VBA code into the Code window of the VBE. When you use the macro recorder, Excel automatically creates the VBA code for you. You can use the VBE to edit macros you create with the macro recorder. Often, it is convenient to use a combination of the two methods to create your VBA code: You record part of the VBA code and then you use the VBE to augment or modify the recorded code.

You can use several methods to activate the VBE: You can press Alt+F11 while in Excel; click the Visual Basic button in the Code group on the Developer tab; or click

the Edit button in the Macro dialog box. When the VBE is open, you can open the Code window by pressing Ctrl+R.

If you create your macros using the macro recorder, Excel defines each macro you create as a procedure and stores each procedure in a module. The VBE lists modules in the Project Explorer under the workbook in which they are located.

If the Personal Macro Workbook, Personal.xlsm, contains macros, the project for the Personal.xlsm workbook opens when you access the VBE. You can view and modify all of the macros in the Personal Macro Workbook. See Chapter 1 to learn more about the Personal Macro Workbook.

Activate the Visual Basic Editor

Open the VBE by Using the Ribbon

1 Click the Developer tab.

Note: See Chapter 1 to learn how to display the Developer tab.

2 Click Visual Basic in the Code group.

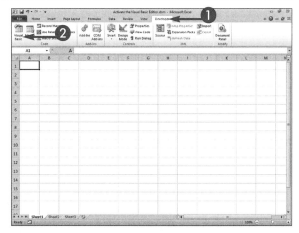

The VBE appears, with the Window layout you last used.

3 Double-click a module name.

Excel shows the macro in the Code window.

● If you placed more than one macro in the module, you can click the down arrow and then select the macro you want to see.

Press Alt+F11 to return to Excel.

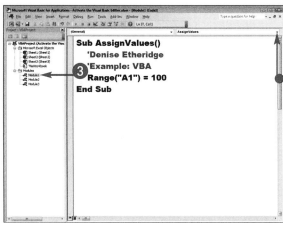

Open the VBE from the Macro Dialog Box

1. Click the Developer tab.

2. Click Macros in the Code group.

   The Macro dialog box appears.

3. Click the macro you want to edit.

4. Click Edit.

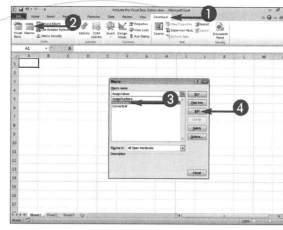

   The VBE appears, with the code for the selected macro in the Code window.

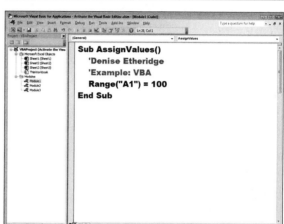

Extra

To make the VBE easier to navigate, Microsoft provides shortcut keys. These shortcuts work when the VBE window is open.

SHORTCUT KEY	DESCRIPTION
F1	When you select an item in the Code window and then press F1, the VBE displays online help for the item you selected.
F4	Press F4 to switch to the Property window and display the properties for the selected object. If the Property window is not open, the VBE opens it in the location where you last viewed it.
F7	You select an object by clicking it in the Project Explorer. If you click an object and then press F7, the Code window for the selected object appears on top of all other Code windows.
Ctrl+G	When you press Ctrl+G, the VBE displays the Immediate window.
Ctrl+R	When you press Ctrl+R, you switch to the Project Explorer. If the Project Explorer window is not open, the VBE opens it in the location where you last viewed it.
Alt+F11	When you press Alt+F11, you toggle between the VBE and Excel.

Open Visual Basic Editor Windows

The VBE contains several windows you can use when creating macros. Microsoft provides a basic window setup; however, you can rearrange, resize, remove, and add windows. The most commonly used windows are the Project Explorer, the Properties window, and the Code window. You may also find the Immediate window useful for quickly testing a statement before adding it to your code.

The View menu lists the available VBE windows. You can select what windows to open and where to open them. When you select a window from the menu, that window appears in the location where you last placed it. For example, if you placed the Project Explorer window in the upper left corner during your previous session, the Project Explorer window reopens in the upper left corner.

You can move windows by using the standard drag-and-drop feature found in all Windows applications. You can resize a window by dragging its edges.

You can also attach windows to specific locations in the VBE by using the docking feature. When you dock a window, it becomes part of another window attached at the specified location. If you set a window to dock, Excel docks it in the location you specified each time it opens. You can dock windows only on the top, bottom, left edge, or right edge of the screen, application window, or another dockable window. Docking a window does not mean that the window always appears in the VBE.

You can have multiple Code windows open at the same time. You can view multiple Code windows simultaneously by tiling or cascading them.

Open Visual Basic Editor Windows

Display a Window

1 Click View.

2 Click the window you want to open.

You can choose from the Immediate Window, Locals Window, Watch Window, Project Explorer, or Properties Window.

The selected window appears in the last viewed location.

You can click and drag the window to a new location.

You can close a window by clicking the Close button () or by right-clicking and selecting Hide.

Dock Individual Windows

1 Click Tools → Options.

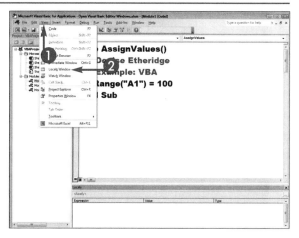

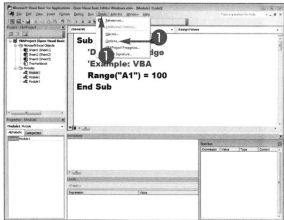

The Options dialog box appears.

② Click the Docking tab.

③ Click the windows you want to dock (☐ changes to ☑).

④ Click OK.

⑤ Dock the window by clicking and dragging it to an edge.

Excel moves the window to its new location.

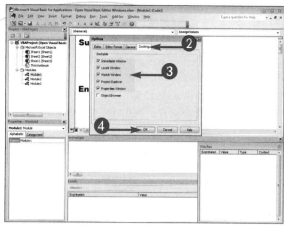

Display Code Windows

① Click Window and then click a tiling option.

You can select Tile Horizontally, Tile Vertically, or Cascade.

The VBE displays your Code windows either tiled or cascading.

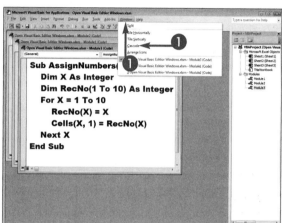

Extra

You can move windows around in the VBE by using the same techniques you use with all Microsoft Windows programs. To move a window, click the title bar and drag it to the desired location. To resize a window, click a corner of the window and drag it to the desired size.

To free up space, you can hide any of the VBE windows. To hide a window, right-click anywhere in the window. In the menu that appears, click Hide.

When you have many lines of code, you may not be able to see all of it. If you click Window → Split, the VBE splits the Code window so you can view different parts of your code simultaneously. When you split your window, the VBE creates two windows with the same code. You can manipulate each window independent of the other.

Set Properties for a Project

Y ou can set the properties, such as the project name and the lock status, for each project you can view in the Project Explorer window. When you lock a project, the project is password-protected so that only people who know the password can view and modify the contents of the project. You can set both the project name and the password in the Project Properties dialog box.

Excel considers each open workbook a project. By default, the VBE gives each project the name VBA Project (WorkbookName). You can change the name of a project. Changing the project's name can help distinguish between projects, especially if you have several workbooks open simultaneously. If you have a workbook that contains macros that perform a specific type of action; you can give your project a name that makes its purpose readily

apparent. For example, if you have a workbook with macros that format a sales report, you can name the project SalesFormat.

If you plan to distribute your workbook to other users, you may want to consider password-protecting your project. If a project is password-protected, the user must enter the password to view or modify any portion of the project. Password-protecting can help protect VBA code that you do not want others to view or modify. Password-protection does not make your code completely secure. There are password recovery utilities on the market that anyone can use to recover your password. Password-protecting the project does not lock the corresponding Excel workbook.

Set Properties for a Project

Change a Project Name

① Click the project name you want to change.

② Click Tools → *Project Name* Properties.

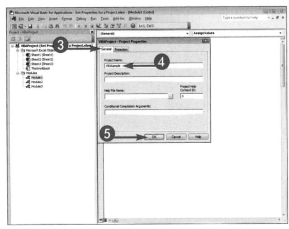

The *Project Name* Properties dialog box appears.

③ Click the General tab.

④ Type the desired project name.

⑤ Click OK.

The project name changes within the Project Explorer window.

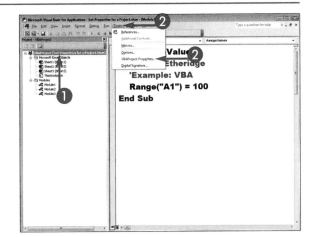

Lock a Project from Editing

⑥ Click the Protection tab.

⑦ Click the Lock Project for Viewing option (☐ changes to ☑).

⑧ Type the password required to unlock the project.

⑨ Type the password again.

⑩ Click OK.

Excel locks your project.

The next time you open the workbook, you will not be able to view the code unless you know the password.

Open a Locked Project

① Save and close your workbook.

② Open your workbook.

③ Press Alt+F11 to open the VBE.

④ Double-click the locked project.

The Password dialog box appears.

⑤ Type the password.

⑥ Click OK.

Excel opens your project.

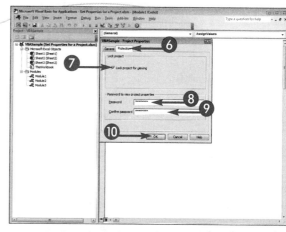

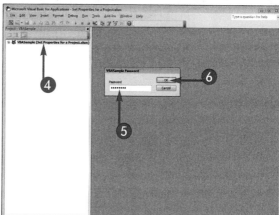

Extra

You can create forms (dialog boxes) to enable users to interact with macros. If you have multiple workbooks open in Excel, you can copy modules and forms by using the Project Explorer window. To copy an object, click the object and drag it to another project. When you release the mouse button, the VBE creates a copy of the selected module or form in the specified project. By default, the VBE gives the copied module the same name as the module in the original project. When you copy an object to another project, if one already exists with that name, the VBE renames the object by adding a number to the end of the name. For example, if you copy Module2 to a project that already contains a Module2, the copied module name becomes Module21. If you have a Module21, the VBE names the copied object Module22.

Set Display Options for the Code Window

As you develop your VBA code, you will spend a lot of time interacting with the Code window. You can use the Editor Format tab in the Options dialog box to adjust many aspects of the Code window. These adjustments can make it easier for you to create and debug your VBA code.

You can enter many different categories of text into the Code window. For example, you can use comments to annotate your code. By using the Format Editor, you can adjust the foreground, background, and indicator color for each type of text listed in the Color Text list. When you use colors, it is easier for you to locate a particular type of text when you are creating or debugging code.

You can use the Font field to select from the fonts installed on your computer. When working with VBA

code, you may find code easier to read if you use a fixed-width font such as Courier New. With a fixed-width font, the characters in the code align vertically, making it easier to detect any spacing problems in your code. Use the Size field to set the size of your font.

The Margin Indicator Bar check box indicates whether a vertical indicator bar appears in the margin when you debug your code. Make sure this option remains selected so you can use the vertical indicator bar to spot appropriate lines of code when you are debugging. The VBE places symbols in the vertical indicator bar to indicate errors and break points. See Chapter 8 for more information on debugging.

As you make changes to the font settings for each of the formatting types, Excel shows you a sample of the changes in the Sample box.

Set Display Options for the Code Window

① Click Tools → Options.

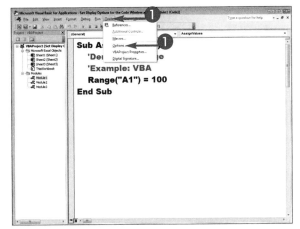

The Options dialog box appears.

② Click the Editor Format tab.

③ Click the type of text for which you want to change the settings.

④ Click the down arrow and select a foreground color.

⑤ Click the down arrow and select a background color.

⑥ Click the down arrow and select an indicator color.

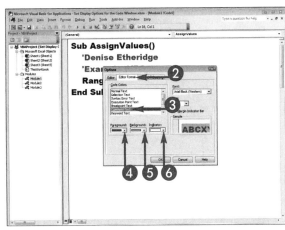

Excel sets the foreground, background, and indicator colors for the category you selected.

● The selection appears in the Sample box.

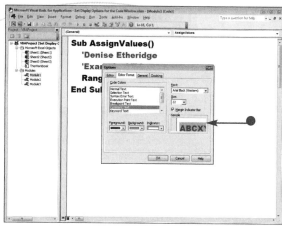

⑦ Click the down arrow and select a font.

⑧ Click the down arrow and select a font size.

⑨ Make sure the Margin Indicator Bar check box remains selected.

⑩ Click OK.

● The text in the Code window changes to reflect your modifications.

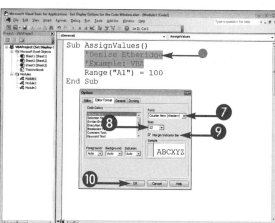

Extra

You can use the Editor tab in the Options dialog box to set the options shown in the table that follows. Click Tools and then click Options to access the Options dialog box.

OPTION	FUNCTION
Auto Syntax Check	Allows the VBE to check the syntax of each line of code immediately after you type it.
Require Variable Declaration	Requires explicit variable declarations within all modules. See Chapter 3 section "Understanding Variables and Data Types" for more information.
Auto List Member	As you type your code, you see a reminder of the next logical value for completing the current statement.
Auto Quick Info	Displays information about functions and their parameters as you type.
Auto Data Tips	Displays the current value of a variable when you position your cursor over the variable while in Break mode. See Chapter 8 for more information about debugging your VBA code.
Auto Indent	After you set a tab location, all following lines start at the same tab location. You specify the width of the tabs in the Tab Width field. You can set tabs from 1 to 32 spaces apart.

Add a New Module

When you write code, you use variables to store information. A *string* is a sequence of characters that does not represent a numeric value. A string can consist of letters, numbers, spaces, and punctuation marks. A variable can hold a number, a string, or some other type of information. When you tell VBA exactly what type of information a variable can contain, you are declaring the variable. A *procedure* is a sequence of code that, when executed, performs an action in Excel. When you record a macro, VBA stores it as a procedure. VBA uses modules to store variable declarations and procedures. Whenever you create a new macro by using the macro recorder, VBA places the procedure in a module and associates the module with the project. The VBE considers every open workbook a project.

When you type VBA code into the VBE, you place it in a module. You must create the module to store your VBA code. As you add new modules to a project, VBA names them Module#. The VBE assigns numbers to the modules, increasing the number by one each time you add a new module. For example, the VBE names the first module in the project Module1, the second Module2, and so on.

The Project Explorer lists all of the modules in a project. When you add a new module, Excel selects that module in the Project Explorer and creates a blank Code window.

You do not have to create a new module for each procedure you add to a workbook. You can add multiple procedures to the same module.

Add a New Module

① Click the project to which you want to add a new module.

② Click Insert → Module.

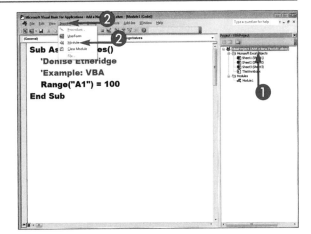

Excel creates a new module and opens the associated Code window.

③ Type the code for your macro.

● This is the macro name.

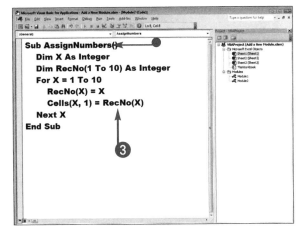

④ Press Alt+F11 to move from the VBE to Excel.

⑤ Click the Developer tab.

⑥ Click Macros in the Code Group.

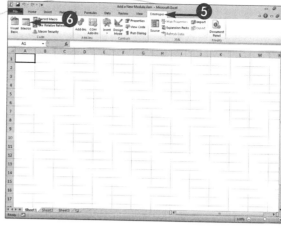

● The Macro dialog box lists existing macros, including the ones you create in the VBE.

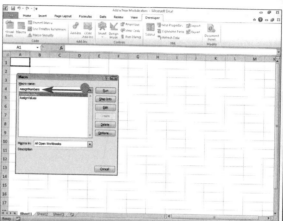

Extra

You can easily change the name of a module. When you create a new module, the VBE automatically names the module Module#, with # representing the sequential number that follows the last module you created — for example, Module1, Module2, and so on. If you have a project with several modules, distinguishing one module from another without reviewing the source code can be difficult. You can rename modules with names that reflect the actions that the contents of the module perform.

Use the Properties window to change the name of a module. In the Project Explorer window, click the name of the module you want to rename. Press F4 to move to the Properties window. Type a new name in the Name field and then press Enter. The name of the module changes on the corresponding node in the Project Explorer window.

Remove
a Module

You can remove modules from the VBE. Generally, you remove modules that contain procedures you no longer need. When you attempt to remove a module, the VBE gives you the opportunity to export the module to a file before removing it. If there is any possibility that you will need to use a procedure in that module in the future, you should export the module before removing it.

Exporting a module creates a file with a .bas extension. These files are text files, and you can open and read them with any text editor.

Once you have exported a module, you can use the Import File dialog box to import the module back into the project from which you exported it or into another project. If you have modules you want to share with other programmers,

you can export them so the other programmers can import them. When you import a module file, the VBE tries to assign it the same name as the original module. If a module already exists with that name, the VBE adds a sequential number to the end of the module name. Therefore, if you named the original module Module1 and a Module1 exists in the project, Excel names the imported module Module11.

When you remove a module that contains code used by a macro, you can no longer access the macro. If you remove a module that contains code referenced by a procedure in another module, an error message appears when you run the code.

When you delete macros within Excel, Excel removes the corresponding VBA code. If a VBA module does not contain any code, Excel removes the entire module.

Remove a Module

① Click the module you want to remove.

If the Project Explorer is not visible, press Ctrl+R to display it.

② Click File → Remove *Module Name*, where *Module Name* is the name of the selected module.

The Remove command always contains the name of the selected module.

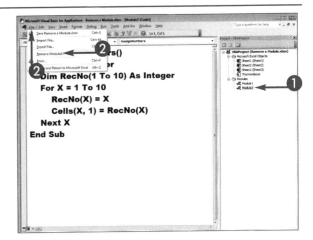

The VBE displays a message, asking whether you want to export the module before removing it.

③ Click Yes to export the module to a file.

Alternatively, click No if you want to delete the module permanently.

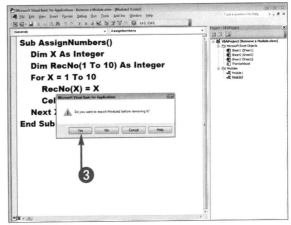

The Export File dialog box appears.

④ Click the down arrow and select the folder in which you want to save the module code.

⑤ Type a name for the module code.

⑥ Click Save.

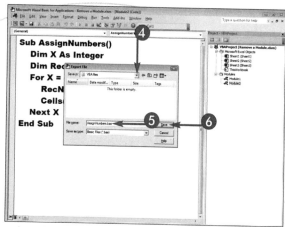

The VBE removes the module from the project and saves the module in the folder and file you specified.

● Module2 no longer exists.

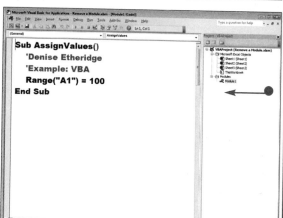

Extra

You do not need to delete a module to save it as a file. If you want to share your code with other VBA developers, you can simply export the module to a file and then distribute the file. To export, select the module and then click File → Export File. The Export File dialog box appears. In the Save In field, select the folder in which you want to save the file. Type a filename in the File Name field and then click Save.

After you export a module to a file, you can import it into any workbook. To import an exported file, click a project name to select the project into which you want to import the file. Click File → Import File. The Import File dialog box appears. Use the Look In field to locate the folder in which you saved the exported module. Click the filename and then click Open. VBA imports the file.

Hide a Macro

You can hide macros so they do not appear in the Excel Macro dialog box. If you create workbooks that you intend to share with others, you may want to hide some of the macros to ensure that users do not inadvertently delete them.

Because Excel cannot execute a hidden macro from the Macro dialog box, you must assign the hidden macro to the Quick Access toolbar, Ribbon, an object, such as a shape or picture, or have another macro call the macro. When you hide a macro, shortcut keys will no longer execute the macro.

To hide a macro, open the module containing the macro within the VBE and place the `Private` statement in front

of the `Sub` statement for the procedure. For example, type the following to hide the Assign_Values procedure:

`Private Sub Assign_Values().`

Hiding a macro does not prevent users from viewing or modifying the macro in the VBE. If you want to keep users from accessing the macro, you must password-protect the project containing the macro by changing the properties of the project. See the section "Set Properties for a Project" for the details on setting project properties. Locking the project prevents users from using the VBE to view and modify the VBA code within that project. To open the project, a user must enter the correct password. Locking a project limits user accessibility, but Excel can still execute any macros in the project.

Hide a Macro

① Click the Developer tab.

② Click Macros in the Code group.

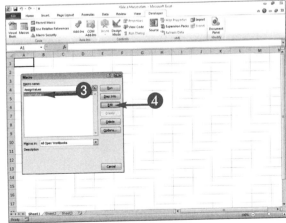

The Macro dialog box appears.

③ Click the macro you want to hide.

④ Click Edit.

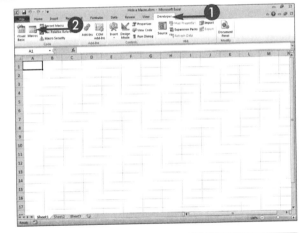

The VBE opens to the macro you selected.

⑤ Type Private before the Sub statement.

⑥ Press Alt+F11 to return to Excel.

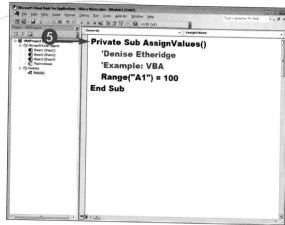

⑦ Repeat Steps 1 and 2 to open the Macro dialog box.

● The macro no longer appears.

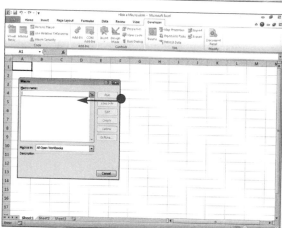

Extra

You should hide macros that are called by other macros if you do not want the user to be able to execute the macro from the Macro dialog box. For example, you have a macro named Change_Cells that calls another macro named Add_Cell_Values. You can hide the Add_Cell_Values macro so users cannot execute it from the Macro dialog box. When you mark a procedure as private by placing the Private statement in front of the Sub statement for the procedure, you can access the procedure only from the same code module. In other words, the hidden macro and the procedure that contains the macro calling the hidden macro must be in the same code module.

To make a hidden macro visible again, you need to access the module containing the procedure in the VBE and delete the Private statement in front of the Sub statement.

Update
a Macro

You can update a macro at any time by adding or removing VBA code. After you record a macro, you can record it again to replace it, but you cannot modify it in Excel. The only way to modify your macro is to change the procedure by using the VBE. If you do not know how to read and write the VBA code required for the step you want to add to the macro, this can be quite an undertaking.

Modifying a macro — even one you create with the macro recorder — requires manually specifying the new VBA code you want to add to the macro. You can quickly update an existing macro by recording the code you want to add to the macro and then using copy and paste to add the new steps to the old macro.

For example, you create a macro that sums the values in a column of cells but you forget to change the formatting of the cell that contains the column total to Currency. You can record a second macro in Excel that formats the cell, and then open the VBE, copy the formatting code you created when you recorded the second macro, and paste it into the procedure for the first macro. When you copy the code, be sure you only copy the portion of the procedure between the Sub and the End Sub statements.

After you copy the code from the second macro into the first macro, you can delete the second macro. You can find out more about deleting macros in Chapter 1.

Update a Macro

① Click the Developer tab.

② Click Macros in the Code group.

The Macro dialog box appears.

③ Click your original macro.

④ Click Edit.

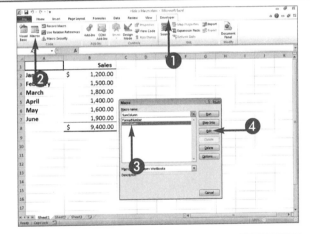

The VBE appears, and opens to the module that contains your macro.

⑤ Click and drag to select the code in your second macro.

⑥ Press Ctrl+C to copy the code.

⑦ Place your cursor at the end of the last line of code in your original macro and then press Enter.

The VBE creates a new line.

⑧ Press Ctrl+V to paste the code.

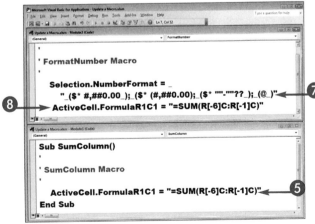

⑨ Click Tools → Macros.

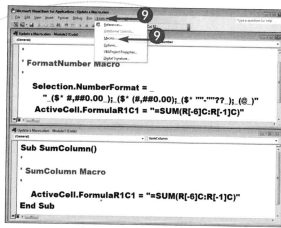

The Macro dialog box appears.

⑩ Click the second macro.

⑪ Click Delete.

The VBE deletes the macro.

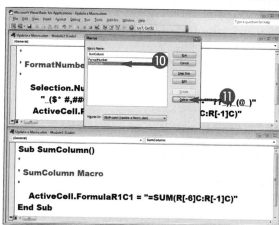

Extra

When you view the VBA code for your macro, you may notice that an apostrophe (') precedes several lines. These are called comment lines. Programmers use comments to provide information about the code, such as what the code does, when it was created, and who coded it. When you use the macro recorder to create a macro, any information you type in the Description box appears as a comment.

Example:
```
Sub Assign_Values()
    'Denise Etheridge
    'Example: VBA
    Range("A1").Value = 100
End Sub
```

Create Sub Procedures

A block of VBA code that performs a task is a *procedure*. A Sub procedure is a special type of procedure that performs a task but does not return a value. Every time you record a macro, Excel creates a Sub procedure. You can view the Sub procedures in the VBE. You can also use the VBE to create Sub procedures.

Every Sub procedure begins with the keyword Sub followed by the name of the Sub procedure and parentheses. If the Sub procedure does not take any arguments, the parentheses are empty. If the Sub procedure does take arguments, you place the arguments between the parentheses, separated by commas. Sub procedures end with the keywords End Sub.

Every Sub procedure must have a name. You can name your Sub procedure anything you want as long as you follow these naming rules: The name must start with a letter. The name can contain only letters, numbers, and underscores and cannot contain any spaces. The name cannot be longer than 255 characters. The name cannot be a cell address; for example, you cannot name your Sub procedure A1. Procedure names in VBA are not case-sensitive. The name of your Sub procedure should describe the function the procedure performs. For example, if your Sub procedure prints a sales report, you might want to name it PrintSalesReport or Print_Sales_Report.

You place Sub procedures inside modules. See Chapter 2 to learn more about modules.

Create Sub Procedures

① Click Insert → Module.

● The VBE creates a new module.

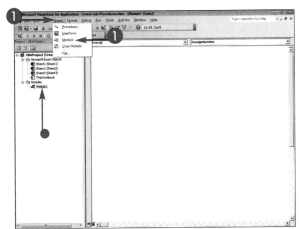

② Type Sub.

③ Type your procedure's name.

④ Type parentheses.

Place arguments the procedure takes between the parentheses separated by commas.

● The VBE automatically adds the words End Sub.

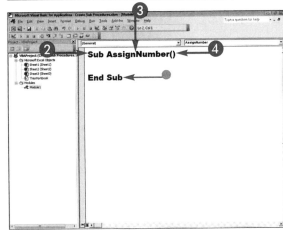

⑤ Type your code.

⑥ Press Alt+F11 to switch from the VBE to Excel, and then run your macro.

Note: See Chapter 1 to learn how to run a macro.

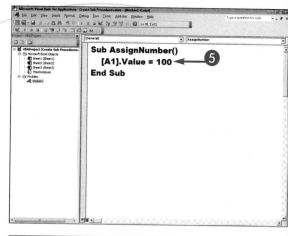

In this example, VBA places the number 100 in cell A1.

Extra

A glossary of Sub procedure terms:

TERM	DEFINITION
Argument	An argument can be a constant, a variable, or an expression that is passed by a calling procedure.
Constant	A value that remains the same.
Function	A type of procedure. This is a block of code that performs a task (usually a calculation) and returns a value.
Expression	A combination of objects, numbers, text, operators, and variables that yield a result. A mathematical equation is an example of an expression.
Procedure	A sequence of code that, when executed, performs a task in Excel. There are several types of procedures.
Sub procedure	A procedure that performs a task but does not return a value.
Variable	A named location where you store information. In the expression x=1, x is a variable that has been assigned the value 1.

Create Functions

You are probably already familiar with functions. Excel has over 300 predefined functions, with SUM being the most commonly used. You use the SUM function to add a list of values. Like a Sub procedure, a function is a special type of procedure. A *function* is a block of code that performs a task — usually a calculation — and returns a value. There are three types of functions: VBA functions, worksheet functions, and custom functions.

VBA functions are functions provided by VBA for use in your VBA code. The MsgBox function is a popular VBA function explained in detail, along with several other VBA functions, in Chapter 7. When executed, the MsgBox function displays a pop-up box with your message. Other VBA functions obtain input from users, execute another program, return the current date, or return the current time.

If an analogous VBA function is not available, you can use an Excel worksheet functions in your code. Chapter 7 explains how to use worksheet functions in detail.

If none of the VBA or worksheet functions suit your needs, you can create a custom function. Every custom function begins with the keyword Function followed by the name of the function and parentheses. If your function takes arguments, you place the arguments between the parentheses, separated by commas. Every Custom Function ends with the keywords End Function. There are two ways to execute a custom function: by using the function in a formula or by calling the function from a procedure. Excel lists custom functions under User Defined in the Insert function dialog box. See Chapter 7 for more information on custom functions.

Create Functions

① Click Insert → Module.

● The VBE creates a new module.

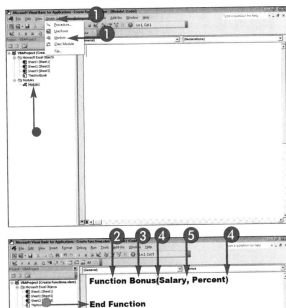

② Type Function.

③ Type your procedure name.

④ Type parentheses.

⑤ Type arguments between the parentheses, separated by commas.

● The VBE automatically adds the words End Function.

6 Type your code.

7 Press Alt+F11 to switch from the VBE to Excel.

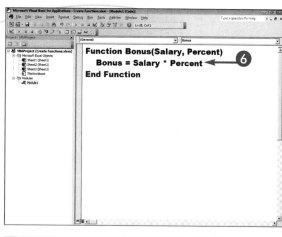

```
Function Bonus(Salary, Percent)
    Bonus = Salary * Percent
End Function
```

● You can use your function to perform calculations.

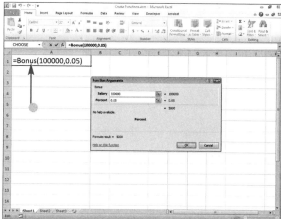

Extra

You can create VBA functions that you can use within Excel to perform calculations. When you create a public function in the VBE, the function is listed in the Insert Function dialog box that appears when you click Formulas ➔ Insert Function within Excel. The VBE places the functions you create under the User Defined category in the Insert Function dialog box. You can use these VBA functions in your worksheet to create formulas in the same way that you use the built-in functions that are standard with Excel. The VBA functions you create are available in the Insert Function dialog box only when the workbook containing the functions is open. Therefore, if you create a specific function you want to use in all your workbooks, you should add the function to your Personal Macro Workbook, Personal.xlsm, to ensure that it is always available from within Excel. The Personal Macro Workbook always opens with Excel, so any macros and functions it contains are always available. See Chapter 1 for more information on the Personal Macro Workbook.

Comment Your Code

With comments, you can document each step of your code. You can use comments to document such things as the person who created the code, the date when the code was last updated, the purpose of the code, and the purpose of each step in the code. When you are working in a collaborative environment, comments are essential.

In VBA, you start a comment by typing an apostrophe (`'`). When you execute the code, VBA ignores everything after the apostrophe. Comments and code appear in different colors. After you add an apostrophe, the VBE changes the color of the commented text.

You can place an apostrophe anywhere in a line of code, and VBA views the text after the apostrophe as a comment. There is an exception to this rule: If you type an apostrophe within double quotation marks, VBA does not view it as a comment. For example, VBA would not view the text after the apostrophe in the following example as code: `Saying = "That's Life!"`.

Comments help only if they provide enough information to describe the code. A reader should be able to read the comments without studying the code and still understand the code. For example, a comment such as "Sums the values" does not provide enough information about the code. A comment such as "Sums the values in cells A1 and A2 and places the result in cell A3" is better because it describes the actual process.

You can turn several lines of code into a comment by using the Comment Block button on the Edit toolbar. Later, if you want to make the commented lines code again, you can click the Uncomment Block button.

Comment Your Code

① Double-click the module that contains the code you want to document.

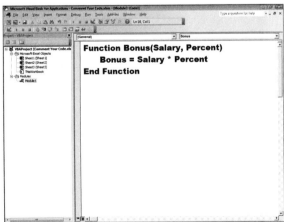

Your code appears in the Code window.

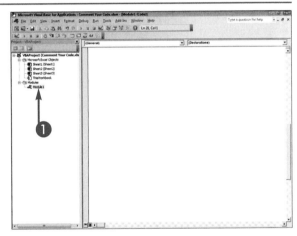

② Type an apostrophe followed by your comments.

You can place your comments anywhere.

③ Press Alt+F11 to switch from the VBE to Excel, and then run the code.

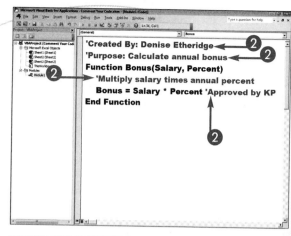

The comments do not affect your code.

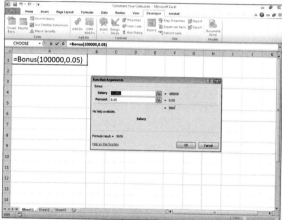

Extra

You can use comments when you are testing your code. If you suspect a line of code is causing your code to run improperly, you can comment it out and run your procedure without it. The process eliminates the need to delete the line of code. You can reactivate the commented-out code by simply removing the apostrophe.

In the VBE, you can use the Edit toolbar to comment out a block of code. To access the Edit toolbar, click View → Toolbars → Edit. The Edit toolbar appears. Select the lines of code you want to comment out. Click the Comment Block button (▦). The VBE comments out your code. When you run your procedure, the lines of code do not execute. To uncomment the lines of code, select them and then press the Uncomment Block button (▦).

Reference Cells and Ranges

As you write your VBA code, you will frequently need to reference cells in an Excel worksheet either to access the information in cells or to put information there. VBA has several methods you can use to reference cells.

One method is the `Cells` method. When using the `Cells` method, you use an index to reference a row and column. For example, if you want to reference cell A1, you type the word `Cells` followed by an open parenthesis, the row reference, a comma, the column reference in quotes, a close parenthesis, a period, and the word `Value`. The period and the word Value are optional. Both of the following assign the value 1 to cell A1: `Cells(1,"A").Value = 1, Cells(1,"A") = 1`.

When using the `Cells` method, you can also use numbers to identify the column. The first column in your worksheet is column 1, and each column thereafter is numbered sequentially. To assign the value 10 to cell E1, you would type either of the following: `Cells(1,5).Value = 10, Cells(1,5) = 10`. Column E is identified by a 5 because it is the fifth column in a worksheet. Using numbers to identify a column is preferable because you can use loops to manipulate your row and column references. To learn more about loops, see Chapter 6.

If you have a simple procedure and you want to access a cell, you can enclose the cell reference in square brackets followed by a period and the word Value. For example, you can use the following to place the number 25 in cell B3: `[B3].Value = 25`.

Reference Cells and Ranges

① Click Insert → Module.

● The VBE creates a new module.

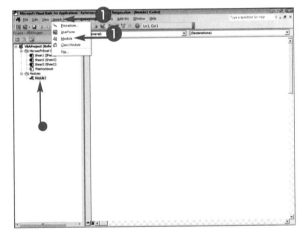

② Name your procedure.

Note: See the section "Create Sub Procedures" to learn how to name a procedure.

③ Reference cells by using the `Cells` method.

● This is a row reference.

● This is a column reference.

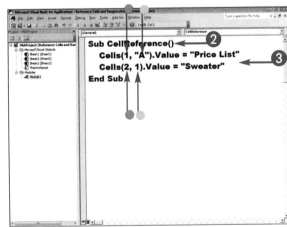

④ Reference a cell by using the cell address.

⑤ Press Alt+F11 to switch from the VBE to Excel, and then run the macro.

Note: *See Chapter 1 to learn how to run a macro.*

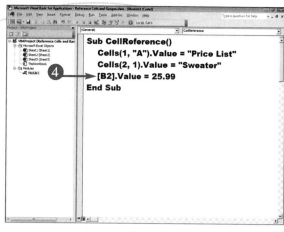

```
Sub CellReference()
    Cells(1, "A").Value = "Price List"
    Cells(2, 1).Value = "Sweater"
    [B2].Value = 25.99
End Sub
```

The VBA places the values in the cells you specified.

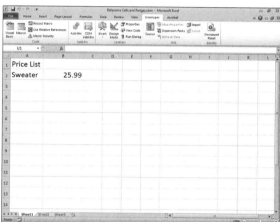

Extra

You can also use the Range property to reference cells. The following table illustrates Range syntax:

SYNTAX	REFERENCE
Range("C4")	Cell C4
Range("B1:B7")	Cells B1 to B7
Range("D1:D8, F1:H2, F7:H8, G2:G6")	Cells D1 to D8, F1 to H2, F7 to H8, and G2 to G6
Range("J:J")	Column J
Range("11:11")	Row 11
Range("L:M")	Columns L to M
Range("14:16")	Rows 14 to 16

See Chapter 11 to learn more about the Range property.

Understanding Variables and Data Types

You use variables to store information for later use. The following syntax stores information to a variable.

```
VariableName = Value
```

`VariableName` represents the name you give to the variable. The equal sign is the assignment operator. The assignment operator tells VBA you want to assign something to a variable. `Value` represents what you want to assign to the variable. Once you assign a value to a variable, VBA retrieves the assigned value whenever you use the variable name. For example, you might make the following assignment:

```
x=2
```

With this assignment, every time VBA sees the variable x, it interprets it to mean 2. You can change the value assigned to a variable many times and at any point in your code.

Variable Names

You can name your variables anything you want; however, you must follow these rules:

- The first character of the variable name must be a letter.
- Your variable name cannot include a space or any of the following: . ! @ & $ or #.
- Your variable name cannot exceed 255 characters.
- Generally, you should not use names that are the same as functions, statements, or methods.
- Your variable name must be unique within its scope.
- You do not need to start each word in your variable name with an uppercase letter; however, that is the convention used in this book. If you develop a convention and use it consistently, you will have an easier time debugging your code.

Data Types

In VBA, a variable can store many data types, including strings, dates, Booleans, and a variety of number types. A string is any sequence of characters consisting of any combination of letters, numbers, or punctuation marks. A Boolean is a value of either `True` or `False`. A number is a value on which you can perform mathematical operations such as addition, subtraction, multiplication, and division.

If you do not declare a data type, VBA assigns the default data type of variant. When a variable is a variant data type, VBA examines the variable to determine if the value is an integer, string, date, Boolean, or other data type. When you change the value assigned to the variable, VBA automatically changes the data type if needed. For example, if you assign x = True, VBA evaluates the expression and determines that x is a Boolean. If

you later change the assignment to x = "George", VBA reevaluates the expression and determines x is a string. Having VBA evaluate your variables slows down your code.

When you declare a variable in VBA, you explicitly tell VBA the variable's data type. In other words, if your variable contains an integer, you declare an integer variable. Because declaring a variable makes your code run faster and more efficiently, you should make a habit of declaring variables. To ensure that variables are always properly declared, type `Option Explicit` as the first statement in your module. If `Option Explicit` is the first statement in your module, your code does not run if you have any undeclared variables. You must place the `Option Explicit` statement at the top of each module you create.

Each Excel workbook is a project. Each `Sub` procedure and function you create is a procedure. You can place multiple procedures in a single module, and you can have many modules in a project. VBA variables can be procedure-only, module-only, or public. Only the procedure in which the variable resides can use a procedure-only variable. Any procedure in a module can use a module-only variable. Any procedure in a project can use a public variable.

Use the `Dim` statement to declare a procedure-only variable. You place the statement after the `Sub` statement but before the procedure code and `End Sub` statement in a `Sub` procedure. In a custom function, you place the `Dim` statement after the `Function` statement but before the procedure code and the `End Function` statement. The following example includes several `Dim` statements that declare procedure-only variables:

Example:
```
Option Explicit
Sub ProcedureOnlyExample()
    Dim EmpLastName As String
    Dim Salary As Long
    Dim StartDate As Date
    'Place procedure code here
End Sub
```

When you want to create a module-only variable that any procedure in a module can use, you place your declarations before the first `Sub` or `Function` statement in the module. You refer to this area of the module as the declarations area. The example shown here includes several `Dim` statements used to declare module-only variables.

Example:
```
Option Explicit
Dim EmpLastName As String
Dim Salary As Long
Dim StartDate As Date
Sub ModuleOnlyExample()
    'Place procedure-only declarations here.
    'Place procedure code here
End Sub
```

When you want to create a public variable that any procedure in your project can use, you place your declarations in the declarations area before the first `Sub` or `Function` statement in the module and precede them with the keyword `Public` instead of `Dim`.

Example:
```
Option Explicit
Public EmpLastName As String
Public Salary As Long
Public StartDate As Date
' Place module-only declarations here
Sub PublicVariableExample()
    ' Place module-only declarations here.
    ' Place procedure code here
End Sub
```

Declare Variables

You use a variable to store information for later use. If you are making an assignment to a variable, you should start by declaring the variable. In its simplest form, declaring your variable consists of telling VBA what data type your variable will use.

You can assign one of several data types. Most are listed in the "Extra" section of this task. Generally, if your data consists of text or numbers you do not intend to use in a mathematical calculation, you should declare your data as a string. If your data is numerical data you do intend to use in mathematical calculations, you should use one of the many numeric data types. Use the data type that uses the least amount of bytes but fully accommodates your needs. If you do not declare your variables, VBA assigns a variable type of variant. A variant data type can hold any type of data. However, declaring your variables

makes your code run faster. You should declare your variables.

You can declare a variable as procedure-only, module-only, or public. To learn more, see the section, "Understanding Variables and Data Types." You use a `Dim` statement to declare a procedure-only or module-only variable. You type the word `Dim` followed by the variable name, the `As` keyword, and then the variable type — for example, `Dim EmployeeName As String`. If you are declaring a public variable, you replace the `Dim` keyword with `Public: Public EmployeeName As String`.

After you have declared a variable, you assign a value to it. Type the variable name, followed by an equal sign and the value you want to assign the variable — for example, `EmployeeName = "John Smith"`.

Declare Variables

① Click Insert → Module.

● The VBE creates a new module.

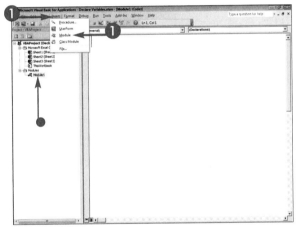

② Type `Option Explicit`.

Note: See the section "Understanding Variables and Data Types" for more information.

● This is the declarations area.

③ Declare your public variables.

④ Declare your module-only variables.

⑤ Name your procedure.

⑥ Declare your procedure-only variables.

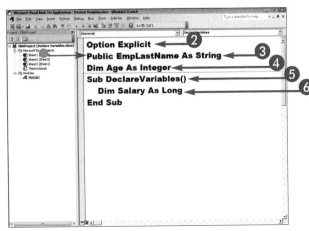

7 Assign values to your variables.

Note: *See the sections "Work with Strings" and "Work with Numbers" to learn more.*

8 Place the values in cells.

9 Press Alt+F11 to switch from the VBE to Excel, and then run the macro.

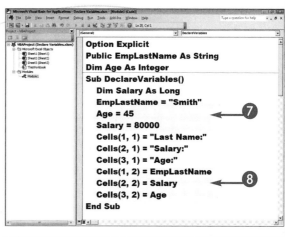

VBA places the values in your variables in the cells you specified.

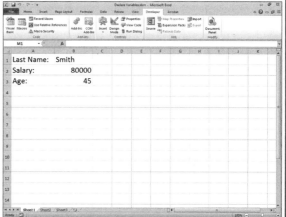

Extra

You should choose the data type that uses the smallest number of bytes but can accommodate your data. Excel provides characters you can use to set the data type for a variable. For example, you can use the following syntax to declare a string: `Dim EmployeeName$`.

DATA TYPE	BYTES USED	RANGE OF VALUE	DECLARATION CHARACTER
Boolean	2 bytes	True or False	
Date	8 bytes	1/1/100 to 12/31/9999	
Double (negative values)	8 bytes	−1.79769313486231E308 to −4.9406564841247E−324	#
Double (positive values)	8 bytes	4.94065645841247E324 to 1.79769313486232E308	#
Integer	2 bytes	−32,768 to 32,767	%
Long	4 bytes	−2,147,483,648 to 2,147,483,647	&
Object	4 bytes	Any defined object	
Single (negative values)	4 bytes	−3.402823E38 to −1.401298E−45	!
Single (positive values)	4 bytes	1.401298E−45 to 3.402823E38	!
String	1 per character	Varies	$
Variant	Varies	Varies	

Work with Strings

You can assign strings to a variable so you can use the string elsewhere in your code. A *string* is any sequence of characters consisting of any combination of letters, numbers, and punctuation marks. A string can have up to two billion characters. When you declare a string variable, you type the `Dim` keyword followed by the variable name and `As String` — for example, `Dim SampleString As String`.

You can assign a string data type to a variable by typing the variable name followed by an equal sign and then the value you want to assign to the variable within quotation marks. For example, you could use the following syntax to assign the name `John Smith` to the string variable `EmployeeName`: `EmployeeName = "John Smith"`.

You can join the contents of two or more strings to create one string. The process of joining strings is called *concatenation*. Use the concatenation operator (`&`) or the plus concatenation operator (`+`) to combine strings. Using the concatenation operator is the better choice because the plus concatenation operator can be confused with the plus arithmetic operator. The expression `FirstName = "David"` assigns the string `David` to the variable `FirstName`. The expression `LastName = "Jackson"` assigns the string `Jackson` to the variable `LastName`. The expression `FullName = FirstName + " " + LastName` and the expression `FullName = FirstName & " " & LastName` both return `David Jackson`. You include the double quotation marks separated by a space (`" "`) to leave a space between the first and last names.

You can assign a string to a cell by enclosing the string in quotes. For example, `Cells(2, 1).Value = "Old Salary"` assigns `Old Salary` to cell A2.

Work with Strings

① Click Insert → Module.

● The VBE creates a new module.

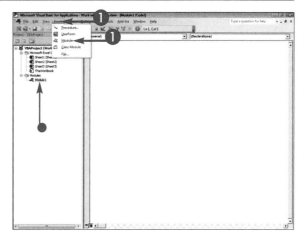

② Name your procedure.

③ Declare your variables.

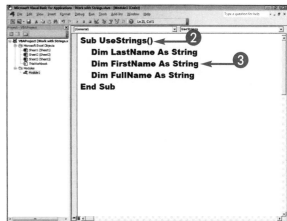

④ Assign string values to variables.

⑤ Concatenate the strings.

⑥ Assign a variable to a cell.

⑦ Assign strings to cells.

⑧ Press Alt+F11 to switch from the VBE to Excel, and then run the macro.

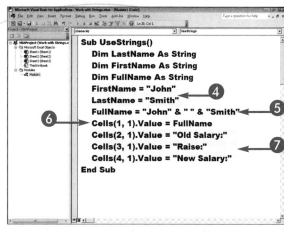

```
Sub UseStrings()
    Dim LastName As String
    Dim FirstName As String
    Dim FullName As String
    FirstName = "John"              ④
    LastName = "Smith"
    FullName = "John" & " " & "Smith"   ⑤
    Cells(1, 1).Value = FullName     ⑥
    Cells(2, 1).Value = "Old Salary:"
    Cells(3, 1).Value = "Raise:"     ⑦
    Cells(4, 1).Value = "New Salary:"
End Sub
```

VBA places the values in your variables in the cells you specified.

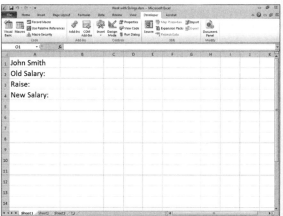

	A
1	John Smith
2	Old Salary:
3	Raise:
4	New Salary:

Extra

When you declare a string, you can declare it as a fixed-length or a variable-length string. A fixed-length string can have between 1 and 65,526 characters. When declaring a fixed-length string, you specify the string's maximum length in characters. For example, you can use the following syntax to declare a fixed-length string with a maximum of ten characters: Dim SampleString As String * 10.

When concatenating fixed-length strings, there is the potential for exceeding the declared or maximum length of the string. VBA does not extend the size of a fixed-length string to store a larger string. If two joined strings form a string larger than the space allows, VBA truncates the string to fit the allotted space. If each of the strings you want to join is ten characters in length, you must make the variable that receives the concatenated string at least 20 characters in length, or VBA truncates the string.

Work with Numbers

To perform mathematical calculations, you can use VBA's seven arithmetic operators: the plus (+), minus (–), multiplication (*), division (/), exponential (^), integer division (\), and Mod operators. You use the plus operator to add, the minus operator to subtract or negate, the multiplication operator to multiply, the division operator to divide, and the exponential operator to raise to a power.

The integer division operator divides two values and returns only the integer portion of the result. VBA discards the remainder when you use this operator. For example, the expression X = 10\3 returns 3. The Mod operator divides two numbers and returns only the remainder. For example, the expression X = 10 Mod 3 returns 1. This operator works well for predetermining if a value divides evenly. If the Mod returns a zero, the value divides evenly.

You can assign the results of a mathematical calculation to a variable, and you can include cells and variables in your calculations. All of the following are valid: A = 5, X = A + 25, X = 5 + 7, X = 9 + Cells(1,1).Value.

When you perform a mathematical calculation in VBA, you must be careful of precedence — the order in which VBA performs calculations. VBA performs calculations from left to right, performing multiplication and division before addition and subtraction. For example, the formula = 3 + 4 * 2 returns 11; VBA multiplies 4 times 2 and then adds 3. If you want to change the order of precedence, use parentheses. Excel calculates numbers in parentheses first. The formula = (3 + 4) * 2 returns 14; VBA adds 3 plus 4 and then multiplies the result by 2.

Work with Numbers

① Click Insert → Module.

● The VBE creates a new module.

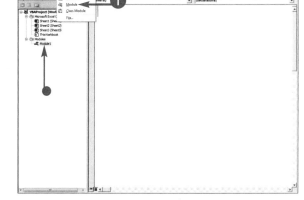

② Name your procedure.

③ Declare your variables.

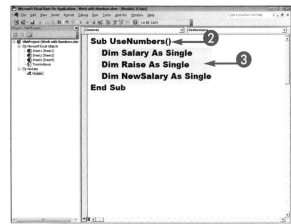

4. Assign numeric values to variables.

● You can perform mathematical calculations.

5. Assign variables to cells.

6. Press Alt+F11 to switch from the VBE to Excel, and then run the macro.

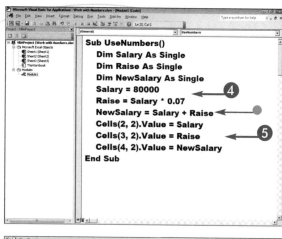

VBA places the values in your variables in the cells you specified.

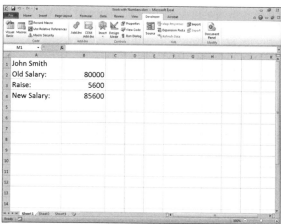

Extra

The following table shows the precedence order, from highest to lowest, that VBA uses to evaluate operators in formulas. If the operators in the formula have the same order of precedence, Excel evaluates the equation from left to right.

PRECEDENCE	OPERATORS	SYMBOL
1	Exponentiation	^
2	Minus sign	– (negates a number before any calculations)
3	Multiplication and division	* /
4	Integer division	\
5	Modulus arithmetic	Mod
6	Addition and subtraction	+ –

You can assign a number to a cell. For example, Cells(2, 2).Value = 80000 assigns 80000 to cell B2. When assigning a number to a cell, do not enclose the number in quotes.

Create a Constant

I f you often use a value that never changes, you can declare it as a constant. For example, there are four quarters in a year. If, in your code, you frequently divide an annual amount by four to allocate amounts to quarters, you can store 4 to a constant named NbrOfQtrs and use the constant when performing calculations. When you review your code and see the constant name, you instantly know you are dividing by the number of quarters, whereas if you use the number 4, the true meaning of the number is not as readily apparent. In short, using constants makes your code easier to understand. After you assign a constant a value, you cannot alter the value.

When you declare a constant, you specify the data type. Constants use the same data types that variables use. As with variables, if you do not specify a data type, VBA treats the value as a variant.

If you want your constant to be available only to the procedure in which it was created, declare your constant after the Sub or Function statement. If you want your constant to be available to all of the procedures in your module, declare your constant in the declarations area. If you want your constant to be available to any procedure in the workbook, declare your constant in the declarations area and use the Public keyword.

Declaration examples: Const NumOfQuarters As Integer = 4, Public Const Region As String = "New York"

To name your constant, you use the same naming rules used for variables. For more information, see the section "Understanding Variables and Data Types" earlier in this chapter.

Create a Constant

① Click Insert → Module.

● The VBE creates a new module.

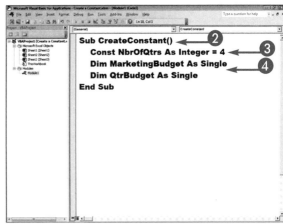

② Name your procedure.

③ Create your constant.

④ Declare your variables.

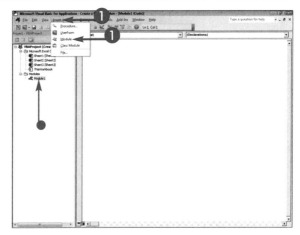

⑤ Assign a value to a variable.

⑥ Use your constant in a calculation.

● The result is stored in a variable.

⑦ Assign values to cells.

⑧ Press Alt+F11 to switch from the VBE to Excel, and then run the macro.

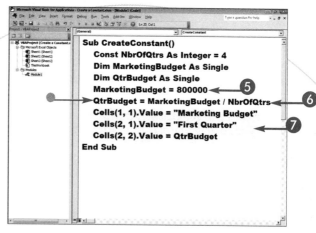

```
Sub CreateConstant()
    Const NbrOfQtrs As Integer = 4
    Dim MarketingBudget As Single
    Dim QtrBudget As Single
    MarketingBudget = 800000          ⑤
    QtrBudget = MarketingBudget / NbrOfQtrs   ⑥
    Cells(1, 1).Value = "Marketing Budget"
    Cells(2, 1).Value = "First Quarter"       ⑦
    Cells(2, 2).Value = QtrBudget
End Sub
```

VBA places the values in the cells you specified.

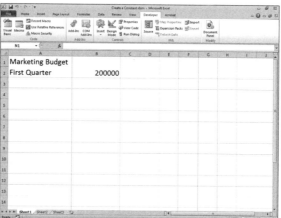

Extra

VBA provides a large number of built-in constants that you can insert into your code at any point without declaring them. The Excel VBA object model adds many more, all of which begin with either xl or vb. Each constant has a numeric value. You can use these constants anywhere, and you do not need to know their numeric value to use them. Two of the most commonly used VBA constants deal with inserting carriage returns, `vbCrLf`, and tab characters, `vbTab`, in your output. Although each of these constants has a numeric equivalent, you simply type the name of the appropriate constant value in your code. To find a list of all VBA and Excel VBA Object Model constants, press F2 to view the Object Browser and search for Constant. Most of the constant values are self-explanatory, based on the name. The appendix also includes many of the constant values used in this book. You can also find a listing of constants by typing **constant** in the Help text box.

Discover the Excel Object Model

Objects are the individual pieces of an application. For example, a worksheet is an object, a range of cells is an object, and a chart is an object. You can use the Excel object model to interact with objects. Using the object model, you can access everything from the entire application to an individual cell in a worksheet.

Objects can have properties and methods. You use methods to perform actions on objects, such as move an object. You use properties to change the characteristics of an object, such as the color of an object.

Excel has an enormous number of objects, properties, and methods, and remembering all of them is virtually impossible. Luckily, the VBE provides a help system to help you quickly locate objects and determine the corresponding methods and properties that are available for the object. You can learn how to work with objects by performing the tasks in this chapter.

Excel Objects

The Excel object model has several hundred objects and thousands of corresponding properties and methods. Each object represents an element of the Excel application. For example, the `Application` object refers to the entire Excel application, and the `Worksheet` object refers to an individual worksheet.

Most objects have child objects. A child object is an object that is part of a larger object. For example, a `Worksheet` object is a child object to a `Workbook` object because worksheets are part of a workbook. All objects in the Excel object model except the `Application` object is a child of at least one other object. The Excel `Application` object is the parent of all objects in Excel.

The object model groups common objects into collections. For example, the `Workbook` object identifies an individual workbook, but the `Workbooks` collection refers to all open workbooks.

Although the list of available objects is extensive, there are six objects that you use frequently: `Application`, `Workbook`, `Worksheet`, `Chart`, `Range`, and `Dialog`. Because you use these objects frequently, it is a good idea to familiarize yourself with them.

Application Object

You usually need to reference the parent object when referencing the child object. For example, to access the second worksheet in the current workbook, you would type `ThisWorkbook.Worksheets(2)`.

The Application object represents the entire Excel program. All other objects are children of the `Application` object in the Excel object model. The `Application` object has several properties and methods. Those that return the most common user-interface values, such as the `ActiveCell` property, do not require the use of the `Application` object in the statement. Both of these statements are valid:

```
Application.ActiveCell
ActiveCell
```

Workbook Object

Every workbook you open in Excel is a `Workbook` object. Every `Workbook` object is part of the `Workbooks` collection. The `Workbooks` collection is part of the `Application` object. You can use the `Workbook` object methods to do things such as save or close a workbook. See Chapter 9 for more information on working with the `Workbook` object.

Worksheet Object

Every worksheet in Excel is a `Worksheet` object. Every `Worksheet` object is part of the `Worksheets` collection. You can use `Worksheet` methods to do things such as add, delete, or copy a worksheet. See Chapter 10 for more information about working with the `Worksheet` object.

Chart Object

Every chart in a workbook is a `Chart` object. You can embed a chart in a worksheet or you can place a chart on a chart sheet. The `ChartObject` object holds `Chart` objects you embed in a worksheet. All `ChartObject` objects are part of a `ChartObjects` object collection. `Chart` objects you place on a chart sheet are part of the `Charts` collection. See Chapter 15 for more information about working with charts.

Range Object

The `Range` object enables you to reference an individual cell or a range of cells. Several different methods and properties use `Range` objects. See Chapter 11 for more information on the `Range` object. The following references cell B3:

```
Range("B3")
```

Dialog Object

The `Dialog` object references each of the built-in dialog boxes available in Excel. Excel stores these dialog boxes in the `Dialogs` collection. VBA identifies each dialog box by assigning it a constant value. The constant value begins with `xlDialog` followed by the name of the dialog box. For example, `xlDialogSaveAs` references the Save As dialog box. You can use the constant value associated with a dialog box to view the dialog box. You view individual dialog boxes by using the `Show` method. The `Dialog` object refers to existing dialog boxes. For information on creating dialog boxes, see Chapter 14.

Excel Properties

Each object in the Excel object model has properties. Properties enable you to view or change the characteristics of an object. For example, you can use the `Value` property to change the value of a cell. You can also use properties to change other aspects of an object. For example, you can use the `Hidden` property to hide or unhide a worksheet. To change an object property, you combine the object name with the property name and then assign a property, as follows:

```
Range("A1").Value = 45
```

Excel Methods

Each object in the Excel object model has methods. You use methods to perform actions on objects. For example, you can use the `Copy` method to copy a worksheet and place the copy in a specified location.

To use a method with an object, you combine the object name with the method name, as in the following example:

```
Worksheets(1).CopyAfter:=Worksheets(3)
```

Object Collections

You can have multiple objects of the same type, such as multiple worksheets in a workbook. To make these objects more accessible, VBA groups them together in an object collection. For example, each `Workbook` object contains a `Worksheets` collection. You access a collection in a manner similar to the way you access an array. You use an index value to reference the desired object in the collection. The following code accesses the second worksheet in the `Worksheets` collection:

```
Worksheets(2)
```

Glossary

TERM	DESCRIPTION
Object	An element in an application, such as a worksheet, chart, or form. You can use VBA to manipulate objects.
Properties	The characteristics of an object, such as its color, size, or location.
Methods	The actions VBA can perform on an object, such as copy, save, or move. For example, you can use methods to copy, save, or move a worksheet.

Access the Excel Object Model Reference

When you want to know what objects are available to you and the properties and methods associated with those objects, you can refer to the Excel Object Model Reference, which is part of the VBA help system. The Excel Object Model Reference provides documentation on every object, method, property, and event in the Excel object model. An *event* occurs in Excel whenever the user performs any type of action. You can use events to trigger the execution of a procedure by creating event-handling procedures. See Chapter 17 to learn more about events.

The Excel Object Model Reference explains every object, and provides you with sample code. You can cut and paste the sample code into the VBE and then run it in Excel. The Excel Object Model Reference explains each

method, provides you with the syntax for each method, explains the parameters associated with each method, and provides you with sample code for most methods. The Excel Object Model Reference also explains each object property and event and provides you with the syntax and sample code for most properties and events.

When using the Excel Object Model Reference, you can access the information you want in several ways. When you type the name of an object, method, property, or event into the Search field, the Excel Object Model Reference brings back a list of topics. You can then click the topic of interest to you. You also can select topics from the Developer Reference Table of Contents, which appears when you access help.

Access the Excel Object Model Reference

① Click Help in the VBE.

A menu appears.

② Click Microsoft Visual Basic for Applications Help.

● The Excel 2010 Developer Reference window appears.

③ Click Excel Object Model Reference.

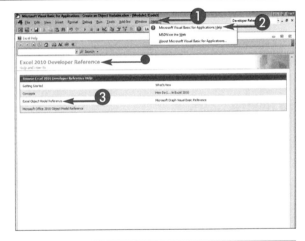

A list of the objects in the Excel object model appears.

④ Click the object for which you want more information.

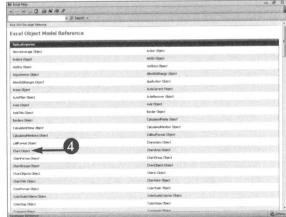

A window with links
to the properties,
methods, and
events appears.

5 Click the
subcategory or
topic in which you
are interested.

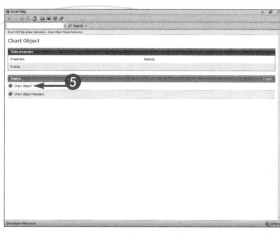

Information on the
topic or a menu of
additional choices
appears.

If a menu appears,
choose an option,
Excel displays
information on the
topic you selected.

Extra

You can use the Object Browser to access a
list of objects, properties, and methods
available for your use. You open the Object
Browser by pressing F2, or by choosing View
→ Object Browser from the menu while in the
VBE. In the field in the upper left corner of the
browser, select Excel to access the Excel
Object Model Reference. Use the Search field
in the upper left corner to search for the object
you want to find. When you find what you are
looking for, click it and then click the question
mark at the top of the window for help.

If you position your cursor over
a keyword in your code and
then right-click, a contextual
menu appears. Click List
Properties/Methods to see a
list of properties or methods
that you can use with the
keyword. Click List Constants
to see a list of constants that
you can use with the keyword.
Click Parameter Info to see a
list of parameters.

As you type your code, the
VBE provides you with a
list of properties, methods,
and constants that you can
use with the object for
which you are creating a
command.

Create an
Object Variable

You can reference objects by typing the complete object reference each time you want to reference the object, or you can assign an object to a variable. You assign objects to variables because variable names are usually shorter and easier to remember, and you can change the objects that variables refer to while your code is running. In addition, VBA code runs faster when you use object variables.

You declare object variables in much the same way as you declare a standard variable. You use the Dim statement to declare the variable and the As statement to identify the variable as an object variable. The data type for the variable is the corresponding object type. For example, the statement Dim SampleVar As Worksheet creates an object variable named SampleVar that is a Worksheet object.

After you create an object variable, you assign an object to the variable by using a Set statement. The following statement assigns Sheet1 to SampleVar:

```
Set SampleVar = ActiveWorkbook. _

Worksheets("Sheet1")
```

When you assign an object to a variable, you are assigning a reference to the object to the variable and not the actual object value. For example, when you assign a range to a variable without using a Set statement, you are assigning the value in the cell to the variable. When you assign a range to a variable using a Set statement, you reference the actual cells. Assigning a range to a variable by using the Set statement enables you to use the variable to set properties for the range.

Create an Object Variable

① Name your procedure.

② Declare your object variable.

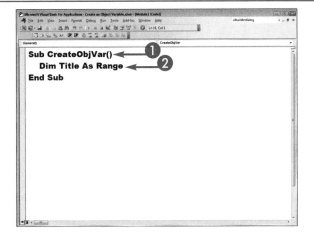

③ Use a Set statement to assign an object to the variable you created.

④ Assign the object properties.

● Assigns a text to a cell.

● Places a thick border at the bottom of the cell.

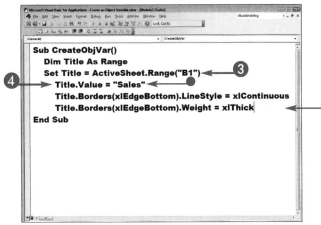

- Makes the font bold.

- Makes the font color blue.

- Right-aligns the text.

⑤ Press Alt+F11 to switch from the VBE to Excel, and run the macro.

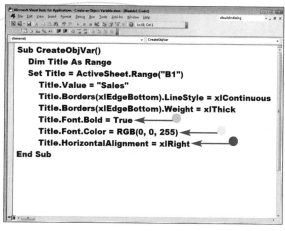

- The macro places the text you specified in the cell you specified, adds a thick border to the bottom of the cell, makes the font bold, and sets the font color to blue.

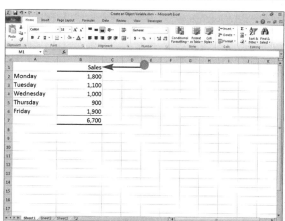

Extra

If you want to refer to the currently selected worksheet, you can use the `ActiveSheet` property. You can use this property in place of an object reference to the worksheet, such as `Worksheets(1)`, which refers to the first worksheet in a workbook. By using the `ActiveSheet` property, you reference the active worksheet at the time your procedure executes. For example, `SheetName = ActiveSheet.Name` assigns the name of the currently active worksheet to the `SheetName` variable.

The `ActiveSheet` property can refer to any type of sheet within a workbook. Therefore, if the currently selected sheet is a chart sheet, the `ActiveSheet` property returns a reference to the chart sheet. See Chapter 10 for more information on working with worksheets.

When you create object variables, you are essentially creating an object reference. Unlike a standard variable, which is the name of a memory location containing the variable's value, an object variable is the memory location that stores a reference to the object. For example, in the following code, `ObjVar` stores the reference to cell B2 in the worksheet.

Example:
```
Dim ObjVar As Range
Set ObjVar = ActiveSheet.Cells(2, 2)
```

Change the Properties of an Object

You can change the value of an object, its appearance, and other characteristics by modifying the properties associated with the object. For example, when working with a cell on a worksheet, you use the `Value` property to change the value of the cell. If you want to change the font style, you modify `Font` object properties, such as `Bold`, `Italic`, `Underline`, and `Size`.

If you want to make several property changes to the same object, you can create a statement for each property you want to change. For example, you can enter the following statements to change the properties of a cell:

```
Active Sheet.Range("B1").Value = "Sales"
```

```
Active Sheet.Range("B1").Borders _
(xlEdgeBottom).LineStyle = xlContinuous
```

```
Active Sheet.Range("B1").Borders _
(xlEdgeBottom).Weight = xlThick
```

```
Active Sheet.Range("B1").Font. _
Bold = True
```

```
Active Sheet.Range("B1").Font. _
Color = RGB(0, 0, 255)
```

You can simplify these statements by assigning `ActiveSheet.Range("B1")` to an object variable and then referencing the variable for each statement. For example, you can assign `ActiveSheet.Range("B1")` to the variable `Title` and type `Title.Value = "Sales"`.

You can simplify the statements even further by using a `With` statement. Instead of typing the object variable reference, you simply type `With VariableName` followed by each property statement. When you complete your list of property settings, you type `End With` to mark the end of your `With` statement. You can nest your `With` statements to further simplify your code.

Change the Properties of an Object

1 Name your procedure.

2 Declare your object variable.

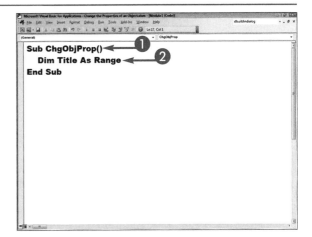

3 Use a `Set` statement to assign an object to the variable you created.

4 Assign the object properties by using a `With` statement.

● Assigns text to a cell.

● Places a thick border at the bottom of the cell.

● Right-aligns a cell.

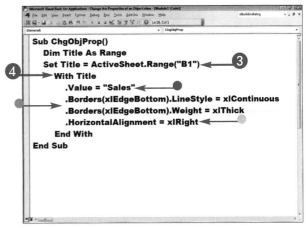

- Makes the font bold.

- Makes the font color blue.

- With statement.

- Nested With.

5 Press Alt+F11 to switch from the VBE to Excel, and run the macro.

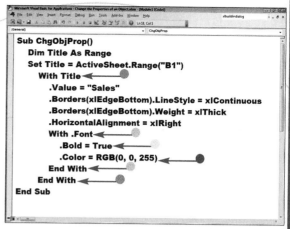

- The macro places the text you specified in the cell you specified, adds a thick border to the bottom of the cell, makes the font bold, and sets the font color to blue.

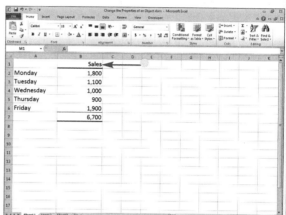

Extra

Some objects, such as the Font object, have a Color property that determines the color of the object. You can use the RGB function to set the font color. When you use this function, you select the desired color by indicating the amount of red, green, and blue in the color. You specify the color values with an integer value between 0 and 255. For example, you type **(0,0,0)** for the color black.

COLOR	RED VALUE	GREEN VALUE	BLUE VALUE
Black	0	0	0
Blue	0	0	255
Cyan	0	255	255
Green	0	255	0
Magenta	255	0	255
Red	255	0	0
White	255	255	255
Yellow	255	255	0

Compare Object Variables

You can use an object comparison to determine if two object variables reference the same object. Unlike standard variables, which actually contain values that you can compare, the object variable does not contain the object, but references it. When you compare two object variables, you are checking to see if they reference the same object. For example, you may want to find out if the currently active worksheet is the first worksheet. If so, you can perform an object comparison.

When you compare standard variables, you use the equals (=) operator to determine if they are the same. For example, If Value1 = Value2 Then compares two standard variables. See Chapter 3 for more information on working with standard variables.

When comparing objects, instead of the equals operator, you use the Is operator. For example, you write an If Then statement to compare two object variables as follows: If ObjVal1 Is ObjVal2 Then.

This statement looks at the object referenced by ObjVal1 and checks to see if it is the same as the object referenced by ObjVal2.

In addition to comparing two objects, you can also use the Is operator to determine if an object variable has an assigned value, as shown in the following example: If ObjVal1 Is Nothing Then. This comparison statement returns a value of True if the object variable does not reference an object. If the object variable references to an object, the comparison statement returns a value of False.

Compare Object Variables

① Name your procedure.

② Declare your variables.

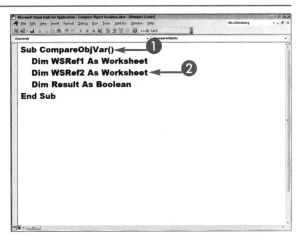

③ Assign objects to your object variables.

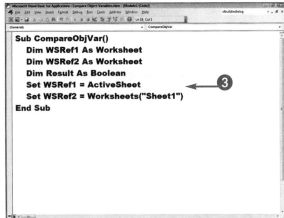

④ Compare the objects and assign the result to a variable.

⑤ Display the result using the `MsgBox` function.

⑥ Press Alt+F11 to switch from the VBE to Excel, and run the macro.

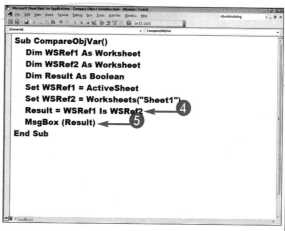

If you are on Sheet1, the macro returns the value `True`; otherwise, it returns the value `False`.

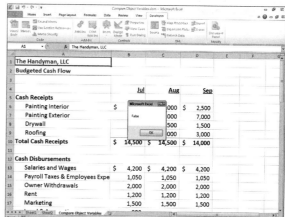

Extra

You can also use the `Is` operator with the `Nothing` keyword to ensure that an object variable points to a valid object. You can compare the value of the object variable to the `Nothing` keyword by using an `If Then` statement, as shown in the following example. If the `If Then` statement returns a value of `True`, the object variable does not contain a reference to a valid object.

Example:
```
If ObjVar Is Nothing Then
    MsgBox ("Variable does not reference a valid object.")
End If
```

You can use the `Nothing` keyword to clear the object variable. By doing so, you free up the memory required to store the object reference in the object variable.

Example:
```
Set ObjVar = Nothing
```

Using an Object Method

You use Excel object methods to modify or perform an action on an object. The Excel object model contains several hundred objects, and each object has a list of methods you can use with it. For example, you can use the `Copy` method to copy a `Worksheet` object and then place the copy in another location.

To use an object method, you specify the appropriate object, followed by a period and the method you want to use. If the selected method has arguments, you place the arguments after the method:

```
Worksheet("Sheet2").Copy Before:=
 Worksheet("Sheet1")
```

In this example, the code copies `Sheet2` and places the copy before `Sheet1` in the current workbook.

`Worksheet("Sheet2")` is the object, `Copy` is the method, and `Before:= Worksheet("Sheet1")` is the argument.

Most methods take arguments. Arguments tell VBA how to modify the object. Usually, at least one argument is required. In this example, the `Copy` method requires you use either the `Before` or `After` argument to tell VBA where to place the copied worksheet. Use the `Before` argument to specify the sheet before which you want to place the copied worksheet. Use the `After` argument to specify the sheet after which you want to place the copied worksheet. See Chapter 10 for more information about copying Excel worksheets.

Using an Object Method

① Name your procedure.

② Declare a `Range` object variable.

③ Store an object to an object variable.

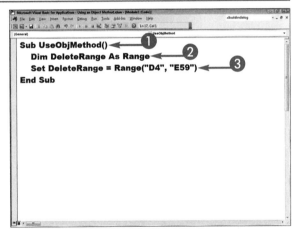

④ Use a method to perform an action on an object.

In this example, you use the `Delete` method to delete a range.

● The `Range` object.

● The `Delete` method.

● Assigns arguments to the method.

This argument is a constant that tells VBA to shift cells to the left after deleting.

⑤ Press Alt+F11 to switch from the VBE to Excel, and run the macro.

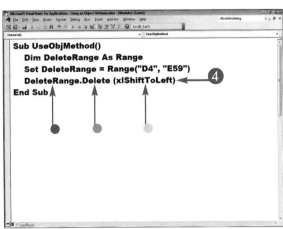

The worksheet before you run the macro.

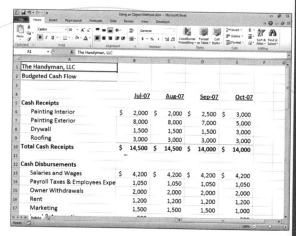

The worksheet after you run the macro.

- The macro deletes the range.

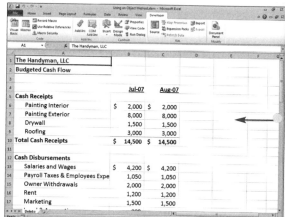

Extra

You can use named arguments with functions, methods, and statements. Using named arguments is an easier way to supply your functions, methods, and statements with the arguments, especially when a large number of arguments are required. If you do not use a named argument, you supply arguments by placing them after the method, enclosed in parentheses and separated by commas in the order VBA expects them. For example, the `Worksheet` object's `Protect` method has 16 optional arguments. If you do not use named arguments, then calling this property requires a placeholder for each argument to specify a value for each parameter, as shown in this example:

Example:
```
Worksheets(1).Protect("Excel", , , , , , , , , , , , , ,True,)
```

If you use named arguments, you can provide the arguments in any order. You assign a value to the argument by using a colon followed by an equals sign (: =).

Example:
```
Worksheets(1).Protect Password:= _
    "Excel", AllowFiltering:=True
```

Display a Built-in Dialog Box

You can incorporate code into your procedure that opens a built-in Excel dialog box. The Excel object model contains a `Dialog` object for each Excel dialog box. These objects are part of the `Dialogs` collection. You can access each of the Excel dialog box objects by specifying its constant value. The constant value for each dialog box begins with `xlDialog` followed by the name of the dialog box. For example, the constant for the Excel Save As dialog box is `xlDialogSaveAs`.

You can find a complete list of the dialog box constants in the help that comes with the VBE by typing `XlBuiltInDialog` in the Search field and then clicking XlBuiltInDialog Enumeration.

You use the `Show` method to display a built-in dialog box. You cannot access the values that a user places in the fields. You can only determine what the user selects by looking at the results after the user dismisses the dialog box. You can use arguments to assign values to a dialog box. For example, the Properties dialog box (`xlDialogProperties`) has the following arguments: `Title`, `Subject`, `Author`, `Keywords`, and `Comments`. You can enter the values for these arguments before you open your dialog box. For a list of the arguments associated with each dialog box, type **Built-In Dialog Box Arguments List** in the Search field and then, in the list of options that appears, click Built-In Dialog Box Arguments Lists. If you want to use named arguments to assign values to the arguments, use `Arg1` for the first argument, `Arg2` for the second argument, and continue in this manner. For example, if you are working with the `xlDialogProperties` dialog box, you can use `Arg1` for Title and `Arg2` for Subject.

Display a Built-in Dialog Box

① Create a new procedure.

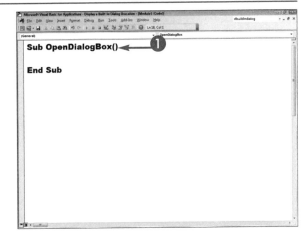

② Type your command.

● The `Show` method.

● The title.

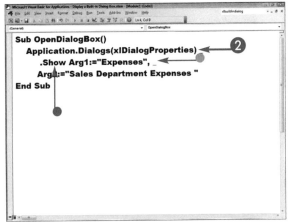

- The subject.

3 Press Alt+F11 to switch from the VBE to Excel, and run the macro.

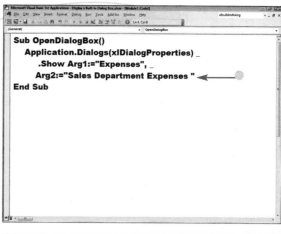

```
Sub OpenDialogBox()
    Application.Dialogs(xlDialogProperties) _
        .Show Arg1:="Expenses", _
        Arg2:="Sales Department Expenses "  ◄────
End Sub
```

The macro adds the arguments to the dialog box and then opens the dialog box.

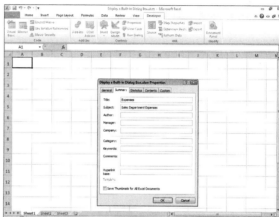

Excel has hundreds of dialog boxes that appear throughout the application. You can display them by using the appropriate constant. The following table lists a few of the most commonly used Excel dialog boxes:

CONSTANT	DISPLAYS
xlDialogFileDelete	The Delete dialog box, where you select files to remove
xlDialogInsert	The Insert dialog box for adding additional cells to a worksheet
xlDialogNew	The New dialog box
xlDialogOpen	The Open dialog box
xlDialogPrint	The Print dialog box
xlDialogSaveAs	The Save As dialog box

Declare an Array

I f you have a group of related values of the same data type, you can declare them as an array. You declare an array in much the same way you declare other variables and, as with other variables, you can declare arrays as either local or global. You set the scope of an array with the Dim or Public statements. See the section "Understanding Variables and Data Types" in Chapter 3 for more information about setting the scope of a variable.

You can use arrays to store a group of related data. Using arrays simplifies your code because you can use one variable to store several values. For example, you can declare an array and use it to store all 12 months of the year instead of creating a separate variable for each month.

When you declare an array, you specify the number of elements in the array. For example, the declaration Dim Month(1 To 12) As String declares 12 elements numbered sequentially 1 through 12. In the example, the Month array has 12 elements with a lower bound of 1 and an upper bound of 12.

An element is a data value in the array. You access the elements in an array by using the index value that represents the desired element. Elements are sequentially numbered. The lower bound of an array is the lowest index value, and the upper bound of an array is the highest index value. To access the second element of the Month array, use the index value of 2, as in Month(2).

Declare an Array

1 Name your procedure.

2 Declare your array.

Note: *For more information on data types, see Chapter 3.*

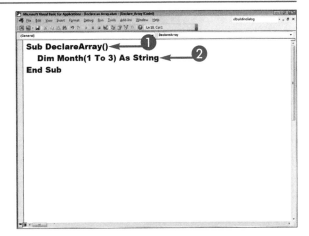

3 Assign values to the array elements.

● A number enclosed in parentheses identifies each element.

④ Use the `Cells` method to assign the values in the array to cells in the spreadsheet.

Note: For more information, see the section "Reference Cells and Ranges" in Chapter 3.

⑤ Press Alt+F11 to switch from the VBE to Excel, and run the macro.

Note: See Chapter 1 to learn how to run a macro.

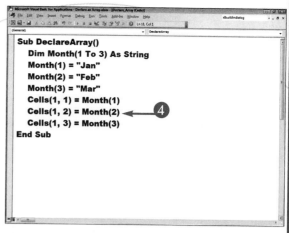

```
Sub DeclareArray()
    Dim Month(1 To 3) As String
    Month(1) = "Jan"
    Month(2) = "Feb"
    Month(3) = "Mar"
    Cells(1, 1) = Month(1)
    Cells(1, 2) = Month(2)          ④
    Cells(1, 3) = Month(3)
End Sub
```

Excel places the values in the array in the specified cells.

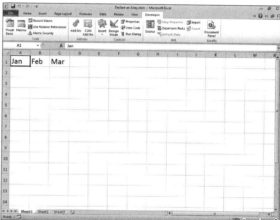

Extra

When you specify the size of an array, you indicate the upper and lower bounds of the array, or the first and last index values. In the example, `Dim NewArray(1 To 45)`, the statement creates an array with 45 elements with a lower bound of 1 and an upper bound of 45. You can omit the lower bound value when you declare an array, as in the example, `Dim NewArray(45)`. If you do not specify the lower bound, VBA assigns a lower bound value of 0. Therefore, the array `NewArray` actually has 46 elements starting with the first element 0 and ending with the final element 45.

If you want all your arrays to have a lower bound value of 1, place the following statement before any procedures in your module: `Option Base 1`. Making your arrays one-based is desirable because Microsoft Excel collections are one-based and the arrays that Excel methods and properties return are one-based. If your arrays are also one-based, your code is easier to debug.

Declare a Multidimensional Array

Y ou can use a multidimensional array to store related values within one array. VBA allows you to create arrays with up to 60 dimensions. However, working with arrays that have more than two or three dimensions is unusual.

By using multidimensional arrays, you can store related values in one location. For example, you can store team numbers and game scores. The first dimension of the array can contain the team's number, and the second dimension can contain the team's score. To help envision a multidimensional array, try thinking of a two-dimensional array as a worksheet, with rows and columns. You access each element of the array by specifying two index values. For example, `MultiArray(1,2)` accesses the value whose first dimension index is `1` and whose second dimension index is `2` — or first row, second column.

As you add a third dimension to an array, it gains depth. Using the worksheet example, you can add a third dimension to the two-dimensional array to make it resemble a cube. Accessing an element of the array now requires three index values, as in the example `MultiArray(1,2,2)` — first row, second column, two deep.

As with other variables, you use the `Dim` statement to declare procedure-only arrays and module-only arrays, and the `Public` statement for arrays that are accessible to the entire workbook.

When you declare a multidimensional array, you indicate the size of each dimension in the array. You do not have to make the dimensions in the array equal. In the example `Dim MultiArray(1 To 4, 1 To 5, 1 To 3)`, the array contains four elements in the first dimension, five in the second, and three in the third.

Declare a Multidimensional Array

① Name your procedure.

② Declare your multidimensional array.

③ Specify the range in your Excel worksheet in which VBA will place the contents of your array.

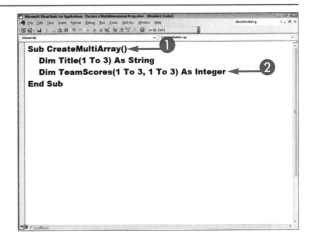

④ Assign values to the array elements.

⑤ Assign the array values to the cells you specified in Step 3.

⑥ Press Alt+F11 to switch from the VBE to Excel, and run the macro.

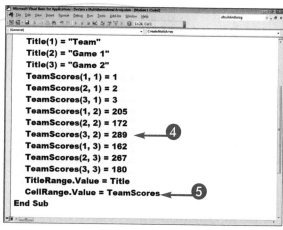

The values in the array appear in cells in your worksheet.

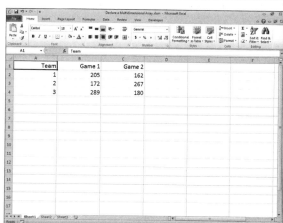

Apply It

You can assign the contents of an array to a series of cells in a worksheet by using the `Value` property of the `Range` object. To learn more about the `Range` object, see Chapter 11. When you create a `Range` object, you can specify the cells you want to include in the range by using the `Set` statement. As the macro runs, VBA places any values you assign to the `Range` object in the corresponding cells in your worksheet.

Example:
```
Dim CellRange As Range
Set CellRange = Range(Cells(2,1), Cells(4,3))
CellRange.Value = TeamScores
```

The `Set` statement assigns the range of cells to the `Range` object. You specify the range by using the `Cells` property to determine the starting and ending cells for the desired range. After you specify the desired range, you assign the contents of an array to the cells in the range by using the `Value` property.

When you use a multidimensional array, all elements of the array must have the same data type. If you plan to use the array to store different types of values, such as strings and numeric values, you must declare your array as variant.

Example:
```
Dim MultiArray (1 To 4, 1
    To 5, 1 To 3) As Variant
```

Convert a List to an Array

By converting a list of values to an array, you can access the individual values quickly using one variable. You can use a variety of methods to convert a list of values to an array.

You can assign values to your array by referencing the index values of each element. Arrays use index values to identify their elements. For example, if an array has ten elements with a lower bound of 1, the third element in the array has an index value of 3. To assign a value to an array, you specify the index values that correspond to the appropriate array element. For example, the following code assigns a value of 45 to the third array element:
`SampleArray(3) = 45`.

With large arrays, assigning values to each element of the array in a statement using the above method can be

cumbersome. Using a `For Next` loop is more efficient; you simply create a `For Next` loop to cycle through the entire array. `For Next` loops work best for adding values either from a series of cells or when values are incremental. See Chapter 6 for more information about working with `For Next` loops.

You can use the `Array` function to add a list of values to an array. The `Array` function adds values to the array by starting at the lower bound of the array and then adding values consecutively. For example, the following code adds the values `"One"`, `"Two"`, and `"Three"` to `SampleArray`:
`SampleArray = Array("One", "Two", "Three")`.

You can produce the same results by specifying each element individually; for example, you can assign a value to the first element of the array, as follows:
`SampleArray(1) = "One"`.

Convert a List to an Array

① Name your procedure.

② Declare your array.

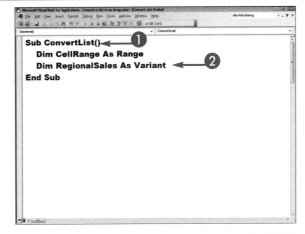

③ Assign values to your array.

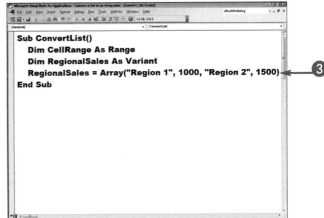

④ Set the `Range` property.

⑤ Assign the values in the array to the range.

⑥ Press Alt+F11 to switch from the VBE to Excel, and run the macro.

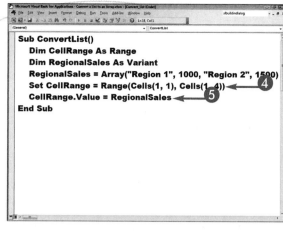

The values in the array appear in cells in your worksheet.

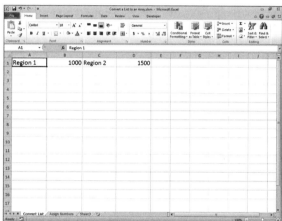

Extra

The `Array` function uses the variant data type. As a result, you can have different data types in a single array. As shown in the example in this section, you can add both strings and numeric values to the same variable when using the `Array` function.

You can use the `ReDim` statement to change the size of the array after you create it. You can also use the `Array` function more than once in the same procedure to reassign the values in the array. See the section "Redimension an Array" for more information on resizing an array.

You can use the following code to assign the numbers 1 to 10 to an array. See Chapter 6 for more information on `For Next` loops.

Example:
```
Sub AssignNumbers()
    Dim X as Integer
    Dim RecNo(1 To 10) As Integer
    For X =1 To 10
        RecNo(X) = X
        Cells(X,1) = RecNo(X)
    Next
End Sub
```

Redimension an Array

VBA lets you declare two types of arrays: fixed-size and dynamic arrays. When you declare a fixed-size array, you specify the number of elements in the array. For example, the following code creates a fixed-size array with seven elements: `Dim NewArray(1,7) As String`.

If you do not know how large to make the array when you declare it, you can use a dynamic array. A dynamic array does not have a size until you use the `ReDim` statement to change the array size. First, use the `Dim` statement without a size to create a dynamic array — for example: `Dim NewArray() As String`.

When you are ready to use the array, use the `ReDim` statement to size the array so you can add values. For example, in the code, `ReDim NewArray(1 To 4)`, an array that was initially declared as a dynamic array with an unknown number of elements is redimensioned to contain four elements.

VBA does not allow you to redimension a fixed-size array. If you attempt to change the size of a fixed-size array, you receive an "Array already dimensioned" error message. However, if you declare your array as a dynamic array, you can use the `ReDim` statement multiple times within a procedure to change the size of the array.

Each time you redimension an array, you destroy the existing elements in the array. If you want to retain the existing values, use the `Preserve` statement. For example, the statement `ReDim Preserve NewArray(7)` instructs VBA to resize the array to seven elements and maintain any existing values. If the array has four values, those values remain the first four values.

Redimension an Array

1. Name your procedure.

2. Declare a dynamic array.

3. Set the initial dimension size.

4. Assign a value to the variable element.

5. Place the contents of the variable in a cell.

6. Redimension the array.

7. Assign values to the variable elements.

8. Place the contents of the variables in cells.

9. Redimension the array.

10. Assign values to the variable elements.

11. Place the contents of the variables into cells.

12. Preserve the first four elements and add space for three more.

13. Assign values to the three new elements.

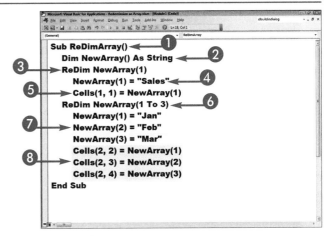

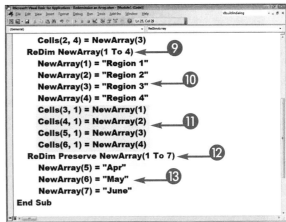

14 Place the values for all of the elements in the worksheet.

15 Press Alt+F11 to switch from the VBE to Excel, and run the macro.

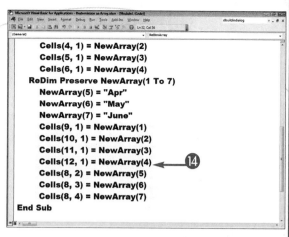

```
        Cells(4, 1) = NewArray(2)
        Cells(5, 1) = NewArray(3)
        Cells(6, 1) = NewArray(4)
    ReDim Preserve NewArray(1 To 7)
        NewArray(5) = "Apr"
        NewArray(6) = "May"
        NewArray(7) = "June"
        Cells(9, 1) = NewArray(1)
        Cells(10, 1) = NewArray(2)
        Cells(11, 1) = NewArray(3)
        Cells(12, 1) = NewArray(4)
        Cells(8, 2) = NewArray(5)
        Cells(8, 3) = NewArray(6)
        Cells(8, 4) = NewArray(7)
    End Sub
```

The values in the array appear in cells in your worksheet.

● These values were preserved.

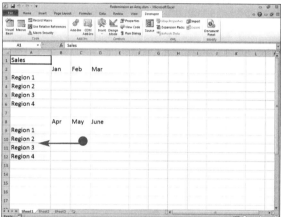

Extra

To find the upper and lower bounds of an array, VBA provides the `UBound` and `LBound` functions. The example finds the upper and lower bounds and assigns them to variables.

Example:
```
UpperBound = UBound(NewArray)
LowerBound = LBound(NewArray)
```

Each of these functions returns a Long data type indicating the upper or lower bounds of the specified array. If the array is multidimensional, you must specify the dimension for which you want the bounds.

Example:
```
UpperBounds = UBound(MultiArray, 2)
```

Create a User-Defined Data Type

U ser-defined data types enable you to create a single variable that records multiple pieces of information. User-defined data types resemble multidimensional arrays in that you can store related values by using one variable name. However, although all elements in the array must contain the same data type, you can create a user-defined data type that contains multiple data types.

You declare user-defined data types at the top of your module in the declarations area. You specify a user-defined data type with the Type and End Type statements. The Type statement indicates the start of the user-defined data type definition, and the End Type statement specifies the end. After the Type statement, you indicate the name of the new data type; for example, Type ItemInfo creates a data type called ItemInfo. To create a user-defined data

type to store a price and description, you can specify a user-defined data type with two components.

After you create the data type, you can declare variables that use the specified data type. You can use a user-defined data type as the data type for an array. For example, to create an array of the ItemInfo data type, you enter Dim NewItems(1 To 10) As ItemInfo.

To assign values to a user-defined array, you not only specify the array element, but you also indicate the component you want to change. For example, this code changes the value of the first component in the array: NewItems(1).ItemDescription = "15 inch Monitor".

Similarly, you can copy the entire contents of one element to another by simply referring to the array element. The following code copies ItemDescription and ItemPrice of the first element of the array to the second array element: NewItems(2) = NewItems(1).

Create a User-Defined Data Type

① Create your user-defined data type in the declarations area.

② Add the Type and End Type statements.

③ Declare the components.

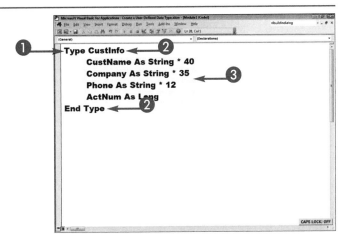

④ Create a new procedure.

⑤ Declare your user-defined data type.

⑥ Assign values to your user-defined data type.

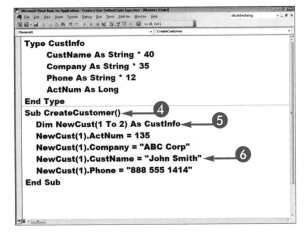

7 Copy the contents of one element to another element.

8 Place the contents of both elements in worksheet cells.

9 Press Alt+F11 to switch from the VBE to Excel, and run the macro.

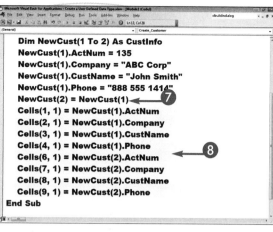

The values from the user-defined data type appear in cells in your worksheet.

● VBA copies the values from the first element to the second element.

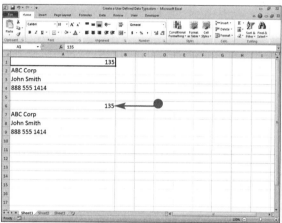

Extra

As you use VBA to develop macros, the complexity of your code may make it difficult to keep track of variables. To simplify the process, many developers use a standard naming convention where the variable name reflects the variable type. When using this type of naming convention, you preface each variable name with a standard lowercase prefix that identifies the data type of the variable. For example, you can identify an integer variable by prefixing it with i to create the variable name iNumVisits. The integer prefix makes it clear at any location in the code that the variable holds an integer value. The following table lists the standard variable-naming conventions for Visual Basic and VBA.

PREFIX	DATA TYPE
b	Boolean
c **or** cur	Currency
dt	Date/Time
d	Double
i **or** int	Integer
l **or** lng	Long
obj	Object
s **or** sng	Single
str	String
u	User-defined
v **or** var	Variant

Create Comparisons

Comparison operators allow you to compare two expressions. Comparison expressions always return either `True` or `False`. For example, the expression, A = B, compares the variable A to the variable B. It then returns `True` if the value stored in variable A is equal to the value stored in variable B, or `False` if the value stored in variable A is not equal to the value stored in variable B.

When writing a comparison expression, you use a comparison operator. You place the comparison operator between the expressions you want to compare. For example, you can use the equal (=) sign to determine if two values are equal or you can use the not equal (<>) sign to determine if values are not equal.

The following table is a summary of the comparison operators:

OPERATOR	FUNCTION
=	Equal to
<>	Not equal
>	Greater than
<	Less than
<=	Less than or equal to
>=	Greater than or equal to

Create Comparisons

① Add a comparison operator to your `Do While` loop.

In this example, if `Counter` is less than 11, VBA executes the code inside the loop.

Note: See the section "Employ Do While Loops" in this chapter to learn more about `Do While` loops.

② Add a comparison operator to your `If` and `ElseIf` statements.

Note: See the section "Create If Then Else Statements" in this chapter to learn more about `If Then` statements.

Make Use of Logical Operators

When writing VBA code, you can use logical operators to link together comparison expressions to create complex comparison expressions. There are six logical operators: Or, And, Xor, Eqv, Imp, and Not.

Using Logical Or

The logical operator Or returns the value True if expression A is true or expression B is true.

EXPRESSION A	EXPRESSION B	RESULT
True	True	True
True	False	True
False	True	True
False	False	False

Example:
```
Sub LogicalOr()
    Dim Result As Boolean
    Result = 10 < 20 Or 30 < 20 'Returns True
    MsgBox (Result)
End Sub
```

Using Logical And

The logical operator And returns the value True if expression A is true and expression B is true.

EXPRESSION A	EXPRESSION B	RESULT
True	True	True
True	False	False
False	True	False
False	False	False

Using Logical Xor

The logical value Xor returns the value True if expression A is true and expression B is false, or if expression A is false and expression B is true.

EXPRESSION A	EXPRESSION B	RESULT
True	True	False
True	False	True
False	True	True
False	False	False

Using Logical Eqv

The Eqv operator returns the value True if expression A is true and expression B is true, or if expression A is false and expression B is false.

EXPRESSION A	EXPRESSION B	RESULT
True	True	True
True	False	False
False	True	False
False	False	True

Using Logical Imp

The Imp operator returns True unless expression A is true and expression B is false.

EXPRESSION A	EXPRESSION B	RESULT
True	True	True
True	False	False
False	True	True
False	False	True

Using Logical Not

The Not logical operator negates an expression. If the expression would normally return True, using a Not operator causes it to return False and vice versa.

Example:
```
Sub LogicalNot()
    Dim Result As Boolean
    Result = Not (10 = 10) 'Returns False
    MsgBox (Result)
End Sub
```

Employ Do While Loops

Y ou can execute a VBA statement or a series of VBA statements as long as a condition is `True` by using a `Do While` loop. The following is the syntax for a `Do While` loop:

```
Do [While condition]
    [statements]
Loop
```

A condition is an expression that evaluates to either `True` or `False`. When VBA encounters a `Do While` loop, it evaluates the condition. If the condition is `True`, it executes the statements. After it executes all of the statements, VBA returns to the `Do While` statement and evaluates the condition again. If the condition is still `True`, it executes the statements again. If the condition is `False`, VBA executes the first statement after the `Loop` statement.

A `Do While` loop consists of four basic parts: The `Do` statement initiates the loop. The `While` statement evaluates the condition that must be met. The body of the loop contains a series of statements to perform as long as the condition is `True`. Finally, the `Loop` statement marks the end of the loop.

You also use the following syntax to create a `Do-Loop While` loop:

```
Do
    [statements]
Loop [While condition]
```

A `Do-Loop While` loop is similar to a `Do While` loop. The primary difference is VBA evaluates the condition at the end of the block of statements so the loop always executes at least once.

Employ Do While Loops

① Name your procedure.

② Declare your variables.

③ Assign values to your variables.

This example assigns the number 1 to the variable `Counter` and then uses the variable as a counter. It also assigns the number 1 to the variable `RowNum` and then uses the variable as the row number.

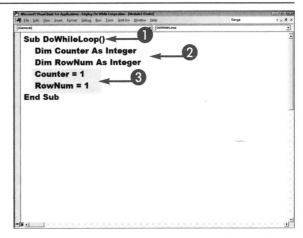

④ Use a `Do While` statement to evaluate whether a condition is `True`.

In this example, the code looks at the value assigned to the variable `Counter` and performs the statements inside the loop if `Counter` is less than 11.

⑤ Place the value of `Counter` in the specified cell.

In this example, the cell row starts at 1 and increases with each loop. The cell column is column 1 (column A).

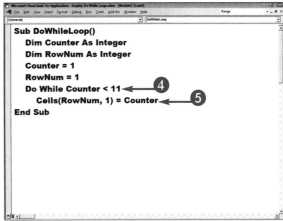

6 Increase the value of the counter.

In this example, VBA adds 1 to the current value of `Counter`.

● This example also adds 1 to the current value of the row number.

7 Add the `Loop` statement.

VBA returns to the `Do While` statement and continues looping until your code no longer meets the condition.

8 Press Alt+F11 to switch from the VBE to Excel, and then run the macro.

Note: See Chapter 1 to learn how to run a macro.

The macro places the numbers 1 to 10 in column A, rows 1 to 10.

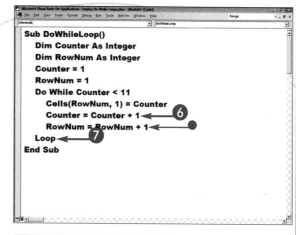

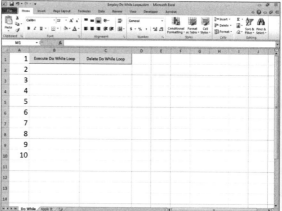

Apply It

A loop must contain a statement that changes the condition, and the condition must eventually evaluate to `False`, or the loop continues endlessly. Programmers refer to this condition as an *infinite loop*.

To avoid an infinite loop, you can use a counter. In the following example, the procedure assigns the variable `Counter` an initial value of 1. The `Do While` loop verifies that it is less than 5, and then executes the loop. The loop assigns a value of 1 to the first cell on the worksheet, cell A1. The variable `Counter` increments by 1, and the loop retests the condition. The looping continues until the condition is `False`. In this example, the loop repeats four times. When `Counter` equals 5, the looping stops.

Example:
```
Dim Counter As Integer
Counter = 1
Do While Counter < 5
    Cells(Counter, 1) = Counter
    Counter = Counter + 1
Loop
```

Create Do Until Loops

I f you need to execute a statement or a series of statements until a condition is met, you can use a Do Until loop. For example, you can use a Do Until loop to apply changes to a series of cells until you encounter an empty cell.

When you use the Do Until loop, the statements you place between the Do Until and Loop statements execute until the specified condition is met. As soon as the looping structure determines that the condition is True, control moves to the next statement outside the loop.

A Do Until loop consists of four basic parts: The Do statement initiates the loop. The Until condition specifies the condition that must be met. The body of the loop contains a series of statements that execute until the

value of the statement meets the condition of the loop. Finally, the Loop statement marks the end of the loop.

When the Until condition follows the Do statement, the Do Until loop checks to see if the condition is True before executing. If the condition is not True, the loop executes. If the condition is True, the loop does not execute. When you use this structure for a Do Until loop, the code inside the loop may never execute.

You can also place the Until condition at the end of the loop. When you place the Until condition at the end of the loop, the Do Until loop always executes at least once before checking the condition. If the condition is True, the Do Until loop stops execution, and control passes to the next VBA statement in your procedure.

Create Do Until Loops

① Name your procedure.

② Declare your variable.

③ Assign a value to your variable.

In this example, the variable RowNum is used to set the row number.

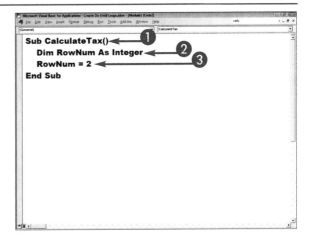

④ Add a Do Until statement.

In this example, the loop continues until it reaches an empty cell.

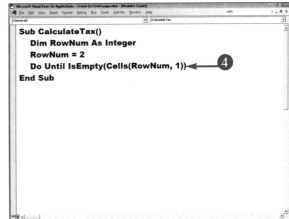

⑤ Type the statements you want to execute.

In this example, VBA multiplies the value in column A by 0.07 and places the result in column B.

⑥ Add the Loop statement.

VBA returns to the Do Until statement and continues looping until the condition is met.

⑦ Press Alt+F11 to switch from the VBE to Excel, and then run the macro.

Note: See Chapter 1 to learn how to run a macro.

The procedure places 7 percent of column A in column B.

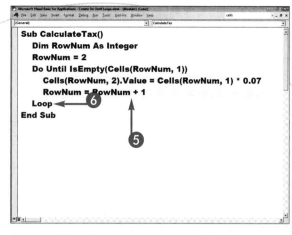

```
Sub CalculateTax()
    Dim RowNum As Integer
    RowNum = 2
    Do Until IsEmpty(Cells(RowNum, 1))
        Cells(RowNum, 2).Value = Cells(RowNum, 1) * 0.07
        RowNum = RowNum + 1
    Loop
End Sub
```

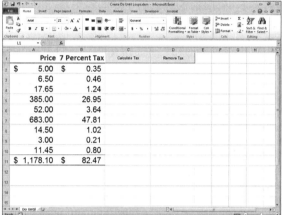

	Price	7 Percent Tax	Calculate Tax	Remove Tax
	$ 5.00	$ 0.35		
	6.50	0.46		
	17.65	1.24		
	385.00	26.95		
	52.00	3.64		
	683.00	47.81		
	14.50	1.02		
	3.00	0.21		
	11.45	0.80		
	$ 1,178.10	$ 82.47		

Extra

When working with loops, you may have situations where you want to jump out of a loop before executing the remaining statements in the loop. You can use an Exit Do statement. You can place an Exit Do statement anywhere within the body of your loop, and you can have multiple Exit Do statements. When VBA encounters an Exit Do statement, the control immediately transfers out of the current loop to the next statement outside the loop.

Typically, a conditional statement such as If Then appears before the Exit Do statement. The conditional statement looks for a condition to meet and then executes the Exit Do statement when your code meets the condition.

Example:
```
Do While Condition1 = True
    If Condition2 = True
        Exit Do
    End If
Loop
```

Create For Next Loops

You can use a For Next loop to execute a statement or a series of statements a specific number of times. For example, by using a For Next loop, you can place text in a specified number of cells.

When you use a For Next loop, you must create a counter variable. The statements you place between the For and Next statements execute until the counter variable exceeds the maximum value. As soon as the looping structure determines that the current value of the counter is greater than the maximum value, control moves to the first statement after the loop.

For Next loops consist of three basic parts: The For statement initiates the loop. The For statement includes a counter variable with an initial and maximum value, such

as X = 1 To 5. The body of the loop consists of a series of statements that perform until the counter exceeds the maximum value of the loop. Finally, you mark the end of the loop with the Next statement.

When the For Next loop starts, it checks to make sure the value of the counter variable does not exceed the maximum value. If the variable is less than or equal to the maximum, the loop executes. The counter variable is a numeric value that increments by default by one each time the loop executes. The loop continues to execute as long as the initial value is less than or equal to the maximum value specified for the counter variable. If the initial value starts out greater than the maximum value, the body of the loop never executes.

Create For Next Loops

① Name your procedure.

② Declare your variable.

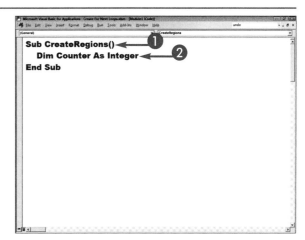

③ Add a For statement.

● Counter variable.

● Initial value.

● Maximum value.

④ Type the statement you want to execute.

This example places the text Region 1 through Region 4 in four consecutive cells starting at the active cell. See Chapter 11 to learn more about the Offset property.

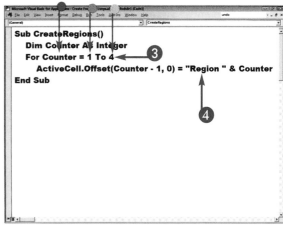

⑤ Add a `Next` statement.

VBA returns to the `For` statement and if the counter exceeds the maximum value, VBA moves to the first line of code after the `Next` statement; otherwise, it executes the statements inside the loop.

⑥ Press Alt+F11 to switch from the VBE to Excel, and then run the macro.

Note: *See Chapter 1 to learn how to run a macro.*

The procedure places the text Region 1 through Region 4 in a column in four consecutive cells.

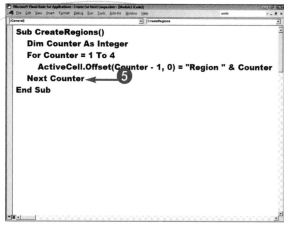

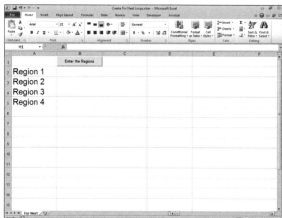

Extra

You can use any value to increment your counter variable. By default, the counter variable for a `For Next` loop increments by one each time the loop executes. If you want to increment or decrement the counter variable by a different value, you can use the `Step` statement to specify the value. If you specify a positive value, the counter variable increments by that value each time the loop cycles. If you specify a negative value, the counter variable decrements by that value each time the loop cycles. In the following example, the `For` loop starts with an initial counter variable of 2 and a maximum value of 20. Each time the loop cycles, the counter variable increments by two. The `TotalVal` variable increments by the value of the loop. The loop executes ten times. When the initial and maximum values of the counter are equal, the loop executes a final time before it passes control to the next statement after the loop.

Example:
```
For J = 2 To 20 Step 2
   TotalVal = TotalVal + J
Next
```

Execute For Each In Loops

You can use a `For Each In` loop to execute a series of statements for each element in an array or each object in a collection. When you use a `For Each In` loop, the statements you place between the `For` and `Next` statements execute for each element in the array or collection. After the statements execute for the last element, control moves to the next statement outside the loop. The following is the syntax for a `For Each In` loop:

```
For Each element In group
    [statements]
Next [element]
```

A `For Each In` loop consists of three parts. The `For Each element In group` statement initiates the loop. An *element* is a variable used to hold an array or collection as you cycle through the `For Each In` loop. *Group* is the name of the array or collection you want to cycle through. The body of the loop contains a series of statements to perform for each element. Finally, the `Next` statement marks the end of the loop.

If you are looping through an array, the variable you use as the element in the `For Each element In group` statement must be defined as a variant data type. If you are working with a collection, you can define the variable as a variant, generic object, or specific object.

Execute For Each In Loops

① Name your procedure.

② Declare your array.

Note: *See Chapter 5 to learn more about arrays.*

③ Declare your variables.

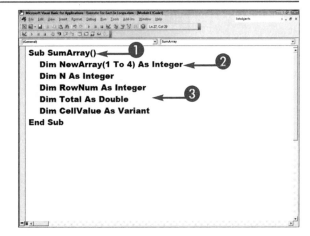

④ Assign values to your array.

In this example, the value in the active cell and three subsequent cells in the same column are assigned to the array.

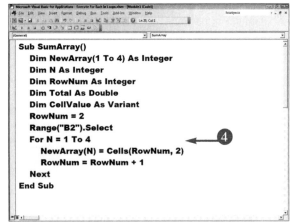

5 Add your `For Each In` statements.

● Variable that holds each element.

● Array or collection name.

● Statements to execute.

6 Add the `Next` statement.

This example totals the elements in the array.

7 Type any statements you want to execute when the `For Each In` loop completes.

8 Press Alt+F11 to switch from the VBE to Excel, and then run the macro.

Note: *See Chapter 1 to learn how to run a macro.*

● In this example, VBA totals the elements in the array and places the total in the cell that follows the array.

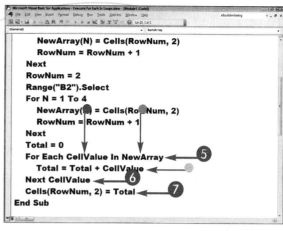

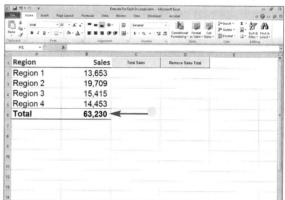

Extra

You can nest loops to populate a multidimensional array. When you nest loops, you place one loop inside another loop. To work with a multidimensional array, you create a separate loop for each dimension of the array. The following code uses two nested `For Next` loops to access elements of the array. Notice that the inside loop, with the Column counter variable, completely cycles each time the loop with Row counter variable runs once. Each `Next` statement has a variable following it. You must exit the inside loop before you can exit the outside loop. Please note that this macro is incomplete. See the file Execute For Each In Loops.xlsm, which is on the Web site for this book for the complete macro.

TYPE THIS:

```
Sub BuildArray()
   Dim NewArray(1 To 3, 1 To 4) As Integer
   Dim Row As Integer
   Dim Column As Integer
   Dim CellValue As Integer
   CellValue = 1
   For Row = 1 To 3
      For Column = 1 To 4
         NewArray(Row, Column) = CellValue
         CellValue = CellValue + 1
      Next Column
   Next Row
End Sub
```

RESULT:

The code creates a two-dimensional array with the values shown in the following table:

1	2	3	4
5	6	7	8
9	10	11	12

Create If Then Else Statements

You can conditionally execute a group of statements by using an `If Then Else` statement. For example, you can calculate a bonus of 5 percent of sales if an employee's sales are greater than $50,000, or enter the text "No Bonus" if an employee's sales are less than or equal to $50,000. The following is the syntax for an `If Then Else` statement:

```
If condition Then
    [statements]
Else
    [statements]
End If
```

An `If Then Else` statement evaluates a condition. A condition is any expression that evaluates to either `True` or `False`. For example: The expression `If Sales > 50000 Then` evaluates the variable `Sales`. If the variable `Sales` is greater than 50,000, the expression returns `True`; otherwise, it returns `False`. If the condition is `True`, the statements that follow the `Then` statement execute. If the condition is `False`, the statements that follow the `Else` statement execute. A null condition evaluates to `False`. An `End If` statement marks the end of an `If Then Else` statement.

If you have multiple conditions that you want to evaluate, you can use `ElseIf`. For example, you can use `ElseIf` when you want to calculate tax at a rate of 5 percent if the state is Texas, 8 percent if the state is Florida, and no tax for all other states. When using `ElseIf`, a single `If Then` statement is followed by several `ElseIf` statements and a final `Else` statement.

Create If Then Else Statements

If Then Else

① Add your `If Then` statement.

● Condition.

● Statement to execute.

② Add your `Else` statement.

● Statement to execute.

③ Type `End If`.

④ Press Alt+F11 to switch from the VBE to Excel, and then run the macro.

Note: See Chapter 1 to learn how to run a macro.

In this example, if the Sales column is over 50,000, VBA calculates a bonus of 4 percent of sales; otherwise, it prints the words "No Bonus."

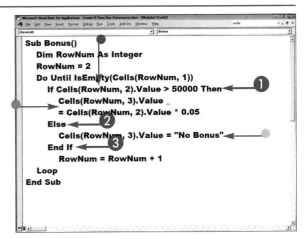

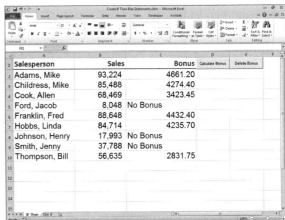

Elself

① Add your If Then statement.

◉ Condition.

● Statement to execute.

② Add your ElseIf statements.

● Statement to execute.

③ Add your Else statement.

◉ Statement to execute.

④ Type End If.

⑤ Press Alt+F11 to switch from the VBE to Excel, and then run the macro.

In this example, the procedure calculates the sales price plus tax, based on the state tax amount.

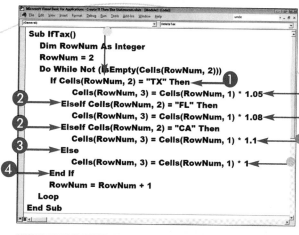

```
Sub IfTax()
    Dim RowNum As Integer
    RowNum = 2
    Do While Not (IsEmpty(Cells(RowNum, 2)))
        If Cells(RowNum, 2) = "TX" Then
            Cells(RowNum, 3) = Cells(RowNum, 1) * 1.05
        ElseIf Cells(RowNum, 2) = "FL" Then
            Cells(RowNum, 3) = Cells(RowNum, 1) * 1.08
        ElseIf Cells(RowNum, 2) = "CA" Then
            Cells(RowNum, 3) = Cells(RowNum, 1) * 1.1
        Else
            Cells(RowNum, 3) = Cells(RowNum, 1) * 1
        End If
        RowNum = RowNum + 1
    Loop
End Sub
```

Total Sale	State	Total with Tax	Calculate Total with Tax	Remove Total with Tax
5.00	TX	5.25		
5.00	CA	5.50		
5.00	FL	5.40		
5.00	UT	5.00		
10.00	TX	10.50		
10.00	TX	10.50		
10.00	CA	11.00		
20.00	FL	21.60		
20.00	TX	21.00		
20.00	CA	22.00		
20.00	UT	20.00		

Extra

Although VBA does not require you to indent your code, you can use indentation to improve readability. Indenting enables you to analyze the structure of the code without reading each line. When working with conditional statements, such as If Then statements and looping statements, most programmers indent the statements that execute. The following example shows how you can indent the code for a For Next loop so you can easily locate the loop's beginning and end. The example also indents an If Then statement.

Example:
```
For I = 1 To 5
    If J < 10 Then
        J = J + 1
    End If
Next
```

If you have an If Then statement that consists of only one statement, you can combine the If statement with the Then statement and eliminate the End If statement.

THIS CODE:
```
If Sum < 10 Then Sum = Sum + 1
```

IS EQUIVALENT TO:
```
If Sum < 10 Then
    Sum = Sum + 1
End If
```

Construct Select Case Statements

Y ou can execute a specific block of code based on a value by using a Select Case statement. Using a Select Case statement is similar to using ElseIf. You can use Select Case when you have different statements to execute and the statements that execute depend upon the value of a cell, variable, number, or string. For example, you can base the calculation of sales tax on the state. You can calculate a tax rate of 5 percent if the state is Texas, 8 percent if the state is Florida, and no tax for all other states. The following is the syntax for Select Case statements.

```
Select Case testexpression
    [Case expressionlist -n
        [statements-n]]
    [Case Else
        [elsestatements]]
End Select
```

The Select Case statement identifies the expression against which you want to test each Case statement. Each Case statement contains a value to test and the statements to execute if the case statement is True. For example:

```
Select Case UserVal
    Case 4
        Statements
. . .
End Select
```

The example determines whether UserVal = 4 is True. Under each Case statement are statements that execute if the expression evaluates to True. The End Select statement marks the end of the Select Case statement.

You can also add a Case Else statement that supplies the statement to run if none of the Case statements evaluate to True.

Construct Select Case Statements

① Name your procedure.

② Declare your variable.

③ Initialize your variable.

④ Create a Do While loop.

Note: See the section "Employ Do While Loops" in this chapter to learn how to create a Do While loop.

⑤ Type your Select Case statement.

● Each Case statement value is compared to this value.

⑥ Type your Case statements.

● If the value in the Select Case statement is equal to the value in the Case statement, the statements that follow the Case statement execute.

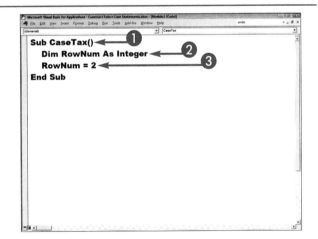

⑦ Add your `Case Else` statement.

The statements after the `Case Else` statement execute if none of the other `Case` statements match the `Select Case` value.

⑧ Add an `End Select` statement.

⑨ Press Alt+F11 to switch from the VBE to Excel, and then run the macro.

Note: *See Chapter 1 to learn how to run a macro.*

In this example, the procedure calculates the sales price plus tax, based on the state tax amount.

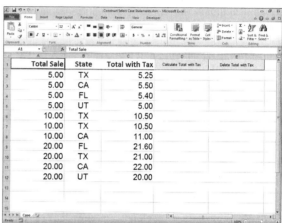

```
Dim RowNum As Integer
RowNum = 2
Do While Not (IsEmpty(Cells(RowNum, 2)))
    Select Case Cells(RowNum, 2)
        Case "TX"
            Cells(RowNum, 3) = Cells(RowNum, 1) * 1.05
        Case "FL"
            Cells(RowNum, 3) = Cells(RowNum, 1) * 1.08
        Case "CA"
            Cells(RowNum, 3) = Cells(RowNum, 1) * 1.1
        Case Else  ⑦
            Cells(RowNum, 3) = Cells(RowNum, 1) * 1
    End Select  ⑧
    RowNum = RowNum + 1
Loop
End Sub
```

Total Sale	State	Total with Tax	Calculate Total with Tax	Delete Total with Tax
5.00	TX	5.25		
5.00	CA	5.50		
5.00	FL	5.40		
5.00	UT	5.00		
10.00	TX	10.50		
10.00	TX	10.50		
10.00	CA	11.00		
20.00	FL	21.60		
20.00	TX	21.00		
20.00	CA	22.00		
20.00	UT	20.00		

Apply It

With the `Select Case` statement, you can use comparison statements to compare a range of values, or multiple values.

TYPE THIS:

```
Select Case NumSales
    Case 1 To 5
        Commission = Total * .05
    Case 6 To 15
        Commission = Total * .1
End Select
```

→

RESULT:

The `Select Case` statement checks the value of `NumSales` to see whether it falls into one of the two specified ranges.

TYPE THIS:

```
Select Case NumStudents
    Case Is < 10
        MsgBox("Not enough students
enrolled.")
End Select
```

→

RESULT:

The `Select Case` statement displays the message box if the value of `NumStudents` is less than 10.

TYPE THIS:

```
Select Case State
    Case "TX", "CA"
        Total = Total * 1.085
End Select
```

→

RESULT:

If the value of `State` equals `TX` or `CA`, the total is calculated using 8.5 percent for the sales tax.

GoTo a Named Location

You can jump to a named location within your macro by using a GoTo statement. However, before you can use a GoTo statement, you must label the line in your procedure to which you want to move. A label is a text string followed by a colon. The GoTo command moves to the label, thereby passing control from the current location in the procedure to the label. The following is the syntax for the GoTo command:

GoTo *label*

As you can see, there are two parts to a GoTo command: the GoTo statement and the label. You can place a label anywhere in your procedure. The GoTo command can jump only to labels within the same procedure. They cannot jump to a label in another procedure, even if both procedures are in the same module. You can add multiple GoTo commands to the same procedure, and each GoTo command can jump to the same or different labels.

You should use GoTo commands only in situations where you cannot obtain the desired results using conditional statements or looping structures. GoTo commands date back to when each line of code had a specific line number, and GoTo commands jumped to the specified line of code. Although GoTo commands are often used for trapping errors in VBA, many programmers consider it bad programming to use GoTo commands too frequently. See Chapter 8 for more information on using a GoTo statement when debugging your code.

GoTo a Named Location

① Create a new procedure.

② Add your code.

③ Add your GoTo statements.

④ Add your GoTo label.

● Label names are followed by a colon.

⑤ Add any additional code.

⑥ Press Alt+F11 to switch from the VBE to Excel, and then run the macro.

Note: See Chapter 1 to learn how to run a macro.

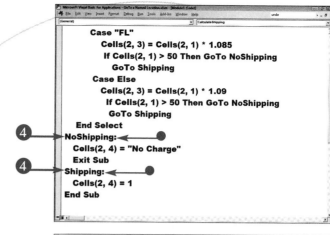

In this example, the procedure calculates a shipping charge if the cost with tax is less than $50.00.

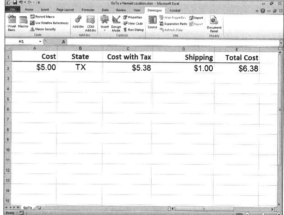

Call a Procedure

I f you are in one procedure and you want to execute another procedure, you can use a Call statement. You simply type the word Call followed by the name of the procedure you want to execute, as well as any arguments the procedure requires, in parentheses and separated by commas. When you call a procedure, VBA moves to the first line of code in the called procedure and begins processing. After the called procedure completes processing, VBA returns to the next line of code after the call and continues processing the original procedure.

You can conditionally call a procedure by using a conditional VBA statement, such as an If Then statement with a Call statement. When you combine the Call statement with a conditional statement, VBA executes the called procedure only if the specified condition is met. The

If Then statement checks the specified condition. If the value of the condition is True, the control passes to the called procedure or function and then, upon the called procedure's completion, returns to the original procedure. If you do not want to continue processing the first procedure after calling the second, you can use an Exit Sub statement to exit the procedure.

The keyword Call is optional when executing a Call statement. You can call a procedure simply by typing the procedure name. If you omit the Call keyword, do not place your arguments in parentheses. Simply type the procedure name followed by its arguments, separated by commas. You can call Sub procedures, Function procedures, or Dynamic-Link Library (DLL) procedures.

Call a Procedure

① Name your procedure.

② Declare and initialize any variables.

You may need to make your variable public.

Note: See Chapter 3 to learn more about public variables.

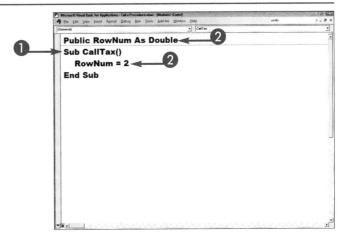

③ Create an If Then condition.

④ Call another procedure.

5 Create called procedures.

6 Type code to run when the procedure is called.

7 Press Alt+F11 to switch from the VBE to Excel, and then run the macro.

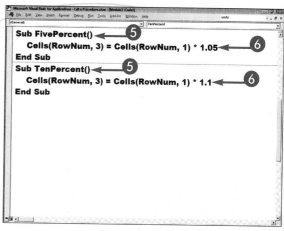

```
Sub FivePercent()            5
    Cells(RowNum, 3) = Cells(RowNum, 1) * 1.05      6
End Sub
Sub TenPercent()             5
    Cells(RowNum, 3) = Cells(RowNum, 1) * 1.1       6
End Sub
```

Note: *See Chapter 1 to learn how to run a macro.*

When the condition is met, the `If Then` statement calls the appropriate procedure.

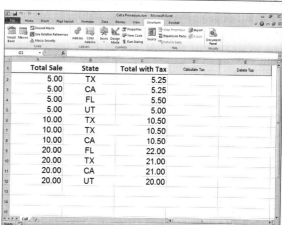

Total Sale	State	Total with Tax	Calculate Tax	Delete Tax
5.00	TX	5.25		
5.00	CA	5.25		
5.00	FL	5.50		
5.00	UT	5.00		
10.00	TX	10.50		
10.00	TX	10.50		
10.00	CA	10.50		
20.00	FL	22.00		
20.00	TX	21.00		
20.00	CA	21.00		
20.00	UT	20.00		

Apply It

You do not need to use the `Call` keyword when you call another procedure or function. However, using the `Call` keyword eliminates confusion by clearly indicating that you are calling a function or `Sub` procedure. When you use the `Call` keyword, you must enclose any arguments passed in parentheses. If you call a procedure without the `Call` keyword, you must omit the parentheses around the argument list, as follows:

THIS CODE:
```
Call NewProc(Var1, Var2)
```

→

IS EQUIVALENT TO:
```
NewProc Var1, Var2
```

Work with Excel Worksheet Functions

A *function* is a block of code that performs a task and returns a value. There are three types of functions: VBA functions, Excel worksheet functions, and custom functions. A VBA function is a function supplied by VBA. An Excel worksheet function is a formula that Excel has predefined. You can use them to do things such as add numbers, find an average, or find the highest number in a list. Excel provides you with more than 300 worksheet functions. Custom functions work like worksheet functions; however, you define the formula the function uses.

Use the `WorksheetFunction` property to place an Excel worksheet function in your VBA procedure. The `WorksheetFunction` property is available through the `Application` object. To access a function in the `WorksheetFunction` object, you type `Application.WorksheetFunction.` followed by the function you want

to use and the function arguments enclosed in parentheses. If you want, you can omit `Application.` from the expression. For example, if you want to sum a range of cells and store the result to a variable, both of these expressions are valid:

```
SumVal = Application.WorksheetFunction _
.Sum(Range("A1:A4"))
SumVal = WorksheetFunction.Sum _
(Range("A1:A4"))
```

Generally, you cannot use an Excel worksheet function that has an equivalent VBA function. For example, both VBA and Excel have a `COS` function that returns a numeric value that represents the cosine of an angle. If you try to use the Excel worksheet function `COS` in your VBA procedure, you receive an error message.

Work with Excel Worksheet Functions

① Name your procedure.

② Declare the variables you want to use to store the results of your worksheet functions.

③ Declare any other variables you will use.

④ Activate the worksheet that uses this procedure by typing `.Activate` after the worksheet reference.

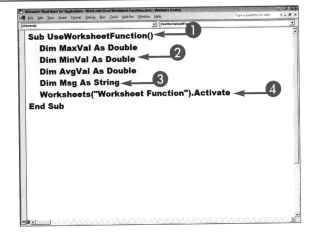

⑤ Create your worksheet functions.

● The underscore indicates that the statement is continued on the next line.

● The name of the function.

● Arguments.

● A VBA function.

⑥ Store the result to a variable.

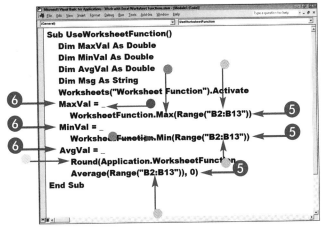

⑦ Use a message box to display the result.

Note: *See the section "Work with a MsgBox Function" to learn more about message boxes.*

● The variable.

● This code creates a blank line.

⑧ Press Alt+F11 to switch from the VBE to Excel, and then run the macro.

Note: *See Chapter 1 to learn how to run a macro.*

● The results of the worksheet functions appear in the message box.

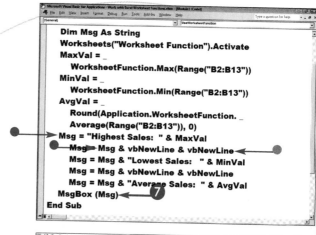

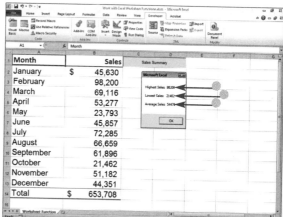

Extra

The Object Browser lists the functions that are part of the WorksheetFunction object. To view this list, use WorksheetFunction as the search criterion in the Object Browser. Press F2 to open the Object Browser. See Chapter 4 for more information on the Object Browser.

If a VBA statement does not fit on a single line, you can use the underscore (_) character to tell Excel you want to continue the statement on another line. The example in this section uses the underscore character as a continue statement indicator.

The remainder of this chapter discusses and illustrates VBA functions. The Round function used in the following example is a VBA function. The Round function takes two arguments: an expression and the number of decimal places to which you want to round the number. If you do not specify the number of decimal places, the Round function rounds to an integer.

Example:
```
Result = Round(124.4589, 2) 'Returns
  124.46
```

You can also use the Excel worksheet function ROUND when writing a VBA procedure.

Work with a MsgBox Function

The `MsgBox` function is a VBA function that makes writing code easier. See Chapter 3 to learn more about functions. You can use the `MsgBox` function to display a dialog box that provides information to the user and, if you want, returns a value to VBA that represents the user's response. The `MsgBox` function has a preset list of values it can return. For example, you can use the `MsgBox` function to prompt the user for a Yes or No response; VBA returns 6 if the user clicks Yes and 7 if the user clicks No.

When using the `MsgBox` function, you use arguments to designate the prompts, buttons, and title that appear in your message box. The `Button` and `Title` arguments are optional. Use the `Prompt` argument to specify the text

that appears in the message box. You can use a text string enclosed in quotes or you can use a variable. You can combine strings and variables by using the concatenation operator (`&`), as in this example:
`MsgBox("Total Sum: " & TotalSum)`.

Use the `Button` argument to specify a constant that indicates the buttons and icons that appear in the message box. If you do not specify a button constant, the `MsgBox` function uses the default `vbOKOnly` and displays only the OK button. Use the `Title` argument to display the title that appears on the title bar of the message box. If you omit this argument, Excel displays the default title, Microsoft Excel.

Work with a MsgBox Function

① Name your procedure.

② Declare the variables you want to use as arguments in the `MsgBox` function.

Alternatively, you can type the arguments directly into the `MsgBox` function.

③ Declare the variable you want to use to store the value returned by the `MsgBox` function.

④ Activate the worksheet that uses this procedure by typing `.Activate` after the worksheet reference.

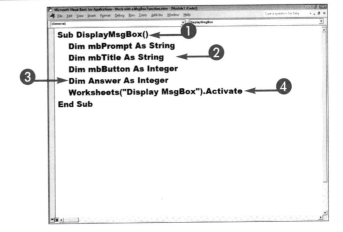

⑤ Store your message to a variable.

⑥ Store the values that represent the buttons you want to use to a variable.

Place a plus sign between each button you want represented.

⑦ Store the title you want your message box to have to a variable.

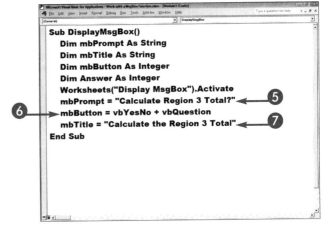

8. Create the `MsgBox` function.
   - Your message.
   - The buttons you want to display.
   - The title.

9. Assign the value returned by the message box to a variable.

10. Write code to execute an action based on the value returned by the message box.

11. Press Alt+F11 to switch from the VBE to Excel, and then run the macro.

Note: See Chapter 1 to learn how to run a macro.

The message box appears when you run the macro.
   - The title.
   - The prompt.
   - The `vbYesNo` buttons.
   - The `vbQuestion` button.

```vba
Sub DisplayMsgBox()
    Dim mbPrompt As String
    Dim mbTitle As String
    Dim mbButton As Integer
    Dim Answer As Integer
    Worksheets("Display MsgBox").Activate
    mbPrompt = "Calculate Region 3 Total?"
    mbButton = vbYesNo + vbQuestion
    mbTitle = "Calculate the Region 3 Total"
    Answer = MsgBox(mbPrompt, mbButton, mbTitle)
    If Answer = 6 Then
        Range("F8").Formula = "=SUM(F2:F7)"
    Else
        Exit Sub
    End If
End Sub
```

Extra

You can use 20 different constant values as the Buttons value for the `MsgBox` function. You can use these values separately, or combine them by placing a plus (+) sign between each constant value. The following code creates a message box containing Yes, No, and Cancel buttons, as well as the Question icon.

Example:
```vba
Response = MsgBox("Select button.", vbYesNoCancel + vbQuestion)
```

The `MsgBox` function returns an integer value between 1 and 7, which represents the button the user clicked. You can interpret the value the `MsgBox` function returns by looking at the integer value. The following table shows the integer values returned by the `MsgBox` function and their associated constant values.

MSGBOX RETURN VALUE	CONSTANT	DESCRIPTION
1	vbOK	OK button clicked
2	vbCancel	Cancel button clicked
3	vbAbort	Abort button clicked
4	vbRetry	Retry button clicked
5	vbIgnore	Ignore button clicked
6	vbYes	Yes button clicked
7	vbNo	No button clicked

Using the InputBox Function

Like `MsgBox`, the `InputBox` function is a VBA function. You can use the `InputBox` function to prompt the user for information during the execution of a procedure. The `InputBox` function displays a dialog box that requests information from the user and returns the user response to your procedure. You capture the user response by assigning the results of the `InputBox` function to a variable. The following is the syntax for the `InputBox` function:

```
InputBox(Prompt[,Title][,Default] [,xPos]
[,yPos])
```

Use the `Prompt` argument to specify the text that appears in the input box. You can combine strings and variables by using the concatenation operator (`&`). The `Title` argument is optional. You can use it to specify the title of

your input dialog box. You can use either a text string enclosed in quotes or a variable. If you omit the `Title` argument, Excel displays the default title, Microsoft Excel.

The `Default` argument is optional. You can use it to specify the default value that displays when your text box appears.

You can specify the display position of the dialog box by using the optional `xPos` and `yPos` arguments. If you omit these arguments, the dialog box appears in the center of the screen. These arguments use units of measurement called *twips*. One twip equals 1/20 of a point, or 1/1,440 of an inch. The `xPos` argument indicates the distance from the left side of the screen to the left side of the dialog box. The `yPos` argument indicates the position from the top of the screen to the top of the dialog box.

Using the InputBox Function

1. Name your procedure.

2. Declare the variable you want to use to store the value returned by the `InputBox` function.

3. Declare the variables you want to use as arguments in the `InputBox` function.

   Alternatively, you can type the arguments directly into the `InputBox` function.

4. Activate the worksheet that uses this procedure by typing `.Activate` after the workbook reference.

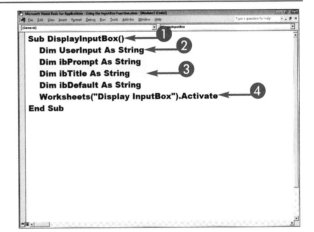

5. Store your prompt to a variable.

6. Store the title you want your message box to have to a variable.

7. Store the default value you want your input box to display to a variable.

8. Create your `InputBox` function.

9. Assign the value returned by the `InputBox` function to a variable.

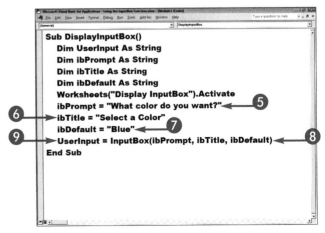

10 Write code that executes based on the value returned by the input box.

Note: See Chapter 6 to learn more about `If Then Else` statements.

11 Press Alt+F11 to switch from the VBE to Excel, and then run the macro.

Note: See Chapter 1 to learn how to run a macro.

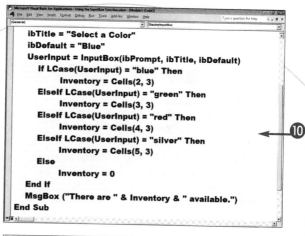

```
        ibTitle = "Select a Color"
        ibDefault = "Blue"
        UserInput = InputBox(ibPrompt, ibTitle, ibDefault)
            If LCase(UserInput) = "blue" Then
                Inventory = Cells(2, 3)
            ElseIf LCase(UserInput) = "green" Then
                Inventory = Cells(3, 3)
            ElseIf LCase(UserInput) = "red" Then
                Inventory = Cells(4, 3)
            ElseIf LCase(UserInput) = "silver" Then
                Inventory = Cells(5, 3)
            Else
                Inventory = 0
        End If
        MsgBox ("There are " & Inventory & " available.")
    End Sub
```

The input box appears when you run the macro.

● The title.

● The prompt.

○ The `default` value.

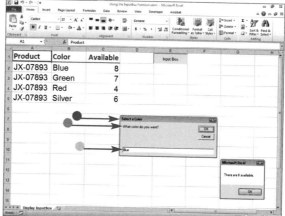

Extra

You can use named arguments to simplify your functions. Many VBA functions have optional arguments. For example, although the `InputBox` function has several arguments, only the first one is required. If you want to include additional arguments, you specify the argument values in order, leaving a space between two commas as a placeholder for any arguments you do not want to use.

Example:
```
UserInput = InputBox("Type a value:", ,"5")
```

Instead of specifying a placeholder for each value, you can use named arguments with the VBA functions. When using a named argument, you specify the name of the argument along with the corresponding value. You type the name of the argument followed by a colon, an equal sign, and the value of that particular argument. You can place named arguments in any order, and you do not have to specify a value for every argument.

Example:
```
UserInput = InputBox(Prompt:="Type a value:", Default:="5")
```

Retrieve the Current Date and Time

VBA includes several date-related, built-in functions that you can add to the procedures and functions you create. You can use these functions to return a system date and/or time, perform date calculations, set a date, or even time a process.

If you want to display the current date or time, you can select from three different functions. The Date VBA function returns the current system date, the Time VBA function returns the current system time, and the Now VBA function returns both the date and time. VBA formats the date and time information in your system's short date format. You can modify the date and time formats by using the Control Panel.

When working with dates, you can avoid displaying a date outside of range by remembering the date range that

Excel accepts. Excel accepts dates between January 1, 1900, and December 31, 9999. If you use Excel on a Macintosh, the date range is even smaller. The acceptable date range begins January 1, 1904. If you need to display a date outside the range, you can do so by placing the date in a string variable. VBA accommodates a much larger date range than Excel. It accepts dates between January 1, 0100, and December 31, 9999.

You can assign the results of the Date or Time function to a variable, a worksheet cell, or another function. The following example stores the Now function to a message box: MsgBox("Current Date and Time: " & Now()).

Retrieve the Current Date and Time

Retrieve the Current Date

1 Name your procedure.

2 Type the Date function.

In this example, the Date function is part of the prompt argument for the MsgBox function.

Note: See the section "Work with a MsgBox Function" in this chapter to learn more about the MsgBox function.

3 Press Alt+F11 to switch from the VBE to Excel, and then run the macro.

Note: See Chapter 1 to learn how to run a macro.

The current system date appears in the message box.

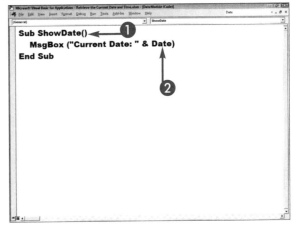

Retrieve the Current Time

1 Name your procedure.

2 Type the `Time` function.

In this example, the `Time` function is part of the prompt argument for the `MsgBox` function.

Note: See the section "Work with a MsgBox Function" in this chapter to learn more about the `MsgBox` function.

3 Press Alt+F11 to switch from the VBE to Excel, and then run the macro.

Note: See Chapter 1 to learn how to run a macro.

The current system time appears in the message box.

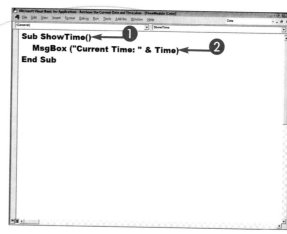

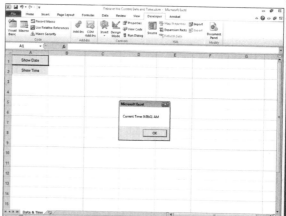

Extra

In Excel, you can convert dates and times into a serial value that Excel can add or subtract and then convert back into a recognizable date or time. Excel calculates a date's serial value as the number of days after January 1, 1900, and represents each date with a whole number. Excel calculates a time's serial value in units of 1/60 of a second. Each time can be represented as a serial value between 0 and 1. A date and time, such as January 1, 2000, at noon, consists of the date to the left of the decimal and a time to the right. In the example August 25, 2011, 5:46 p.m., the date and time serial value is 40780.74028.

VBA uses the same serial number system for dates and times as Excel. Each date and time is stored as a numeric value. Because VBA stores dates and times as numeric values, you can add and subtract to perform date calculations.

Perform Date and Time Calculations

You can determine the amount of time between two dates by using the `DateDiff` VBA function. With this function, you can obtain time intervals between two date values, such as the number of months, days, hours, minutes, or seconds.

The `DateDiff` function takes five arguments: `Interval`, `Date1`, `Date2`, `Firstdayofweek`, and `Firstweekofyear`. The first three arguments are required. Use the `Interval` argument to specify the unit of time to use when returning the difference between the two dates. Use a constant value to specify the interval.

Use the `Date1` and `Date2` arguments to specify the dates you want to compare. You can use a date string, a value returned by a function, or the contents of a cell, as long as you use a valid date. To ensure the date is valid, you can use the `IsDate` VBA function, which returns the value `True` if an expression is a date. Use the `CDate` function to coerce a date data type.

You can use the optional `Firstdayofweek` argument if you want to use a day other than Sunday as the first day of the week. To create the constant value you use as this argument, type **vb** before the appropriate day of the week. For example, to use Monday as the first day of the week, type `vbMonday` as the argument value.

You can use the optional `Firstweekofyear` argument to indicate what you want to treat as the first week of the year. If you omit this argument, VBA considers the week that contains the date January 1 as the first week of the year. If you want to have the first week contain at least the first four days, specify a value of `vbFirstFourDays`. See the appendix for a list of `Firstweekofyear` constant values.

Perform Date and Time Calculations

① Name your procedure.

② Declare the variables you want to use to store your dates.

③ Declare any other variables you need.

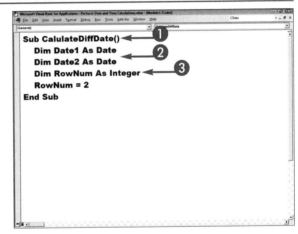

This example uses a `Do While` loop and an `If Then Else` statement.

Note: See Chapter 6 to learn more about loops and `If Then Else` statements.

● This example evaluates two columns of cells, starting at row 2.

④ Store the cell values to variables.

⑤ Use the `IsDate` VBA function to make sure the cells contain valid dates.

⑥ Use the `MsgBox` function to display an error message if the dates are not valid.

⑦ Use the `DateDiff` function to determine the amount of time between two dates.

● The Interval.

◐ Date1.

◔ Date2.

⑧ Place the results in a cell.

⑨ Press Alt+F11 to switch from the VBE to Excel, and then run the macro.

Note: *See Chapter 1 to learn how to run a macro.*

The procedure calculates the difference between two times.

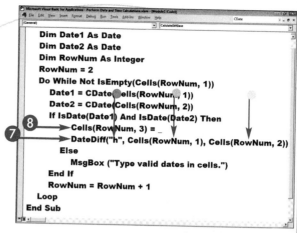

```
Dim Date1 As Date
Dim Date2 As Date
Dim RowNum As Integer
RowNum = 2
Do While Not IsEmpty(Cells(RowNum, 1))
    Date1 = CDate(Cells(RowNum, 1))
    Date2 = CDate(Cells(RowNum, 2))
    If IsDate(Date1) And IsDate(Date2) Then
        Cells(RowNum, 3) = _
        DateDiff("h", Cells(RowNum, 1), Cells(RowNum, 2))
    Else
        MsgBox ("Type valid dates in cells.")
    End If
    RowNum = RowNum + 1
Loop
End Sub
```

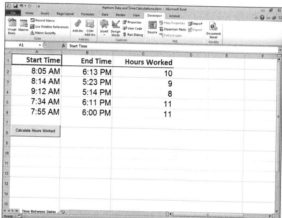

	Start Time	End Time	Hours Worked
1	Start Time	End Time	Hours Worked
2	8:05 AM	6:13 PM	10
3	8:14 AM	5:23 PM	9
4	9:12 AM	5:14 PM	8
5	7:34 AM	6:11 PM	11
6	7:55 AM	6:00 PM	11

Calculate Hours Worked

Extra

You can use one of ten constant values to specify the `Interval` argument and the type of date interval to return.

INTERVAL	VALUE	DESCRIPTION
yyyy	Year	Only compares the year portion of both dates. The dates 12/31/1999 and 1/1/2000 return a value of 1 year.
q	Quarter	Divides the year into four quarters and returns the number of quarters between dates.
m	Month	Compares only the month portion of both dates. The dates 12/31/1999 and 1/1/2000 return a value of 1 month.
d	Day	The number of days between two dates.
y	Day of Year	The same results as using d.
w	Weekday	Determines the day of the week of the first date — for example, Wednesday — and then counts the number of Wednesdays between the dates.
ww	Week	Relies on the value specified as the `Firstdayofweek` argument to determine the number of weeks between two dates.
h	Hour	The number of hours between two times. If a time is not specified, it uses midnight or 00:00:00.
n	Minute	The number of minutes between two times.
s	Second	The number of seconds between two times.

Format a Date Expression

You can format an expression that uses a date or time by using the FormatDateTime VBA function. The FormatDateTime function takes two arguments: Date and NamedFormat. The Date argument is required. It identifies the date expression that you want to format and accepts cell references, variable references, string expressions, or numeric values. You can reference a cell using any of the cell range reference options discussed in Chapter 11. For example, if the date you want to format is located in cell A1, you can use the following code to reference that cell:

```
X = FormatDateTime(Range("A1"))
```

You use the NamedFormat argument to specify the formatting you want to use. You can use any of the predefined formatting constants. If you omit the

NamedFormat argument, the FormatDateTime function uses the vbGeneralDate constant.

The vbGeneralDate constant instructs Excel to format the date portion of the expression in the system short date format, and to format the time portion of the date in the system long time format. Windows maintains your default date and time settings in the Regional and Language Options dialog box, which you can access through the Control Panel. When you use a constant as the NamedFormat argument, you specify which of these settings you want to use to format your date and time values. By changing the values in the Regional and Language Options dialog box, you affect how the dates and times appear when you use the FormatDateTime function.

Format a Date Expression

① Name your procedure.

② Declare the variables you want to use to store your unformatted dates.

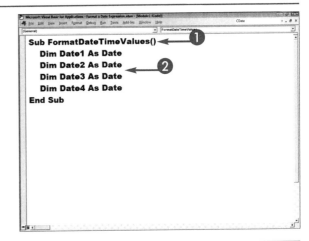

③ Store the contents of the cells with unformatted dates to variables.

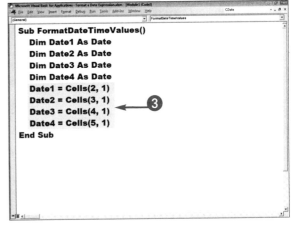

4 Use the `FormatDateTime` function to format the variables in which you stored the dates.

● The variable containing the date.

● The format you want to apply.

5 Assign the results to cells.

6 Press Alt+F11 to switch from the VBE to Excel, and then run the macro.

Note: See Chapter 1 to learn how to run a macro.

The procedure formats the dates in column A and places the results in column B.

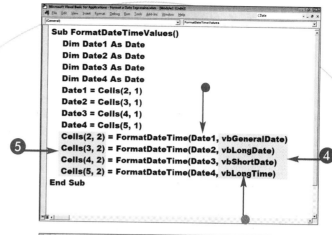

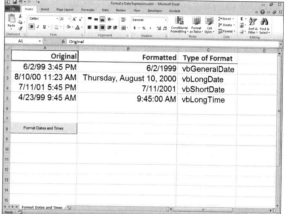

Extra

You can specify the formatting for a date and time by using the `NamedFormat` argument. If it is omitted, Excel uses the `vbGeneralDate` constant. When you use the `NamedFormat` argument, you can pass it a constant value or the numeric value that corresponds to the constant, as outlined in the following table. The actual formats used as a result of specifying these constant values are based upon the system date and time settings in the Regional and Language Options dialog box.

CONSTANT	VALUE	DESCRIPTION
vbGeneralDate	0	The default value if the `NamedFormat` argument is omitted. This value displays the date using the short date format and the time using the long time format.
vbLongDate	1	Displays the date using the system long date format.
vbShortDate	2	Displays the date using the system short date format.
vbLongTime	3	Displays the time using the system long time format.

Format a Numeric Expression

You can format a numeric expression by using the `FormatNumber`, `FormatCurrency`, or `FormatPercentage` function. These functions all take a numeric value and return the value formatted in the format you specify. The `FormatNumber` function returns a formatted number, the `FormatCurrency` function returns a formatted number preceded by a currency symbol, and the `FormatPercentage` function returns a number followed by a percentage sign.

Each function takes the same five arguments: `Expression`, `NumDigitsAfterDecimal`, `Include`, `LeadingDigit`, `UseParensForNegativeNumbers`, and `GroupDigits`. The `Expression` argument is required.

The `Expression` argument specifies the numeric value to format. The `NumDigitsAfterDecimal` argument indicates the number of decimal places to display on the right side of the decimal. The `IncludeLeadingDigit` argument determines whether a zero appears before fractional values. The `UseParensForNegativeNumbers` argument specifies whether to place parentheses around negative numbers. Finally, the `GroupDigits` argument determines whether Excel groups numbers to make them more readable. With this argument, you can specify whether to display fifty thousand as 50,000 or 50000.

The last three arguments, `IncludeLeadingDigit`, `UseParensForNegativeNumbers`, and `GroupDigits`, all use the same three constant values. Use `vbTrue` as the argument if you want to use the formatting, and `vbFalse` if you do not want to use the formatting. If you do not specify a value, or if you specify `vbUseDefault`, the function uses your computer's regional settings.

Format a Numeric Expression

① Name your procedure.

② Declare the variables you want to use to store your formatted numbers.

③ Declare any other variable you need.

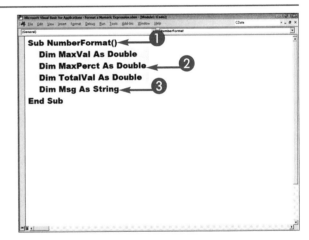

④ Store the numeric values you want to format to variables.

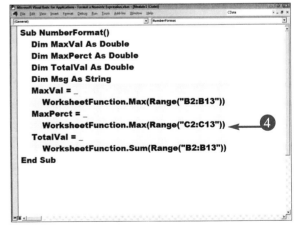

5 Apply a format to the variables.

In this example, the formatted numbers are part of the message box prompt.

6 Press Alt+F11 to switch from the VBE to Excel, and then run the macro.

Note: *See Chapter 1 to learn how to run a macro.*

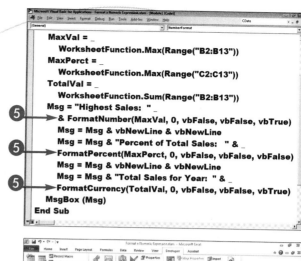

In this example, the procedure formats the numbers and displays the results in a message box.

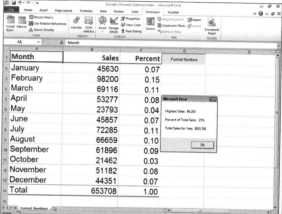

Extra

If you want to customize the way a number appears, you can use the `Format` function. You can create your own number formats by combining specific characters along with symbols that represent the numbers, as in the following example: `Format(NumVal, "##.##")`.

NUMERIC CHARACTERS	DISPLAYS
0	A numeric digit or a zero if the number does not have a digit in that place. Use this character to ensure that a digit appears in a specific place. For example, 0000 always displays a four-digit number. If there are fewer digits, a 0 appears for the non-specified digits.
#	A numeric digit if the number has a digit in that place. If there is no digit, a value does not appear in that place.
.	A decimal-point placeholder.
%	An expression as a percentage by multiplying by 100 and adding a percent sign.
,	A thousands separator.
E-, E+, e-, e+	A numeric expression in scientific format. The number of digits on the right side of the symbol indicates the number of digits in the exponent.
\	The character that follows a backslash or is enclosed in quotes. For example, to place a plus sign (+) in the number string, you would type \+ in the desired location.

Change the Case of a String

You can use the LCase and UCase VBA functions to change the case of your text. This is useful when you are formatting output or when you want to compare strings without regard to case. The LCase function changes all characters that are not already lowercase to lowercase. The UCase function changes all characters that are not already uppercase to uppercase.

To use the LCase function, simply type LCase followed by the expression you want to convert to lowercase in parentheses.

Example:
```
MyVariable = "HELLO"
SampleText = LCase(MyVariable)
```

Result:
```
hello
```

The syntax for the UCase function is similar to the syntax for the LCase function. To use the UCase function, you type UCase followed by the expression you want to convert to uppercase in parentheses.

Example:
```
MyVariable = "hello"
SampleText = UCase(MyVariable)
```

Result:
```
HELLO
```

Both the LCase and the UCase functions ignore numbers and symbols. The expression can be an actual string enclosed in quotes, or a reference to a string such as a cell or variable name. If the string contains no data, both functions return Null.

Change the Case of a String

① Name your procedure.

② Declare your variable.

③ Use an InputBox function to retrieve a user entry.

④ Use the UCase function to change the entry to uppercase.

Alternatively, you can use the LCase function to change the entry to lowercase.

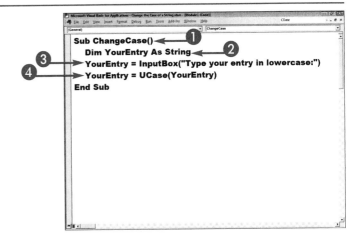

⑤ Use a message box to display the entry.

⑥ Press Alt+F11 to switch from the VBE to Excel, and then run the macro.

Note: See Chapter 1 to learn how to run a macro.

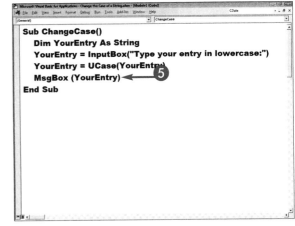

⑦ Make an entry using lowercase text.

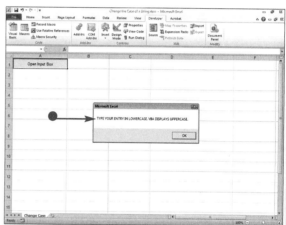

● The message box displays the text in uppercase.

Apply It

The example used in the section "Using the InputBox Function," earlier in this chapter, converts the user's entry to lowercase and then compares the entry to a string. Converting the entry to lowercase allows you to make a comparison without regard to case. For example, if the user types GREEN, green, or GrEen, the procedure returns the value `True` when it compares the user input to green.

Example:
```
If LCase(UserInput) = "blue" Then
     Inventory = Cells(2, 3)
   ElseIf LCase(UserInput) = "green" Then
     Inventory = Cells(3, 3)
   ElseIf LCase(UserInput) = "red" Then
     Inventory = Cells(4, 3)
   ElseIf LCase(UserInput) = "silver" Then
     Inventory = Cells(5, 3)
   Else
     Inventory = 0
End If
```

To see this function in action, refer to the Chapter 7 example file, "Using the InputBox Function," which is on the Web site for this book.

Return a Portion of a String

nstead of an entire string, you can use the built-in functions available in VBA to return a portion of a string. You can use three different functions: `Left`, `Right`, and `Mid`. The `Left` function returns the specified number of characters starting at the left side, or beginning, of the string. The `Right` function returns the specified number of characters starting at the right side, or end, of the string. These functions use similar syntax: `Left(string, length)` and `Right(string, length)`.

The `string` argument specifies the string from which you want to return the specified number of characters. You can make the argument an actual string enclosed in quotes, a variable that contains a string, or a cell reference. The `length` argument indicates the number of characters to return from the string.

The third built-in function for returning a portion of a string is the `Mid` function. Use this function to retrieve characters from the center of a string. When you use this function, you indicate the character with which to start and how many characters to return. There are three `Mid` function arguments: `Mid(string, start, [length])`.

Similar to the `Left` and `Right` functions, the `Mid` function `String` argument specifies the string to use with the function. The `start` argument indicates the position of the first character in the string to return. The `length` argument is the only optional argument when using the `Mid` function. If you omit the `length` argument, the function returns the remaining portion of the string. Otherwise, the `length` argument indicates the number of characters to return.

Return a Portion of a String

① Name your procedure.

② Declare your variables.

③ Use an `InputBox` function to capture a user entry.

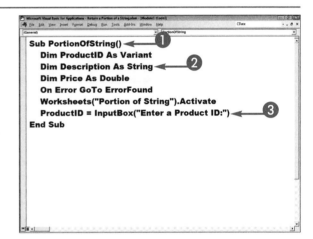

④ Use the `Left` function to retrieve the left portion of a user entry.

● The variable that you want to examine.

● The number of characters from the left you want to retrieve.

In this example, if the first two characters of the user entry are not "OS", then the user receives an error message.

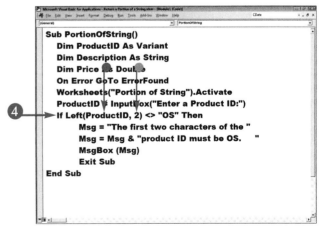

5 Use the `Mid` function to retrieve a portion of a string.

● The variable you want to examine.

● The position of the first character you want to return.

● The number of characters you want to return.

In this example, if the third character of the user entry is not a "-", then the user receives an error message.

6 Use the `Right` function to retrieve the right portion of the user entry.

● The variable that you want to examine.

● The number of characters from the right you want to retrieve.

● This example uses the `IsNumeric` function.

In this example, if the last four characters of the user entry are not numbers, then the user receives an error message.

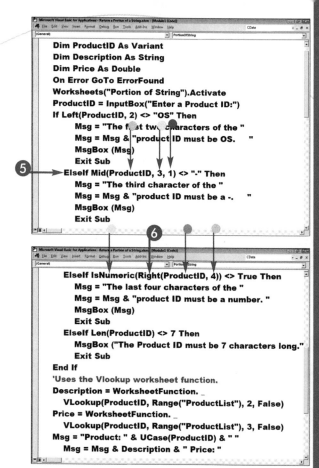

```
Dim ProductID As Variant
Dim Description As String
Dim Price As Double
On Error GoTo ErrorFound
Worksheets("Portion of String").Activate
ProductID = InputBox("Enter a Product ID:")
If Left(ProductID, 2) <> "OS" Then
    Msg = "The first two characters of the "
    Msg = Msg & "product ID must be OS.    "
    MsgBox (Msg)
    Exit Sub
ElseIf Mid(ProductID, 3, 1) <> "-" Then
    Msg = "The third character of the "
    Msg = Msg & "product ID must be a -.    "
    MsgBox (Msg)
    Exit Sub
```

```
    ElseIf IsNumeric(Right(ProductID, 4)) <> True Then
        Msg = "The last four characters of the "
        Msg = Msg & "product ID must be a number. "
        MsgBox (Msg)
        Exit Sub
    ElseIf Len(ProductID) <> 7 Then
        MsgBox ("The Product ID must be 7 characters long."
        Exit Sub
End If
'Uses the Vlookup worksheet function.
Description = WorksheetFunction. _
    VLookup(ProductID, Range("ProductList"), 2, False)
Price = WorksheetFunction. _
    VLookup(ProductID, Range("ProductList"), 3, False)
Msg = "Product: " & UCase(ProductID) & " "
    Msg = Msg & Description & " Price: "
```

Apply It

You can use the `IsNumeric` VBA function to determine if a value is a number. The `IsNumeric` function takes one argument, the value you want to examine. The `IsNumeric` function returns `True` when the value is a number, and `False` when the value is not a number.

You can determine the length of a string with the `Len` function, `Len(string)`, which takes one argument, `string`. You can make the string argument an actual string, or the name of a variable that contains a string. The following example checks to see if the length of the string is not equal to 7. If the length of the string is not equal to 7, the procedure displays an error message.

Example:
```
Dim ProductID As String
ProductID = InputBox("Enter a ProductID:")
If Len(ProductID) <> 7 Then
    MsgBox("The Product ID must be 7 characters long.")
    Exit Sub
End If
```

Debug a Procedure with Inserted Breakpoints

Correcting errors, often referred to as debugging, is a normal part of writing a program. VBA has several tools you can use to debug your procedures. For example, you can insert breakpoints in your procedures. Breakpoints suspend the execution of a procedure at the points you specify. Once the program stops, you can examine the results and then continue the execution of the program.

You set a breakpoint by clicking the margin of the Code window next to the line where you want to insert the breakpoint. The VBE places a circle in the margin and highlights the line of code using the display options you set for the Code window. See Chapter 2 for more information on setting the display options for the Code window. While in the Break mode, if you position your cursor over a variable name, the value of the variable appears.

The VBE has a Locals window, which displays the expressions in your procedure, their current value, and their type. When you are debugging your code, you should dock the Locals window at the bottom of the VBE. You can then use the Locals window to view the value of expressions and variables at each breakpoint. See Chapter 2 for more information on using the VBE windows.

When your procedure stops at a specified breakpoint, VBA places you in Break mode and stops the procedure. You can then choose to continue running the procedure until it encounters another breakpoint or the procedure ends. Each time VBA encounters a breakpoint, the current value of the local variables appear in the Locals window.

Debug a Procedure with Inserted Breakpoints

① In Project Explorer, double-click the module name to open the module.

② Click View → Locals Window.

● You can click the Close button to close the Project Explorer.

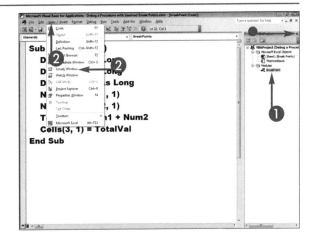

● The Locals window appears.

③ Click in the margin where you want to add a breakpoint.

● You can add additional breakpoints as needed.

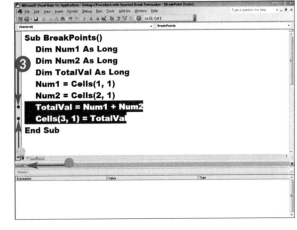

④ Click Run → Run Sub/UserForm.

Alternatively, press F5.

If the Macros dialog box appears, click the macro you want to run and then click Run.

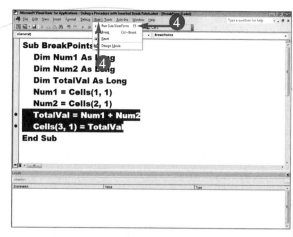

The values for the locally declared variables appear in the Locals window.

⑤ Position your cursor over a variable name to see the current value.

■ The value for the variable appears.

⑥ Press F5 to run the procedure.

Click Run → Reset to stop.

Click Debug → Clear All Breakpoints to clear all breakpoints.

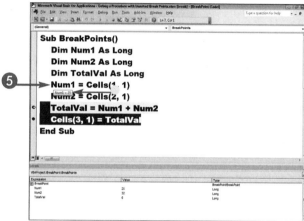

Extra

The VBE has three different modes: Design, Run, and Break. You use the Design mode to create new VBA procedures. You use the Run mode to execute a procedure. To activate the Run mode, click Run → Run Sub/UserForm, or press F5. The VBE runs your procedure.

The VBE places you in the Break mode whenever a procedure stops running due to a breakpoint, a Stop statement, or a Watch statement, or when it encounters an error during execution. When the VBE places you in the Break mode, it highlights the line of code that caused the error and places the word *break* in the caption of the title bar. To exit the Break mode, click Run → Reset.

You can toggle breakpoints on and off by selecting a line of code and then pressing F9 or by clicking Debug → Toggle Breakpoint. You can remove a breakpoint by clicking it with your mouse. You can clear all breakpoints from your code by pressing Ctrl+Shift+F9 or by clicking Debug → Clear All Breakpoints. Remember to clear all breakpoints after you finish debugging your code.

Using the Watches Window to Debug a Procedure

If you suspect an error occurs at a particular breakpoint, when a variable or expression reaches a certain value, or when the value of a variable or expression changes, the Watches window can be of use to you.

You can use the Add Watch dialog box to set up a watch. You start by entering an expression in the Expression field. For example, if you suspect that an error occurs when the variable RowNum is equal to 2, you can enter the expression RowNum = 2 to have your procedure break when the variable RowNum is equal to 2. In the Procedure field of the Add Watch dialog box, select the proper procedure. In the Module field, select the proper module. If you have multiple procedures or modules that call one another and you are not sure which procedure is causing the error, you can opt to monitor all procedures and/or all modules.

The Add Watch dialog box offers three watch types: Watch Expression, Break When Value Is True, and Break When Value Changes. You can set a breakpoint and then select Watch Expression to display the expression you are evaluating and its current value in the Watches window when your procedure breaks. You can select Break When Value Is True to have your procedure break when an expression evaluates to True. For example, by using this option, you can break when the variable RowNum is equal to 2. You can select Break When Value Changes to have your procedure break when the value of an expression changes. For example, if you are using a counter, you can break every time the variable you are using to count changes.

Using the Watches Window to Debug a Procedure

1 In Project Explorer, double-click the module name to open the module.

2 Click View →Watch Window.

● You can click the Close button to close the Project Explorer.

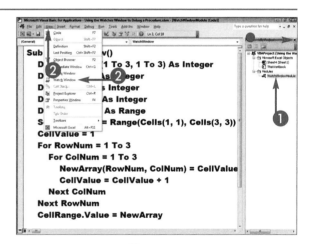

● The Watches window appears.

3 Click Debug → Add Watch.

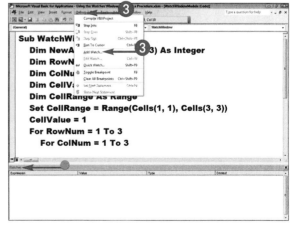

The Add Watch dialog box appears.

④ Type the expression to watch in the Expression field.

⑤ Click the down arrow and select a procedure.

⑥ Click the down arrow and select a module.

⑦ Click to select a watch type (◯ changes to ◉).

⑧ Click OK.

● The Watches window lists each watch.

⑨ Press F5 to run your procedure.

If the Macros dialog box appears, click the macro you want to run and then click Run.

● The procedure breaks when the expression you entered evaluates to True.

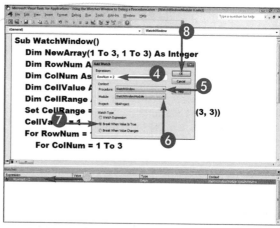

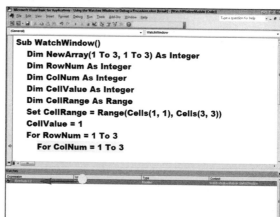

Extra

When you are in the Break mode, you can find the current value of a variable or expression by using VBA's Quick Watch feature. Select the variable or expression for which you want to find the value. Click Debug → Quick Watch or press Shift+F9. The current value of the expression appears in the Quick Watch dialog box. If you want to continue to monitor the variable or expression value, click Add to add the item to the Watches window.

To delete a watch, right-click the watch you want to delete and then click Delete Watch on the context menu that appears. To edit a watch, right-click the watch you want to edit and then click Edit Watch on the context menu. The Edit Watch dialog box appears. Use it to edit your watch.

When evaluating an expression, such as $X > 5$, the value in the Watches window is either True or False, indicating whether the expression is valid. For example, if the current value of X is 6, the expression $X > 5$ has a value of True because 6 is greater than 5.

Step through a Procedure

Programmers call the process of stepping through code one line at a time *tracing*. With breakpoints, VBA executes the code until it encounters a breakpoint. With tracing, VBA executes one line of code and waits for you to indicate that you want to execute the next line of code. Tracing is an excellent way to debug your code when you do not know where your error is located.

As you step through your code, you can use the Watches and Locals windows to monitor the value of variables and expressions. See the section "Using the Watches Window to Debug a Procedure" to learn more about the Watches window. See the section "Debug a Procedure with Inserted Breakpoints" to learn more about the Locals window.

You start tracing by executing the Step Into command on the Debug menu, or by pressing F8. When you are ready to move to the next statement, you execute the Step Into command or press F8 again. You can continue executing the Step Into command or pressing F8 for each line of code you want to execute.

Each time you execute the Step Into command or press F8, the VBE highlights the next line of code. The Locals window updates the value of the local variables, and the Watches window monitors the values of any watch expressions created for the procedure.

As you step through a procedure, if a code statement calls another procedure, the VBE also steps through the called procedure. After that procedure runs, the control returns to the original procedure.

Step through a Procedure

① In Project Explorer, double-click the module name to open the module.

② Click View → Watch Window.

③ Click View → Locals Window.

● You can click the Close button to close the Project Explorer.

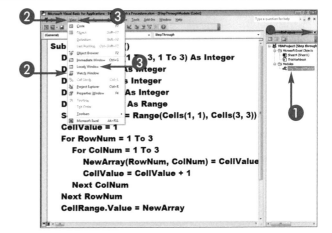

● The Locals and Watches windows appear.

④ Set up a watch.

Note: *See the section "Using the Watches Window to Debug a Procedure" to learn how.*

⑤ Press F8.

Alternatively, click Debug → Step Into.

● As you begin stepping into the code, VBA highlights the first line of code.

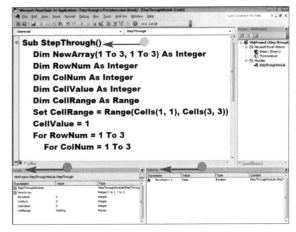

6 Continue pressing F8 to step through the entire procedure.

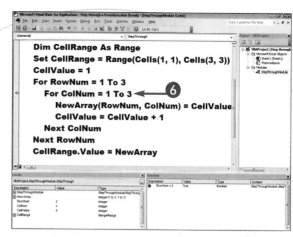

As you step through the code, local variable values appear in the Locals window, and any watches that are set appear in the Watches window.

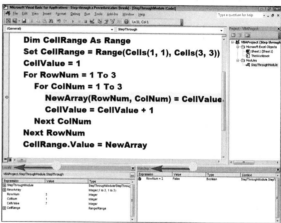

Extra

You step into procedures by pressing F8 or by clicking Debug → Step Into. If your procedure contains calls to other procedures, you can step through those procedures by using the Step Into command. VBA executes the entire called procedure without stopping and then returns control to the next line in the original procedure. If you do not want to step through called procedures, you can step over them. To step over a called procedure, click Debug → Step Over or press Shift+F8.

If you decide to step through the called procedure, you still have the option of stepping out of it at any time. To step out of a called procedure, click Debug → Step Out or press Ctrl+Shift+F8. The remainder of the called procedure runs, and then control returns to the next line of code after the called procedure in the original procedure.

If your code is running and you need to break, press Ctrl+Break. This feature is useful when you find yourself in an infinite loop.

Using the Immediate Window

The Immediate window is useful when you want to evaluate expressions, find out the value of a variable, or quickly test a procedure. You can open the Immediate window by pressing Ctrl+G.

You can print values to the Immediate window by placing a `Debug.Print` command in your code. When VBA executes the `Debug.Print` command, it prints the value you indicate to the Immediate window. For example, if you place `Debug.Print Val1` in your code, and then you step through your code, when VBA executes the `Debug.Print Val1` command, the value of the variable `Val1` appears in the Immediate window.

You can use the Immediate window to return a value. Use the `Print` statement or a question mark (?) to return the

value of a variable or expression. For example, if you want to display the value of the variable `Val1`, you can go to the Immediate window and type:

```
Print Val1
```

or

```
? Val1
```

You can also use the Immediate window to execute commands. Type the command in the Immediate window. As soon as you press Enter, VBA executes the command. When using the Immediate window, control statements must appear on a single line. For example, you would use the following code for a `For Next` loop:

```
For X = 1 to 4: Print X: Next X
```

Using the Immediate Window

Use Debug Print

① Add the `Debug.Print` command to your code.

② Press Ctrl+G.

   Alternatively, click View → Immediate Window.

● The Immediate window appears.

③ Press F8 to step through your code.

   As you step through your code, the values you requested with the `Debug.Print` command appear in the Immediate window.

● The `Val1` value.

● The `Val2` value.

● The `TotalVal` value.

Use Print

① Create a breakpoint.

② Press F5 to run your code.

③ Type `Print` followed by the variable you want to retrieve.

④ Press Enter.

● The Immediate window retrieves the value.

⑤ Type `?` followed by the value you want to retrieve.

● The Immediate window retrieves the value.

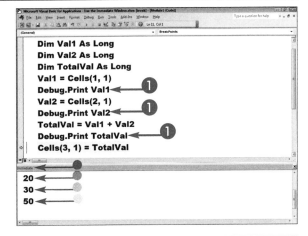

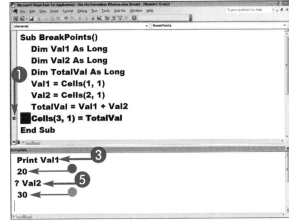

Evaluate an Expression

1. Type your expressions.

● The Immediate window evaluates the expressions.

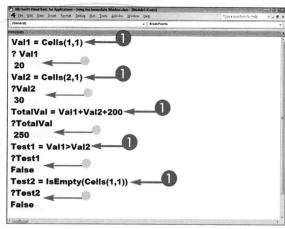

Evaluate a For Next Loop

1. Type your For Next loop.

   All of the statements must be on one line.

● The results appear in the Immediate window.

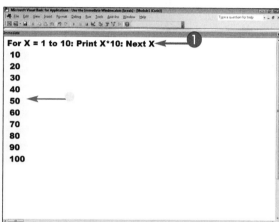

Extra

The VBE has a toolbar you can use when debugging your code. To view the toolbar, click View → Toolbars → Debug. The toolbar appears below the menu. The following table lists the functions that the buttons on the toolbar perform.

BUTTON	FUNCTION
▶	Run Macro
❚❚	Break
■	Reset
✋	Toggle Breakpoint
▤	Step Into
▥	Step Over
▦	Step Out
▤	Open Locals Window
▥	Open Immediate Window
▦	Open Watches Window
▦	Open Quick Watch

Resume Execution When an Error Is Encountered

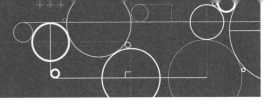

A *runtime error* is an error that occurs when your code attempts to perform an invalid operation, such as trying to access a value that does not exist. If you do not provide a way for VBA to handle runtime errors, when VBA encounters them, it stops running your code and displays an error message to the user, or it acts in an unpredictable way.

VBA has special code you can use to handle runtime errors. You can instruct VBA to continue the execution of a procedure when it encounters an error by using the On Error GoTo statement. The following is the syntax for the On Error GoTo command:

```
On Error GoTo label
```

When you use this command, control jumps to a labeled section of code whenever VBA encounters a runtime error. A label is a text string followed by a colon. The On Error GoTo command moves to the label, thereby passing control from the current location in the procedure to the label. Usually, you place your labeled code at the end of your procedure. For example, you can use ErrorFound: as a label for the code you want to run if VBA encounters an error.

An Exit Sub or Exit Function statement causes VBA to end the execution of your procedure. You can place an Exit Sub or Exit Function statement prior to the labeled section of your code to keep the procedure from executing the labeled code when VBA does not encounter an error.

Resume Execution When an Error Is Encountered

① Name your procedure.

② Type your On Error GoTo command.

● This is the label.

③ Type the VBA code for the procedure.

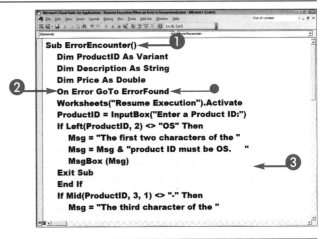

④ Type Exit Sub at the end of the main procedure code.

The Exit Sub statement causes the procedure to exit without running the error code.

⑤ Create a label.

VBA moves to the label when a runtime error occurs.

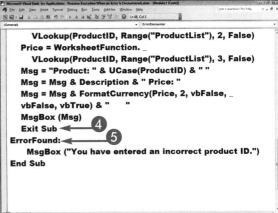

6 Type the VBA code to execute when an error occurs.

7 Press Alt+F11 to switch from the VBE to Excel, and then run the macro.

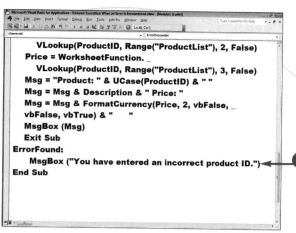

If a runtime error occurs, the appropriate VBA code executes.

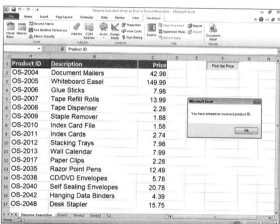

Process a Runtime Error

Whenever VBA encounters a runtime error, it places the error information, which includes an error code and description, in the `Err` object. You can use this information to correct the error.

To capture the error without halting the execution of your code, you can place the `On Error Resume Next` statement immediately after the `Sub` statement for your procedure. This statement instructs VBA to capture the error and continue processing.

The `Err.Number` property contains the most recent runtime error code. The error codes for runtime errors are always numbers. Essentially, if the `Err.Number` property has a value greater than 0, then an error has occurred. You can quickly check to see if an error exists by checking the `Number` property of the `Err` object. If an error exists, you can use `If Then` statements or `Case` statements to respond to the error, as in the following code: `If Err.Number = 13 Then`.

You can design your error-processing code to react to the specific runtime error encountered. For example, if the `Err.Number` property has a value of 13, the value passed to a variable is not the correct data type; the user may have entered a string for a variable that requires a number. You can write code that examines the runtime error and prompts the user for the correct data type.

If you want to see the error description, use the `Err.Description` property. The following code creates a Division by Zero error and then displays the error number and code in a message box:

```
On Error Resume Next
X = 1/0
MsgBox (Err.Number & " " & Err.Description)
```

Process a Runtime Error

1. Name your procedure.

2. Type the `On Error GoTo` command.

   ● This is the label.

3. Type `Exit Sub` at the end of the main body of code.

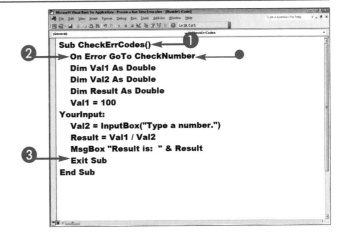

4. Create a label.

5. Create a conditional statement to check the value of the `Err.Number` object property.

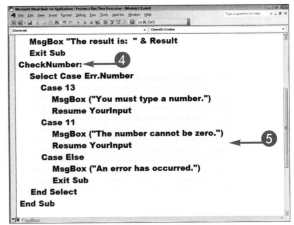

6 Type the code to execute if a specific error occurs.

7 Press Alt+F11 to switch from the VBE to Excel, and then run the macro.

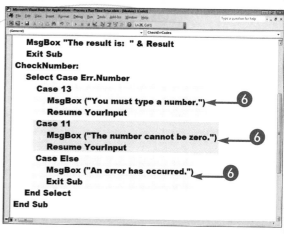

If a runtime error occurs, the appropriate VBA code executes.

In this example, an error occurs if you enter a 0 into the input box.

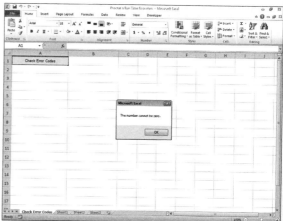

Extra

The following table lists some of the most common errors that VBA returns when it encounters a runtime error. Each error code has a description message you can display using the `Err.Description` property. You can also capture the code and display your own custom messages.

CODE	ERROR	REASON
3	Return without GoSub	The `Return` statement exists without a corresponding `GoSub` statement.
5	Invalid procedure call	The call to another procedure or function cannot be made. This is usually due to a problem with the arguments; either not calling with a valid number of arguments, or the value of an argument is not valid for the procedure.
9	Subscript out of range	An attempt was made to access an array element that does not exist.
10	The array is fixed or temporarily locked	This occurs when you try to redimension a fixed-length array.
11	Division by zero	This occurs when the divisor is zero.
13	Type mismatch	The value passed to a variable is not the correct data type.
35	Sub, Function, or Property not defined	This occurs when you attempt to call a procedure, function, or property that does not exist.

Open a Workbook

Y ou can use the Open method with the WorkBooks object to open a workbook. This is similar to clicking the File tab and using the menu to open a workbook. Each time you open a new workbook, Excel adds the workbook to the Workbooks collection.

The Open method has 16 parameters. This section discusses the FileName, WriteResPassword, Password, ReadOnly, IgnoreReadOnlyRecommended, and AddToMru parameters. Refer to VBA help for a discussion of the remaining parameters.

Use the FileName parameter to specify the workbook you want to open. You can use the name of the workbook if the workbook is located in the current folder. If the workbook is located in another folder, enter the path to

the workbook. You must enclose the workbook name or path in quotes.

If you want users to enter a password before they can modify the workbook, set the WriteResPassword parameter to the password you want them to enter. If you want users to enter a password before they can open a protected workbook, set the Password parameter to the password you want them to enter.

Set the ReadOnly parameter to True to make a workbook read-only. If the workbook is Read-Only Recommended, Excel prompts users to open the file as read-only each time the workbook opens. To eliminate the prompt, set the IgnoreReadOnlyRecommended parameter to True.

Set the AddToMru parameter to True to add the workbook to the Recent Workbooks list.

Open a Workbook

① Name your procedure.

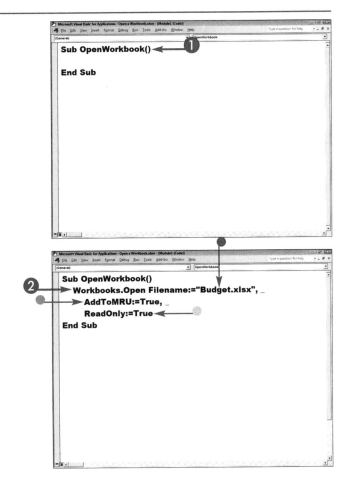

② Create your Open command.

● The workbook you want to open.

● Adds the file to the Recent Workbooks list.

● Sets the file to read-only.

③ Press Alt+F11 to switch from the VBE to Excel, and run the macro.

The macro opens the file and adds the filename to the Recent Workbooks list.

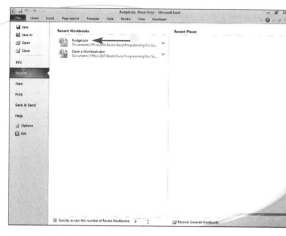

If users make a change and then try to save the file, Excel warns that the file is read-only.

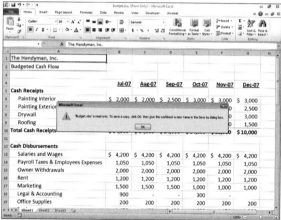

Extra

When working in Excel, you can use the Save As dialog box to set a password for your file, to set your file to read-only recommended, or to set your file to read-only. To open the Save As dialog box, click the File tab and then click Save As. The Save As dialog box appears. In the lower right corner of the Save As dialog box, click the Tools button. The Tools menu appears. Click General Options. The General Options dialog box appears. Enter a password in the Password to Open or Password to Modify field to password-protect your file. Select the Read-Only Recommended option to set your file to read-only recommended. Click OK to close the dialog box.

Open a Text File as a Workbook

Many software applications have an option for exporting the application's data to a text file. You can use VBA's OpenText method with the Workbooks object to import a text file. You can then use all of Excel's data-analysis capabilities to analyze the file. With the OpenText method, Excel opens the text file as a single worksheet in a new workbook. The file remains a text file. Users can modify the workbook and save it as a text file or as an Excel worksheet.

The list of parameters for the OpenText method is extensive. Only the FileName parameter is required. Use the FileName parameter to tell VBA the name of the file to open. You can enter the name of a file as the parameter if the workbook is located in the current folder. If the file is located in another folder, enter the path to the file.

Make sure you enclose the name of the file or path in quotes.

The OpenText method can handle any delimited or fixed-width file. A delimited file uses a comma, space, semicolon, tab, or other character to mark the end of each column. A fixed-width file aligns the columns and gives each column a defined width. Use the DataType parameter to tell VBA whether your file is a delimited file or a fixed-width file. Use the constant xlDelimited for delimited files, and the constant xlFixedWidth for fixed-width files.

If your file is delimited, you specify what the delimiter is. For example, if the delimiter is a comma, then you set the Comma parameter to True.

Open a Text File as a Workbook

① Name your procedure.

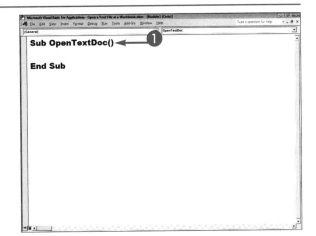

② Create your OpenText command.

● The file you want to open.

● The file type. Type xlDelimited or xlFixedWidth.

● The delimiter. In this example, a comma separates each column.

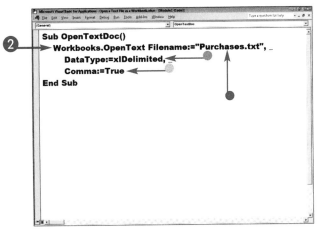

③ Press Alt+F11 to switch from the VBE to Excel, and run the macro.

The text file.

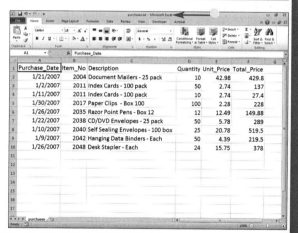

You can open the file in Excel.

The macro opens the text file as a worksheet in Excel.

The file remains a text file.

Extra

Use the following parameters with the OpenText method to open a text file in a workbook.

PARAMETERS	DESCRIPTION
FileName	The name and location of the text file.
Origin	Indicates the original file platform: xlMacintosh or xlWindows.
StartRow	The first row to import.
DataType	The format of the text file, either xlFixedWidth or xlDelimited.
TextQualifier	The character that identifies text.
ConsecutiveDelimiter	Set to True to treat consecutive delimiters as one delimiter.
Tab, Semicolon, Comma, Space	Set each of these parameters to True if they are a delimiter.
Other	Set to True to specify the delimiter.
OtherChar	If Other is set to True, use this parameter to specify the character to use as a delimiter.
FieldInfo	The column number followed by an XlColumnDataType constant.
DecimalSeparator	The character VBA recognizes as a decimal separator.
ThousandsSeparator	The character VBA recognizes as a thousands separator.
TrailingMinusNumbers	Set to True to designate trailing minus signs as negative numbers.
Local	Set to True to use the computer's regional settings.

Open a File Requested by the User

You can retrieve the name of the file a user wants to open by prompting the user with the Open dialog box and then using a method to open the file.

To display the Open dialog box from an Excel procedure, use the GetOpenFilename method. This method does not open the file when the user clicks OK. Instead, the method passes the name of the file the user selects to a variable you assign to the statement. If you want to open the selected file, you must use either the Workbooks. Open method or the Workbooks.OpenText method. If the user does not select a file, the statement returns False.

The GetOpenFilename method has several optional parameters. The FileFilter parameter lets users select the type of file they want to open. You can create a list of

values for the Files of Type drop-down menu in the Open dialog box. For example, "XML Files (*.xml), *.xml" tells VBA that Excel should open only XML files. You can specify multiple file types by separating the file types with commas. Users can then select the file type they want to use.

Use the FilterIndex parameter to indicate the default FileFilter option. You can specify a filter value between 1 and the number of filters you selected. If you omit this parameter, VBA uses the first filter specified as the default value.

Use the Title parameter to place a title on the Open dialog box. For example, for a dialog box that opens text files, you can make the title "Open Text Files."

To enable users to select and open multiple files at once, set the MultiSelect parameter to True.

Open a File Requested by the User

① Name your procedure.

② Create a variable to store the filename returned by the GetOpenFilename method.

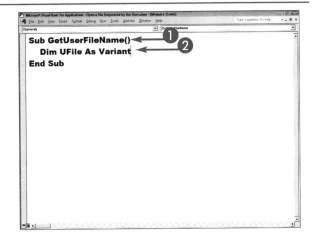

③ Create your GetOpenFilename command.

● Types of files the user can open.

● The title of the Open dialog box.

④ Create a command to open the workbook.

⑤ Press Alt+F11 to switch from the VBE to Excel, and run the macro.

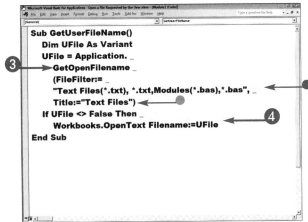

The macro opens the Open dialog box.

● The list of file types the user can open.

● The title of the dialog box.

6 Double-click the file you want to open.

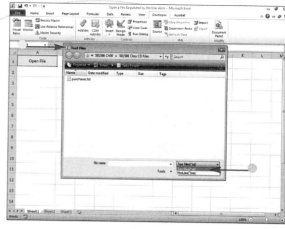

The macro opens the file.

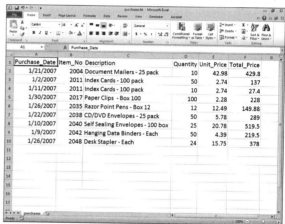

Extra

The `FileFilter` parameter enables you to create a list of files users can select in the Open dialog box. You describe the file and follow the description with a comma and a wildcard file specification. If you do not set this parameter, VBA lists all of the file types Excel can open.

Example:
```
Text Files (*.txt), *.txt
```

An asterisk (*) is a wildcard character that represents any string of characters, and a question mark (?) is a wildcard character that represents a single character. The notation *.txt means any filename that ends with .txt.

FILE TYPE	DESCRIPTION
*.txt, *.prn, *.csv	Text files
*.xls, *.xlm, *.xl, *.xlc, *.xlsx, *.xlsm	Microsoft Excel files
*.htm	Web pages
*.xml	XML files
*.odc, *.udl, *.dsn	Data sources
*.mdb, *.mde	Access databases
*.wk?	Lotus files
*.wks	Microsoft Works 2.0 files
*.dbf	dBase files

Save a Workbook

To save an Excel workbook, you can use the `Save` or `SaveAs` methods of the `Workbook` object. VBA creates a workbook object for each workbook you open. You can reference a specific workbook object by name. For example, `Workbooks("Sample.xlsx")` refers to the Sample.xlsx workbook.

If you do not know the name of the workbook you want to save, you can make the workbook you want to save the active workbook, and then use the `ActiveWorkbook` property to save the workbook. For example, the code `ActiveWorkbook.Save` saves the active workbook.

If the workbook you want to save contains the macro that is currently running, you can use the `ThisWorkbook` property. For example, the code `ThisWorkbook.Save` saves the workbook in which the macro is located. The workbook that contains the macro is often the active workbook. However, if you open a new workbook during the execution of a macro, the new workbook can become the active workbook.

To set save specifications for a workbook, use the `Workbook.SaveAs` method, which has the following parameters: `FileName`, `FileFormat`, `Password`, `WriteResPassword`, `ReadOnlyRecommended`, `CreateBackup`, `AccessMode`, `ConflictResolution`, `AddToMru`, and `Local`.

Use the `FileName` parameter to specify the name of the workbook and the folder in which to save the workbook. If you do not set this parameter, Excel uses the workbook's current name.

Use the `FileFormat` parameter to specify a format for the saved file. You can use any of the file formats that Excel supports by entering one of the `XlFileFormat` constant values. See the appendix for a list of the `XlFileFormat` constant values. Set the `AddToMru` parameter to `True` if you want to add the workbook to the Recent Workbooks list.

Save a Workbook

① Name your procedure.

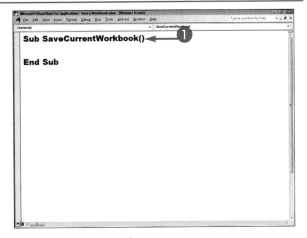

② Create your `SaveAs` command.

● The name you want to give the saved file.

● The file format.

● Adds the file to the Recent Workbooks list.

③ Press Alt+F11 to switch from the VBE to Excel, and run the macro.

○ The macro saves your file.

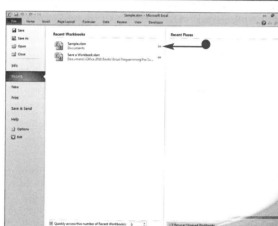

● The macro adds your file to the Recent Workbooks list.

The `Workbook.SaveAs` method has several optional parameters that determine how the file is saved.

SAVEAS PARAMETER	DESCRIPTION
FileName	Indicates the name and location to save the file.
FileFormat	The `XlFileFormat` constant that indicates the format of the saved file. See the appendix for a list of `XlFileFormat` constant values.
Password	The up to 15-character password required to open the file.
WriteResPassword	The password for write-restricting the file.
ReadOnlyRecommended	Set to `True` to display a message that recommends that the user open the file as read-only.
CreateBackup	Set to `True` to create a backup file.
AccessMode	A constant value of `xlExclusive`, `xlNoChange`, or `xlShared`. Indicate the access mode.
ConflictResolution	A constant that indicates how to resolve conflicts. A value of `xlUserResolution` displays a Conflict Resolution box, `xlLocalSessionChanges` accepts a local user's changes, and `xlOtherSessionChanges` accepts changes from other users.
AddToMru	Set to `True` to add a workbook to the Recent Workbooks list.
Local	Set to `True` to save files in the language used by Excel; set to `False` to save files in the language used by VBA.

Save a Workbook in a Format Specified by the User

You can use the `GetSaveAsFilename` method to request the name, location, and format to use when saving a workbook file. This method displays the Save As dialog from which users select the file they want to save. The `GetSaveAsFilename` method does not save the file; instead, VBA returns the user's selection to the variable you assign to the `GetSaveAsFilename` statement. If the user does not make an entry, the variable returns `False`. To save the file, use the `SaveAs` method. See the section "Save a Workbook" for more information.

The `GetSaveAsFilename` method has the following optional parameters: `InitialFilename`, `FileFilter`, `FilterIndex`, and `Title`. Use the `InitialFilename` parameter to suggest a name for the file. If you do not suggest a name, Excel uses the name of the active

workbook. Use the `FileFilter` parameter to create a list of file formats users can use to save the file. If you do not include this parameter, Excel lists all available formats. To create the list, describe the file type, place a comma after the description, and then place a wildcard specification after the comma. For example:

```
Text Files (*.text), *.txt
```

An asterisk (*) is a wildcard character that means any string of characters. The notation *.txt means any file that ends with .txt.

Use the `FilterIndex` parameter to select a default file-filtering option from the `FileFilter` parameter options. You can use a filter value between 1 and the total number of filters. If you omit this parameter, VBA uses the first filter as the default value. Use the `Title` parameter to place a title on the dialog box.

Save a Workbook in a Format Specified by the User

① Name your procedure.

② Declare your variables.

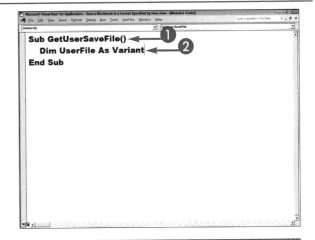

③ Create a `GetSaveAsFilename` command.

● The filter list.

● The dialog box title.

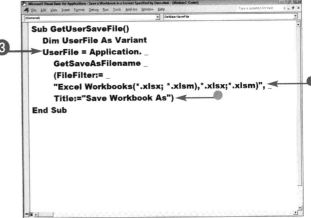

④ Create a command to save the file.

⑤ Press Alt+F11 to switch from the VBE to Excel, and run the macro.

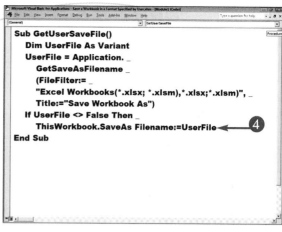

```
Sub GetUserSaveFile()
    Dim UserFile As Variant
    UserFile = Application. _
        GetSaveAsFilename _
        (FileFilter:= _
        "Excel Workbooks(*.xlsx; *.xlsm),*.xlsx;*.xlsm)", _
        Title:="Save Workbook As")
    If UserFile <> False Then _
        ThisWorkbook.SaveAs Filename:=UserFile    ④
End Sub
```

The macro opens the Save Workbook As dialog box and then saves the file using the name you specify.

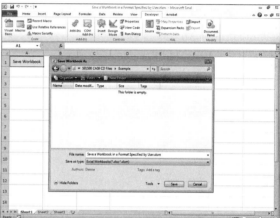

Extra

Instead of saving an individual workbook, you can save the entire workspace. Saving workspaces enables you to save all open workbooks as a group. When you open a workspace, all of the workbooks open. Workspace files have an .xlw filename extension.

To save a workspace, use the SaveWorkspace method of the Application object. The SaveWorkspace method has one parameter: FileName. To save your file in the current folder, enter the name of the file as the FileName parameter. To save to another folder, enter the path to the file as the FileName parameter. Enclose the filename or path quotes.

Examples:
```
Application.SaveWorkspace("Sample")
Application.SaveWorkspace("C:\Workbooks\Sample")
```

Determine if a Workbook Is Open

The `Workbooks` collection contains all of the workbooks that are open in Excel. You can determine if a workbook is open by examining the workbooks in the `Workbooks` collection. Every time you open a workbook, it becomes a `Workbook` object and Excel adds it to the `Workbooks` collection. Excel stores workbooks in the `Workbooks` collection sequentially and assigns each workbook an index value based on its sequence. For example, the first workbook opened is the first workbook in the collection, and VBA assigns it an index value of 1; the next workbook opened is the second workbook, and VBA assigns it an index value of 2. If you know the order in which a workbook opened, you can access the workbook by using the associated index value.

The code `MyWorkbook = Workbook(1).Name` uses the `Name` property to return the name of the first workbook in the collection to the `MyWorkbook` variable. The `Name` property is read-only. You can use it to return the name of a workbook, but you cannot use it to change the name of a workbook. To learn how to change the name of a workbook, see the section "Save a Workbook."

To locate a workbook, look at each workbook in the `Workbooks` collection. With a `For Each Next` loop statement, you can cycle through all open workbooks. See Chapter 6 for more information about using a `For Each Next` loop statement.

Within a looping structure, you can compare the name of each workbook with the name of the desired workbook. With an `If Then` statement, you can check the name of each workbook and then execute a series of statements when the workbook you want is found. See Chapter 6 for more information on using an `If Then` statement.

Determine if a Workbook Is Open

① Name your procedure.

② Declare your variables.

● Handles errors. See Chapter 8.

③ Assign `False` to a Boolean variable.

 You set this variable to `True` if the active workbook is the workbook that you want to activate.

④ Assign the file you are looking for to a variable.

⑤ Create a `For Each In` loop.

 This statement enables you to review every open workbook.

⑥ Create an `If Then` statement.

 The code looks at every open workbook; if it finds the workbook you requested, it activates the workbook and displays a message.

● If the macro does not find the workbook, it looks in the current folder and opens the workbook.

● Handles errors. See Chapter 8.

⑦ Press Alt+F11 to switch from the VBE to Excel, and run the macro.

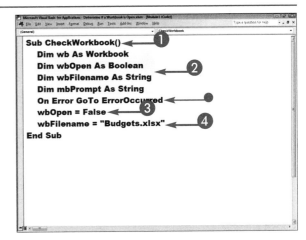

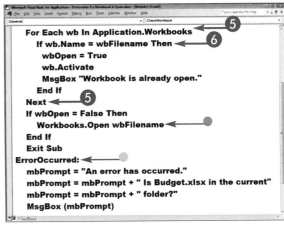

The macro opens the file you specified and activates it.

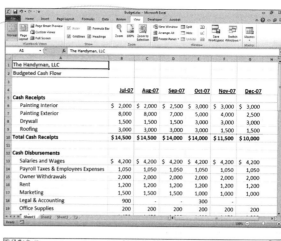

If the file is already open, the macro displays the message "Workbook is already open."

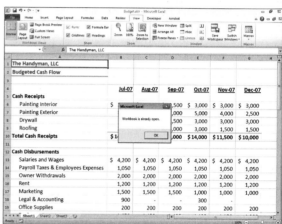

Extra

If a workbook is open, you can activate it by using the `Activate` method of the `Workbook` object. The activated workbook becomes the currently selected workbook in Excel. The `Activate` method has no parameters. Specify the workbook to activate, followed by the method.

Example:
```
Workbooks("Budget.xlsx").Activate
```

Using `Application.Workbooks` returns all workbooks, including hidden workbooks, but it does not return any open add-ins. To return a specific add-in, reference the add-in by name.

Example:
```
Workbooks("OpenAddin.xla").
```

The `Open` method opens the specified add-in file. If you do not specify the path, Excel looks for the workbook in the current folder. See Chapter 18 for more information on add-ins.

Close a Workbook

You can close a workbook by using the `Close` method and referencing the `Workbook` object that contains the workbook you want to close. When you open a workbook, VBA assigns the workbook an index value. For example, VBA assigns the first workbook you open an index value of `1`, and the next workbook you open an index value of `2`. The `Workbooks` collection contains all open workbooks as individual `Workbook` objects. You can reference a workbook by using an index value, the name of the workbook, the `ActiveWorkbook` property, or the `ThisWorkbook` property. If you close a workbook that is running the macro and you have code after the `Close` statement, Excel may ignore the code. The following examples close a workbook:

```
Workbooks(1).Close
```

```
Workbooks("Budget.xlsx").Close
```

```
ActiveWorkbook.Close
```

```
ThisWorkbook.Close
```

The `Close` method has three optional parameters: `SaveChanges`, `Filename`, and `RouteWorkbook`. Set the `SaveChanges` parameter to `True` to save changes to a workbook as it closes. A `SaveChanges` value of `False` closes the workbook without saving, and you lose any changes you have made since your last save. Use the `FileName` parameter to tell VBA the name you want to give your file when you save it.

If you set up the workbook to route, you can use the `RouteWorkbook` parameter to route the workbook to the next recipient on the routing list. You specify a value of `True` to route the workbook; you specify a value of `False` if you do not want route the workbook to the next recipient.

Close a Workbook

① Name your procedure.

② Create your `Close` command.

● The workbook that you want to close.

● Saves any changes.

● The new filename.

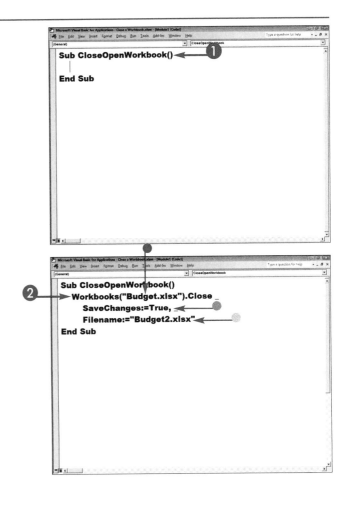

3 Create a message for the user.

Note: *This procedure assumes that Budget. xlsx is open.*

4 Press Alt+F11 to switch from the VBE to Excel, and run the macro.

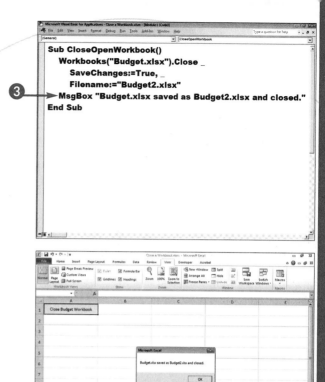

3

```
Sub CloseOpenWorkbook()
    Workbooks("Budget.xlsx").Close _
        SaveChanges:=True, _
        Filename:="Budget2.xlsx"
    MsgBox "Budget.xlsx saved as Budget2.xlsx and closed."
End Sub
```

The macro closes the file specified in the macro, saves it under the name specified in the macro, and then displays a message to the user.

Extra

By using the Close method with the Workbooks object, you can close all workbooks that you have open in Excel. If the SaveChanges parameter does not have a value specified, Excel checks to ensure that you have saved each workbook since its last modification. If a workbook contains modifications, Excel prompts you to save the workbook. The following example closes all open workbooks.

Example:
```
Workbooks.Close
```

When you close all workbooks, Excel remains open. If you want Excel to close, use the Quit method with the Application object.

Example:
```
Application.Quit
```

Before closing Excel, the Quit method first closes the open workbooks. If any of the workbooks contain changes, Excel prompts you to save the changes. If you do not want to save modified worksheets and you do not want the dialog box to ask you to save changes, set the DisplayAlerts property to False. This property determines whether the alert message appears when Excel performs a task.

Example:
```
Application.DisplayAlerts = False
```

Create a New Workbook

To create a new Excel workbook, use the `Add` method with the `Workbooks` collection. The `Add` method has one optional parameter: `Template`. The following is the syntax for the `Add` method:

`Workbooks.Add(Template)`

To tell VBA how to create a workbook, use the `Template` parameter. You can use one of the four `XlWBATemplate` constant values or another workbook as the template parameter. Use `xlWBATWorksheet` to create a workbook containing one worksheet; `xlWBATChart` to create a workbook containing one chart sheet; `xlWBATExcel4MacroSheet` to create an Excel 4.0 macro sheet; and `xlWBATExcel4IntMacroSheet` to create an international macro sheet.

When you use a workbook as the template, Excel copies the workbook into a new workbook. You can use the name of the workbook as the parameter if the workbook is located in the current folder. If the workbook is located in another folder, use the path to the workbook.

When you use the `Add` method without the template parameter, Excel creates a new workbook with the name Book1.xlsx. If a workbook already exists with that name, Excel assigns the name Book2.xlsx. You can use the `Title` property to specify the title of the workbook. To name and save the new workbook, you can use the `SaveAs` method. See the section "Save a Workbook" for more information on the `SaveAs` method.

Create a New Workbook

① Name your procedure.

② Declare a new `Workbook` object.

③ Create your `Add` command.

● The workbook that you want to use as a template.

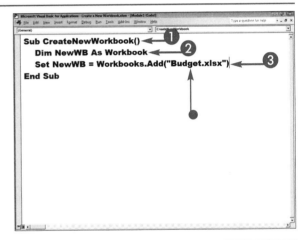

④ Assign a title to your workbook.

⑤ Name and save your workbook.

⑥ Press Alt+F11 to switch from the VBE to Excel, and run the macro.

- The macro creates and saves the new workbook.

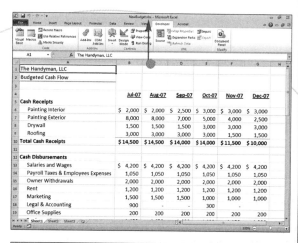

- The macro adds the title to the Document Properties pane.

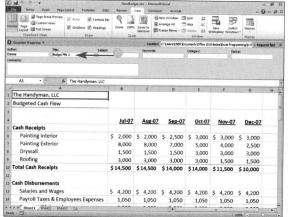

Extra

You can use the following properties with the `Workbook` object.

PROPERTY	DESCRIPTION
ActiveSheet	A string indicating the name of the active sheet in the workbook.
FileFormat	A read-only value indicating the format of the workbook. This value returns an `XlFileFormat` constant; see the appendix for more information.
FullName	A read-only string indicating the name and complete path to the workbook.
HasPassword	A read-only Boolean value indicating whether the workbook is password-protected.
Name	A string indicating the name of the workbook.
Password	Returns or sets the password string for the workbook.
Path	Returns the complete Excel application path.
ProtectStructure	A read-only Boolean value indicating whether the order of the sheets in the workbook is protected. If `True`, you cannot move, delete, or add worksheets.
ReadOnly	A read-only Boolean value indicating whether the workbook was opened as read-only.
ReadOnlyRecommended	A read-only Boolean value indicating whether the workbook was saved as read-only.
Saved	Contains a Boolean value indicating whether changes were made since the workbook was saved.

Delete a File

The VBA `Kill` statement deletes a workbook or file. You can use this statement to have VBA delete any file that the user has permission to delete. The following is the syntax for the `Kill` statement:

`Kill(Pathname)`

The `Kill` statement has one parameter: `Pathname`. The `Pathname` parameter is a string referencing the files you want to delete. You can use the name of a workbook as the parameter if the workbook is located in the current folder. If the workbook is located in another folder, use the path to the workbook. Make sure you enclose the filename or path in quotes.

You can specify the name of a single file by typing the complete filename, including the extension. You can

remove multiple files at once by using wildcard symbols to specify multiple characters. An asterisk (*) represents multiple characters, and a question mark (?) represents a single character. For example, you can remove the entire contents of a folder by using the *.* specification. The statement `Kill "C:\Excel Files\*.*"` deletes every file in the Excel Files folder. If you only want to remove the Excel workbooks, you can use `Kill "C:\Excel Files\*.xls?"`.

You cannot delete open files. If you attempt to delete an open file, a Permission Denied error appears. You also cannot delete read-only files. If you attempt to delete a read-only file, Excel displays a Path/File access error message.

Delete a File

1 Name your procedure.

2 Declare your variables.

This example uses the `DeleteWB` variable to store the name of the file to delete.

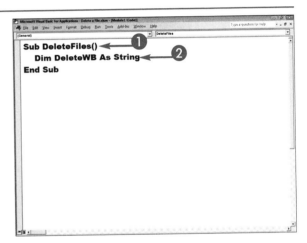

3 Use the `GetSaveAsFilename` method to request from the user the file that the user wants to delete.

Note: See the section "Save a Workbook in a Format Specified by the User" to learn more about the `GetSaveAsFilename` method.

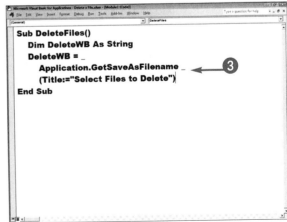

④ Delete the file.

⑤ Press Alt+F11 to switch from the VBE to Excel, and run the macro.

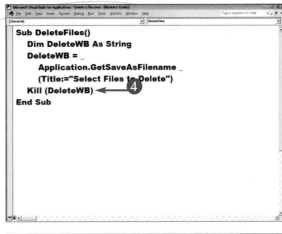

```
Sub DeleteFiles()
    Dim DeleteWB As String
    DeleteWB = _
        Application.GetSaveAsFilename _
        (Title:="Select Files to Delete")
    Kill (DeleteWB) ← ④
End Sub
```

The macro requests a filename and then deletes the file.

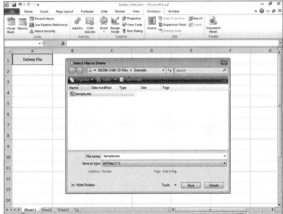

Extra

The `Kill` statement removes files; it does not remove folders. To delete a folder, use the `RmDir` statement. The `RmDir` statement has one parameter: `Path`. If you omit the parameter, VBA tries to delete the current folder. For the path parameter, specify the location of the folder that you want to remove. For example, the code `RmDir("Excel Files")` removes the Excel Files folder. The `RmDir` statement removes only folders; it does not remove any files. If the folder you are deleting contains any files, an error appears telling you that Excel cannot remove the folder.

When working with folders, you may need to know the current path. To determine the path to the current folder, use the `CurDir` function. The `CurDir` function returns a string containing the path to the current folder. You can assign the value returned by the function to a variable, as shown in following example.

Example:
```
CurrentFolder = CurDir
```

Add a Sheet

To add a new sheet to a workbook, you can use the Add method with the Sheets object. You can use this method to add a worksheet, chart sheet, or macro sheet. The Add method has four optional parameters that specify where in the workbook to place the sheet, the number of sheets to add, and the type of sheet to create. The following is the syntax for the Add method:

`expression.Add(Before, After, Count, Type)`

Use the expression portion of the statement to identify the workbook to which you want to add sheets. Use the Before parameter to tell VBA the sheet before which you want to place the new sheet, or use the After parameter to tell VBA the sheet after which you want to place the new sheet. You can use the Sheets collection to reference a sheet. Excel uses an index value to refer to sheets in the

Sheets collection. In a workbook, the first sheet on the left has an index value of 1 and is referred to as Sheets(1). To reference a sheet, you can use the sheet name or the Sheets collection with an index value, as in this example: `ThisWorkbook.Sheets.Add Before:= Sheets(1)`.

Use the Count parameter to add multiple sheets to a workbook. If you do not specify a value for the Count parameter, Excel adds one sheet.

By default, the Add method creates a worksheet. You can also use this method to create chart or macro sheets. You specify the type of sheet you want to create by using one of the four XlSheetType constant values: You use xlWorksheet to add a new worksheet, xlChart to add a chart sheet, xlExcel4MacroSheet to add a macro sheet, and xlExcel4IntMacroSheet to add an international macro sheet.

Add a Sheet

① Name your procedure.

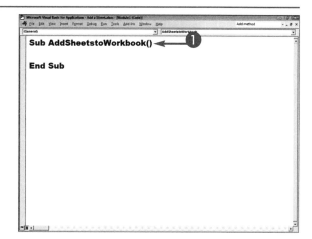

② Create your Add command.

● The sheet before which you want to add the new sheets.

● The number of sheets you want to add.

● The type of sheet you want to add.

③ Press Alt+F11 to switch from the VBE to Excel, and run the macro.

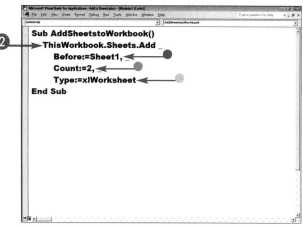

The workbook before you run the macro.

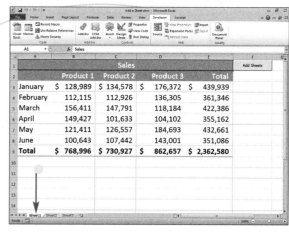

The workbook after you run the macro.

The macro adds two worksheets before the first worksheet in the workbook.

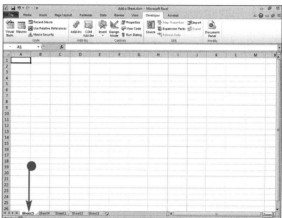

Apply It

If you know that you want Excel to add new sheets before the first sheet in the workbook or after the last sheet, reference an element of the Sheets collection. Excel always makes the first sheet in the workbook the first element in the Sheets collection. You can refer to it as Sheets(1). You can use the Count method with the Sheets object to determine the last sheet in the workbook. The expression Sheets.Count returns the total number of Sheets in the Sheets collection. The following example places a Sheet after the last sheet in the workbook.

Example:
```
ThisWorkbook.Sheets.Add _
   After:=Sheets(Sheets.Count)
```

You can also reference a sheet by name. For example, by default, Excel names worksheets Sheet1, Sheet2, and so on. If you want to place new sheets before Sheet1, use the following as the Before parameter: Before:= Sheets("Sheet1").

Delete a Sheet

You can delete or remove from a workbook any sheet you can modify. If you open the workbook in read-only mode or if a sheet is protected, you may not be able to delete a sheet.

To delete sheets, use the Delete method with the Sheets object. You can delete worksheets, chart sheets, and macro sheets. To use the Delete method, you simply specify the sheet you want to remove. The following example removes the first sheet in a workbook:

```
Sheets(1).Delete
```

Every sheet has an index value. This example deletes the sheet with the index value of 1. Excel numbers worksheets and charts as you add them to the workbook as follows: Sheet1, Sheet2, and so on (or Chart1, Chart2, and so on). However, the VBA index number does not always correspond with the number given to the sheet by Excel.

VBA assigns index values numerically, starting with the first sheet on the left. If you move sheets within your workbook, Excel reorders them in the Sheets object. The first sheet on the left always has an index value of 1.

You can also use the sheet name to reference the sheet you want to delete. You must enclose the name of the sheet in quotes, as in the following example:

```
Sheets("Sheet3").Delete
```

When a Delete statement executes, Excel displays an alert and asks you to verify that you really want to delete the sheet. Click Yes to remove the specified sheet from the workbook. If you do not want Excel to display an alert, use the following code to set the DisplayAlerts property to False: Application.DisplayAlerts = False. Remember that if the sheet contains any data, when you delete Excel permanently removes the data.

Delete a Sheet

① Name your procedure.

② Declare your variables.

● Handles Errors.

③ Create an input box.

Users enter the name of the sheet they want to delete into the input box, and VBA stores the name to a variable.

④ Create a Delete command.

● The variable containing the worksheet that the user wants to delete.

⑤ Press Alt+F11 to switch from the VBE to Excel and then run the macro.

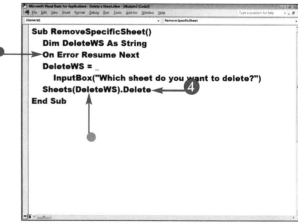

The macro displays the message box requesting the sheet the user wants to delete.

● The macro deletes the sheet.

Extra

If you want to create a procedure that removes only worksheets from the workbook, you can use the `Delete` method with a `Worksheets` object instead of the `Sheets` object. The `Sheets` object contains all worksheets, chart sheets, and macro sheets that are open in a workbook, whereas the `Worksheets` object only keeps track of the open worksheets. If you use the `Worksheets` object to remove the first worksheet in the workbook, Excel ignores any chart sheets before the first worksheet. The following statement deletes the first worksheet in the workbook and ignores any other sheet types.

Example:
```
Worksheets(1).Delete
```

If you want to create a procedure that removes only chart sheets from a workbook, you can use the `Delete` method with the `Charts` object. The `Charts` object contains all of the chart sheets that are contained in a workbook. This method works only with chart sheets, not charts embedded in worksheets. When you use the `Charts` object with the `Delete` method, Excel considers only actual chart sheets and ignores any worksheets, even if they exist before the specified chart sheet. The following statement deletes the first chart sheet in the workbook and ignores any other sheet types.

Example:
```
Charts(1).Delete
```

Move a Sheet

You can use the `Move` method with the `Sheets` object to rearrange sheets within a workbook. When you move a sheet, you indicate the new location by specifying the name of the sheet before or after which you want to place the sheet you are moving.

The `Move` method has two optional parameters: `Before` and `After`. Although both parameters are optional, you can use only one of them at a time. Use the `Before` parameter to specify the sheet in front of which you want to place a sheet, and the `After` parameter to specify the sheet after which you want to place a sheet. For example, the following statement moves the first sheet in a workbook and places it after the third sheet:

```
Sheets(1).Move After:=Sheets(3)
```

If you do not specify a `Before` or `After` parameter value, Excel creates a new workbook and places the worksheet in that workbook. The worksheet becomes the only worksheet in the new workbook.

The `Sheets` object references all sheets in the workbook, including all worksheets, chart sheets, and macro sheets. As shown in the example, you can use index values to reference sheets based on their order in the workbook. You can also reference a sheet by using the name on the sheet tab.

Moving a sheet before or after a nonexistent sheet causes VBA to display a "Subscript out of range" error. To avoid this error, you can use the `Count` method to determine the number of sheets in the workbook before you attempt to move sheets.

Move a Sheet

① Name your procedure.

② Declare your variables.

③ Count the number of sheets in your workbook and store the result to a variable.

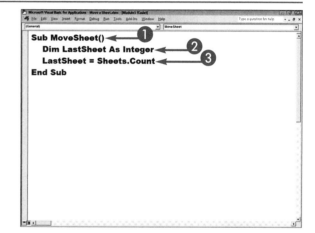

④ Create your `Move` command.

● The sheet you want to move.

● The location where you want to move your sheet.

⑤ Press Alt+F11 to switch from the VBE to Excel, and run the macro.

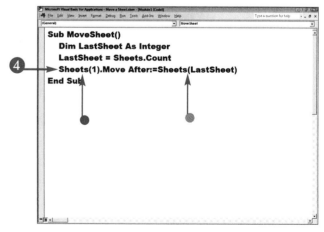

● The worksheet before the move.

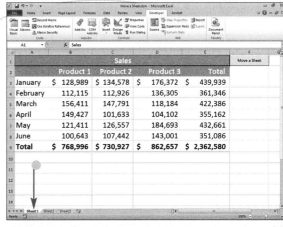

● The worksheet after the move.

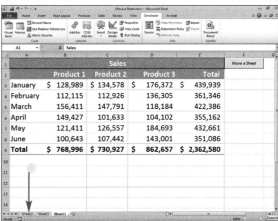

Apply It

When you work with Excel objects in VBA, especially collection objects that contain several objects, you frequently must determine the number of objects in the collection. Because the number of objects in a collection can vary, you may need to determine the number of objects as your code runs. The best way to do this is by using the Count property, which works with virtually all VBA collection objects and returns the number of items in the collection.

Example:
```
NumWrkSheets = Worksheets.Count
```

The Count property is read-only, meaning you can use it to obtain the number of sheets in a workbook, but you cannot use it to change the number of sheets in a workbook.

Copy a Sheet

I f you want to copy a sheet, you can use the Copy method with the Sheets object. When you copy a sheet, you indicate where you want to place the copy by specifying the name of the sheet before or after which you want the copy to appear.

The Copy method has two optional parameters: Before and After. Although both parameters are optional, you can use only one of them at a time. Use the Before parameter to specify the sheet in front of which you want to place the copy of the sheet, or use the After parameter to specify the sheet after which you want to place the copy of the sheet. The following statement copies the first sheet in a workbook and places the copy after the third sheet: Sheets(1).Copy After:=Sheets(3). If you do

not specify a Before or After value, Excel creates a new workbook and places the copy in the new workbook.

When you use the Sheets object, you can reference all sheets within a workbook, including worksheets, chart sheets, and macro sheets. You can use index values to reference sheets based on their order in the workbook, or you can reference sheets by using their sheet names.

Be careful with the sheet references you use. If you try to place a copy of a sheet before or after a nonexistent sheet, VBA displays a "Subscript out of range" error. To avoid this error, consider using the Count method to determine exactly how many sheets you have in a workbook before you copy a sheet.

Copy a Sheet

① Name your procedure.

② Declare your variables.

③ Count the number of sheets in your workbook and store the result to a variable.

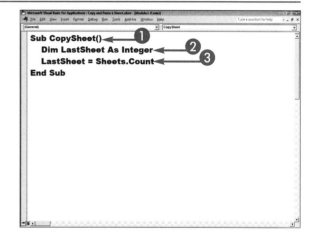

④ Create your Copy command.

● The sheet you want to copy.

● Where you want to place the copy.

⑤ Press Alt+F11 to switch from the VBE to Excel, and run the macro.

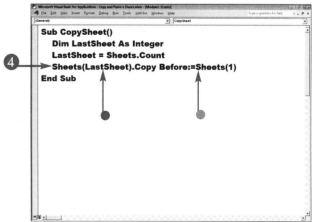

- The workbook before you run the macro.

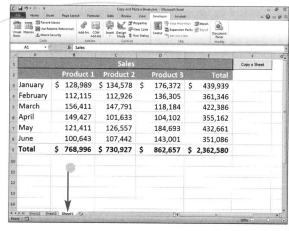

- The workbook after you run the macro.

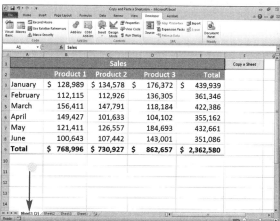

Apply It

The Copy method produces the same results when you use it with a Chart object, Charts collection object, Worksheet object, or Worksheets collection object instead of the Sheets object. You can use these other objects when you want to work with a specific type of sheet. For example, to make a worksheet the first worksheet in a workbook, you can type Worksheet(3).Copy Before:=Worksheets(1). This code places a copy of the third worksheet in front of the first worksheet. If the first sheet in the workbook is a chart, the copied sheet comes after the chart but before the first worksheet. You can copy chart sheets the same way, by using the Charts collection object to specify the chart sheet to copy. You can combine your object references within a Copy statement. For example, you can place a copy of the first worksheet before the first chart sheet.

Example:
```
Worksheets(1).Copy Before:=Charts(1)
```

When you copy a sheet in a workbook, Excel indicates the sheet is a copy by placing a number in parentheses after the sheet name. For example, for Sheet3, Excel indicates the copied sheet as Sheet3 (2), with the number in parentheses indicating that the sheet is the second version. Copying the worksheet again creates Sheet3 (3).

Hide a Sheet

If you want to hide sheets, use the `Visible` property with the `Sheets` object. You may want to hide sheets to prevent users from viewing them. These sheets might contain the raw values that you use to calculate data.

Hiding a sheet does not always keep users from accessing it. Users can unhide sheets in Excel by using the Unhide option on the Format menu. If you want others to be able to unhide a sheet but not be able to change a sheet, protect the sheet. See the section "Protect a Worksheet" for more information about protecting sheets.

Using the `Visible` property, you can determine the current state of a sheet — visible or not visible — or you can change the state of a sheet. To determine the current

state of a sheet, you assign the `Visible` property to a variable as follows: `SheetProps = Sheets(1).Visible`. If you declare the `SheetProps` variable as a Boolean value, the variable receives a value of `True` if the specified sheet is visible; otherwise, it receives a value of `False`. If you do not declare the variable as Boolean, Excel assigns a numeric value of -1 if the sheet is visible and 0 if the sheet is not visible.

To change the visibility of a sheet, you can assign a Boolean value of `True` or `False` to the sheet's `Visible` property. You can hide all but one sheet in a workbook, because Excel requires that a workbook have at least one visible sheet. The following example hides a sheet:

```
Sheets(2).Visible = False
```

Hide a Sheet

1. Name your procedure.

2. Declare your variables.

3. Count the number of sheets in your workbook and store the result to a variable.

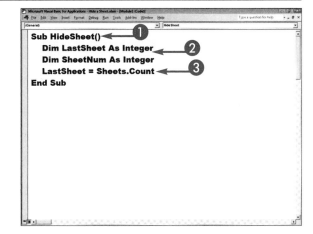

4. Set the `Visible` property to `False`.

- This example uses a For Next loop to hide every worksheet except the first one.

5. Press Alt+F11 to switch from the VBE to Excel, and run the macro.

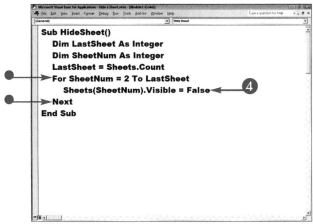

- The workbook before you execute the macro.

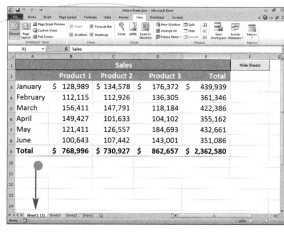

- The workbook after you execute the macro.

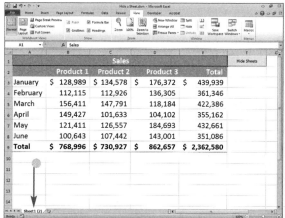

Extra

Sheets that you hide by setting the Visible property to False are still accessible to users from within Excel. To see hidden sheets, on the Home tab click Format → Hide & Unhide → Unhide Sheet. The Unhide dialog box appears, listing all of the sheets that you have hidden. To unhide a sheet, click the sheet and then click OK. This is equivalent to setting the Visible property for a sheet to True.

There are three XlSheetVisibility constant values. You can use them to set the visibility status of a sheet.

CONSTANT VALUE	FUNCTION
xlSheetHidden	Hides a sheet. The Ribbon can be used to unhide the sheet.
xlSheetVeryHidden	Hides a sheet. The Ribbon cannot be used to unhide the sheet.
xlSheetVisible	Displays a sheet.

Example:
```
Sheets("Formulas").Visible =
  xlSheetVeryHidden
```

Change the Name of a Sheet

f you have a number of sheets in a workbook, naming your sheets enables your users to easily determine which sheet they want to access. For example, if you keep your budget on a sheet named Budget and your sales figures on a sheet named Sales, when users open your workbook, they can quickly determine the sheet they want to access.

To change the name of a sheet in a workbook, use the Name property of the Sheets object. By default, Excel names all worksheets Sheet#, replacing # with the order in which you add the sheet to your workbook. For example, a typical workbook contains three worksheets: Sheet1, Sheet2, and Sheet3. If you add a worksheet, Excel names it Sheet4. Excel uses the name Chart# for chart sheets. Again, Excel assigns chart sheets numbers,

based on the order in which you add them, with the first chart sheet being Chart1.

You can change the name of a sheet by assigning a name to the Name property of the Sheet object. For example, the following code changes the name of Sheet1 to Budget:

```
Sheets(1).Name = "Budget"
```

You can assign a string or a variable to the Name property.

You can determine what the current name of a sheet is by assigning the Name property to a variable, as in the following example:

```
SheetName = Sheets(1).Name
```

This example returns the name of Sheet(1) to the variable SheetName.

Change the Name of a Sheet

① Name your procedure.

② Declare your variables.

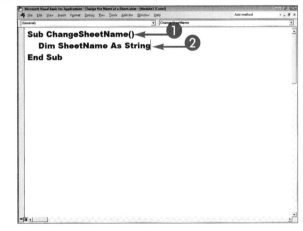

● Handles Errors.

③ Create an input box.

    In the input box, users enter the name they want to change the active sheet to, and VBA stores the name to a variable.

④ Create a Name command to rename the sheet.

● The variable containing the name the user wants to give to the worksheet.

● The sheet to be renamed.

    In this example, the code is renaming the active sheet.

⑤ Press Alt+F11 to switch from the VBE to Excel, and run the macro.

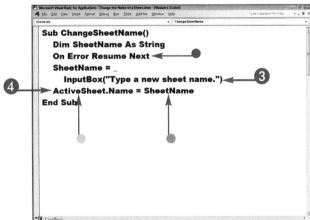

The macro displays a input box requesting the name the user wants to give the active sheet.

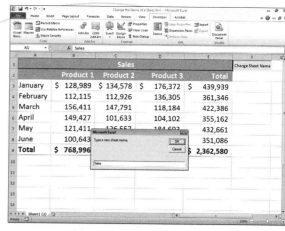

The macro renames the sheet.

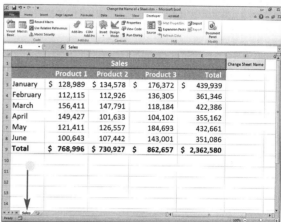

Extra

You can manually change the name of a sheet in Excel by clicking the Home tab and then selecting Format → Rename Sheet. Excel highlights the sheet's name tab. You click the tab and then type the new name. After you modify the name, click elsewhere on the sheet and Excel updates the sheet name.

Because users can easily modify the name of a worksheet, be careful when referencing sheet names in your macros. If you reference a sheet name that Excel cannot find, Excel returns an error message.

Regardless of what sheets are named, Excel keeps track of them based on the order in which they exist within the `Sheets` collection.

You can also use the `Name` property in conjunction with the `Parent` property to determine the name of the workbook that contains the current sheet. To determine the name of the corresponding workbook, use the code `CurrentWB = ActiveSheet.Parent.Name`.

Save a Sheet to Another File

You can save any sheet to another file by using the SaveAs method with a Sheets collection object. The SaveAs method has several parameters that tell VBA how to save the sheet: FileName, FileFormat, Password, WriteResPassword, ReadOnlyRecommended, CreateBackup, AddToMru, and Local.

The FileName parameter is required. Use the FileName parameter to specify the name of the file you want to save the sheet to, and the folder in which you want to save the sheet. If you do not specify a path, Excel saves the file to the current folder.

Use the FileFormat parameter to specify the file format in which you want to save the file. You can save in any file format supported by Excel, by using one of the XlFileFormat constant values. See the appendix for a list of the XlFileFormat constant values. If you do not specify a file format, Excel uses the format that was

previously used to save the file if the file was previously saved, or the file format used by the current version of Excel if the file has never been saved. Use the Password parameter to set a password of up to 15 characters for opening the file. Use the WriteResPassword parameter to restrict the file to open as read-only, unless the user has the password.

The remaining parameters accept the Boolean values True or False. You set ReadOnlyRecommended to True to display a message to users when the file opens, suggesting that they open the file as read-only. You set CreateBackup to True to create a backup file; AddToMru to True to add the file to the Recent Workbooks list; Local to True if you want to save the file in the language used by Excel; and Local to False if you want to save the file in the language used by VBA.

Save a Sheet to Another File

① Name your procedure.

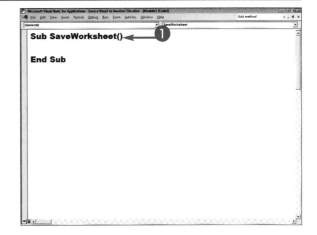

② Create your SaveAs command.

● The name of the new file.

● The format in which you want to save the file.

This example saves the file in HTML format.

○ Creates a backup.

○ Adds the file to the Recent Workbooks list when the file is saved.

③ Press Alt+F11 to switch from the VBE to Excel, and run the macro.

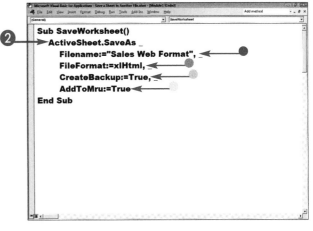

- The macro saves the file in HTML format, adds the file to the Recent Workbooks list, and creates a backup.

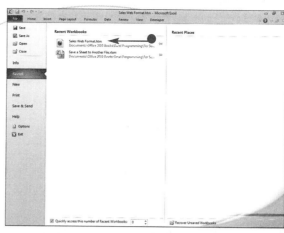

The HTML file that the macro created, open in a browser.

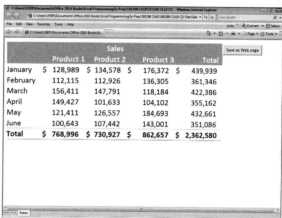

	Sales			
	Product 1	Product 2	Product 3	Total
January	$ 128,989	$ 134,578	$ 176,372	$ 439,939
February	112,115	112,926	136,305	361,346
March	156,411	147,791	118,184	422,386
April	149,427	101,633	104,102	355,162
May	121,411	126,557	184,693	432,661
June	100,643	107,442	143,001	351,086
Total	$ 768,996	$ 730,927	$ 862,657	$ 2,362,580

Extra

The FileFormat parameter accepts any of the XlFileFormat constant values that are listed in the appendix. The list of available file formats is rather extensive. You can save a worksheet to another workbook by specifying the xlWorkbookNormal constant. This constant creates a new workbook based on the default workbook format for the current version of Excel. If you need to save the workbook in a format used by an earlier version of Excel, you need to specify the appropriate format parameter. For example, xlExcel5 saves the workbook in a format that you can open in Excel 5.0 or later. To save an Excel 2010 file in a macro-enabled format, use xlOpenXMLWorkbookMacroEnabled.

Protect a Worksheet

Protecting your worksheets enables users to make certain types of changes while disallowing others. For example, you can allow users to make changes to formats; insert or delete columns, rows, or hyperlinks; sort; filter; use PivotTables; and edit objects or scenarios.

You use the `Worksheet.Protect` method to protect a worksheet. The `Worksheet.Protect` method has several parameters, all of which are optional. With the exception of the `Password` parameter, you use the Boolean value `True` to activate a parameter and the Boolean value `False` to deactivate a parameter. The parameters are `Password, DrawingObjects, Contents, Scenarios, UserInterfaceOnly, AllowFormattingCells, AllowFormattingColumns, AllowFormattingRows, AllowInsertingColumns, AllowInsertingRows, AllowInsertingHyperlinks, AllowDeletingColumns, AllowDeletingRows, AllowSorting, AllowFiltering,` and `AllowUsingPivotTables`.

If you want to password-protect your worksheet, set the `Password` parameter to the password you want to use. You can use any string as a password, but remember passwords are case-sensitive. In other words, Excel interprets "password" and "PASSWORD" differently.

Set the `DrawingObjects` parameter to `False` if you want the user to be able to modify shapes. The default value is `True`. By default, Excel protects locked cells; to remove this protection, set the `Contents` parameter to `False`. To unprotect scenarios, set the `Scenarios` parameter to `False`. If you set the `UserInterfaceOnly` parameter to `False`, Excel applies protection to macros and to the user interface. If you want only the user interface protected, set the `UserInterfaceOnly` parameter to `True`.

The remaining parameters are self-explanatory and they all have a default value of `False`. To allow any of these options, set the parameter to `True`.

Protect a Worksheet

1 Name your procedure.

2 Create your `Protect` command.

● Sets the password.

● Protects the user interface only.

● Allows format changes.

3 Press Alt+F11 to switch from the VBE to Excel, and run the macro.

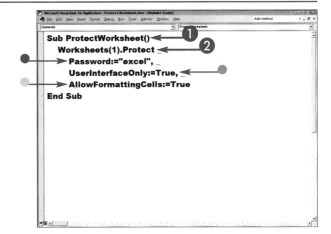

If the user tries to change a cell, Excel does not permit the change.

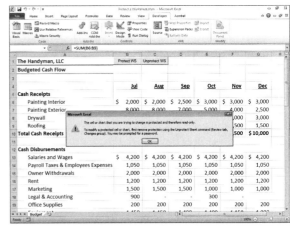

The user can make permitted changes.

In this example, the user can change the formats.

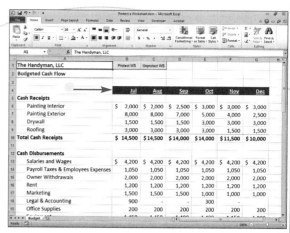

If users know the password, they can enter the password to unprotect the worksheet.

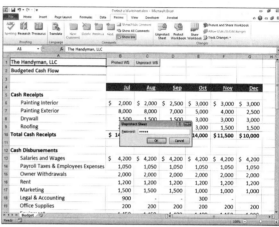

Extra

After you password-protect a worksheet, a user can unprotect the worksheet by clicking the Review tab, clicking Unprotect Sheet in the Changes group, and then typing the correct password in the Unprotect Sheet dialog box that appears.

You can unprotect the worksheet from within a procedure by using the Unprotect method. The only parameter the Unprotect method takes is the Password parameter. You set the parameter to the worksheet password.

Example:
```
ActiveSheet.Unprotect Password:="excel"
```

This example unprotects the active worksheet by passing it the correct password. Remember to keep track of the passwords that you have assigned to worksheets. If you lose your password, you cannot access the password-protected document.

Protect a Chart

Y ou can use the `Chart.Protect` method to protect a chart so that a user cannot modify it. The `Chart.Protect` method takes several parameters that you can use to select the type of protection you want to assign to the chart. All of the parameters are optional. With the exception of the `Password` parameter, you use the Boolean value `True` to activate a parameter and the Boolean value `False` to deactivate a parameter. The following is the syntax for the `Chart.Protect` method:

```
expression.Protect(Password, DrawingObjects,
Contents, UserInterfaceOnly)
```

Use the `expression` portion of the statement to identify the chart you want to protect. If you want to password-protect your chart, set the `Password` parameter to the password you want to use. You can use any string as a

password, but remember that passwords are case-sensitive. In other words, Excel interprets "password" and "PASSWORD" differently.

If you set the `DrawingObjects` parameter to `False`, the user can add shapes to the chart and modify the shapes in the chart. The default value is `True`. If you set the `Contents` parameter to `False`, the user can modify the chart. If you set the `UserInterfaceOnly` parameter to `False`, Excel applies protection to macros and to the user interface. If you want only the user interface protected, set the `UserInterfaceOnly` parameter to `True`.

To unprotect a chart using a procedure, use the `Unprotect` method. You must include the password if the chart is password-protected, as follows:

```
Charts(1).Unprotect Password:="excel"
```

Protect a Chart

① Name your procedure.

② Create your `Protect` command.

● Sets the password.

● Protects the user interface only.

● Allows the user to draw objects.

③ Press Alt+F11 to switch from the VBE to Excel, and run the macro.

● Excel grays out the Ribbon options to indicate that they are not available.

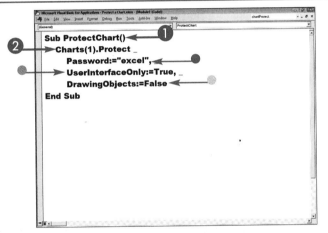

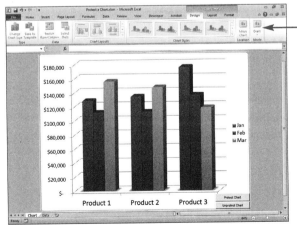

The user can make permitted changes.

- In this example, the user can add shapes.

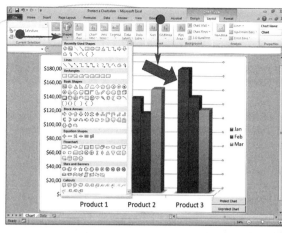

- If users know the password, they can enter the password to unprotect the worksheet.

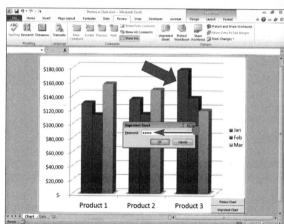

VBA provides properties that you can use with `Worksheet` and `Chart` objects to determine if parts of a sheet are protected. This helps eliminate errors caused by attempting to modify a protected sheet. Each of these properties is read-only.

PROPERTY	DESCRIPTION
ProtectContents	Returns a value of `True` if the sheet is protected. For a chart, the property looks to see if the entire chart is protected. For a worksheet, the property looks to see if the cells are protected. To turn off this property, set the `Contents` parameter of the `Protect` method to `False`.
ProtectDrawingObjects	Returns a value of `True` if the shapes in the sheet are protected. To turn off this property, set the `DrawingObjects` parameter of the `Protect` method to `False`.
ProtectScenarios	Returns a value of `True` if the scenarios are protected. To turn off this property, set the `Scenarios` parameter of the `Protect` method to `False`.
ProtectionMode	Returns a value of `True` if the user interface is protected.

Print a Sheet

You can use the `PrintOut` method to create a procedure to print the contents of a sheet. The `PrintOut` method has several parameters for specifying how Excel prints the sheet: From, To, Copies, Preview, ActivePrinter, PrintToFile, Collate, and PrToFileName.

Use the `From` and `To` parameters to indicate the range of pages within the specified sheet that you want to print. Indicate the page number of the first page to print as the value of the `From` parameter, and the page number of the last page as the value of the `To` parameter. If you omit these parameters, Excel prints the entire sheet.

By default, Excel prints one copy of the sheet. For multiple copies, use the `Copies` parameter to specify the desired number. You can specify a value of `True` for the

`Collate` parameter to have Excel collate the copies.

If you want the Excel preview window to show the contents of the print selection, set the value of the `Preview` parameter to `True`. The Print button on the Print Preview screen prints the copy, and the Close button cancels the print.

To specify a printer, use the `ActivePrinter` parameter. If you do not set the `ActivePrinter` parameter, VBA uses the computer's default printer.

You can send the printout to a file instead of a printer by setting the `PrintToFile` parameter to `True`, and specifying the name of the file to which you want to send the printout by setting the `PrToFileName` parameter. If you do not specify a filename, Excel prompts you for one when your procedure runs.

Print a Sheet

① Name your procedure.

② Set up your page.

● Sets the orientation to landscape.

● Sets the print area.

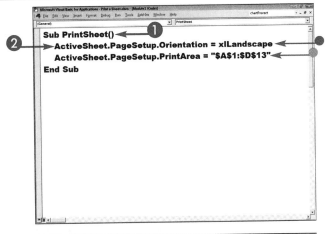

③ Create your `PrintOut` command.

● The number of copies to print.

● Displays the Print Preview before printing.

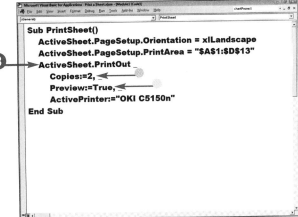

- The printer to which you want to send the report.

4 Press Alt+F11 to switch from the VBE to Excel, and run the macro.

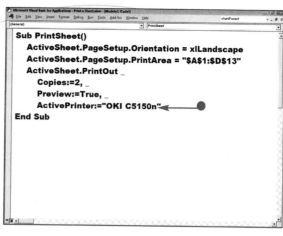

The macro displays the Print Preview screen.

- The Print button prints the file.

- The Close button cancels the printing.

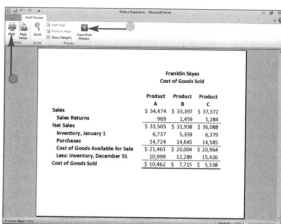

Apply It

You can set a print area for a worksheet by using the PageSetup object with the PrintArea property. Assign the PrintArea property a range of cells as the print area. For example, ActiveSheet. PageSetup.PrintArea = "$A$1:$D$13" sets the range of cells in the print area to A1 to D13. If cells outside that range contain data, Excel does not print them.

When you use the PrintArea property to set the range of cells to print, you can omit the From and To parameters of the PrintOut method.

To clear the print area, assign the PrintArea property a value of False or an empty string. Both of the following lines of code clear the print area:

Examples:
```
ActiveSheet.PageSetup _
  PrintArea = False
ActiveSheet.PageSetup _
  PrintArea = " "
```

When printing, you can set the orientation by using the PageSetup object with the Orientation property. Use the xlLandscape constant value to set the orientation to landscape. Use the xlPortrait constant value to set the orientation to portrait.

Sort Sheets by Name

You can use VBA to sort worksheets in a workbook based on the worksheet names. When you first create a new workbook, Excel lists the sheets in order: Sheet1, Sheet2, Sheet3. However, as you add sheets, the order of the sheets can change dramatically. For example, if your active sheet is Sheet2 and you instruct Excel to add a new sheet, Excel adds it before Sheet2 and names it Sheet4, making the order of your sheets Sheet1, Sheet4, Sheet2, Sheet3.

You can easily resolve this problem by manually renaming or moving the sheets within the workbook. Alternatively, you can create a procedure that sorts the worksheets and lists them in alphabetical order. You start by using the Count property to determine the number of

sheets in the workbook. When you know the number of sheets in a workbook, you can use a For Next loop to cycle through the sheets so that Excel can compare the names and place the sheets in order. You use nested looping, which is the process of placing one loop inside another loop. The inside loop executes completely, and then control returns to the outside loop. See Chapter 6 for more information on using For Next loops.

Within the second For Next loop, use an If Then statement to compare the name of a sheet to the sheet currently considered the alphabetically lowest sheet name. If the compared name is alphabetically lower, it becomes the new alphabetically lowest name. Excel does an alphabetical comparison when you are working with strings.

Sort Sheets by Name

① Name your procedure.

② Declare your variables.

③ Count the number of sheets and store the result to a variable.

④ Create a For Next loop to loop through each index position.

IndexNum1 starts at 1 and increments with each loop.

⑤ Store the name of the sheet with the index value of IndexNum1 to the variable SheetName.

⑥ Create a For Next loop within the previous loop, assign the value of IndexNum1 to IndexNum2, and loop through the total number of sheets, starting at the value of IndexNum2.

⑦ If the name of the sheet with an index value of IndexNum2 is less than SheetName, store the name of the sheet with an index value of IndexNum2 to the variable SheetName and then keep looping; otherwise, do nothing and keep looping.

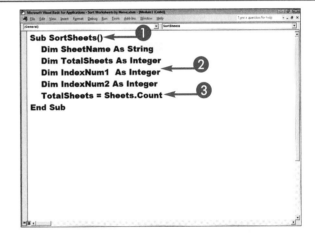

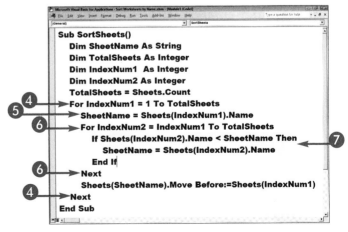

172

When the loop has finished, `SheetName` contains the lowest value.

⑧ Move the sheet identified by the variable `SheetName` before the sheet with an index value of `IndexNum1`.

⑨ Move to the next index value and perform the loop again.

⑩ Press Alt+F11 to switch from the VBE to Excel, and run the macro.

● The macro sorts the sheets.

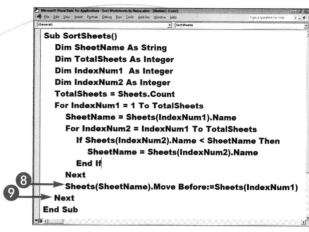

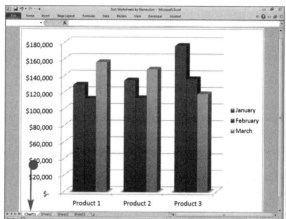

Apply It

The steps in this section determine the sheet with the lowest name in the inside loop and places that sheet before the index value that it is evaluating. Although this code works correctly, it is not the most efficient method for sorting a large list of items. The code attempts to move the sheet without first checking to see if the lowest name is also the current sheet. To make the execution of the code more efficient, add a conditional `If Then` statement that compares the two sheets and performs the move only if they are not the same sheet. The code runs more effectively because it determines that no move is required if the sheets are already in the correct order.

TYPE THIS:

```
If Sheets(SheetName) <> Sheets(N) Then
    Sheets(SheetName). Move Before:=Sheets(N)
End If
```

RESULT:

This code checks that the sheet you are moving and the sheet before which you intend to move it are not the same sheet. If the sheets are the same, Excel ignores the `Move` statement and continues with the looping statements.

Using the Range Property

When working in Excel, a lot of the work that you do involves ranges. You can define a range by using the Range property. Defining a range creates a Range object, which can be a single cell, a column, a row, or a group of cells.

If you use the range property without an object qualifier, Excel assumes you are referencing the active sheet. If you apply the Range property to a range object, the property is relative to the object. For example, the code Range("B11:D11").Formula = "=Sum(B6:B10)" sums in a relative fashion.

You can use two syntax forms with the Range property. The first form requires two parameters: Cell1 and Cell2. This form references the upper left corner of the desired range with the Cell1 parameter, and the lower

right corner of the range with the Cell2 parameter. For example, to specify a range of cells between A1 and E15, you would use the code Range("A1", "E15").

The other form of the Range property requires a Name parameter. This required parameter indicates a range. You place a colon between two cells to specify a range. For example, Range("A3:F5") refers to the range of cells from A3 to F5. You place a comma between the range definitions to refer to two or more noncontiguous ranges. For example, Range("A3, A1, B4:C10") specifies the range of cells A3, A1, and B4 to C10. You leave a space between the two range definitions to specify the location where two ranges intersect. For example, Range("A3:F3 D2:G5").Select selects the cells where the range A3 to F3 intersect with the range D2 to G5, which happens to be cells D3 to F3.

Using the Range Property

① Name your procedure.

② Define a range and select it.

● The range.

③ Ask users if they want to calculate a total.

④ If the user responds "Yes," then calculate the total.

● This same range was selected in Step 2 using a different syntax.

⑤ Press Alt+F11 to switch from the VBE to Excel, and run the macro.

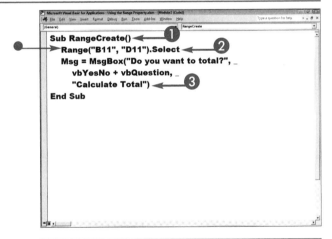

- The macro selects the range and then displays a message box.

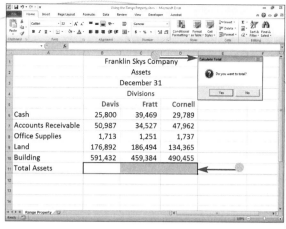

- If the user clicks the Yes button, the macro totals the columns.

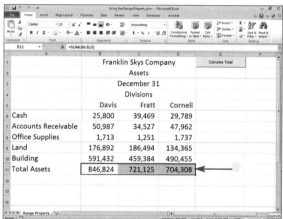

Extra

To select a cell or range of cells in a worksheet, use the Select method with a Range object. For example, to select the range of cells from A3 to A6, you would type Range("A3:A6").Select.

When you use the Select method with a Range object, the first cell in the specified range becomes the active cell. If you specify individual cells with the Select method, the first cell specified becomes the active cell. For example, Range("A3, A1, A5").Select makes cell A3 the active cell.

You can use the Activate method to highlight a cell or range of cells. With the Activate method, the first cell referenced in the range becomes the active cell, but VBA highlights all of the other cells in the range to indicate that VBA has selected them as well. For example, the code Range("B4:C6").Activate makes B4 the active cell and highlights cells B4 to C6. The Select method and the Activate method are often interchangeable.

Using the Cells Property

You can use the `Cells` property to reference specific cells in a worksheet and make changes to the values or properties of the cells, such as the font settings. The Excel object model does not contain a `Cells` object. To reference specific cells, use either the `Cells` property or the `Range` property, each of which returns a `Range` object with the specified cells. See the section "Using the Range Property" for more information about the `Range` property.

You can use the `Cells` property with the `Application`, `Range`, and `Worksheet` objects. Using the `Cells` property with the `Application` and `Worksheet` objects returns the same result. For example, you can type `X = Application.Cells(1,1)` or `X = ActiveSheet.Cells(1,1)` to obtain the content of cell A1.

The `Cells` property has two parameters. The first parameter, `Row`, contains a value indicating the row index. The second parameter, `Column`, contains a value indicating the column index. For example, to reference cell B5, you assign a value of 5 for the row parameter, because you want row 5, and a value of 2 for the column parameter, because you want column 2.

`Cells(5,2)`.

One advantage of using the `Cells` property over using the `Range` property is that you can use variables to change the values. For example, you can use a variable to represent either the row or column, as shown in the code `Cells(RowNum,1) = 5`, which sets the value of a cell in column A and a row specified by `RowNum` to 5.

Using the Cells Property

① Name your procedure.

② Declare your variable.

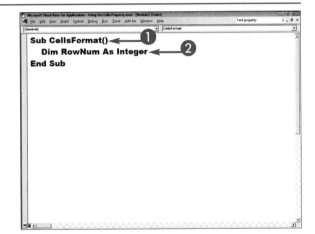

③ Create a `For Next` loop.

④ Use the `Cells` property to indicate the cells you want to format.

⑤ Format the cells.

⑥ Press Alt+F11 to switch from the VBE to Excel, and run the macro.

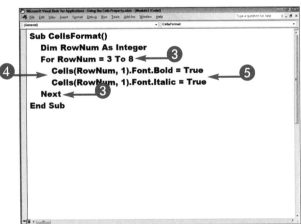

The worksheet before
you run your macro.

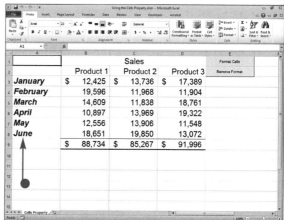

The worksheet after
you run your macro.

- The macro moves
  down the first column
  and adds bold and italic
  formatting to each cell.

Extra

To set the font attributes for objects in Excel, use the Font object. You typically use the Font object to modify the attributes of a cell or a range of cells. The Font object has several properties for obtaining or modifying the attributes of a specified object. Some of these properties are listed in the following table.

FONT PROPERTY	DESCRIPTION
Bold	A Boolean value indicating whether the font for the object is bold.
Color	Indicates the color of the font. Use the RGB function to set the font color.
FontStyle	Indicates the font style. For example, to set both a bold and an underline font style, specify Font.FontStyle = "Bold Underline".
Italic	A Boolean value indicating whether the font for the object is italic.
Shadow	A Boolean value indicating whether the font is a shadow font.
Size	Indicates the size of the font.
Strikethrough	A Boolean value indicating whether to use a strikethrough font to draw a horizontal line through each character.
Subscript	A Boolean value indicating whether the font is subscript.
Superscript	A Boolean value indicating whether the font is superscript.
Underline	A Boolean value indicating whether the font is underlined.

Combine Multiple Ranges

To create a multiple area range, you can use the Union method. A multiple area range contains more than one block of cells, and the blocks of cells are noncontiguous. For example, you can use the Union method to create a Range object containing the cells A1 to B5 and D1 to E5.

When you use the Range property in conjunction with the Union method, you can specify up to 30 ranges. You must specify at least two ranges. You assign the ranges by using any option that returns a valid Range object, such as the Range property or the Cells property. See the sections "Using the Range Property" and "Using the Cells Property" for more information. The following example specifies two ranges:

```
Dim RangeVar As Range
Set RangeVar = Union (Range("A1:A3"), _
Range("A5:A15"))
```

The code Set RangeVar = Union (Range("A1:A3"), Range("A5:A15")) uses the Union method to combine two Range objects created with the Range property and assigns the result to a Range object variable. The new range contains the cells A1 to A3 and A5 to A15. Notice that the two blocks of cells are noncontiguous.

Because you must declare the variable to which you assign the multi-area range as a Range object, you use the Set statement when creating the assignment statement. You must use the Set statement whenever you assign an object to an object variable. See Chapter 4 for more information on assigning objects to variables.

Combine Multiple Ranges

① Name your procedure.

② Declare the Range object variables that you will use to store your ranges.

③ Store each range to a variable.

④ Use the Union method to create a single range object that contains multiple ranges.

⑤ Apply formats to multiple ranges using one Range object.

⑥ Press Alt+F11 to switch from the VBE to Excel, and run the macro.

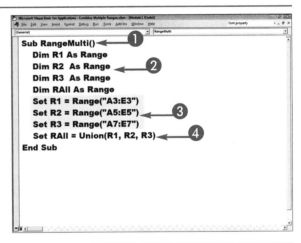

The worksheet before
you run your macro.

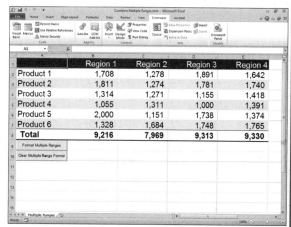

The worksheet after
you run your macro.

The macro uses a
Union range to
apply a format to
multiple ranges.

Extra

When you use the Union method, you combine multiple ranges. Each range is a Range object and is part of the Areas collection. Each member of the Areas collection represents a contiguous block of cells, with one Range object representing each contiguous block of cells.

You cannot apply some VBA operations to ranges that contain multiple areas; for that reason, you may need to determine the number of areas in a range. The Count property counts the number of areas in the range; if the Count property returns a value greater than 1, the range contains more than one area. The following example uses the Count property to determine the number of areas in the range RAll:

Example:
```
NumOfRanges = RAll.Areas.Count
```

Each range in an Areas collection has an index value. The first range added to the collection has an index value of 1, the next 2, and so on. You can reference an area by its index value.

Using the Offset Property

U sing the `Offset` property is another way to specify a range of cells. The `Offset` property defines a range as an offset from another range, with the offset being the distance in rows and columns from the existing range to the new range.

The `Offset` property has two parameters. Although both are optional, if you do not specify at least one parameter, the `Offset` property returns the current range. Use the `RowOffset` parameter to indicate the number of rows to offset the new range from the current range. A positive number offsets the range downward. A negative number offsets the range upward. The `Offset` property bases the offset on the upper left cell in the active range. For example, if the active range is cells A1 to B4, the `Offset` property bases the offset values on the number of rows

and columns from cell A1. Use the `ColumnOffset` parameter to specify the number of columns to offset the range from the current range. A positive number offsets the range to the right. A negative number offsets the range to the left. The default value for both parameters is 0.

If you assign a value to only one of the parameters, Excel gives the other parameter a value of 0. For example, with a value of 5 for the `RowOffset` and no `ColumnOffset` parameter value, the property returns the range that is five rows down from the current range selection.

If you specify a value outside the valid number of rows and columns in a worksheet (for example, if you specify `Offset(-1, -1)` and the current cell is A1, VBA returns an error.

Using the Offset Property

1. Name your procedure.

2. Declare the `Range` object variables that you will use to store your ranges.

3. Store your range to an object variable.

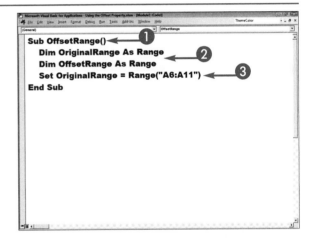

4. Use the `Offset` property to define the range.

- The same row.

- Four columns to the right.

5. Place a formula in the offset range.

6. Press Alt+F11 to switch from the VBE to Excel, and run the macro.

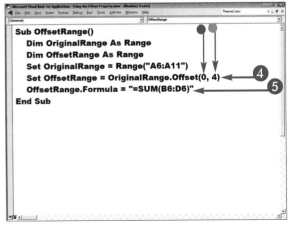

The worksheet before you run the macro.

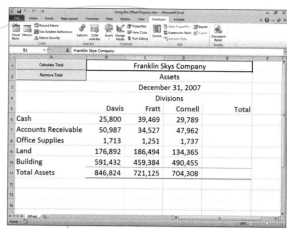

The worksheet after you run the macro.

● The macro uses the `Offset` property to create the values under the Total column.

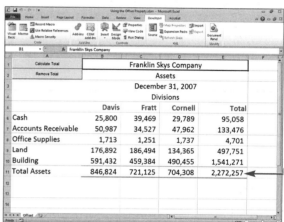

You can use the `Offset` property in a `For Next` loop to cycle through a range of cells.

Example:
```
Dim Counter As Integer
For Counter = 1 To 4
    ActiveCell.Offset(Counter -1, 0) = "Region" & Counter
Next Counter
```

The initial value of `Counter` is 1. `Counter -1` is equal to 0. The code starts executing from the active cell because `ActiveCell.Offset(Counter -1, 0)`, resolves to `ActiveCell.Offset(0,0)`. With each loop, the value of `Counter` increases by 1, and so VBA stays in the same column, but moves down one row. See Chapter 6 to learn more about using a `For Next` loop and to see this code in action.

Delete a Range of Cells

To remove a range of cells from a worksheet, use the `Delete` method. Excel completely removes the cells and adjusts the remaining values in the worksheet to fill the gap left by the deletion. For example, if you remove column B, Excel shifts the values in column C to the left to become the new column B values, and all remaining column values shift to the left as well. Conversely, if you delete a row, Excel shifts all values up one row. You can reference an entire column by using the syntax `Columns(ColumnNumber)`. You can reference an entire row by using the syntax `Rows(RowNumber)`. The following examples delete column B and row 3, respectively:

```
Columns(2).Delete
```

```
Rows(3).Delete
```

Excel easily determines how to shift the cells when you remove entire rows and columns, but if you remove a block of cells, you must specify how the remaining values fill by using the `Shift` parameter with the `Delete` method. When you use the `Shift` parameter, you assign it one of the `XlDeleteShiftDirection` constant values. The `xlShiftToLeft` constant value tells Excel to shift values to the left to fill the gap created by the deletion. The `xlShiftUp` constant value tells Excel to shift values up to fill the gap. For best results, specify how to shift the cells.

Excel ignores the parameter value if it is not a valid shift direction for the deleted range. For example, the code `Columns(2).Delete Shift:=xlShiftUp` deletes a column, but Excel shifts the cells to the left because there are no cells to shift up.

Delete a Range of Cells

① Name your procedure.

② Declare a `Range` object variable.

③ Store your range to an object variable.

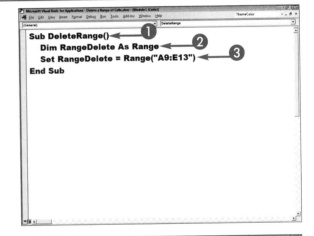

④ Delete your range.

● The range you want to delete.

● The instruction to shift up.

⑤ Press Alt+F11 to switch from the VBE to Excel, and run the macro.

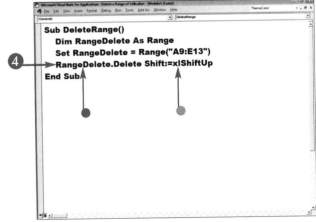

The worksheet before you run your macro.

- The rows that the macro will delete.

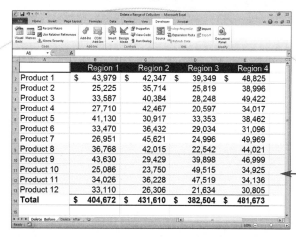

The worksheet after you run your macro.

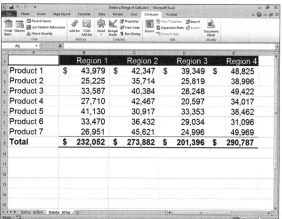

Extra

If a workbook is protected, you may not be able to modify a range by adding or removing cells. You can use the AllowEdit property to determine if you can modify a range. The AllowEdit property returns a Boolean value of True if you can modify the specified range. In the example code, the AllowEdit property checks a range to make sure you can modify the range before it calls the Delete method.

Example:
```
If Columns(6).AllowEdit Then
    Columns(6).Delete
End If
```

The code checks the AllowEdit property for column F and then deletes column F if you can modify it. If you cannot modify column F, the code ignores the Delete statement.

To protect worksheets, use the Protect method. See Chapter 10 for more information on using the Protect method.

Hide a Range of Cells

You can use the `Hidden` property with the `Range` object to hide a range of cells. Generally, you hide portions of a worksheet so that you can focus in on other data. For example, a worksheet may contain monthly data and quarterly summaries. You can hide the monthly data so you can focus on the quarterly summaries.

With the `Hidden` property, the range of cells you hide must consist of an entire row or column. You hide a column or row by assigning `True` to the `Hidden` property. You make the column or row visible again by assigning `False` to the `Hidden` property. The following examples hide row 2 and column C respectively:

```
Rows(2).Hidden = True

Columns(3).Hidden = True
```

You can also hide column C by using the following syntax:

```
Columns("C").Hidden = True
```

When you hide a column or row, Excel sets either the width of the columns or height of the rows to 0. You can use the `Hidden` property to determine if a range is hidden. For example, you can check to see if column A is hidden by typing `HiddenRange = Columns(1).Hidden`. If you declare the `HiddenRange` variable as a Boolean value, the variable receives a value of `True` if the specified range is hidden; otherwise, it receives a value of `False`. If you do not declare the variable as Boolean, Excel assigns a numeric value of –1 if the range is hidden and 0 if the range is visible.

Hide a Range of Cells

① Name your procedure.

② Create `For Next` loops.

In this example, the `For Next` loop enables you to hide multiple columns — columns 2 to 4 in the first loop and columns 6 to 8 in the second loop.

③ Set the `Hidden` property to `True` to hide the columns.

You can set the `Hidden` property to `False` to unhide the columns.

④ Press Alt+F11 to switch from the VBE to Excel, and run the macro.

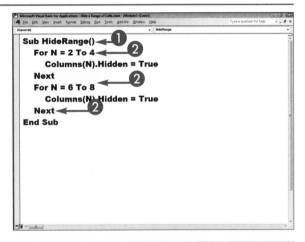

The worksheet before
you run the macro.

● The columns that the
macro will hide.

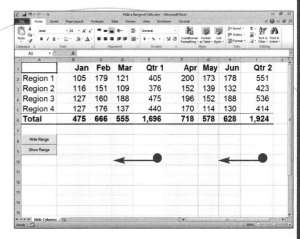

The worksheet after
you run the macro.

The macro hides
the columns you
specified.

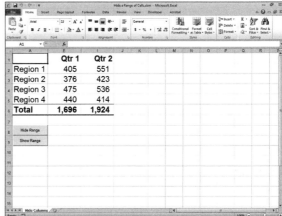

Extra

When you hide a row or column in Excel, you can still access the values contained in the cells by referencing them in functions and macros. Excel indicates the existence of hidden rows and columns by skipping over the hidden rows and columns in the row and column headings. For example, if you hide columns C and D, you see the column labels for columns A, B, E, F, and so on. To unhide a row or column in a worksheet, set the Hidden property to False.

You can use the following code to unhide all of the columns in a worksheet.

Example:
```
Columns.Hidden = False
```

You can use the following code to unhide all of the rows in a worksheet.

Example:
```
Rows.Hidden = False
```

Create a
Range Name

I n Excel, you can name ranges. Range names are easier to remember than cell addresses. When you name a range, you can refer to the range using the range name when creating formulas or performing other tasks. When you move a range to a new location, Excel automatically updates any formulas that refer to it.

When you use a named range in a procedure, you do not need to know the location of the cells that contain the desired values. For example, if cell B3 contains the sales tax rate, assign the name Tax_Rate to the cell so you can reference the cell by name when you want to use it.

In VBA, you use the Name property to assign a name to a range of cells, as follows:

```
Columns(3).Name = "May_Sales"
```

This example assigns the name May_Sales to Column C in the active worksheet. To view the assigned name in Excel, you can select the range, and the name will appear in the Name box on the Formula bar.

Whenever you need to reference the range in your procedure, you can use its range name. You can reference range names created by your procedure and range names created manually in Excel. You can use Excel to modify and delete the range names you define in VBA.

You can use the Delete method to delete a range name. The following example deletes the range name May_Sales:

```
ActiveWorkbook.Names("May_Sales").Delete
```

Create a Range Name

1 Name your procedure.

2 Declare your variable.

3 Assign a name to a range.

● The range to which you want to assign a name.

● The name that you want to assign the range.

4 Use the range name.

In this example, the worksheet function Sum totals the range.

5 Assign the result of the worksheet function to a cell.

6 Press Alt+F11 to switch from the VBE to Excel, and run the macro.

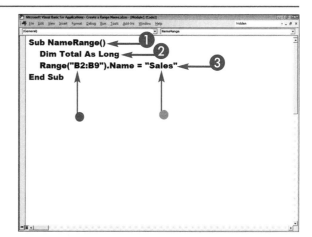

The worksheet before
you run your macro.

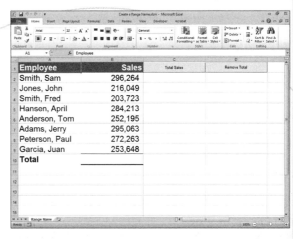

The worksheet after
you run your macro.

● The macro uses the
named range to sum
a range of cells.

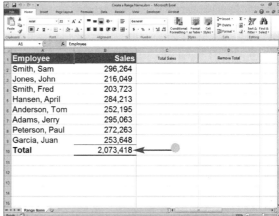

Extra

To create a named range in Excel, select the range, click the Formulas tab on the Ribbon, and then click Define
Name in the Defined Names group. The New Name dialog box appears. Type a name in the Name field, and then
click OK.

Click Name Manager on the Formulas tab to open the Name Manager. The Name Manager contains a list of all
named ranges. To see which cells a named range includes, select the range name in the Name Manager; the
corresponding range appears in the Refers To field. If you want to delete a named range, highlight the range name
and then click Delete. If you delete a named range, any macros that reference the named range will not work.

You can also use the Name Manager to modify a named range. In the Name Manager, click the Edit button. The
Edit Name dialog box appears. Use the Refers To field to define the range of cells to which the range name refers.

Resize a Range

You can use the `Resize` property to change the size of a range. When you resize a range, you change the number of rows and/or columns included in the range. You can specify either more or fewer rows or columns.

The `Resize` property has two optional parameters. You should set at least one of the two parameters. If you do not set either parameter, Excel returns the original range. The first parameter, `RowSize`, sets the number of rows in the new range. The second parameter, `ColumnSize`, sets the number of columns in the new range.

When you resize the range, the upper left corner of the original range remains the same. For example, if the original range is B1 to C4 and you resize the range to contain only two rows and two columns, then B1 remains the upper left cell value. VBA adjusts the range based on

that cell, creating a new range of cells from B1 to C2.

You may need to know how many rows and columns currently exist in a range before you resize it. If you are working with a range that is defined elsewhere, such as a named range, use the `Count` property to determine the number of rows and columns in the range, as shown in the following code:

```
NumberOfRows = _
    Range("Named_Range").Rows.Count.
```

The `Count` property counts the number of rows in `Named_Range` and assigns the result to the `NumberOfRows` variable. You use the same syntax with the `Columns` property to count the number of columns in a range. Once you know the size of the range, you can use the `Resize` property to modify the number of rows and/or columns.

Resize a Range

① Name your procedure.

② Declare your variables.

③ Count the number of rows in a range and assign the result to a variable.

④ Count the number of columns in a range and assign the result to a variable.

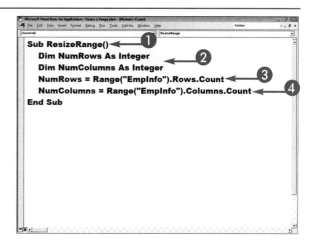

⑤ Add 2 to the values stored in your variables.

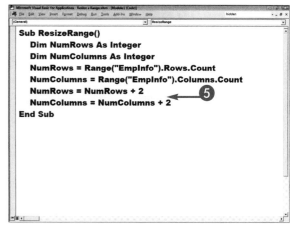

6 Resize your range.

● The range you want to resize.

● Sets the number of rows to the value in your `NumRow` variable.

● Sets the number of columns to the value in your `NumCol` variable.

7 Press Alt+F11 to switch from the VBE to Excel, and run the macro.

The macro resizes the range.

● The original size of the range.

● The current size of the range.

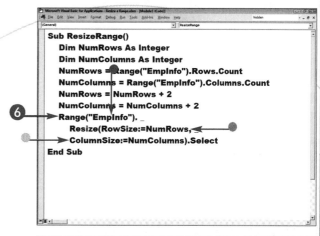

```vba
Sub ResizeRange()
    Dim NumRows As Integer
    Dim NumColumns As Integer
    NumRows = Range("EmpInfo").Rows.Count
    NumColumns = Range("EmpInfo").Columns.Count
    NumRows = NumRows + 2
    NumColumns = NumColumns + 2
    Range("EmpInfo"). _
        Resize(RowSize:=NumRows, _
        ColumnSize:=NumColumns).Select
End Sub
```

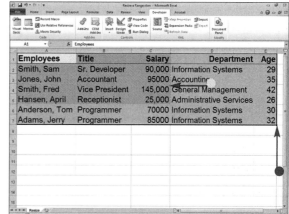

Extra

Besides determining the number of rows and columns in a range, you may need to know the exact row or column that begins the range. To find this, use either the `Row` property or the `Column` property. The following code determines the number of the first row in a range:

Example:
```
FirstRowNum = Range("EmpInfo").Row
```

The code assigns the integer value representing the first row in the specified range to the `FirstRowNum` variable. You can also determine the first column in the range by using the `Column` property, as shown in this code:

Example:
```
FirstColNum = Range("EmpInfo").Column
```

Insert a Range

You can use the `Insert` method to insert a range of cells into a worksheet. When you insert a range of cells, VBA adjusts the values in the existing cells by moving them either down or to the right so that it can insert the new cells into the specified location. For example, if you insert a new range of cells in row 3, VBA shifts the existing values in row 3 down to row 4 and shifts all of the values in cells below row 3 down as well. If you add a new column, Excel shifts all existing values to the right. The following examples insert a column and a row, respectively:

`Columns(2).Insert`

`Rows(3).Insert`

How the cell values in the worksheet should shift when you add an entire row or column is obvious. With a smaller block of cells, you must use the `InsertShift` parameter to tell VBA how the cells shift. To make sure the cells shift correctly, assign the parameter one of the `XlInsertShiftDirection` constant values. You can use the `xlShiftToRight` constant value to shift the cell values to the right. You can use the `xlShiftDown` constant value to shift the cell values down. The following example shifts cells to the right:

`Range("B5:B7").Insert:=xlShiftToRight`

You use the `Copy` method to paste data to the Office Clipboard. You can insert data that is on the Office Clipboard into your worksheet by placing a `Copy` command before the `Insert` command in your procedure. See Chapter 12 to learn more about the `Copy` method.

Insert a Range

① Name your procedure.

② Copy a range.

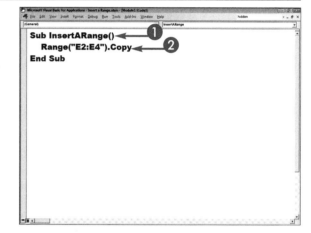

③ Insert the range.

● The point at which to begin the insertion.

● The shift direction.

④ Press Alt+F11 to switch from the VBE to Excel, and run the macro.

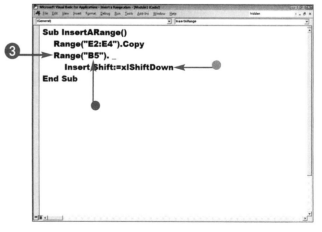

190

The worksheet before you run the macro.

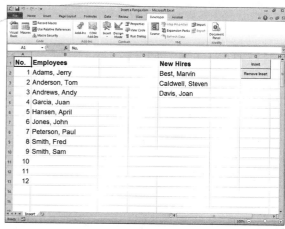

The worksheet after you run the macro.

● The macro places the copied data in the insert location.

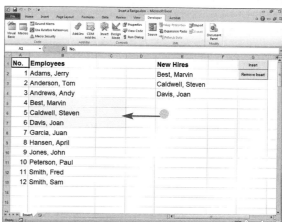

Extra

You can also use the `Insert` method to insert a value in a cell. To insert a value in a cell, use the `Insert` method with the `Characters` object. You can insert a string of characters at the beginning of a cell or at any location in the cell. For example, to insert the words "New String" in cell B1 and replace the contents, type the following code:

Example:
```
Range("B1").Characters.Insert("New String")
```

To place new characters within the existing string of characters, indicate the location and the number of characters. For example, in the string "Excel 2011 Worksheet," you can replace the "2011" with "2012" by using the `Insert` method. The following code illustrates how to make the replacement when the string is located in cell A1.

Example:
```
Range("A1").Characters(7,4).Insert("2012")
```

The `Characters` object has two parameters, `Start` and `Length`. The `Start` parameter indicates the number of the character at which to start the insert — in this case, character 7. The `Length` parameter indicates the number of characters to replace.

Set the Width of Columns in a Range

By default, Excel assigns a width of 8.43 characters to each column. Excel bases this width size on the number of zeros it can place in the cell using the Normal style. One unit is equal to one character.

To set the width of a column, use the `ColumnWidth` property. In the following example Excel sets column 1 to 15 characters in the Normal style:

```
Columns(1).ColumnWidth = 15
```

You can also use the `ColumnWidth` property to determine the width of the columns in a range. If all columns in the range have the same width, the `ColumnWidth` property returns the number of characters that can appear in each column using the Normal style. If the column widths in

the selected range vary, the `ColumnWidth` property returns `Null`. The following example, returns the width of column 1.

```
ColWidth = Columns(1).ColumnWidth
```

Every worksheet has a default width, commonly referred to as the standard width. You can use the `StandardWidth` property to set the columns in a worksheet to the standard width. The following example sets every column in a worksheet to the standard width:

```
Columns.ColumnWidth = _
    ActiveSheet.StandardWidth
```

Set the Width of Columns in a Range

Set a Column Width

① Name your procedure.

② Create a `For Next` loop.

③ Create a `ColumnWidth` command.

● The column for which you want to set the column width.

● The amount to which you want to set the column width.

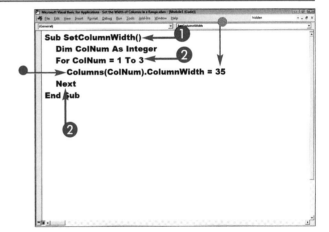

Set Columns to a Standard Width

① Name your procedure.

② Create a `For Next` loop.

③ Create a `ColumnWidth` command.

○ The column for which you want to set the column width.

○ The amount to which you want to set the column width.

④ Press Alt+F11 to switch from the VBE to Excel, and run the macros.

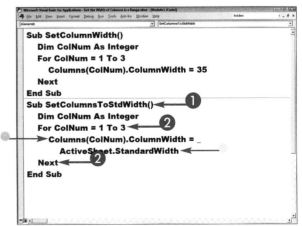

When you run the
`SetColumnWidth`
macro, the macro
sets columns 1, 2,
and 3 to 35.

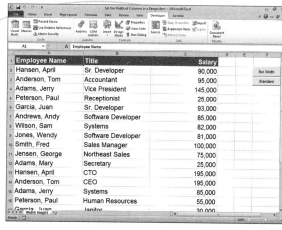

When you run the
`SetColumnsToStdWidth`
macro, the macro sets
columns 1, 2, and 3 to the
standard width.

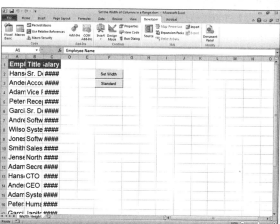

Extra

You can also use the `Width` property to obtain the width of a column. The `Width` property returns the measurement of the column width in points, unlike the `ColumnWidth` property, which returns characters. You typically use points to reference font sizes (1 point is equivalent to 1/72 of an inch).

The `Width` property is read-only, meaning that you can use it only to obtain the width of a column. To obtain the `Width` property of a column, assign the value to a variable, as shown in the following code.

Example:

```
ColWidth = Column(4).Width
```

The `Width` property is useful when you want to compare a column width to a row height because Excel stores row heights in points.

Set the Height of Rows in a Range

To modify the height of rows in a range, you can use the RowHeight property. By default, Excel assigns a height of 15.75 points to each row. Excel measures font sizes in points, with each point equal to approximately 1/72 of an inch. Because the default font size in Excel is 12 points, the default row size of 15.75 points is usually adequate for displaying text. For a larger font size or for text that wraps in a cell, you can specify a larger row height by using the RowHeight property.

You can set the height of the row by assigning a numeric value to the RowHeight property. For example, to change the height of row 2 to 25 points, use the following code:

```
Rows(2).RowHeight=25
```

If the row height you specify is not high enough to display the entire font, the text appears cut off when you view it in Excel.

You can also use the RowHeight property to obtain the height of the rows in a range. If all rows in the range have the same height, the height is returned as the number of points. If all the rows in the selected range do not have the same height, the RowHeight property returns Null. The following example demonstrates how to use the RowHeight property to obtain the height of a row:

```
RowHeight = Rows(1).RowHeight
```

Every worksheet has a default height, commonly referred to as the standard height. You can use the StandardHeight property to set the standard height for a worksheet or to set a range of rows in a worksheet to the standard height. The following example sets every row in a worksheet to the standard height:

```
Rows.RowHeight = ActiveSheet.StandardHeight
```

Set the Height of Rows in a Range

Set the Row Height

1. Name your procedure.

2. Create a For Next loop.

3. Create a RowHeight command.

● The rows for which you want to set the height.

● The amount to which you want to set the row height.

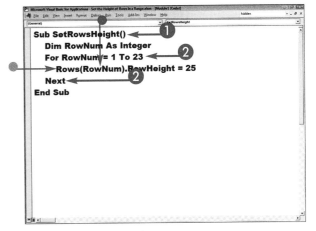

Set Rows to the Standard Height

1. Name your procedure.

2. Create a For Next loop.

3. Create a RowHeight command.

● The row for which you want to set the height.

● The amount to which you want to set the row height.

4. Press Alt+F11 to switch from the VBE to Excel, and run the macros.

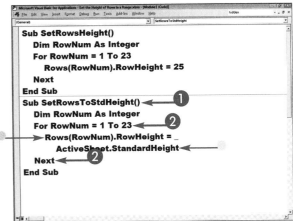

When you run the
`SetRowsHeight`
macro, the macro sets
rows 1 to 23 to 25.

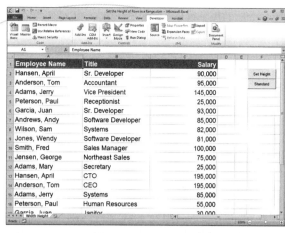

When you run the
`SetRowstoStdHeight`
macro, the macro sets
rows 1 to 23 to the
standard height.

Extra

You can also use the `UseStandardHeight` property to set a row to the standard height. The following example
sets row 1 of the active sheet to the standard height.

Example:
```
ActiveSheet.Rows(1).UseStandardHeight = True
```

You can use the `Height` property to determine the total height of a range of cells. Excel returns the height of the
range in points. The `Height` property is read-only. You can obtain the range height by assigning the height value to
a variable, as shown here.

TYPE THIS:
```
HeightOfRange = Range("A1:A10").Height
```

RESULT:

The code assigns the height of all the
rows specified by the `Range` object to
the `HeightOfRange` variable.

Cut and Paste Ranges of Cells

C ut, Copy, and Paste are among the most commonly used commands, and you can find them in almost every application. When writing VBA code, you can use the Cut and Copy methods to cut, copy, and paste a range of cells. The following is the syntax for the Cut method (see "Copy and Paste Ranges of Cells" for an explanation of the Copy method):

expression.Cut(*Destination*)

The Cut method enables you to cut a range of cells and paste them either to the Windows Clipboard or to another range of cells. You can use the Cut method's optional Destination parameter to tell VBA where you want to paste. If you do not include a destination, VBA pastes to the Windows Clipboard.

If you include a destination, you can use a Range object to specify the location to which you want to paste. The following example uses the Cut method to cut and paste a range of cells:

Range("A1:A5").Cut Range("C1:C5")

When using this syntax, you must make the cut range and the destination range the same size or VBA returns an error. Alternatively, you can specify a single cell as the destination range. VBA makes the cell you specify the upper left corner of the paste range.

Cut and Paste Ranges of Cells

Cut and Paste by Using a Single Cell

1 Create your Cut statement.

● The range you are cutting.

● The upper left corner of the range where you are pasting.

● This code resizes columns to ensure that the contents appear in the cells.

Cut and Paste by Using a Range of Cells

1 Create your Cut statement.

● The range you are cutting.

● The range where you are pasting.

Note: *The range you cut must be the same size as the range where you paste.*

2 Press Alt+F11 to switch from the VBE to Excel, and run the macro.

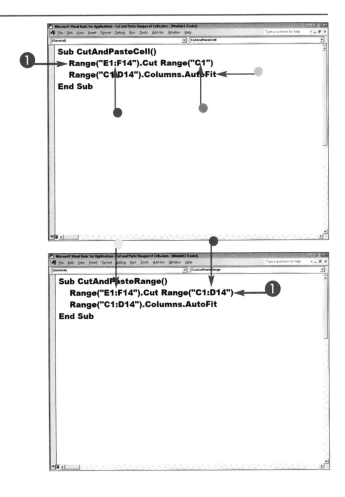

The original worksheet.

- The macro cuts and pastes this information.

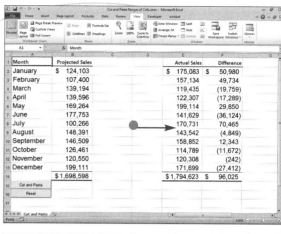

The worksheet after the cut-and-paste macro has executed.

Both of the macros shown in this example yield the same result.

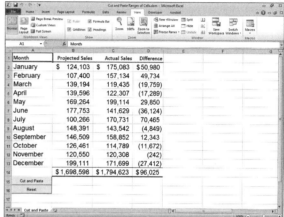

Apply It

When you paste values in cells, the cells may not be able to hold the new content. If the values you paste are numeric and the cells are not wide enough for the numbers, Excel displays pound signs (####) in the cells. When you write a VBA procedure, VBA provides formatting options you can use to resize cells so that your values fit into the cells to which you paste them. For example, you can use the `AutoFit` method to resize the rows and columns in a range automatically to allow the contents to appear. The `AutoFit` method uses the following syntax:

Example:
```
Range("C1:D14").Columns.AutoFit
```

You can use the `ShrinkToFit` property to reduce the font size of the text so the entire contents of the cell appear. You set the `ShrinkToFit` property by assigning the `Range` property the value of `True`, as shown in the following example:

Example:
```
Range("C1:D14").ShrinkToFit = True
```

You can also use the `WrapText` property to ensure text appears properly. Assigning a value of `True` to the `WrapText` property causes text to wrap within the cell.

Example:
```
Range("C1:D14").WrapText = True
```

Copy and Paste Ranges of Cells

In this section, you learn how to copy and paste a range of cells. You can copy and paste cell ranges by using the Copy method. The Copy method is essentially the same as the Copy and Paste commands within Excel. The following is the syntax for the Copy method:

`expression.Copy(Destination)`

The Copy method enables you to copy a range of cells and paste them either to the Windows Clipboard or to another range of cells. You can use the Copy method's optional Destination parameter to tell VBA where you want to paste the cells. If you do not include a destination, VBA pastes the cells to the Windows Clipboard.

If you include a destination, you can use a Range object to specify the location to which you want to paste. The

following code illustrates using the Copy method to copy and paste a range of cells:

`Range("A1:A5").Copy Range("C1:C5")`

When using this syntax, you must make the copy range and the destination range the same size or VBA returns an error. Alternatively, you can specify a single cell as the destination range. VBA makes the cell you specify the upper left corner of the paste range.

A block of cells surrounded by blank cells is called the *current region*. You can use the CurrentRegion property to copy and paste or to cut and paste when using VBA. When entering the range, you specify any cell within the block of cells you want to cut or copy as the range, and then follow the range specification with .CurrentRegion.

Copy and Paste Ranges of Cells

Copy and Paste by Using a Single Cell

① Create your Copy statement.

● The range you are copying.

● The CurrentRegion property enables you to manipulate a range of cells without specifying the entire range.

● The upper left corner of the range where you are pasting.

② Press Alt+F11 to switch from the VBE to Excel, and run the macro.

The macro copies and pastes the information.

● The range you copied.

● The pasted data.

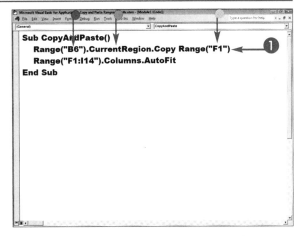

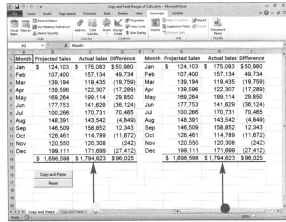

Copy and Paste by Using a Range of Cells

1 Create your Copy statement.

● The range you are copying.

○ The range where you are pasting.

The range you copy must be the same size as the range where you are pasting.

Formats the range.

This example changes the color of the interior of cells, the border that surrounds cells, and the font.

2 Press Alt+F11 to switch from the VBE to Excel, and run the macro.

The macro copies and pastes the information.

● The range you copied.

○ The pasted data.

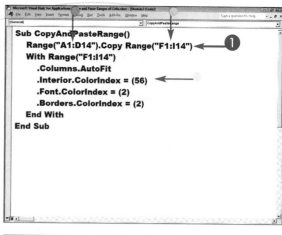

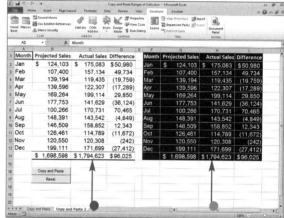

Extra

You can use the `ColorIndex` property with the `Interior`, `Borders`, and `Font` objects to change the color of the interior of cells, the border that surrounds cells, and the font. You can assign an index value of 1 to 56 to the `ColorIndex` property. The following example demonstrates the `ColorIndex` property.

Examples:
```
Range("F1:I14").Interior.ColorIndex = (1)
Range("F1:I14").Borders.ColorIndex = (2)
Range("F1:I14").Font.ColorIndex = (2)
```

The following table lists 16 of the possible colors you can use with the `ColorIndex` property. Refer to VBA help for a complete list.

INDEX	COLOR	INDEX	COLOR
1	Black	9	Brown
2	White	10	Forest Green
3	Red	11	Navy Blue
4	Green	12	Yellow-Brown
5	Blue	13	Maroon
6	Yellow	14	Blue-Green
7	Fuchsia	15	Light Gray
8	Light Blue	16	Gray

Using Paste Special Options When Pasting

Cells can contain a lot of information. When you use the `PasteSpecial` method, you decide exactly what information you want to paste. You can choose to paste everything, or you can choose to paste just one element of the cell's contents, such as the formula, value, or column width. You can also use the `PasteSpecial` method to perform simple arithmetic operations on each cell in a range. For example, in a list of salaries, you may want to increase every salary by five percent. You can use the `PasteSpecial` method to make the change quickly. Just copy the value by which you want to multiply to the Clipboard and then use `xlPasteSpecialOperationMultiply` when you paste with the `PasteSpecial` method.

You can use the `PasteSpecial` method with values you have added to the Windows Clipboard using the `Copy` method. The following is the syntax for the `PasteSpecial` method:

```
expression.PasteSpecial(Paste, Operation,
  SkipBlanks, Transpose)
```

Use the `Paste` parameter to indicate how you want to paste the information into the new range. By default, Excel uses the `xlPasteAll` constant value for this parameter, which pastes the entire contents of the copied cells into the new range.

Use the `Operation` parameter to perform a mathematical operation, such as multiplying the current value of a cell by the pasted value. The default constant value used by Excel is `xlPasteSpecialOperationNone`, which does not perform any mathematical operations.

Set the `SkipBlanks` parameter to `True` if you do not want to overwrite a destination cell with a blank cell if the destination cell has data in it and the copied cell does not. If you want to transpose the data values from rows to columns or vice versa, set the `Transpose` parameter to `True`.

Using Paste Special Options When Pasting

Paste Parameter

1. Copy a range of cells to the Clipboard.

   Do not include the `Destination` parameter.

2. Type your `PasteSpecial` command.

● The range where you are pasting.

● This statement pastes the column widths, thereby making sure that the source column widths match the destination column widths.

● This statement pastes the data.

Operation Parameter

1. Copy a cell to the Clipboard.

   In this example, cell B1 contains the number needed to calculate an annual salary increase.

2. Type your `PasteSpecial` command.

● The range where you are pasting.

   In this example, range B5 to B10 contains the salaries you want to increase.

● The Operation parameter.

3. Press Alt+F11 to switch from the VBE to Excel, and run the macro.

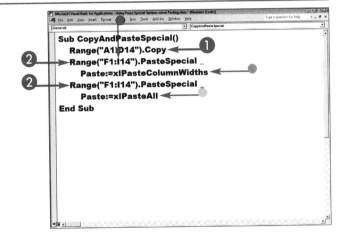

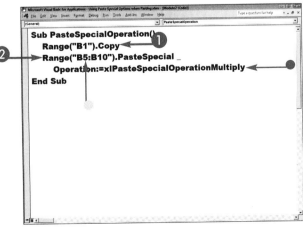

The worksheet before you run the macro.

● The cell you copied.

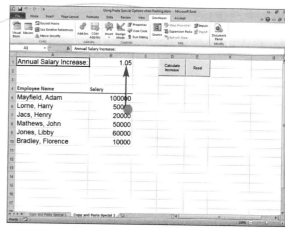

The worksheet after you run the macro.

● The PasteSpecial range.

The macro multiplies each cell in the PasteSpecial range by the value in the cell you copied.

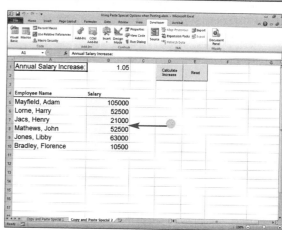

Extra

The Paste parameter requires one of the following constant values.

NAME	DESCRIPTION
xlPasteAll	The default value, which pastes the entire contents of the cells.
xlPasteAllExceptBorders	Pastes everything except border settings.
xlPasteAllUsingSourceTheme	Pastes everything using the source theme.
xlPasteColumnWidths	Pastes the column widths.
xlPasteComments	Pastes the cell comments only.
xlPasteFormats	Pastes the formats only.
xlPasteFormulas	Pastes the formulas only.
xlPasteFormulasAndNumberFormats	Pastes the formulas and number formats.
xlPasteValidation	Pastes the cell validation only.
xlPasteValues	Pastes the cell values only.
xlPasteValuesAndNumberFormats	Pastes the cell values and number formats.

The Operation parameter requires an XlPasteSpecialOperation constant value. See the appendix for a list.

Add Comments to a Cell

When several people work on a single workbook, comments can provide useful information. Excel associates a comment with an individual cell and indicates its presence with a small, red triangle in the cell's upper right corner. You can view a comment by clicking in the cell or by positioning your mouse pointer over the cell. In VBA, by using the AddComment method with the Range object, you can add a comment to any cell in your worksheet.

When the user creates a comment, Excel adds the user's name to the comment. When you create a comment by using the AddComment method, VBA does not automatically include a username. The following is the syntax for the AddComment method:

`expression.AddComment(Text)`

The expression is the variable or range object that represents the cell to which you want to add a comment. The following code adds a comment to cell A1:

`Cells(1,1).AddComment "Sample Comment Text"`

If you want to add the same comment to multiple cells, you can use a looping statement, such as a Do Until loop, to cycle through a range of cells. See Chapter 6 to learn more about loops.

If you attempt to add a comment to a cell that already contains a comment, Excel returns an error message. To avoid errors, you can use the ClearComments method to clear existing comments. The following is an example of the ClearComments method:

`Cells(1,1).ClearComments`

Add Comments to a Cell

① Add a loop, if you are going to loop through a series of cells.

② Add Case statements, if you are going to add comments selectively.

Note: See Chapter 6 to learn more about loops and Case statements.

```
Sub AddComments()
    Dim RowNum As Integer
    RowNum = 2
    Do Until IsEmpty(Cells(RowNum, 4))        ①
        Select Case Cells(RowNum, 4)
            Case Is < 0        ②
                Cells(RowNum, 4).ClearComments
                Cells(RowNum, 4).AddComment _
                    "Bob, please review."
            Case Is >= 0        ②
                Cells(RowNum, 4).ClearComments
        End Select
        RowNum = RowNum + 1
    Loop        ①
End Sub
```

③ Add a ClearComments statement.

● The range.

The ClearComments statement clears any comments that are already in the cell.

④ Add an AddComment statement.

● The range.

● The comment.

The AddComment statement adds comments to your worksheet.

⑤ Press Alt+F11 to switch from the VBE to Excel, and run the macro.

```
Sub AddComments()
    Dim RowNum As Integer
    RowNum = 2
    Do Until IsEmpty(Cells(RowNum, 4))
        Select Case Cells(RowNum, 4)
            Case Is < 0
                Cells(RowNum, 4).ClearComments        ③④
                Cells(RowNum, 4).AddComment _
                    "Bob, please review."
            Case Is >= 0
                Cells(RowNum, 4).ClearComments
        End Select
        RowNum = RowNum + 1
    Loop
End Sub
```

The worksheet before
you run the macro.

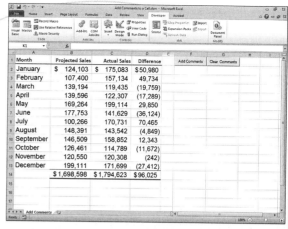

The worksheet after
you run the macro.

The macro adds the
comments to your
worksheet.

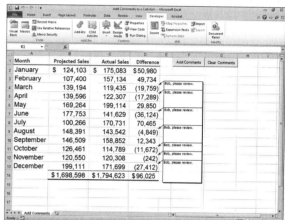

Apply It

When you add a comment to a cell, Excel creates a Comment object for that cell. The Comment object is part of the Comments collection, which contains all comments in a worksheet. You can reference comments using an index value. For example, to access the second comment in a worksheet, you would type the following:

Example:
```
SecondComment=ActiveSheet.Comments(2).Text
```

You may want to delete comments that a particular author created. The Comment object provides an Author property that you can use to return the author. Excel adds the author when it creates a comment. The following example deletes a comment by a particular author:

Example:
```
CountComments = ActiveSheet.Comments.Count
For N = 1 To CountComments
    If Comment(N).Author = "John Smith" Then
        Comment(N).Delete
    End If
Next
```

Automatically Fill a Range of Cells

In Excel, AutoFill helps you quickly enter data when a data series has an intrinsic order such as days of the week, months of the year, or numeric increments. You can use the `AutoFill` method to create an AutoFill using VBA. The following is the syntax for the `AutoFill` method:

expression.AutoFill(*Destination, Type*)

The `expression` is the variable or range object that represents the cell or cells you want to use when you create an AutoFill. VBA uses the values in this source range to determine the type of values to add to the cells in the destination range. For example, if the source range is cells A1 and A2 and the cells contain the values January and February, respectively, Excel fills the cells in the destination range with the months of the year starting with March.

The `AutoFill` method has two parameters, `Destination` and `Type`. The `Destination` parameter, which is required, must contain a range indicating which cells to fill. The `Destination` range must encompass the source range. For example, if the source range is A1 and A2, these cells must be included in the destination range, as shown in the following example:

```
Range("A1:A2").AutoFill _
    Destination:=Range("A1:A12").
```

VBA uses the values in the source range to determine the pattern you want to use when adding values to the cells in the destination. If you want to tell VBA the pattern to use to add values to the destination, you must include the `Type` parameter. The `Type` parameter accepts an `XlAutoFillType` constant, which specifies the type of fill.

Automatically Fill a Range of Cells

Fill a Range

1. Type your `AutoFill` command.

- The range you want to use as the source.

- The cells you want to fill.

- The fill type.

   This example uses months.

2. Press Alt+F11 to switch from the VBE to Excel, and run the macro.

   The worksheet after you run the macro.

- The source cells.

- The destination cells.

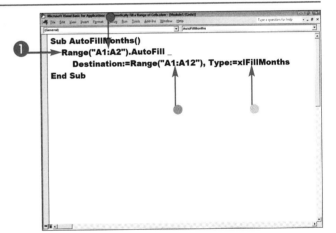

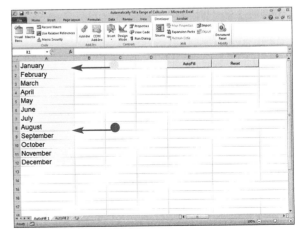

Create an AutoFill

① Create your `AutoFill` command.

● The range you want to use as the source.

◉ The cells you want to fill.

No fill type is given because VBA bases the fill type on the cell you use as the source.

② Press Alt+F11 to switch from the VBE to Excel, and run the macro.

The worksheet after you run the macro.

The macro fills the cells.

◉ The source cell.

● The fill.

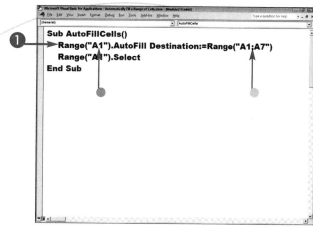

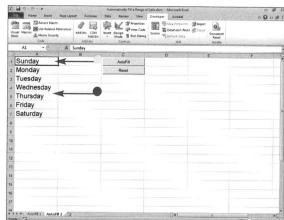

Extra

The `XlAutoFillType` constant values specify how Excel fills the range of cells for the `Destination` parameter. The following table describes each of the `XlAutoFillType` constant values.

CONSTANT	DESCRIPTION
xlFillDays	Increments the values by days. If only one date is specified for the source, it increments by one day. If multiple dates are specified, it uses those dates to determine the increment value.
xlFillFormats	Applies the formats of the source cells to the destination cells.
xlFillSeries	Creates a series based upon the contents of the source range.
xlFillWeekdays	Increments based on weekdays, omitting dates that fall on Saturday or Sunday.
xlGrowthTrend	Fills cells based on a growth trend.
xlFillCopy	Copies the formatting and values, and increments based on source values.
xlFillDefault	The default value. Excel determines the fill type based upon values in the source cells.
xlFillMonths	Increments by month.
xlFillValues	Copies the values in the source cells.
xlFillYears	Increments the year portion of the date.
xlLinearTrend	Fills cells based on a linear trend.

Copy a Range to Multiple Sheets

You can copy a range of cells and place the contents in the same location on multiple sheets with the FillAcrossSheets method. When you use this method, Excel copies the cells you specify to each worksheet you specify. You can copy everything in the range of cells, just the values in the cells, or just the formatting. The following is the syntax for the FillAcrossSheets method:

expression.FillAcrossSheets(*Range, Type*)

The expression is the variable or object that represents the worksheets to which VBA copies the range of cells. The worksheets must exist within the current workbook and you must include the worksheet that you are copying from in the list.

The FillAcrossSheets method has two parameters: Range and Type. The Range parameter, which is

required, specifies the range of cells you want to copy to the other worksheets. You can specify the range of cells using any valid range statement. See Chapter 11 for more information on specifying ranges.

The Type parameter is optional. Use this parameter to tell VBA what you want to copy. The Type parameter accepts one of the three xlFillWith constant values. If you do not specify a Type parameter, VBA uses the default value of xlFillWithAll, which copies the entire contents of the range of cells, including the formatting. If you want to copy only the cell contents, use the xlFillWithContents constant value. This constant value instructs Excel to copy everything but the cell formatting. If you want to copy only the formatting, use the xlFillWithFormats constant value. When you use xlFillWithFormats, Excel ignores the values and applies the formatting only.

Copy a Range to Multiple Sheets

1 Declare a variable to store your array.

You use an array to store the list of worksheets to which you want to copy.

2 Create your array and store it to the variable you created.

3 Activate the sheet you want to copy.

Note: *See Chapter 5 to learn more about arrays.*

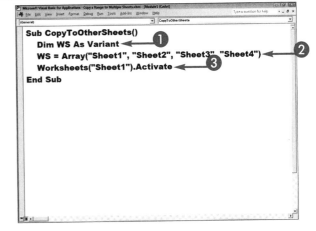

4 Add your FillAcrossSheets command.

● The sheets to which you want to copy.

● The range you want to copy.

● What you want to copy.

Use xlFillWithAll to copy everything.

Use xlFillWithContents to copy the contents only.

Use xlFillWithFormats to copy the formats only.

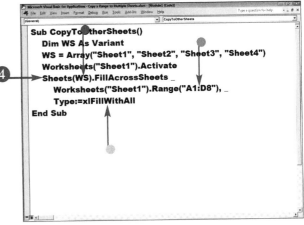

⑤ Move to one of the sheets to which you copied.

⑥ Select range A1.

⑦ Press Alt+F11 to switch from the VBE to Excel, and run the macro.

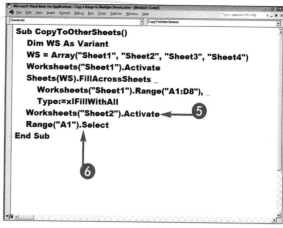

```vba
Sub CopyToOtherSheets()
    Dim WS As Variant
    WS = Array("Sheet1", "Sheet2", "Sheet3", "Sheet4")
    Worksheets("Sheet1").Activate
    Sheets(WS).FillAcrossSheets _
        Worksheets("Sheet1").Range("A1:D8"), _
        Type:=xlFillWithAll
    Worksheets("Sheet2").Activate
    Range("A1").Select
End Sub
```

● Your macro copies the range you specified to the worksheets you specified.

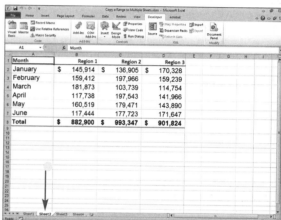

Apply It

You can fill a range of cells in a specific direction within a worksheet using one of the fill methods. For example, you may want to fill across a worksheet with the first value in the left corner of the range. VBA offers four Range object methods for filling in a specific direction: FillUp, FillDown, FillRight, and FillLeft.

You can use the FillUp method to fill a range of cells with the value in the last cell of the range. For example, if you have the range A1:A10 and you apply the FillUp method, as shown here, the value in cell A10 copies and pastes to cells A1:A9.

Example:
```
Range("A1:A10").FillUp
```

The FillDown method works opposite to the FillUp method. This method takes the value in the first cell of the range and copies it to all other cells.

You can use the FillRight method to fill across rows. For example, if you use this method with the range A1:G1, Excel takes the value in cell A1 and pastes it into cells B1 to G1. The FillLeft method works opposite to the FillRight method. This method takes the value in cell G1 and pastes it into cells A1 to F1.

Add a Border

When creating an Excel worksheet, you can highlight important information by adding a border. In VBA, you can add borders to a range of cells by using the `Range.Borders` property. Use an `XlBordersIndex` constant to specify where you want to place the border. The following is a list of `XlBordersIndex` constant values: `xlEdgeTop`, `xlEdgeBottom`, `xlEdgeRight`, `xlEdgeLeft`, `xlInsideHorizontal`, `xlDiagonalDown`, and `xlDiagonalUp`. If you do not specify an `XlBordersIndex` constant, Excel places a border around the outside edge of every cell in the range.

You can set the line style, weight, and color of a border. Use an `XlLineStyle` constant value to set the style of the line. Use an `XlBorderWeight` constant value to set the `Weight` of the line. See the appendix for a list of

`XlLineStyle` and `XlBorderWeight` constant values. You can use a `ColorIndex`, `RGB` function, or theme color to set the color of a border.

Use a `ColorIndex` value between 1 and 64. See the section "Copy and Paste Ranges of Cells" for a partial list of `ColorIndex` values. Set the `ColorIndex` to `xlColorIndexAutomatic` to use the default line color. If you want to use an RGB color value, use the `RGB` function. To assign a theme color, use the `Border.ThemeColor` property with an `XlThemeColor` constant. See the "Extra" portion of this section for a list of `XlThemeColor` constants. Use the `Border.TintAndShade` property to lighten or darken a color. The `Border.TintAndShade` property can be set to any value between –1 and 1. A value of –1 produces the darkest color, a value of 0 produces a neutral color, and a value of 1 produces the lightest color.

Add a Border

① Create a border.

- The range.

- The line style.

- The weight.

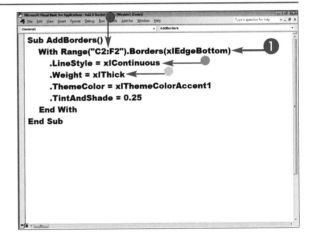

- The theme color.

- The tint and shade.

- Color index.
- RGB color.

2 Press Alt+F11 to switch from the VBE to Excel, and run the macro.

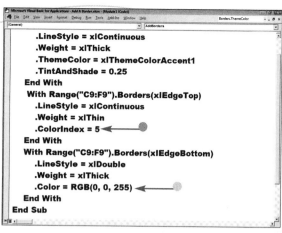

The worksheet after you run your macro.

VBA places a border around the ranges you specified.

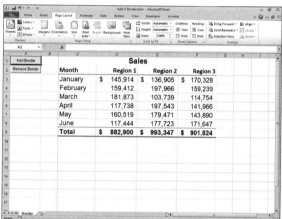

Extra

You can set the color of your border to a theme color. In Excel, whenever you choose an option that gives you the ability to apply a color, theme colors appear at the top of the gallery. For example, if you click the Home tab, click the down arrow next to the Borders button, and then click Line Color, a gallery appears with Theme Colors at the top. You can use XlThemeColor constants to apply these colors to your borders. When you position your mouse pointer over a color below the first row, a Lighter Value appears. To match these colors, set the TintAndShade value to the Lighter Value. For example, if the Lighter Value is 25%, set the TintAndShade to .25.

The following is a partial list of XlThemeColors.

VALUE	DESCRIPTION
xlThemeColorAccent1	The 5th column in the theme color gallery
xlThemeColorAccent2	The 6th column in the theme color gallery
xlThemeColorAccent3	The 7th column in the theme color gallery
xlThemeColorAccent4	The 8th column in the theme color gallery
xlThemeColorAccent5	The 9th column in the theme color gallery
xlThemeColorAccent6	The 10th column in the theme color gallery
xlThemeColorLight1	The 1st column of the theme color gallery
xlThemeColorDark1	The 2nd column of the theme color gallery
xlThemeColorLight2	The 3rd column of the theme color gallery
xlThemeColorDark2	The 4th column of the theme color gallery

Find Specific Cell Values

You can use the Find method to search for a value within a range of cells. This method is similar to the Find command in Excel. The following is the syntax for the Find method:

```
expression.Find(What, After, LookIn, LookAt, SearchOrder, SearchDirection, MatchCase)
```

The What parameter is the only required parameter. Use the What parameter to tell VBA what you want to find. You can use the After parameter to specify the cell after which you want to start searching. If you omit this parameter, Excel starts the search after the top left cell in the range. The LookIn parameter tells VBA what you want to search. You can assign one of the XlFindLookIn constants: xlValues searches cell values, xlComments searches comments, and xlFormulas searches formulas.

The LookAt parameter tells VBA how to match your search criteria. Assign the LookAt parameter xlWhole if you want your search criteria to match the contents of the cell exactly; assign xlPart if you want VBA to return a match if your search criteria is found anywhere in the cell.

The SearchOrder parameter tells VBA the order in which you want to search. Assign the value xlByRows if you want to search by rows, or assign the value xlByColumns if you want to search by columns.

Use the SearchDirection parameter to indicate the direction you want to search. A value of xlNext finds the next matching value. A value of xlPrevious finds the previous matching value.

Assign True to the MatchCase parameter if you want your search to be case-sensitive.

Find Specific Cell Values

In this example, the user enters a value in a cell and VBA searches a range for the value.

① Declare the variable VBA uses to store the search criteria.

② Type On Error Resume Next.

This statement tells VBA to continue processing if an error occurs.

Note: See Chapter 8 to learn more about handling errors.

③ Activate the relevant worksheet.

If a procedure works only with a particular worksheet, you should activate the worksheet.

④ Store to a variable the contents of the cell in which the user enters the search criteria.

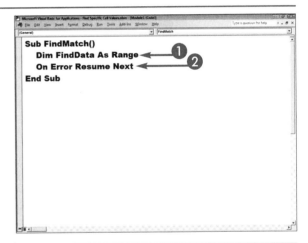

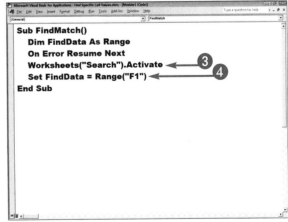

⑤ Type your `Find` command.

● The range you want to search.

● The data for which you are searching.

In this example, the data is stored in the `FindData` variable.

● What you want to search.

● How you want to match your search criteria.

● The search order.

● Your instruction as to what VBA should do when it finds the item.

⑥ Press Alt+F11 to switch from the VBE to Excel, and run the macro.

● The cell in which the user places the search criteria.

● When you execute the macro, if VBA finds the item, Excel moves to the first instance of the item.

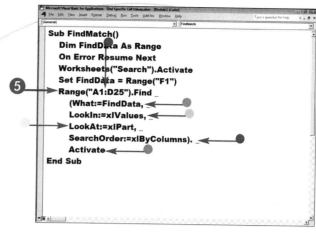

```vba
Sub FindMatch()
    Dim FindData As Range
    On Error Resume Next
    Worksheets("Search").Activate
    Set FindData = Range("F1")
    Range("A1:D25").Find _
        (What:=FindData, _
        LookIn:=xlValues, _
        LookAt:=xlPart, _
        SearchOrder:=xlByColumns). _
        Activate
End Sub
```

Region	Qtr	Product	Units Sold	What are you looking for?	Q2
Region 1	Q1	R6790	7000		
Region 1	Q2	R6790	5000		Find
Region 1	Q3	R6790	4000		Find Next
Region 1	Q4	R6790	6000		Find Previous
Region 1	Q1	X5495	4300		
Region 1	Q2	X5495	5450		
Region 1	Q3	X5495	6975		
Region 1	Q4	X5495	2004		
Region 1	Q1	Y7746	5196		
Region 1	Q2	Y7746	5123		
Region 1	Q3	Y7746	5248		
Region 1	Q4	Y7746	4222		

Extra

The introduction to this task does not mention two `Find` method parameters: `MatchByte` and `SearchFormat`. If you have installed double-byte language support on your computer, assign the value `True` to the `MatchByte` parameter.

The `SearchFormat` parameter enables you to match formats. If you assign the value `True` to this parameter, you must specify the format for the `Application.FindFormat` object.

VBA remembers the values specified for the `What`, `LookIn`, `LookAt`, `SearchOrder`, and `MatchByte` parameters. If you run a search again without setting these parameter values, Excel uses the settings from the previous `Find` or `Replace` method execution. These values are also set when you run a Find or Replace from within Excel. To avoid running searches that have unexpected results, you should set these parameters each time you run the `Find` method.

You can continue a search and find the next match using the `FindNext` or `FindPrevious` methods. When using these methods, you must specify an `After` parameter. The `After` parameter tells Excel the cell after which you want to execute the next search.

Example:
```
SearchRange.FindNext(After)
SearchRange. _
  FindPrevious(After)
```

Find and Replace Values in Cells

You can use the `Replace` method to search for and replace values within a range of cells. This method is similar to the Find and Replace command in Excel. The following is the syntax for the `Replace` method:

```
expression.Replace(What, Replacement, LookAt,
  SearchOrder, MatchCase, SearchFormat,
  ReplaceFormat)
```

The `Replace` method has two required parameters: `What` and `Replacement`. The `What` parameter tells VBA what you want to find. The `Replacement` parameter tells VBA with what you want to replace the data you find.

The `LookAt` parameter tells VBA how to match your search criteria. You can assign the `LookAt` parameter `xlWhole` if you want your search criteria to match the contents of the cell exactly. You can assign `xlPart` if you want VBA to return a match if your search criteria is found anywhere in the cell.

The `xlSearchOrder` parameter tells VBA the order in which you want to search. You can assign the value `xlByRows` if you want to search rows, or assign the value `xlByColumns` if you want to search by columns.

You can assign `True` to the `MatchCase` parameter if you want your search to be case-sensitive.

The `SearchFormat` and the `ReplaceFormat` parameters tell VBA the format you want to search for or replace. If you want to search for or replace a format, then you must set the appropriate parameter to `True` and specify the format properties for the `Application.FindFormat` object or the `ReplaceFormat` object, or both. For example, to replace text with a bold format, you can use the following code:

```
Application.ReplaceFormat.Font.FontStyle = _
  "Bold"
```

Find and Replace Values in Cells

① Type `On Error Resume Next`.

This statement tells VBA to continue processing if an error occurs.

Note: See Chapter 8 to learn more about handling errors.

② Activate the relevant worksheet.

If a procedure works only with a particular worksheet, activate the worksheet.

③ Type your `ReplaceFormat` or `FindFormat` command.

In this example, you make the replacement text bold and italic.

④ Type your `Replace` command.

- The range you want to search.
- The data for which you are searching.
- Your replacement.
- Set your `ReplaceFormat` object to `True`.

  VBA uses your `ReplaceFormat` command.

- How you want to match your search criteria.

⑤ Press Alt+F11 to switch from the VBE to Excel, and run the macro.

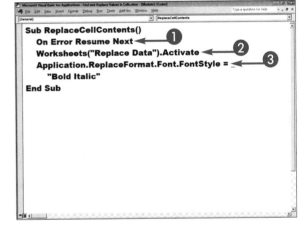

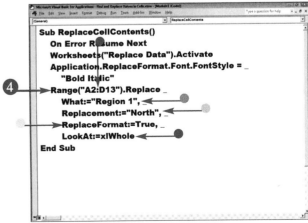

Your worksheet before
you execute your macro.

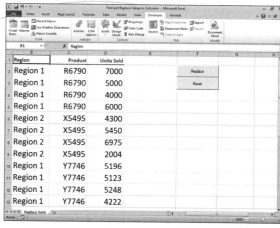

Your worksheet after you
execute your macro.

The macro replaces the
Region 1 text with North
and applies bold and italics.

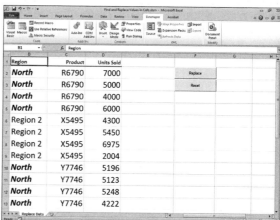

Extra

When you specify a value of `True` for the `SearchFormat` parameter or for the `ReplaceFormat` parameter, VBA looks for the search and replacement format settings. If you want to use formatting as part of the search criteria, you need to specify the format settings by using the `FindFormat` property of the `Application` object. With the `ReplaceFormat` parameter, you need to specify the replacement format settings by using the `ReplaceFormat` property. Set these properties at the top of the procedure, before the code that sets the associated parameter. You can use these properties to set the `Font` object properties for searching and replacing text. You can use the `With` statement to set the property values. For example, to set replacement text properties, you can type code similar to the following:

Example:
```
With Application.ReplaceFormat.Font
    .Name = "Arial"
    .FontStyle = "Bold"
    .Size = 12
End With
```

Convert a Column of Text into Multiple Columns

When you need to break a column of text into multiple columns, you can use the TextToColumns method. For example, if a list contains both first and last names in one column, you can use the TextToColumns method to break the list into two columns — one for the first name and one for the last name. When using the TextToColumns method, use the Range object to specify the column you want to parse into multiple columns.

The TextToColumns method provides several optional parameters you can use to specify how to separate the text. Use the Destination parameter to specify the range where VBA should place the results.

A *delimiter* is a character, such as a comma or space, which indicates a separation between strings. Use the DataType parameter to specify a constant value of xlDelimited if the text has a delimiter. Use the constant value of xlFixedWidth if each column of text is a fixed width.

Use one of the XlTextQualifier constants, xlTextQualifierDoubleQuote, xlTextQualifierNone, or xlTextQualifierSingleQuote, to indicate the text qualifier character.

Specify a value of True for the ConsecutiveDelimiter parameter to have consecutive delimiters treated as one. For the Tab, Semicolon, Comma, Space, and Other parameters, set the value to True for each delimiter that is used in the specified range. If you specify Other as the delimiter, set the value for the OtherChar parameter to the delimiter character.

The FileInfo parameter contains information pertaining to parsing individual columns in the range, with the first element being the column number, and the second element being one of the XlColumnDataType constants.

Specify the character used to separate decimals with the DecimalSeparator parameter, and the character used to separate thousands with the ThousandsSeparator parameter.

Convert a Column of Text into Multiple Columns

1. Name your procedure.

2. Declare a Range object variable.

3. Store the column you want separate to the Range object variable.

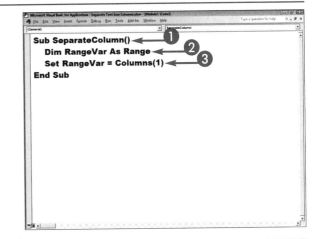

4. Create your TextToColumns command.

● Where you want to place the separated text.

● The type of data.

● The delimiter.

5. Press Alt+F11 to switch from the VBE to Excel, and run the macro.

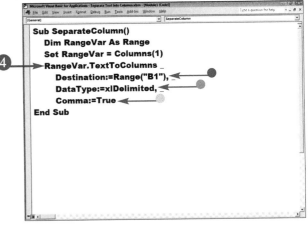

214

The worksheet before
you run your macro.

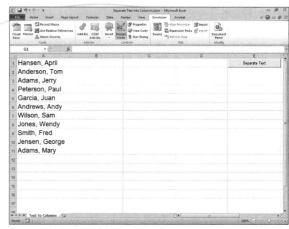

The worksheet after you
run your macro.

The macro separates
one column of data into
two columns of data.

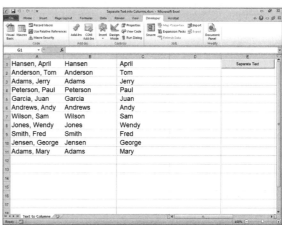

Apply It

You can use the `Parse` method to separate data values into multiple columns. When using the `Parse` method, you specify how the string should break. The `Parse` method has two optional parameters. The first parameter, `ParseLine`, is a string containing left and right brackets, indicating where the columns should split. For example, [xx][xxxx] breaks each string so that the first two characters are placed in the first column and the second four characters are placed in the second column. VBA ignores any other characters. For example, for the string "OS1024Y26," Excel would place the first two characters (OS) in the first column and the second four characters (1024) in the second column. Excel would ignore the remaining characters. The second parameter, `Destination`, specifies the range where the `Parse` method places the data. If the range has more than one cell, Excel uses the upper left corner of the range as the first cell.

Example:
```
Worksheets(1).Range("A1").Parse _
    ParseLine:="[xx][xxxx]", _
    Destination:=Range("B1")
```

Perform a Sort

ou can use VBA to sort your data, and you can have several levels of sort. For example, you can sort a list by last name and within last name by first name.

If you have imported your data or if you constantly update your data, you may not know the exact range the data encompasses. If you know the location of any cell in the range, you can use Selection.CurrentRegion to determine the range. Activate any cell in the range and use Selection.CurrentRegion to select the block of cells that surround the active cell. VBA selects everything above, below, to the left, and to the right until it reaches a blank column or row.

Use the Add method to add each level of sort. Create your highest level first and then create each additional level in

the order you want to sort. For example, if you want to sort by last name, then within last name by first name, create the last name sort, and then create the first name sort. You may want to assign a range name to each column.

The Add method has five parameters: Key, SortOn, Order, CustomOrder, and DataOption. Use the Key parameter to specify the sort field. You can use a range name or a range object. Use the SortOn parameter to specify the attribute to sort on. You can sort on values, cell color, font color or icons by specifying the proper XlSortOn constant value. See the "Extra" portion of this section for a list of XlSortOn constant values. Use the Order parameter to specify the sort order. Set the Order parameter to xlAscending to sort in ascending order or xlDescending to sort in descending order.

Perform a Sort

1 Declare a Range object.

2 Activate the worksheet containing the data you want to sort.

3 Activate a cell in the range you want to sort.

4 Assign the data range to the Range object you declared.

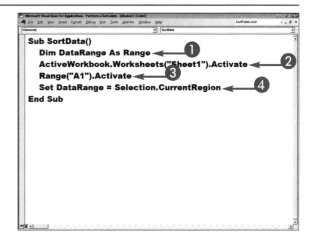

5 Assign a range name to each field.

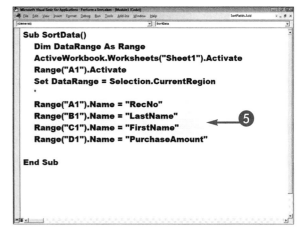

6 Clear any Sorts on the range.

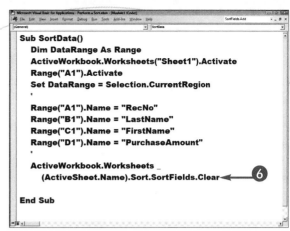

7 Add the first sort level.

● Field you want to sort.

● The attribute you want to sort on.

● The sort direction.

● The data option.

8 Add any additional sort levels.

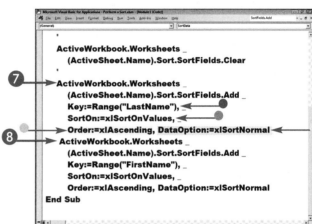

Extra

You can use the `SortField.SortOn` property to retrieve or set the sort attribute. The syntax for the `SortField.SortOn` property is *expression*.`SortOn`. The expression can be any variable that represents the `SortField` object. Use an `XlSortOn` constant value to tell Excel the attribute to sort on.

XLSORTON CONSTANT	VALUE	ATTRIBUTE
xlSortOnValues	0	Values
xlSortOnCellColor	1	Cell Color
xlSortOnFontColor	2	Font Color
xlSortOnIcon	3	Icon

You can use an `XlSortDataOption` constant to specify how to treat numeric data when you perform a sort.

XLSORTDATAOPTION CONSTANT	DESCRIPTION
xlSortNormal	Sort text and numeric data separately.
xlSortTextAsNumbers	Treat text as numeric data for sort.

continued ➡

U se the CustomOrder parameter if you want to sort by a custom order such as days of the week or months of the year. Use the DataOption parameter with one of the XlSortDataOption constants to specify how to treat numeric data. See the Extra section for a list of XlSortDataOption constant values.

You can use a With statement to set the methods and properties associated with a sort. See the Chapter 4 section "Change the Properties of an Object" to learn more about the With statement. Use the Sort.SetRange method to set the range of the sort. Use the Sort.Header property to specify whether the sort range has headers. Set the Sort. Header property to xlGuess to have Excel determine if there is a header, xlNo if the range does not have headers,

or xlYes if the range has headers. The default value is xlNo. Use the Sort.MatchCase property to specify whether the sort is case sensitive. Set the property to True for a case-sensitive sort or False for a non-case-sensitive sort. Use the Sort.Orientation property to set the orientation of the sort. Set the Sort.Orientation to xlSortColumns to sort by columns or to xlSortRows to sort by rows. The Sort.SortMethod property sets the sort method for Chinese languages; xlPinYin is the default and works with the English language. Use xlStroke to sort by the quantity of stokes for each character. Use xlPinYin for a phonetic Chinese sort order. Use the Sort. Apply method to apply the sort. VBA does not sort if you do not include the Sort.Apply method.

Perform a Sort (continued)

⑨ Use a With statement to set the methods and properties.

⑩ Set the range you want to sort.

⑪ Specify whether the range has headers.

⑫ Specify whether the sort should be case-sensitive.

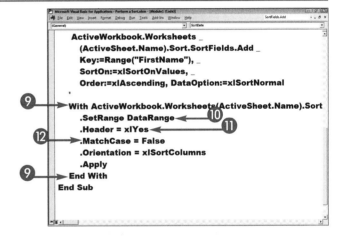

⑬ Specify the orientation.

⑭ Apply the sort.

⑮ Press Alt+F11 to switch from the VBE to Excel, and run the macro.

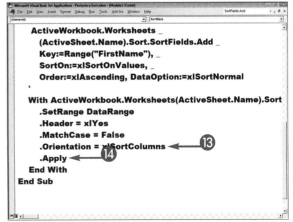

The worksheet before
you run the macro.

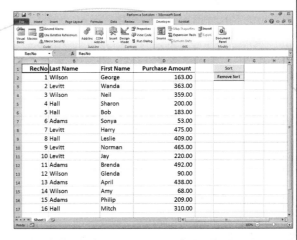

The worksheet after you
run the macro.

The macro sorts the data.

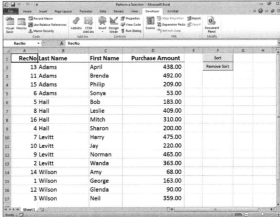

If you want to add a custom sort, you must list each of the sort values in the order you want to sort as shown in the
following code, which sorts by months in a year:

Example:
```
ActiveWorkbook.Worksheets("Sheet1").Sort.SortFields.Add _
    Key:=Range("Month"), _ ' Month is a named range
    SortOn:=xlSortOnValues, _
    Order:=xlAscending, _
    CustomOrder:= _
    "Jan,Feb,Mar,Apr,May,Jun,Jul,Aug,Sep,Oct,Nov,Dec", _
    DataOption:=xlSortNormal
```

You can use the `Range.AutoFilter` method to filter the data in your worksheet. For example, if you have four quarters of data for regions one to four and you want to look at regions one and two and quarters one, two, and three, you can use the `Range.AutoFilter` method. The following is the syntax for the `Range.AutoFilter` method:

`Range.AutoFilter(Field,Criteria1, Operation, Criteria2, VisibleDropDown)`

Use the `Field` parameter to specify the column you want to filter. VBA numbers the columns in your list. The leftmost column is column 1, the next column is column 2, and so on.

Use the `Criteria1` parameter to specify the criteria you want to use to filter a column. Use the `Operator` parameter

to specify an `XlAutoFilterOperator`. These operators tell VBA the type of filter to apply. For example, the `xlOr` operator causes VBA to use a logical `Or`, and the `xlAnd` operator causes VBA to use a logical `And`. See the Chapter 6 section "Make Use of Logical Operators" to learn more about logical operators. You can use an `XlAutofilterOperator` such as `xlTop10Items` or `xlFilterCellColor` to find the highest values or the cell color, respectively. Use the `Criteria2` parameter with a logical operator to construct multiple criteria.

Use the `VisibleDropDown` parameter to tell VBA whether to display an AutoFilter drop-down arrow for the filtered field. Set the parameter to `True` to display the drop-down arrow. Set the parameter to `False` to hide the drop-down arrow. The default is `True`.

Perform a Filter

① Declare a `Range` object.

② Activate the worksheet containing the data you want to filter.

③ Activate a cell in the range you want to filter.

④ Assign the data range for the list to the `Range` object you declared.

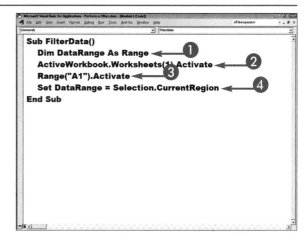

⑤ Create a column filter.

● The field you want to filter.

● Filter `Criteria1`.

● The `Operator`.

● Filter `Criteria2`.

⑥ Add additional column filters.

Note: *This filter uses an array and the* `xlFilterValues` *constant.*

⑦ Press Alt+F11 to switch from the VBE to Excel, and run the macro.

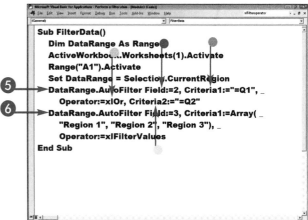

The worksheet before
you run the macro.

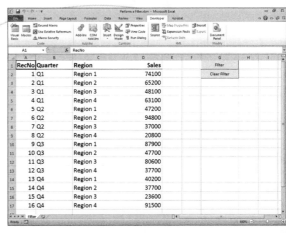

The worksheet after you
run the macro.

The macro filters the data.

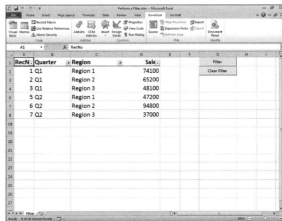

Extra

You can use XlAutoFilterOperators to specify the type of filter to apply. The following is a list of
XlAutoFilterOperators.

CONSTANT	VALUE	DESCRIPTION
xlAnd	1	Logical And
xlOr	2	Logical Or
xlTop10Items	3	Items with highest value. Use the criteria parameter to specify the number of items.
xlBottom10Items	4	Items with lowest value. Use the criteria parameter to specify the number of items.
xlTop10Percent	5	Items with highest value. Use the criteria parameter to specify the percentage.
xlBottom10Percent	6	Items with lowest value. Use the criteria parameter to specify the percentage.
xlFilterValues	7	Filter values
xlFilterCellColor	8	Color of the cell
xlFilterFontColor	9	Color of the font
xlFilterIcon	10	Filter icon
xlFilterDynamic	11	Dynamic filter

You can use the `Range.AdvancedFilter` method to filter your data. With the `Range.AdvancedFilter` method, you can create two or more filters and easily coordinate filters within and among columns. For example, you can filter a list to find all females with an income more than $100,000 and all males with an income less than $100,000. The syntax for the `Range. AdvancedFilter` method is:

expression`.AdvancedFilter(`*Action, CriteriaRange, CopyToRange, Unique*`)`

You have two options when you create a filtered list using the `Range.AdvancedFilter` method. You can have your filtered list appear in place — under the column heads of your unfiltered list — thereby hiding the unfiltered list. Or, you can have your filtered list appear in another location, thereby enabling you to keep your original list in your worksheet. If you want to filter your list in place, set

the `Action` parameter to `xlFilterInPlace`. If you want to keep your unfiltered list in your worksheet, set the `Action` parameter to `xlFilterCopy`.

When using the `Range.AdvancedFilter` method, you must have a criteria range. To create a criteria range, copy one or more column labels from a list. In the cell below each label, type the criteria by which to filter each column, such as **>100000** to find people with an income greater than $100,000 and **M** to find all males. Use the `CriteriaRange` parameter to specify the criteria range.

If you specified `xlFilterCopy` as the action, use the `CopyToRange` parameter to specify where you want to place the filtered data. Make sure your copy to range has enough room below it to include all the values in the filtered list.

If you want to include only unique records set the Unique parameter to `True`. The default is `False`.

Perform an Advanced Filter

① Declare your ranges.

② Set your ranges.

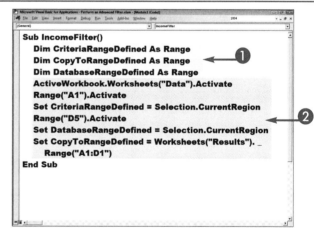

③ Activate the sheet where the results will appear.

④ Create an `AdvancedFilter`.

● Set the `Action` parameter.

● Set the `CriteriaRange`.

● Set the `CopyToRange`.

● Set the `Unique` parameter.

⑤ Press Alt+F11 to switch from the VBE to Excel, and run the macro.

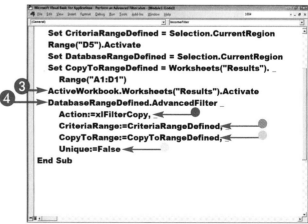

The worksheet before
you run the macro.

The results.

The macro filters the data.

Extra

At any time after you create a procedure that performs an advanced filter, you can change the criteria. The example finds all females with an income more than $100,000 and all males with an income less than $100,000. You can change the criteria to find, for example, all females. In the example, the criteria appear on two rows. If you want to find all females, the criterion would appear on one row. For that reason, your code for finding the criteria range must be flexible. You can create a flexible criteria range by activating any cell in the region and then using a `Selection.CurrentRegion` statement.

Example:
```
Range("D5").Activate
Set DatabaseRangeDefined = Selection.CurrentRegion
```

If you include a blank row in your criteria range, Excel returns all the records in the list.

Create Subtotals

After you sort, you can group your data into categories, such as quarters, and you can perform calculations so that you can compare one category with another. If you have a sort defined for at least one column, you can find the average, sum, min, max, number of items, and more for that column and/or other columns. Excel calls this feature *subtotaling*. In VBA, you can use the Range.Subtotal method to subtotal. The following is the syntax for the Range.Subtotal method:

Range.Subtotal(Groupby, Function, TotalList, Replace, PageBreaks, SummaryBelowData)

The Range portion of the statement can be any expression that returns a range object. Use the Groupby parameter to specify the column you want to group. VBA numbers each column in your list. The leftmost column is column 1, the next column is column 2, and so on.

Use the Function parameter to specify an XlConsolidationFunction. XlConsolidationFunctions tell VBA how to subtotal. For example, if you want to calculate a sum, use the xlSum function.

Use the TotalList parameter to create an array that identifies the columns you want to subtotal. Set the Replace parameter to True to replace any existing subtotals with the newly defined subtotal, or set the parameter to False to add an additional subtotal to the existing subtotals. The default is True. If you want every subtotal to appear on a separate page when you print, set the PageBreaks parameter to True. The default setting is False.

Your subtotals and grand totals can appear below or above each category. If you want them to appear below each category, set the SummaryBelowData parameter to True. If you want them to appear above each category, set the parameter to False.

Create Subtotals

① Activate the worksheet where you want to create a subtotal.

② Create a Subtotal.

● The column you want to group.

● The function you want to use to summarize your data.

◦ An array that identifies the columns you want to summarize.

◦ Indicates whether you want to replace the existing subtotal.

● Determines whether a page break is created after each summary.

● Places summary data below the category. Set to False to place summary data above the category.

③ Press Alt+F11 to switch from the VBE to Excel, and run the macro.

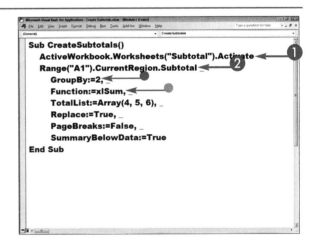

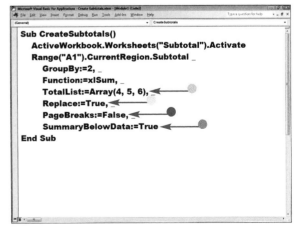

The worksheet before
you run the macro.

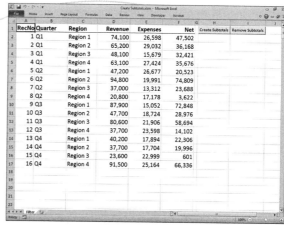

The results.

The macro subtotals the data.

Extra

You can use XlConsolidationFunctions
to specify the type of function to use when
summarizing data. See Chapter 16 section
"Add Fields to a PivotTable" for a list of
XlConsolidationFunctions.

After you create a subtotal, you can use code similar to the
following to remove it.

Example:
```
Sub RemoveSubtotals()
    ActiveWorkbook.Worksheets("Subtotal").Activate
    Range("A1").CurrentRegion.RemoveSubtotal
End Sub
```

Create Groups

With the `Range.Subtotal` method, you can create groups based on sorted data. If you want to group data that you have not sorted, use the `Group` method. When using the group method, you must specify the rows and/or columns that you want to group. For example, you can group the details related to cash receipts and cash disbursements so that you can compare total cash receipts with total cash disbursements.

When you create a group, Excel places Collapse and Expand buttons to the left side of the worksheet row labels if you group rows, or above the worksheet column labels if you group columns. When you click a Collapse button, Excel hides the columns or rows and the Collapse button turns into an Expand button. When you click an Expand button, Excel reveals the columns or rows and the Expand button turns into a Collapse button.

When you create a group, Excel places it on a level. Excel places the group that encompasses the most data on Level 1; it places any groups that fall within Level 1 on Level 2, and any groups that fall within groups on Level 2 on Level 3, and so on. Each time you run a macro that creates groups, Excel attempts to add the groups to the existing groups. To avoid this, you may want to include code that removes any existing groups to the beginning of your `Sub` procedure.

When creating a group, you can use the `Range` property to identify the columns or rows you want to group. For example, if you want to group columns A through C, you can use the syntax `Range("A:C").Group`. If you want to group rows 1 through 3, you can use the syntax `Range("1:3").Group`.

Create Groups

① Remove any existing groups.

● A cell anywhere in the grouped range.

② Group columns.

● The columns you want to group.

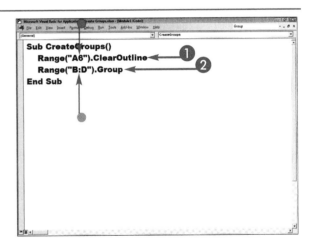

③ Group rows.

● The rows you want to group.

● You can create several levels.

④ Specify the level you want to display.

⑤ Press Alt+F11 to switch from the VBE to Excel, and run the macro.

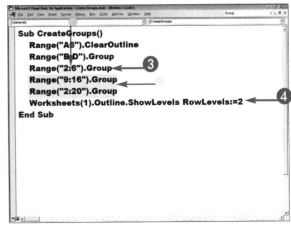

The worksheet before
you run the macro.

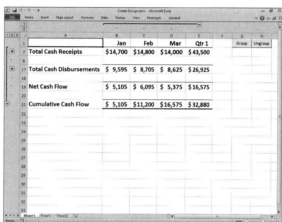

The results.

The macro groups the
data and displays the
level you indicated.

Apply It

You can use the `Range.ClearOutline` method
to remove groups from your data. The `Range.`
`ClearOutline` method consists of a range object
followed by `ClearOutline`. The range object can
be any range within the grouped data. The following
statement removes the groups created by the sample
code.

Example:
```
Range("A6").ClearOutline
```

Excel places grouped data on levels. You can use the
`Outline.ShowLevels` method to specify the level you
want to display. The `Outline.ShowLevels` method
has two parameters: `RowLevels` and `ColumnLevels`.
Use the `RowLevels` parameter to specify the row level
you want to display. Use the `ColumnLevels` parameter
to specify the column level you want to display. If the
group has fewer levels than you specify, Excel displays
all levels.

Example:
```
Worksheets(1).Outline.ShowLevels RowLevels:=2
```

Define a List as a Table

In Excel, a table is a special type of list. Like all lists, a table is a set of columns and rows where each column represents a single type of data. When you define a list as a table, Excel adds AutoFilter buttons to each column label, enabling you to readily sort and filter your data. To create a table, you use the ListObjects.Add method.

The ListObjects.Add method has five optional parameters: SourceType, Source, LinkSource, TableStyleName, and Destination. Use the SourceType parameter to specify your data's source type. The source type can be a SharePoint Services site, a query, a range, or an XML file. Use the Source parameter to specify your data source. If your SourceType is a range, specify a Range object. If you do not specify a Range object, Excel uses internal code to detect the range. If the SourceType is a SharePoint Services site, you must use an array to specify the URL to the SharePoint site, the ListName, and the ViewGUID.

Use the LinkSource parameter to specify a Boolean value indicating whether you want to link the data source to the ListObject object. If the data source is a SharePoint Services site, the default is True. Use a XlYesNoGuess constant with the TableStyleName parameter to indicate whether imported data has headers. Do not set the LinkSource or the TableStyleName parameter if the SourceType is a range. Use the Destination parameter to specify a Range object that is a single cell, indicating the upper left corner of where you want to place the new table. If your source is a SharePoint Services site, you must specify a destination. If your source is a range, VBA ignores this parameter.

You can use a With statement to set the properties for a ListObject object.

Define a List as a Table

① Declare a ListObject.

② Add the ListObject.

● The SourceType.

● The Source.

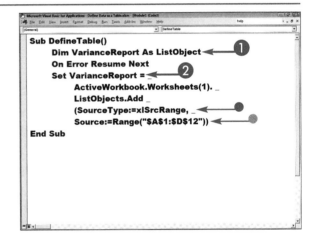

③ Set the ListObject properties.

● The name.

● Display a totals row.

● Set the table style.

④ Press Alt+F11 to switch from the VBE to Excel, and run the macro.

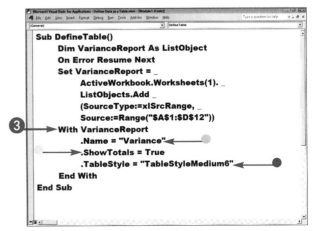

228

The worksheet before you run the macro.

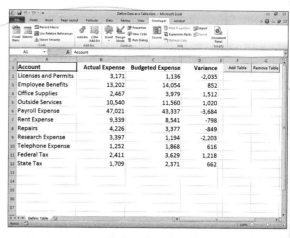

The results.

• The name.
• The totals row.

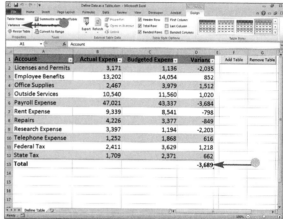

Extra

You can use the TableStyle property to assign a style to a ListObject. To find a style's name, click the Home tab. Click Format as Table in the Styles group. A gallery of styles appears. When you position your mouse pointer over a style, the style's name appears. You can assign the name to a ListObject by assigning the name, without spaces between the words, to the TableStyle property.

In Excel, tables have names. The default name is Table #. You can use the Name property to assign a name to a table.

If you add a totals row to your table, Excel can automatically calculate the sum, count, max, min, or other value for a column. Set the ShowTotals property to True to add a totals row.

Use an XlListObjectSourceType constant to specify the SourceType.

CONSTANT	VALUE	DESCRIPTION
xlSrcExternal	0	SharePoint Services site
xlSrcRange	1	Range
xlSrcXml	2	XML
xlSrcQuery	3	Query

UserForm Basics

very Windows application uses dialog boxes to gather information from the user, and Excel is no exception. For example, you can use the Open dialog box in Excel to select a file to open. VBA has two ready-made dialog boxes, MsgBox and InputBox, that you can use with your code. In addition, you can create your own custom dialog boxes. See Chapter 7 for more information on the MsgBox and InputBox dialog boxes.

Use the Visual Basic Editor to Create Custom Dialog Boxes

By using the VBE, you can create custom dialog boxes to use with your Excel procedures. The VBE refers to these custom dialog boxes as UserForms. When you create a UserForm, you design it by using the various controls available in the UserForm Toolbox.

Select Objects

Label Button

TextBox Button

ComboBox Button

ListBox Button

CheckBox Button

Option Button

Toggle Button

Frame Button

Command Button

TabStrip Button

MultiPage Button

Scrollbar Button

Spin Button

Image Button

RefEdit Button

The UserForm Toolbox appears when you select a UserForm in the VBE. The Toolbox contains controls that you can add to your custom UserForm. See the section "Create a Custom Dialog Box" for more information about adding Toolbox controls.

The Toolbox contains several standard controls. You can also create custom controls and add them to the Toolbox. See the section "Create Custom UserForm Controls" for more information on adding custom controls.

Select Objects For resizing and moving controls that have been drawn on a user form.	**CommandButton** A user clicks the button to perform a specific action. When you create a CommandButton control, you specify the text that appears on the button by setting a control property.
Label For adding text to a UserForm. This control does not interact with the UserForm; you add labels for informational purposes only.	**TabStrip** A multiple-page area for a section of your UserForm.
TextBox Enables the user to type text.	**MultiPage** Tabbed dialog boxes a user can use to switch between pages of options. By default, when you add the MultiPage control to your UserForm, it creates two pages. To add additional pages, right-click one of the page tabs and then select the New Page option.
ComboBox A user can either click an item from the list or type the appropriate value.	
ListBox Presents a list of items from which a user can select the desired item.	**ScrollBar** A user can scroll through information that is not shown on the screen, or indicate a position on a scale.
CheckBox A user can select or deselect options. Typically, a CheckBox control returns a value of True if it is selected, and False if it is not selected.	**SpinButton** A user can specify a value by clicking one of the arrow buttons to increment or decrement the value.
OptionButton A user can select from a list of items. You place Option Button controls in a group. When the user selects a control, the other controls are automatically deselected.	**Image** Use this control to add a graphic to the UserForm. Excel stores the graphic in the worksheet. If you distribute the worksheet, Excel includes the graphic. You can use a graphic that is in any of the following file formats: BMP, CUR, GIF, ICO, JPEG, and WMF.
ToggleButton The button appears to be either pressed or unpressed. When pressed, the button returns a value of True; when unpressed the button returns a value of False.	**RefEdit** A text field and a button with which a user can select a range of cells from a worksheet. When the user clicks a button, the corresponding dialog box minimizes so that the user can drag the pointer across the worksheet to select the desired range of cells.
Frame This control is a container for grouped controls.	

Create a Custom Dialog Box

ou can use VBA to create custom dialog boxes to use with your macros. Dialog boxes are user interfaces that enable users do such things as click buttons to indicate a desired selection or type appropriate values in a field. VBA refers to these dialog boxes as Forms or UserForms.

To create a custom dialog box, in the VBE select the UserForm option on the View menu. The VBE creates a new UserForm called UserForm# and creates a Forms folder in the Project Explorer window. The Forms folder appears only if you have created UserForms. See Chapter 2 for more information about the Project Explorer window.

You can use the Properties window to make changes to the properties associated with a UserForm. For example, you can change the name of a UserForm to make it

easier to identify when you look at the UserForms list in the Project Explorer window. To open the Properties window, press F4.

After you create a UserForm, you can custom design it by using the Toolbox controls, which appear only when you select the UserForm. You add controls to the UserForm by dragging them from the Toolbox to the appropriate location on the UserForm. For example, to create a list box to request a value from the user, you drag the ListBox control onto the UserForm. After you add a control, you can resize it as needed. The VBE assigns default values to the control's properties. You can change the assigned values in the Properties window for the control. You must select the control before you can change its properties.

Create a Custom Dialog Box

① In the Project Explorer window, click the project to which you want to add a UserForm.

② Click Insert → UserForm.

● The VBE creates a blank UserForm with a default name of UserForm1, and the Toolbox appears.

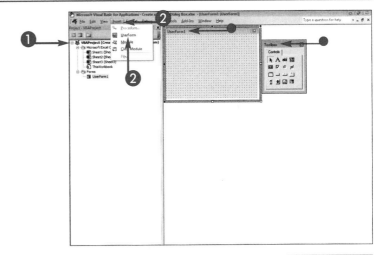

③ Press F4.

● The Properties window appears.

④ Type a form name in the Name field of the Properties window.

⑤ Click the UserForm.

● The Toolbox reappears.

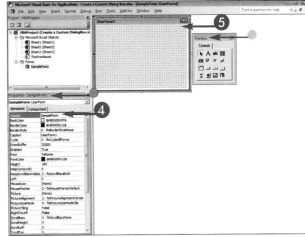

6 Click a control.

7 Click and drag to create the control on the UserForm.

Repeat Steps 6 and 7 and to add additional controls.

8 Click the UserForm or a control on the form.

9 Use the Properties window to modify any properties you want to change.

※ This example changed the Caption on the UserForm.

10 Press F5.

The VBE moves you to Excel and provides you with a preview of the dialog box.

11 To return to the VBE, click the Close button.

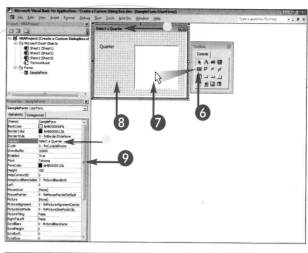

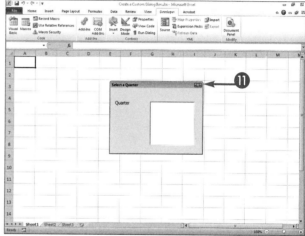

Extra

For each control you add to a UserForm, you can set several properties. Although each control type has unique properties, most of the properties are common to all controls. To change the value of a control property, either type a new value or select a value from the drop-down list. The following table describes some common control properties.

CONTROL PROPERTY	DESCRIPTION
(Name)	The name of the control.
BackColor	The background color of the control.
Caption	The text that appears on the control, such as the button or label text.
Font	The font used to display the text on the control.
Height	The height of the control in pixels.
Text	The text on the control.
TextAlign	The way text aligns on the control.
Width	The width of the control in pixels.

Call a Custom Dialog Box from a Procedure

You can call, display, and use custom dialog boxes to obtain user input. For example, you can use a custom dialog box to request the values you need to perform a calculation from the user.

To display a custom dialog box, use the Show method of the UserForm object. The Show method instructs Excel to display the specified UserForm. The following is the syntax for the Show method:

UserForm.Show *modal*

The Show method has one optional parameter, Modal. The Modal parameter determines whether the UserForm appears as a modal or modeless dialog box in Excel. The default value of vbModal makes the dialog box modal, which means that users must either close or hide the dialog box before selecting any other options in Excel.

When Excel opens a modal dialog box, Excel passes control to the dialog box, and the user can interact only with the dialog box. A value of vbModeless means that although the dialog box remains open until a user closes it, the user can perform other actions.

Dialog boxes contain a Close or Cancel button a user can click to close the dialog box. In a procedure, you can also close a dialog box by using the Unload method. You must use a Click event with CommandButton controls to create a procedure that calls the Unload method. See the section "Capture Input from a Custom Dialog Box" for more information about specifying the code to run when a user clicks a button.

Call a Custom Dialog Box from a Procedure

① Create a UserForm.

Note: See the section "Create a Custom Dialog Box" to learn how to create a UserForm.

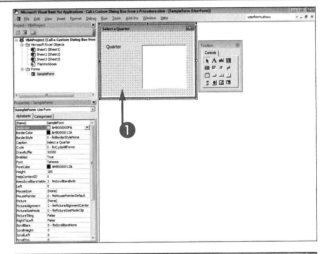

② Create a new Sub procedure.

③ Create a Show command.

④ Press Alt+F11 to switch from the VBE to Excel, and run the macro.

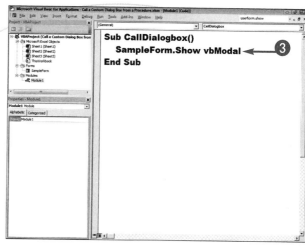

Excel displays the dialog box.

⑤ Click the Close button to close the dialog box.

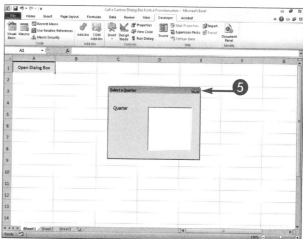

Extra

You can use the Unload statement to remove the UserForm from memory. When you call the Unload statement, VBA resets all the controls on the UserForm to their default values; as a result, you cannot access the options specified by the user after the UserForm unloads from memory. To maintain access to the values, you can either store the values in public variables or hide the UserForm until your procedure terminates. To unload a UserForm, use the Unload statement followed by the name of the UserForm that you want to unload, or use the code Unload Me:

THIS CODE:		IS EQUIVALENT TO:
Unload UserForm1	→	Unload Me

You can use the Hide method to hide a UserForm so that it is no longer visible. When you hide a UserForm, you can still access it from your procedure.

TYPE THIS:		RESULT:
UserForm1.Hide	→	Excel hides the form.

After hiding a form, Excel may appear to freeze as your code continues to access the UserForm. This condition clears as soon as the code that accesses the UserForm finishes processing.

Capture Input from a Custom Dialog Box

Dialog boxes in Excel gather input from the user. The input can be anything, from what button the user clicks to text the user types into a field. You can capture user input by using `UserForm` events. For example, when the user clicks an OK `CommandButton` control, you can use a `CommandButton_Click Sub` procedure to tell Excel what to do next.

Excel considers every user interaction that occurs in a dialog box an event. For example, scrolling through a list of items, clicking an OK button, and typing text in a text box are all events. Each `UserForm` control has several events that you can capture. The most common event is the `Click` event, which occurs each time a user clicks a control. To make `UserForms` interactive, you can create procedures that execute when specific events occur.

Each `UserForm` has two views: a graphical layout window and a code window. The graphical layout window is where you add controls that appear in the dialog box. See the section "Create a Custom Dialog Box" for more information on designing custom dialog boxes. The code window contains the code associated with the `UserForm`. You can use the code window to create event procedures for each control. To create event code, you double-click the control. By default, the VBE creates a private click event for a control when you double-click it. If a `Click` event already exists, the VBE simply displays the code window. Users cannot execute private click event procedures by using the Macro dialog box. The only way execute a private click event procedure is to click the appropriate control.

Capture Input from a Custom Dialog Box

1 Create a `UserForm`.

Note: See the section "Create a Custom Dialog Box" to learn how to create a `UserForm`.

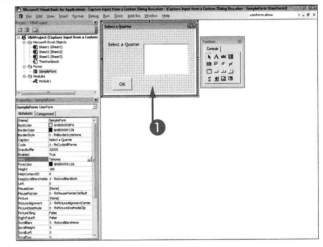

2 Double-click a control.

In this example, you write code for the OK button, and so you double-click OK.

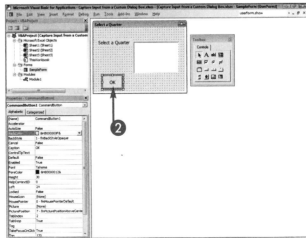

- VBA creates a Sub procedure.

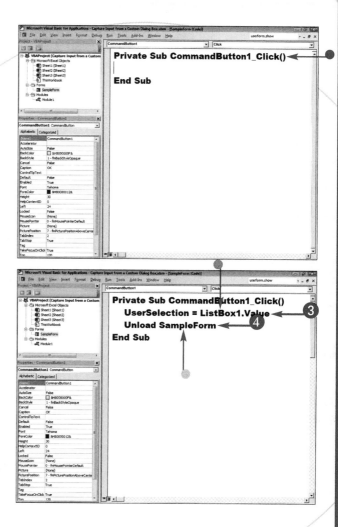

3 Assign the user selection to a variable.

- Name of the control.

  You can find the name of the control in the Properties window's Name field.

4 Close the dialog box.

- Name of the form.

  You can find the name of the form in the Properties window's Name field.

Extra

A Click event occurs when the user clicks a control or a value in a control. For most controls, you can write a procedure to handle the Click event, by simply placing _Click after the control name.

Example:
```
Sub CommandButton1_Click()
```

If you need to capture the Click event to determine the page or tab selected with a MultiPage or TabStrip control, you can use an index parameter value to specify the index value of the page or tab.

Example:
```
Sub MultiPageQtr_Click(1)
```

When working with MultiPage and TabStrip controls, create a separate procedure to handle the selection of each page or tab by using the proper index value.

A Click event also occurs when the user presses Enter while a control has focus, when the user presses the accelerator key that corresponds to the control, or when the user presses the spacebar while a CommandButton has focus.

continued ➡

You can create code to monitor events and execute code when a specific event occurs. Each control has its own events, and the VBE lists them for you in the Procedure list box. You can quickly create an event procedure in the code window by selecting the appropriate control name in the Object list box and then selecting the corresponding event from the Procedure list box. When you select an event, the VBE creates a procedure with the name of the control followed by the event name.

Control values on a `UserForm` are active only as long as the dialog box is open. If you close the dialog box prior to saving user input values, you lose the user input. To avoid potential problems related to lost data, consider saving user responses to public variables that can pass into other procedures. For example, you can call a

`UserForm` from a procedure to capture user responses and then pass the values back to the main procedure.

You declare public variables at the top of your module, before any procedure code, by using the `Public` statement. Declaring public variables enables you to declare variables that all procedures in a project can access. See Chapter 3 for more information on declaring variables.

When working with a single-column list box or combo box, you can use the `AddItem` method to create the list of choices that appears in the box. The following is the syntax for the `AddItem` method:

`object.AddItem Item`

You can use the `With` statement to shorten the code required to create the list. See Chapter 4 for more information on using the `With` statement.

Capture Input from a Custom Dialog Box *(continued)*

⑤ Create a new module.

Note: *See Chapter 2 to learn how to create a new module.*

⑥ Declare a public variable to hold the user selection.

⑦ Create a `Sub` procedure.

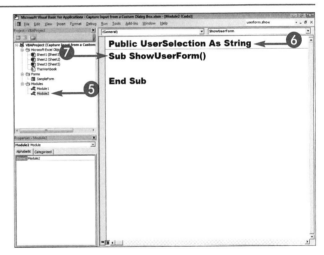

⑧ Add items to the list box.

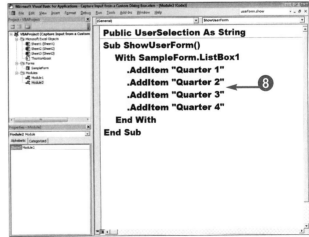

⑨ Show the dialog box.

⑩ Press Alt+F11 to switch from the VBE to Excel, and run the ShowUserForm macro.

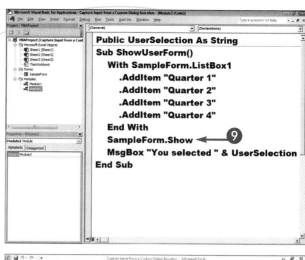

The dialog box displays and returns the data you requested.

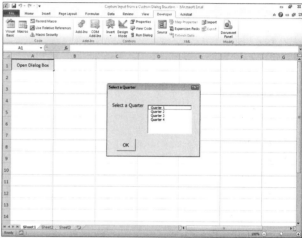

Apply It

You use control events to determine when to execute specific code. The following list identifies the most common events that occur with the various controls placed on UserForms. Not all events are available for each control. In the code window, check the Procedure list box to see the events that are associated with the selected control.

CONTROL EVENT	OCCURRENCE
BeforeDragOver	The user is dragging-and-dropping data onto a control.
BeforeUpdate	Before data on a control is changed.
Change	The Value property of the control changes.
Click	The user clicks the control.
DblClick	The user clicks the control twice.
Enter	Before a control receives focus.
KeyDown	The user presses a key.
MouseDown	The user presses the left mouse button.

Validate Input from a Dialog Box

You can validate the values returned by controls in a dialog box before passing them to your procedure. You validate the data values for two reasons: First to ensure that the user enters a value. Second, and probably more important, to ensure that errors do not occur in your code because the wrong data passes to a procedure.

You can create code that validates the user input for any event that occurs in a `UserForm`. The best time to validate is prior to closing the dialog box. For example, if a `CommandButton` control, such as an OK button, passes values to variables and closes the dialog box, the OK button is the ideal place to validate your data. When you create the validation code, you can use a conditional statement, such as an `If Then` statement, to check the

properties of each control. For example, to make sure the user typed a string in the Name text field of a dialog box, you can add the following `If Then` statement to your procedure: `If TextBox1.Text = "" Then`.

The `If Then` statement checks the `Text` property for the specified `TextBox` control to ensure that it contains a value. If the `TextBox` control does not contain a value, your VBA code can call the `MsgBox` function and display a message telling users that they must enter a value.

When working with a list box, you can use the `ListIndex` property to find out if the user typed a value. The `ListIndex` property returns -1 if the user did not type in a value, 0 if the user selected the first value in the list, 1 if the user selected the second value in the list, and so on.

Validate Input from a Dialog Box

① Double-click the control to which you want to add validation code.

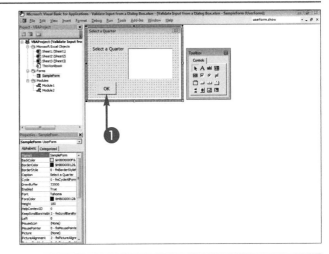

The code window opens.

2 Add the validation code.

In this example, if the user does not make a selection, a message box appears.

3 Press Alt+F11 to switch from the VBE to Excel, and run the macro.

If the user does not make a selection, a message box appears.

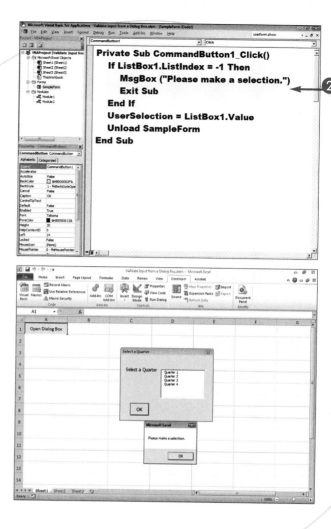

```vba
Private Sub CommandButton1_Click()
    If ListBox1.ListIndex = -1 Then
        MsgBox ("Please make a selection.")
        Exit Sub
    End If
    UserSelection = ListBox1.Value
    Unload SampleForm
End Sub
```

Extra

The `QueryClose` event takes two arguments, `Cancel` and `CloseMode`. The `Cancel` argument accepts an integer value. If the value of the argument is anything other than 0, the `QueryClose` event stops and the associated dialog box remains open. The `CloseMode` argument contains a constant value indicating the cause of the `QueryClose` event, as shown in the following table.

CONSTANT	VALUE	DESCRIPTION
vbFormControlMenu	0	The user selected the Close button in the dialog box.
vbFormCode	1	The code initiated an Unload statement.
vbAppWindows	2	The Windows operating session is ending.
vbAppTaskManager	3	The Windows Task Manager is closing Excel.

Create Custom UserForm Controls

You can customize the Toolbox to suit your needs. The Toolbox that appears when you select a UserForm in the Visual Basic Editor contains all of the standard controls you can add to a UserForm. These controls appear on a single tabbed page called Controls. By using the Properties window, you can change the tip text that appears when a user drags across the icon, the color of the control, and many other features. You can also create new controls and add them to the Toolbox.

To create new controls, you customize and combine the existing controls. For example, if you add an OK button to all of your UserForms, you can create a custom button and set the appropriate properties, such as Caption, Width, Height, and Default. If you place the button in the Toolbox, the VBE adds it as a new control. Alternatively, you can create new controls by combining multiple controls. For example, you can create a new control that consists of an OK and a Cancel button.

To keep your custom controls separate from the existing controls in the Toolbox, you can add a new page to the Toolbox. You add a new page to the Toolbox by using the New Page option. You can assign a name to the new page by using the Rename option.

When you create a custom control by dragging a control from a form to the Toolbox, you transfer only the properties. Code that you have added to the control does not transfer. Each time you use a custom control you must add the necessary code.

Create Custom UserForm Controls

① In the Toolbox, click the control you want to customize.

② Drag the control to the UserForm.

③ Set the control properties.

● In the Properties window, type the control name in the Name field.

● Type the text you want to appear on the control in the Caption field.

● Enter the tip that appears when the user drags across the control in the ControlTipText field.

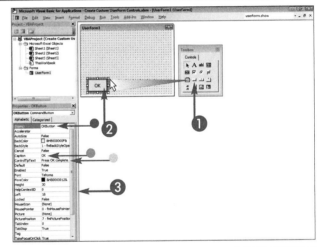

④ In the Toolbox, right-click the Controls tab.

⑤ Click New Page.

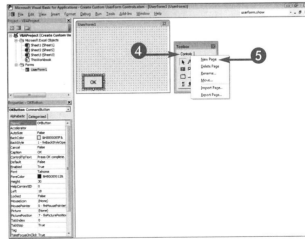

The VBE adds a new page to the Toolbox.

6 Click the control on the UserForm and drag the control to the Toolbox.

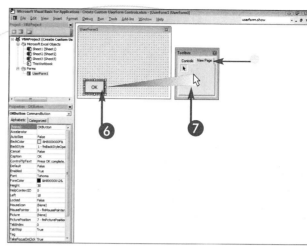

● The control appears on the new page of the Toolbox.

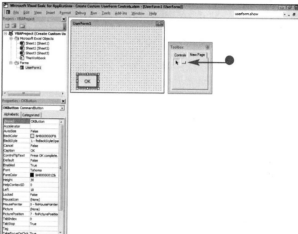

Create a UserForm Template

I f you find that you create the same basic UserForm repeatedly, you can create a UserForm template and use that template as a basis for creating new forms. When you create UserForms, the Visual Basic Editor attaches them to the project in which you create them. Each time you create a new project, you must re-create the UserForm.

With a UserForm template, you design a basic UserForm and save it as a template. You can then import the template to add the UserForm to any other project you create. You create a template by using the Export File command on the File menu. In the Export File dialog box, you specify the name and location for saving the template. You may want to create a special folder in which to save all your templates.

When you create a UserForm for use as a template, you should keep it generic so you can customize it for each new project. For example, if you frequently create a UserForm that contains a TextBox control for gathering user input, as well as two CommandButton controls, OK and Cancel, you can create a generic version of the form with the three controls on it. If you do not place the Label control for the text box in the template version, you can import the form and add a label that reflects the type of data you want to gather from the user.

To add a UserForm template to a project, you use the Import option on the File menu. The VBE imports the file into your project.

Create a UserForm Template

Create a Template

① Create a UserForm.

Note: *See the section "Create a Custom Dialog Box" to learn how to create a* UserForm.

② Click File → Export File.

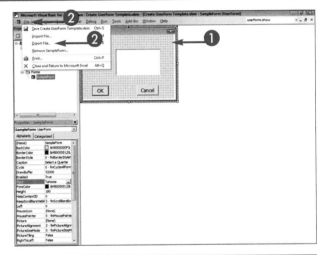

③ Locate the folder in which you want to save the file.

④ Type the filename.

⑤ Click Save.

VBA exports the file.

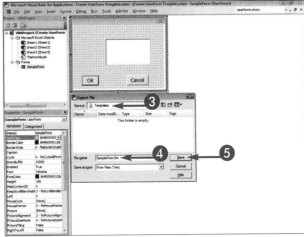

Import a Template

① Click the project to which you want to add a template.

② Click File → Import File.

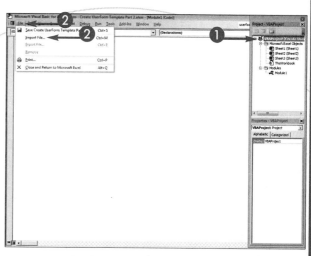

The Import File dialog box appears.

③ Locate the folder in which you saved the template.

④ Click the file containing the template.

⑤ Click Open.

The VBE adds the template to the project.

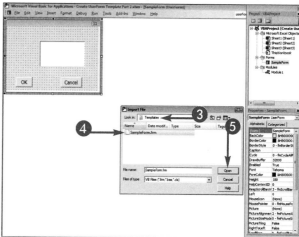

Extra

You can specify the order that Excel uses to move between controls on a UserForm by setting each controls' tab order. Tab order is the order in which the VBE selects the control to move to when a user presses Tab. By default, the tab order is the order in which you add controls to a UserForm.

Each control has two properties that relate to tab order. You can use the Properties window to set these properties. The first property, TabStop, determines whether focus stops on the control when the user presses Tab. If you set the TabStop property to False, when the user tabs through the controls, Excel skips the control. The second property, TabIndex, is a value between 0 and the number of controls, and sets the order in which Excel moves from control to control when the user presses Tab. You can use the Tab Order dialog box to set the tab order. This dialog box appears when you right-click the UserForm and then click Tab Order.

Customize the Ribbon

S tarting with Office 2007, Microsoft introduced a new user interface for many of its Office products, including Excel. Earlier versions of Excel used toolbars and menus to provide access to Excel commands; Office 2007 and later use the Ribbon. You can customize the Ribbon. You can add tabs, groups, commands, and buttons. You can also delete tabs, delete groups, rearrange commands, and rearrange buttons.

You can add command groups and commands to existing Ribbon tabs. For example, if you frequently use the Format Cells dialog box, you can add it to the Home tab next to the Styles group. You can rename tabs and groups. For example, if you do not like the name Home tab, you can change the name to Basic Commands or some other name. You can also choose what tabs appear

and the order in which they appear. For example, if you never use the Review tab, you can remove it from view. If you frequently use the Formulas tab, you can have it display first.

Excel divides commands into the following categories to make it easier for you to find the commands you want: Popular Commands, Commands Not in the Ribbon, All Commands, Macros, Office Menu, All Tabs, Main Tabs, Tool Tabs, and Custom Tabs and Groups. Main Tabs are the tabs that you see when you use Excel without any customizations. Tool tabs are the context-sensitive tabs that appear when you work on objects such as charts or PivotTables. You select a command category from the Choose Command From drop-down list.

Customize the Ribbon

① Right-click the Ribbon.

A menu appears.

② Click Customize the Ribbon.

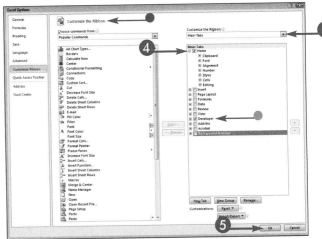

● The Customize the Ribbon pane appears.

③ Click the down arrow and then select the type of tab you want to customize.

④ Click to select or deselect the tabs you want to display or not display (☐ changes to ☑ or ☑ changes to ☐).

● To display the Developer tab, make sure you select the Developer check box.

⑤ Click OK.

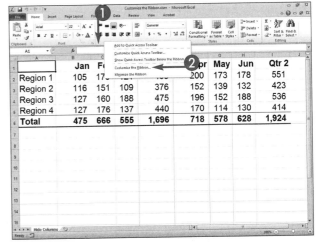

- Only selected tabs appear.

6 Right-click the Ribbon.

A menu appears.

7 Click Customize the Ribbon.

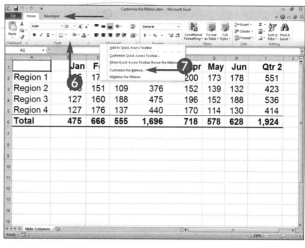

- The Customize the Ribbon pane appears.

8 Click the down arrow and then select Macros.

- All the macros in open workbooks appear.

To add a command, click the down arrow and then select the category from which you want to select commands.

9 Click New Tab.

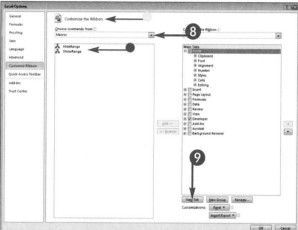

Apply It

Tabs, groups, and commands display in the order they appear in the Customize the Ribbon pane. To change the order, open the Customize the Ribbon pane. Click a tab, group, or command and then use the Move Up ( ) or Move Down ( ) buttons to change the location. Move Up moves the tab, group, or command up, and Move Down moves the tab, group, or command down.

If you no longer want a tab, group, or command to appear, you can remove it. Open the Customize the Ribbon pane. Click the tab, group, or command you want to remove and then click the Remove button. Excel removes the tab, group, or command.

You can restore the Excel Ribbon back to the way it was before you made any customizations. To remove all customizations, click the Reset button. A menu appears. Click Reset All Customizations. A prompt appears. Click Yes. Note that the Quick Access toolbar customizations are also removed. To restore a specific tab, click the tab. Click the Reset button. A menu appears. Click Reset Only Selected Ribbon Tab. Excel restores the tab.

continued ➡

You can place buttons on the Ribbon to execute your macros. To access the macros you have created, choose Macros from the Choose Commands From drop-down list. All of the macros in open workbooks appear. You click a macro and then click Add to add the macro to the Ribbon.

You can use the Customize the Ribbon drop-down list to tell Excel the type of tab you want to a modify. Choose from All Tabs, Main Tabs, or Tool Tabs. Once you choose a tab type, the options appear in the box below the Customize the Ribbon field. A check box appears next to each tab listed. Only the selected tabs appear in the Ribbon. To access the VBE, you must display the Developer tab, which is unselected by default and does

not appear. You can find the Developer tab under Main Tabs. To display the Developer tab, select the Developer tab check box.

You can click the New Tab button to add a new tab. You can click the New Group button to add a new group. When you click the New Tab button or the New Group button, Excel usually places the new tab or group under the highlighted tab or group. Tabs and groups appear in the order listed on the Customize the Ribbon pane. You can change the order of tabs and groups.

You can use the Rename button to rename any tab or group. You can also use the Rename button to assign a button to a macro.

Customize the Ribbon (continued)

- A new tab and a new group appear.

  If a new group does not appear, click New Group.

⑩ Click a macro.

  To add a command, click the command

⑪ Click Add.

  Repeat Steps 10 and 11 for every macro or command you want to add.

- Excel adds the macro or command to the new group.

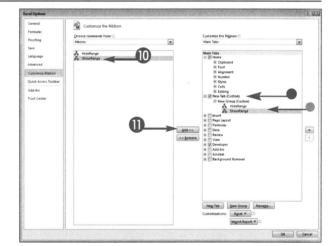

⑫ Click a tab or group name.

⑬ Click Rename.

  The Rename dialog box appears.

⑭ Type a new name.

⑮ Click OK to close the Rename dialog box.

  Excel renames the tab or group.

  Repeat Steps 8 to 11 for every tab and group you want to rename.

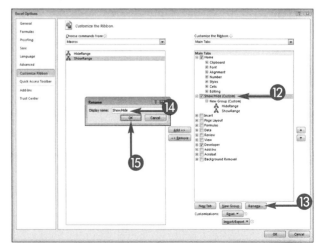

⑯ Click a macro.

⑰ Click Rename.

The Rename dialog box appears.

⑱ Click the button you want to use to represent your macro.

⑲ Type a name for your macro.

⑳ Click OK to close the Rename dialog box.

㉑ Click OK to close the Excel Options pane.

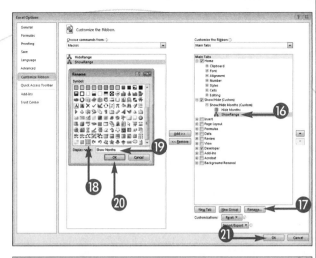

● The new tab and group appear.

㉒ Click a button to run a macro.

If you added a command, you can click the command to run it.

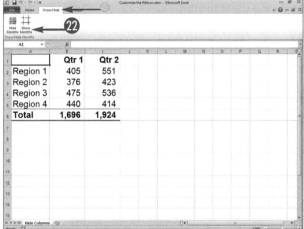

Apply It

To add a new group to a standard Excel tab, follow these steps: Open the Customize the Ribbon pane. Click the down arrow next to the Choose Commands From field and then choose the category from which you want to choose commands. Click the down arrow next to the Customize the Ribbon command and then choose the type of tab you want to customize. Click the tab to which you want to add the new group. Click New Group. Excel adds the new group. Click Rename. The Rename dialog box appears. Type the name you want to give the new group and then click OK. Excel renames the group.

Click the command you want to add. Click the Add button. Excel adds the command. Repeat the process to add additional commands. Groups display in the order they appear in the Customize the Ribbon pane. Click the new group's name. Click the Move Up button (▲) to move the group up. Click the Move Down button (▼) to move the group down. Click OK. The group and the commands appear on the Ribbon on the tab you selected.

Create a CustomUI.xml File

Y ou can use XML to customize the Ribbon. Using XML is a bit more difficult than using the Customize the Ribbon pane, but it offers some features that are not available there. For example, using XML you can add drop-down lists and check boxes to the Ribbon. Microsoft refers to the XML markup system as RibbonX. You create and use a file named customUI.xml to modify the Ribbon. Because you write XML in plain text, you can use any text editor to create a customUI.xml file. To learn more about XML, see Chapter 19.

Creating a basic Ribbon modification requires that you use control markups. The ribbon control markup represents the Ribbon. The tab control markups represent the tabs on the Ribbon. All tab control markups are contained within the tabs control markup.

The tabs control markup does not have any attributes. You can set an id attribute and a label attribute for a tab control. An id attribute uniquely identifies a control. A label attribute assigns a label to a control.

The group control markup identifies a group on a tab. You can set an id attribute and a label attribute for the group markup.

The button control markup creates a button on a tab. You can set id, label, imageMso, size, onAction, and screenTip attributes for a button control. The imageMso attribute identifies the built-in image you want to use as the button. The size attribute determines the size of the button. You can set the size attribute to either normal or large. The customUI.xml file can call the onAction attribute when the user clicks a control. The screenTip attribute specifies the screen tip that appears when the user positions the mouse pointer over the button.

Create a CustomUI.xml File

① Create a file named customUI.xml.

You can use Notepad or another text editor to create the file.

② Type `<customUI xmlns= "http://schemas. microsoft.com/ office/2006/01/ customui">`.

You start every customUI. xml file with this code.

③ Create a ribbon control markup.

④ Create a tabs control markup.

⑤ Create a tab control markup, include attributes.

6 Create a group, include attributes.

7 Create buttons, include attributes.

● A button.

● A label.

● Executes the procedure.

○ Name of the procedure

8 Save your file with the filename customUI.xml.

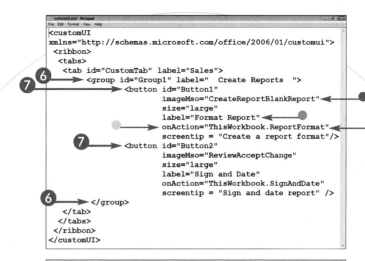

```xml
<customUI
xmlns="http://schemas.microsoft.com/office/2006/01/customui">
  <ribbon>
    <tabs>
      <tab id="CustomTab" label="Sales">
        <group id="Group1" label="  Create Reports  ">
          <button id="Button1"
                  imageMso="CreateReportBlankReport"
                  size="large"
                  label="Format Report"
                  onAction="ThisWorkbook.ReportFormat"
                  screentip = "Create a report format"/>
          <button id="Button2"
                  imageMso="ReviewAcceptChange"
                  size="large"
                  label="Sign and Date"
                  onAction="ThisWorkbook.SignAndDate"
                  screentip = "Sign and date report" />
        </group>
      </tab>
    </tabs>
  </ribbon>
</customUI>
```

After you add your file to a workbook, your Ribbon should look like the one shown here.

● A new tab. The tab label appears on the tab.

● Two buttons with button labels.

○ The group label.

This is how the file appears after you perform the steps outlined in "Add a CustomUI.xml File to a Workbook."

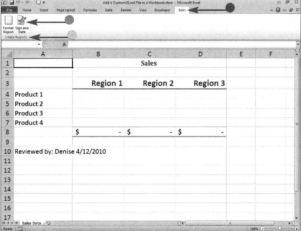

Extra

You use the `imageMso` attributes to identify the built-in image you want to appear on the Ribbon by using the following syntax:

Example:
```
imageMso = "ImageName"
```

To obtain the name of the image, click the File tab and then Options. The Excel Options dialog box appears. Click Customize Ribbon. In the Choose Commands From field, select All Commands. Position the mouse pointer over the command with the button that you want to use. A screen tip appears. The name of the image appears at the end of the screen tip in parentheses.

You can also download the 2007 Icons Gallery from the Microsoft Web site. The Icons Gallery is an Excel workbook. When you open the workbook, galleries containing built-in images appear on the Developer tab. When you position your mouse pointer over an image or click an image, the name of the image appears. You can specify the size of the image by using the `size` attribute. Set the `size` attribute to `large` to display a large button. Set the `size` attribute to `normal` to display a normal size button.

Add a CustomUI.xml File to a Workbook

To integrate the procedures that you create with VBA into the Excel Ribbon, you can use a customUI.xml file to place buttons on the Ribbon that execute your macros when the user clicks them. You place the customUI.xml file in your workbook file, and then create a relationship between the workbook and the customUI.xml file. See the section "Create a CustomUI.xml File" to learn more about creating a customization file.

You can open an Excel workbook file by changing the filename extension to .zip and then double-clicking the file. When the file opens, you will see several files and folders. You refer to this Zip file as a package, and the files in the Zip file as parts. To modify the Ribbon, you place your customUI.xml file in a folder named customUI and then place the folder and file in the package.

Relationships define how the parts of a document come together to form the document. To modify the Ribbon,

you must create a relationship between the workbook and the customization file by adding a relationship to the RELS file under _rels in the root directory. You create the relationship by placing the following code between the last `Relationship` tag and the `Relationships` tag.

```
<Relationship Id="AnyIDYouWant" Type="http://
  schemas.microsoft.com/office/2006/
  relationships/ui/extensibility"
  Target="CustomUI/customUI.xml"/>
```

If you are going to execute a procedure by using a Ribbon button, you can use the `onAction` attribute. Assign the `onAction` attribute the name of the procedure you want to execute. Place the procedure in a module and place `(ByVal control As IRibbonControl)` after the procedure name and between the parentheses, as follows:

```
Sub SubName (ByVal control As _
IRibbonControl)
```

Add a CustomUI.xml File to a Workbook

① Create a folder on your desktop and name it customUI.

② Place your customUI.xml file in the folder.

Note: See the section "Create a CustomUI.xml File" to learn how to create a customUI file.

③ Open the file that will contain the macros you want to execute.

④ In the Project Explorer, double-click `ThisWorkbook`.

The workbook module opens.

⑤ Name your `Sub` procedures and type `ByVal control As IRibbonControl` in parentheses.

⑥ Type your `Sub` procedures.

⑦ Save and close your file.

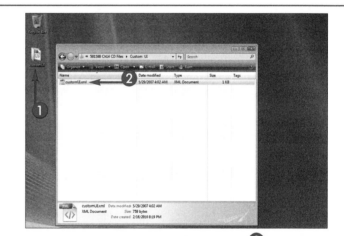

8. Locate your file in Windows Explorer.

9. Change the extension on the filename to .zip.

10. Double-click the file to open it.

11. Drag the customUI folder from the desktop to the Zip file.

12. Drag the _rels folder from the Zip file to the desktop.

13. Double-click the _rels folder to open it.

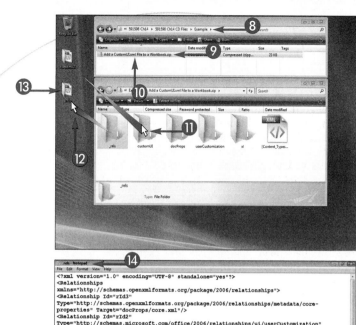

The RELS file appears.

14. Open the RELS file in Notepad or another text editor.

15. Create a relationship.

16. Save and close the file.

17. Delete the RELS file in the Zip file and replace it with the new RELS file.

18. Rename the Zip file back to its original name.

A new tab appears in the file.

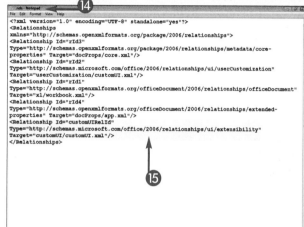

Extra

The process outlined in the steps modifies the Ribbon for an individual workbook. If you want to modify the Ribbon for multiple workbooks using VBA, you can use an add-in. You create an add-in by saving a workbook in add-in format. Add-ins enable you to integrate additional functionality into Microsoft Excel. You can create an add-in and distribute it to others. See Chapter 18 to learn more about add-ins.

If you are planning to convert a workbook with a modified Ribbon to an add-in, do not place your code in ThisWorkbook. Place you code in standard modules.

The examples in this book introduce modifying the Ribbon with XML. For complete coverage of the topic, refer to a book dedicated to the topic. There are many more things that you can do in addition to what is presented here.

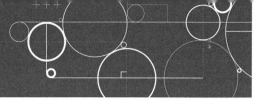

Add Additional Options to the Ribbon

You can create a customUI.xml file, use that file to create a new Ribbon tab, add buttons to the tab, and use the buttons to execute your procedures. You can also add control markups to your customUI.xml file that will create launchers, drop-down lists, toggle buttons, check boxes, and more.

When creating your Ribbon modification, you use callbacks to run procedures based on the information returned when the user interacts with a control. For example, check boxes return a Boolean value of either True or False when you use the onAction callback. Your procedure can perform one action if the value returned is True, and another action if the value returned is False.

Excel uses dialog boxes to enable users to access advanced features. The user is able to open the dialog

box by clicking a launcher located in the lower right corner of the group. You can create launchers to open the dialog boxes you create for your custom applications. Dialog boxes are useful when you want to obtain information from the user. Use the dialogBoxLauncher element to create a launcher. Each group can have one launcher. The launcher element must be the last element in the group and must contain a button attribute. You can use the onAction callback to tell VBA what procedure to execute when the user clicks the launcher.

Use the dropDown element to present the user with a list of options. When you present the user with a list, the procedure that executes depends on the option the user selects. You typically use conditional statements with a drop-down list.

Add Additional Options to the Ribbon

Add a Launcher

1. Add a launcher.

   This example adds additional code to the file started in "Create a CustomUI.xml File."

   ● The dialogBoxLauncher tag.

   ● The required button tag.

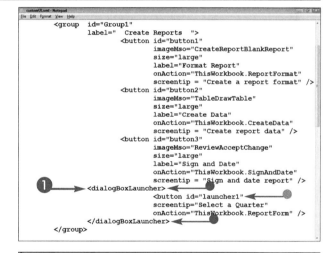

2. Open the VBE.

3. Add the code that will execute to ThisWorkbook.

   ● Opens an input box.

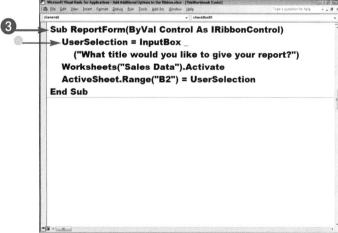

Add a Drop-down List

1 Add a tag to end the previous group.

2 Add tags for the new group.

○ This label will appear at bottom of the group.

3 Create your drop-down list tags.

● List of options.

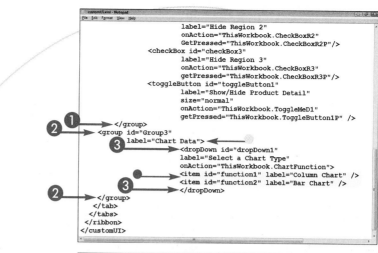

4 Open the VBE.

5 Add the code that will execute to `ThisWorkbook`.

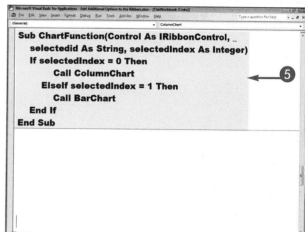

Chapter 14: Creating Dialog Boxes and Customizing the Ribbon

Extra

Prior to Office 2007, developers used command bars to modify the user interface. In most cases, this code works in Office 2007 and higher without any modification. The changes appear on the Add-ins tab. If the developer added an item to a menu in Office 2003, then Office 2007 and higher creates a Menu Commands group and places the information there. If the information was assigned to a toolbar, then Office 2007 and higher places the information in a Toolbar Commands group.

When the user checks a check box, the Boolean value `True` is returned to the variable `pressed`; when the user unchecks the check box, the Boolean value `False` is returned to the variable `pressed`. You can use a check box to set a property to `True` or `False`. For example, you can use a check box to set the `Hidden` property for a worksheet column. If the `Hidden` property is `False`, the column is visible. If the `Hidden` property is set to `True`, the column is not visible.

Example:
```
Sub PressCheckBox(control As IRibbonControl,
    pressed as Boolean)
    Columns(2).Hidden = pressed
End Sub
```

You can use the `toggleButton` element to add a toggle button to the Ribbon. Toggle buttons are useful when you want to enable the user to turn an option on and off with a single mouse click. For example, if your worksheet has detail and summary data, you can use a toggle button to hide the detail data so that you can focus on the summary data. Use an `onAction` callback to specify the procedure to execute. Use the label attribute to label the button. In Excel, enter VBA code similar to the following:

```
Sub ToggleMeD1(Control As IRibbonControl, _
    pressed As Boolean)
    Dim RowNum As Integer
    Dim Counter As Integer
    RowNum = 4
    For Counter = RowNum To 7
```

```
        Rows(Counter).Hidden = pressed
    Next
End Sub
```

When used with a toggle button, the `onAction` callback returns `True` when a toggle button is pressed, and `False` when it is not. The value is returned to the variable `pressed`. The code hides the detail when the button is in a pressed state, and unhides the detail when the button is in an unpressed state. Toggle buttons are always in one of two states, pressed or unpressed. In Excel, bold is an example of a toggle button.

You can use the `checkBox` element to add check boxes. For example, if your data consists of three columns with data for Region 1, Region 2, and Region 3, then you can create a check box that hides and unhides the information for each of the regions.

Add Additional Options to the Ribbon *(continued)*

View Changes to the Ribbon

① Click the launcher to open a dialog box.

The dialog box appears.

● Notice that there are multiple groups.

● Notice the custom tab.

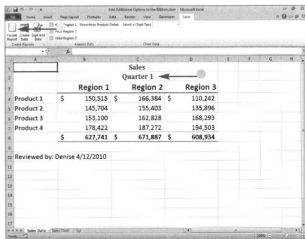

● The dialog box adds a title to your worksheet when the user clicks OK.

● Click this button to add a format to your worksheet.

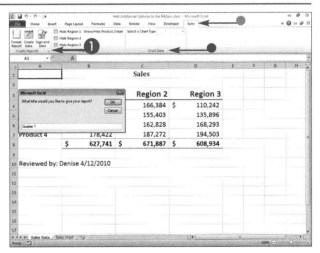

③ Click the drop-down list to see a list of options.

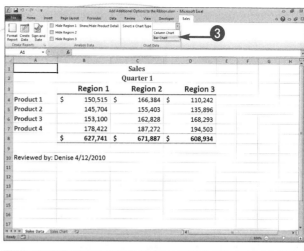

The Bar Chart option displays a bar chart.

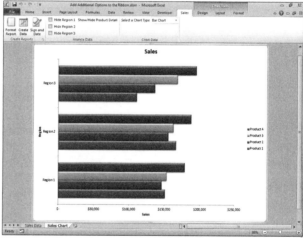

Extra

The following XML script creates a toggle button:

Example:
```
<toggleButton id="toggleButton1"
   label="Show/Hide Product Detail"
   size="normal"
   onAction="ToggleMeD1"/>
```

The following XML script creates a check box:

Example:
```
<checkBox id="checkBox1"
   label="Hide Region 1"
   onAction="CheckBoxR1"/>
```

Create a
Chart Sheet

You can use VBA to create a chart. When you create a chart, VBA creates a new Chart object. You can then set the properties such as the title, name, font, type, and style.

You can create a new chart sheet or embed a chart in a worksheet. When you create a new chart sheet, you use the Chart object directly. When you create an embedded chart, you use a ChartObjects object. See the section "Embed a Chart in a Worksheet" for more information on creating embedded charts.

To create a new chart sheet, use the Add method with the Charts object. After you create the chart, you can use a With statement to set chart properties such as chart type, the name you want to place on the chart's tab, the title of

the chart, and the chart style. You select a chart type by assigning an XlChartType constant value to the ChartType property. You use the Name property to assign a name to the chart tab. If you want to place a title on the chart, set the HasTitle property to True and then use the ChartTitle property to assign the title. If you want to apply a style, assign a style number to the ChartStyle property. Every style in the Excel style gallery has a number. Position your mouse pointer over the style to find out what the number is.

Use the SetSourceData method to tell VBA where the data is located. The SetSourceData method has two parameters: Source and PlotBy.

Create a Chart Sheet

① Create a Chart object variable.

② Set the Chart object variable.

● Use the Add method to add the new chart.

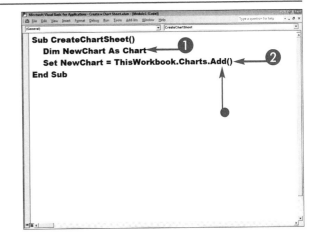

③ Create a With statement.

④ Use the ChartType property to specify a chart type.

⑤ Name the chart sheet tab.

⑥ Set HasTitle to True and then assign a title to the chart.

⑦ Assign a chart style.

⑧ Specify your data source.

● The worksheet tab name.

⑨ Press Alt+F11 to switch from the VBE to Excel, and run your macro.

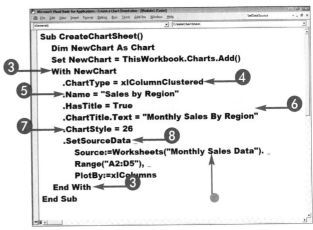

- Your source data.
- The worksheet tab name.

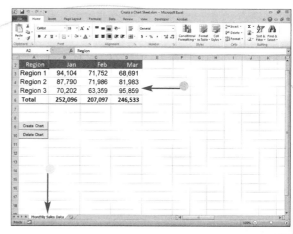

The macro creates a chart.

- The tab name.
- The title.

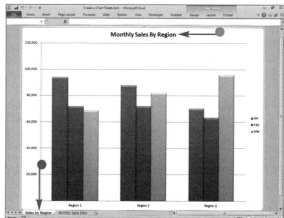

Apply It

When creating a chart, you should specify the chart's data source. Use the `SetSourceData` method. The following is the syntax:

Example:
```
NewChart.SetSourceData(Source, PlotBy)
```

Use the `Source` parameter to specify the actual data range your chart will use. The `Source` parameter can reference any valid data range. See Chapter 11 for more information on defining a range of values. When working with a chart sheet, you must indicate the name of the worksheet containing the data as part of the range reference. For example, the following code references the range of cells contained in Sheet1 in the same workbook.

Example:
```
NewChart.SetSourceData Source:=Worksheets("Sheet1").Range("A1:B15")
```

With the `SetSourceData` method, you can use the `PlotBy` parameter to tell VBA how to plot the data in the specified range. You assign `PlotBy` one of the `XlRowCol` constant values.

Embed a Chart in a Worksheet

You can use VBA to embed a chart in a worksheet. When you embed a chart, Excel creates a new Chart object. You can then set the properties such as the title, name, font, type, and style.

When you embed a chart in a worksheet, the corresponding Chart object that Excel creates becomes a part of the Worksheet object. Because you can embed multiple charts in one worksheet, the Worksheet object contains a ChartObjects collection object that contains all Chart objects on the worksheet. When you add or remove embedded charts, you must use the ChartObjects collection object.

To add a chart to a worksheet, use the Add method with the ChartObjects object. The Add method has four

parameters you can use to set the location and size of the chart in points: Left, Top, Width, and Height. Use the Left parameter to specify the location of the chart in relation to the left edge of column A. Use the Top parameter to specify the location of the chart in relation to the top edge of row 1. Use the Width and Height parameters to specify the initial width and the height of the Chart object.

You specify the type of chart that Excel creates by using the ChartType property with one of the XlChartType constant values. For example, to create a line chart, you use the constant xlLine. See the appendix for a list of the XlChartType constants.

Embed a Chart in a Worksheet

① Create a Chart object variable.

② Set the Chart object variable to the new chart.

● The name of the worksheet in which you want to place the chart.

● Sets the chart position and size.

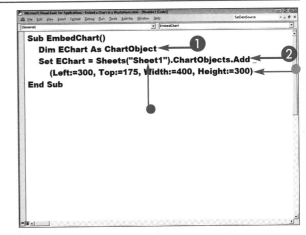

③ Create a With statement.

④ Use the ChartType property to specify a chart type.

⑤ Set HasTitle to True and then assign a title to the chart.

⑥ Assign a chart style.

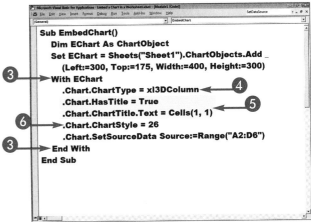

7 Specify your data source.

8 Press Alt+F11 to switch from the VBE to Excel, and run your macro.

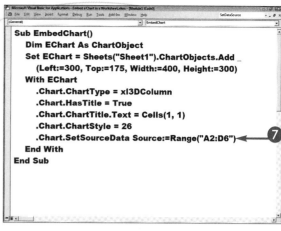

```
Sub EmbedChart()
    Dim EChart As ChartObject
    Set EChart = Sheets("Sheet1").ChartObjects.Add _
        (Left:=300, Top:=175, Width:=400, Height:=300)
    With EChart
        .Chart.ChartType = xl3DColumn
        .Chart.HasTitle = True
        .Chart.ChartTitle.Text = Cells(1, 1)
        .Chart.ChartStyle = 26
        .Chart.SetSourceData Source:=Range("A2:D6")    ← 7
    End With
End Sub
```

The macro creates your chart.

◉ Your source data.

◉ The tab name.

● The title.

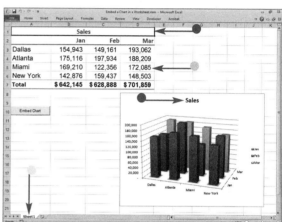

Extra

The only real difference between embedded charts and chart sheets is that the Chart object for an embedded chart is part of the ChartObjects collection for the worksheet, whereas the Chart object for a chart sheet is part of the Workbook object. If you compare the code that creates an embedded chart to the code that adds a chart sheet, you will notice that with an embedded chart, specifying chart methods and properties requires reference to the Chart object. This is because when you create a new chart sheet, you create a new Chart object, but when you create an embedded chart, you add a Chart object to the ChartObjects collection for the worksheet; therefore, the Chart object becomes a child of the ChartObjects collection object. To set the chart type of an embedded chart, you can use the following code:

Example:
```
Worksheets("Sheet1").ChartObject(1).Chart.ChartType = xlColumnStacked
```

This code sets the chart type of the first Chart object in the worksheet named Sheet1 to a stacked column chart. If you compare this code to the code required for changing the chart type of a chart sheet, you can see the similarities.

Example:
```
Sheets("Chart1").ChartType = xlColumnStacked
```

Apply Chart Wizard Settings to a Chart

When writing VBA code, you can use the ChartWizard method to format or reformat a chart quickly. The method has 11 optional parameters that enable you to set chart properties. The following is the syntax:

`expression.ChartWizard(Source, Gallery, Format, PlotBy, CategoryLabels, SeriesLabels, HasLegend, Title, CategoryTitle, ValueTitle, ExtraTitle)`

Use the Source parameter to specify or modify the chart's data source. When you are working with a chart sheet, you must specify the name of the worksheet that contains the data source. Use the Gallery parameter to specify the chart type. Assign one of the XlChartType constant values to indicate the desired chart type. See the appendix for a list of XlChartType constants.

Specify a value of 1 to 10 for the Format parameter. The Format parameter applies one of VBA's built-in formats. The format that it uses depends on the chart type you select. The PlotBy parameter tells VBA whether the data series is in rows or columns. Assign the PlotBy parameter xlRows if the data series is in rows. Assign it xlColumns if the data series is in columns.

Assign an integer value to the CategoryLabels and SeriesLabels parameters to indicate the number of rows or columns in the category or series that have labels. Assign the HasLegend parameter the value True if you want your chart to have a legend.

Use the Title parameter to assign a title to your chart, the CategoryTitle parameter to assign a title to the axis that displays categories, and the ValueTitle parameter to assign a title to the axis that displays values. For a 3-D chart, use the ExtraTitle parameter to assign a title to your depth axis. You must set any additional properties individually.

Apply Chart Wizard Settings to a Chart

1 Create a Chart object variable.

2 Set the Chart object variable to the chart you want to modify.

● The name of the chart sheet.

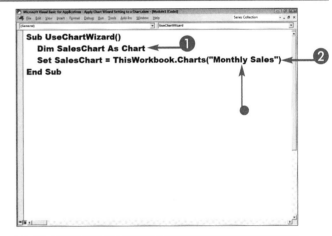

3 Create your ChartWizard command.

4 Set your parameters.

5 Press Alt+F11 to switch from the VBE to Excel, and run the macro.

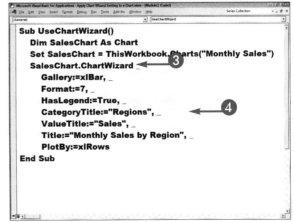

Your chart before
you apply the macro.

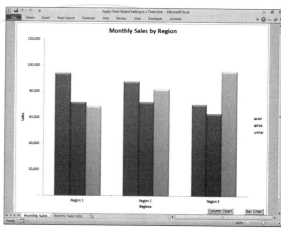

Your chart after you
apply the macro.

Your macro changes
the format of your
chart.

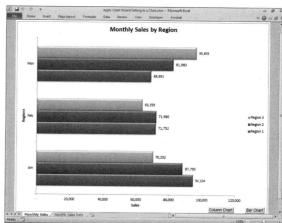

When working in Excel, once you have your chart designed exactly the way you want it, you can save your design as a template. You can also use VBA to save your design as a template.

Example:
```
Sub CreateTemplate()
   Dim SalesChart as Chart
   Set SalesChart = ThisWorkbook.Charts("Monthly Sales")
   SalesChart. _
      SaveChartTemplate("Sales Chart Template")
End Sub
```

To apply your template to an existing chart, in Excel, click your chart. The Chart tools become available. Click the Design tab. Click Change Chart Type in the Type group. The Change Chart Type dialog box appears. Click Templates, click your template, and then click OK. Excel applies your template to your chart.

Add a New Data Series to a Chart

A data series is a group of data values that Excel displays in your chart. Each data series appears as a legend item. After you create a chart, you can redefine the range of data Excel uses to display values in your chart by adding a new data series. For example, if you have a bar chart showing the sales in Regions 1, 2, and 3 for January, February, and March, you can add another data series that contains the sales data for April.

The SeriesCollection collection object contains all of the data series that Excel plots on a specific chart, with each data series representing a Series object. To define a new data series, create a new Series object and add it to the SeriesCollection collection object by using the Add method.

When used with the SeriesCollection object, the Add method has five parameters: Source, Rowcol, SeriesLabels, CategoryLabels, and Replace. Use the Source parameter to specify the data series you want to add to the chart. Use the Rowcol parameter to tell VBA whether the new series is in a row or a column. Use xlRows if the data series is in a row, or use xlColumns if the data series is in a column.

Set the SeriesLabels to True if the first row or column of the data series contains a label. Set the CategoryLabels to True if the first row or column of the data series contains a category label. If you specify a value of True for the CategoryLabels parameter and for the Replace parameter, VBA replaces the current category labels with the labels from the new range.

Add a New Data Series to a Chart

① Create your
SeriesCollection
Add statement.

● The worksheet name.

● Identifies the chart.

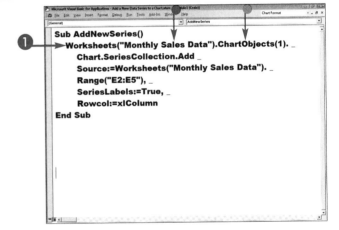

● The data series you want
to add.

● Tells VBA that the series
has labels.

● Tells VBA the data is
organized in columns.

② Press Alt+F11 to switch
from the VBE to Excel,
and run the macro.

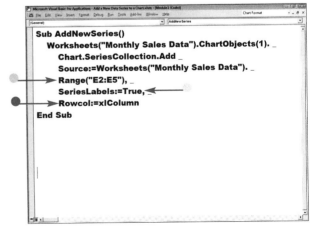

Your chart before
you apply the macro.

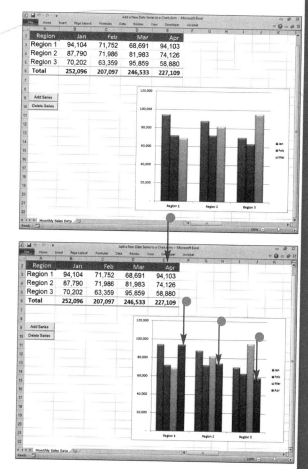

Your chart after you
apply the macro.

● The macro adds a
new data series.

Extra

Each chart embedded in a worksheet is a member of the worksheet's `ChartObjects` collection. Each chart in the worksheet's `ChartObjects` collection has an index number. The first chart is `ChartObjects(1)`, the second chart is `ChartObjects(2)`, and so on. You can refer to a chart by its index number. You can also refer to a chart by its name. To find a chart's name, in Excel, click your chart. The Chart tools appear. Click the Layout tab. The chart name appears in the Properties group.

Each chart sheet in a workbook is part of the `Charts` collection. Each member of the `Charts` collection has an index number. The leftmost chart is `Chart(1)`, the next chart is `Chart(2)`, and so on. You can refer to `Chart` objects by their index number.

You can remove a series from a chart by using the `Delete` method. The following code removes the series that was added in the example.

Example:
```
Worksheets("Monthly Sales Data")._
    ChartObjects(1)._
    Chart.SeriesCollection("Apr") _
    .Delete
```

Format Chart Text

As with all text elements in a workbook, you can format the text that appears in your chart by changing the `Font` properties. When Excel adds text to a chart, such as a chart title, axis label, or even data label, it applies default formatting. You can reformat the text by using the `Font` object properties. By setting the `Font` properties, you can make your chart easier to read.

The chart area encompasses everything in your chart. By applying `Font` object properties to the `ChartArea` object, you can set the font attributes for all of the text in the chart. For example, if you want to change the font color for the entire chart, you apply the `Font` object `Color` property to the `ChartArea` object.

Excel also enables you to format individual elements of text that appear in your chart. For example, if you use the `Font` object properties with the `ChartTitle` object, you can modify the chart title. To change how Excel displays legend text, use the `Font` object properties with the `Legend` object.

You can use the `ChartArea` object to set the font settings for the entire chart and then use the individual objects to customize various portions of the chart. You can set the properties for any of the following objects by using the `Font` object: `ChartTitle`, `DataTable`, `Legend`, `Characters`, `AxisTitle`, `DataLabel`, and `TickLabels`. See the Chapter 11 section "Using the Cells Property" to see a partial list of the `Font` properties you can set.

Format Chart Text

① Create a `Chart` object variable.

② Set the `Chart` object variable to the chart you want to format.

● The name of the chart sheet tab.

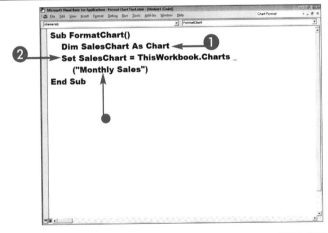

③ Format the text in the chart area.

④ Format the chart title.

⑤ Press Alt+F11 to switch from the VBE to Excel, and run the macro.

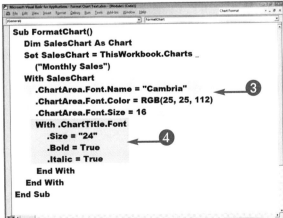

The chart without formatting.

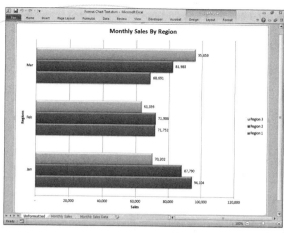

The macro formats the data.

The chart with formatting.

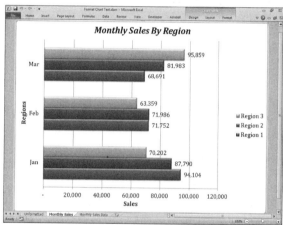

Apply It

You may not want to apply the same font settings to an entire Chart object. For example, you may want to underline the first character in the chart title. With the ChartTitle, AxisTitle, and DataLabel objects, you can use the Characters object to specify the character within the text string where formatting should start, as well as the number of characters to format. For example, to underline the first two characters in a chart title, type code similar to that shown in the example. The Characters object has two parameters: Start and Length. Use the Start parameter to indicate the character in the text string at which VBA should begin applying the format. Use the Length parameter to indicate the number of characters to which VBA should apply the format.

TYPE THIS:

```
ThisWorkbook.Charts(1).ChartTitle.
  Characters(1,2).Font.Underline = True
```

RESULT:

Excel underlines the first and second characters in the chart title, but all remaining characters maintain their original font settings.

Create Charts with Multiple Chart Types

I f you show more than one type of data in your chart, you may want to create a chart that uses a different chart type for each data series. For example, if your chart displays the population of various cities and the average income in those cities, you may want to create a column chart to display population, and a line chart to display average income. A chart that uses more than one chart type is called a *combination chart*.

To set the chart type for a data series, you use the Series Collection collection object. The SeriesCollection collection object contains each of the data series in the range of data shown in your chart as an individual SeriesCollection object. You reference an individual object by using an index value. VBA numbers each data series. The first data series is SeriesCollection(1), the second is SeriesCollection(2), and so on.

To set the chart type for a data series, you set the ChartType property for the SeriesCollection object. When you initially create your chart, you can set the chart type for each individual data series, or you can set the chart type for the entire chart, and then modify the ChartType property for the individual data series you want to change. You assign the ChartType property, an XlChartType constant value that represents the chart type you want to use for the data series. See the appendix for a list of the XlChartType constant values that you can assign to the ChartType property.

Create Charts with Multiple Chart Types

① Create a Chart object variable.

② Set the Chart object variable.

● Use the Add method to add a new chart.

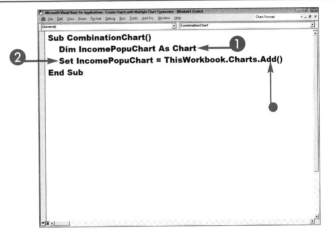

③ Set your data source.

④ Assign a chart type to your chart.

⑤ Assign a chart style to your chart.

⑥ Tell VBA whether your data is in columns or rows.

⑦ Assign a new chart type to a data series.

In this example, you assign a new chart type to SeriesCollection(1).

⑧ Format your chart.

⑨ Press Alt+F11 to switch from the VBE to Excel, and run the macro.

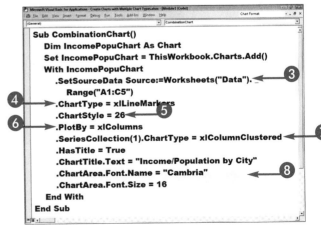

Your data source.

● Series 1.

● Series 2.

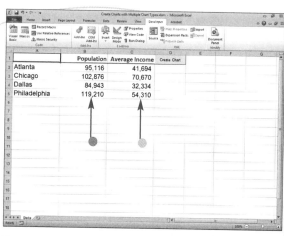

The macro creates a combination chart.

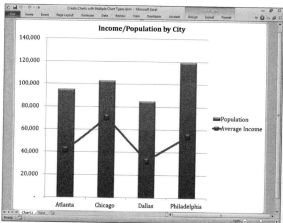

Extra

You can use a different chart type for each data series. Excel keeps track of the data series chart types, and groups the common types together as ChartGroup objects. Each ChartGroup object contains one or more data series with the same chart type. Excel stores all ChartGroup objects within the ChartGroups collection object, which you can access through the ChartGroup property.

The ChartGroups object provides methods for returning the collection of the ChartGroup objects that correspond to a particular type. For example, if you want to access the line chart type ChartGroup objects, you can use the LineGroups method. The example that follows illustrates how to count the number of column chart types in a chart.

Example:
```
DataSeriesCount = ThisWorkbook.Charts(1).ColumnGroups.Count
```

METHOD	DESCRIPTION
AreaGroups	Determines the number of series with an area data type
BarGroups	Determines the number of series with a bar chart data type
ColumnGroups	Determines the number of series with a column chart data type
DoughnutGroups	Determines the number of series with a doughnut chart data type
LineGroups	Determines the number of series with a line chart data type
PieGroups	Determines the number of series with a pie chart data type

Add a Data Table to a Chart

A data table displays the values in your chart. You can add data tables to any chart you create. VBA stores the data table associated with a chart in the `DataTable` object.

Use the `HasDataTable` property to tell VBA whether you want to include a data table in your chart. This property accepts the Boolean values `True` and `False`. If you want to display a data table, set this property to `True`. Conversely, if you do not want to display a data table, set this property to `False`.

After you set the `HasDataTable` property, you can format your data table by using the methods and properties associated with the `DataTable` object. You specify the font by using the `Font` properties. For example, `DataTable.Font.Name = "Arial"` tells VBA to use an

Arial font in the data table. See the section "Format Chart Text" for more information on working with the `Font` object in a chart.

You can choose to display or not display borders in and around your data table by using the `HasBorderHorizontal`, `HasBorderOutline`, and `HasBorderVertical` properties. By default, Excel displays all borders on a data table. If you do not want to display one or more of these borders, set their value to `False`. For example, the following code removes the horizontal border from a data table: `DataTable.HasBorderHorizontal = False`.

A legend key tells the user what each data series represents. You can use the `ShowLegendKey` property to tell VBA whether you want to show a legend key in your data table.

Add a Data Table to a Chart

① Create a `Chart` object variable.

② Set the `Chart` object variable to the chart to which you want to add a data table.

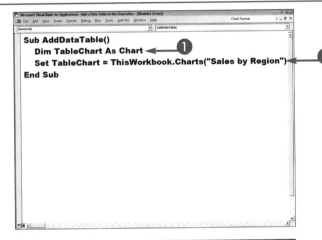

③ Create a `With` statement.

④ Set the `HasDataTable` property to `True`.

⑤ Assign a font to your data table.

⑥ Assign a border color.

⑦ Set the `ShowLegendKey` property for the data table to `True`.

This code shows a legend in the data table.

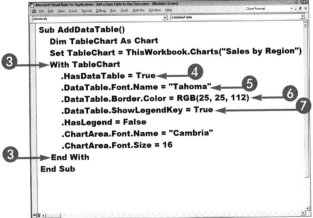

8 Set the `HasLegend` property for the chart to `False`.

This code suppresses the chart legend.

9 Set the chart area properties.

10 Press Alt+F11 to switch from the VBE to Excel, and run the macro.

The macro creates a chart with a data table.

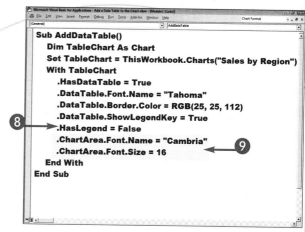

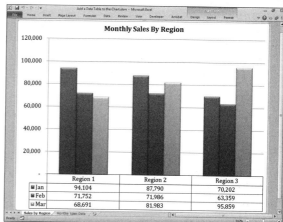

Extra

When you add a data table to a chart, you can include the chart legend with the data table. To create a data table that contains a chart legend, set the `ShowLegendKey` property to `True` for the `DataTable` object. The following example sets the value of the `ShowLegendKey` property.

Example:
```
ThisWorkbook.Charts(1).DataTable.ShowLegendKey = True
```

If you display the legend as part of your data table, you typically do not want the legend to appear separately on your chart. To hide the chart legend, set the `HasLegend` property for the `Chart` object to `False`.

Example:
```
ThisWorkbook.Charts(1).HasLegend = False
```

Create a PivotTable

PivotTables help you answer questions about your data. A PivotTable shows how data is distributed across categories. For example, you can use a PivotTable to see how different products sell by region or by quarter. You base PivotTables on lists. You can use a worksheet list or you can connect to a list from another data source, such as Access.

A `PivotCache` object represents the memory cache for a PivotTable report. You must create a `PivotCache` object for your PivotTable. Use the `PivotCaches.Create` method. The `PivotCaches.Create` method has three parameters: `SourceType`, `SourceData`, and `Version`. Use an `XlPivotTableSourceType` to specify the `SourceType`. Use `xlconsolidation` if the source is a consolidation, use `xlDatabase` if the source is a list in your workbook, or use `xlExternal` if the source is another application. The `SourceType` parameter is required.

Use the `SourceData` parameter to specify the location of the data. If your `SourceType` is `xlconsolidation` or `xlDatabase`, the `SourceData` can be a `Range` object and is required. If your `SourceType` is `xlExternal`, the `SourceData` can be an Excel Workbook Connection object. Use the optional `Version` parameter to specify the version of Excel by using an `XlPivotTableVersionList` constant.

Use the `PivotCache.CreatePivotTable` method to create a PivotTable. The `PivotCache.CreatePivotTable` method has four parameters: `TableDestination`, `TableName`, `ReadData`, and `DefaultVersion`. Use the `Table Destination` parameter to specify a cell that represents the upper left corner of the range where you want to place the PivotTable. Use the `TableName` parameter to name the PivotTable. Use the `ReadData` parameter to specify whether records from an external database are held in cache. Use the optional `DestinationVersion` parameter to specify the version of Excel by using an `XlPivotTableVersionList` constant.

Create a PivotTable

1. Declare your variables.

2. Store the location of the data to a `Range` object.

3. Add the worksheet on which you want to place the PivotTable.

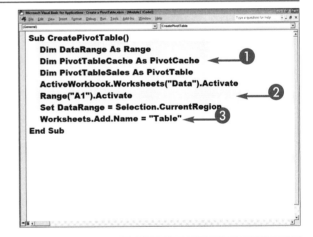

4. Create a PivotTable cache.

● The `SourceType`.

● Where the data is located.

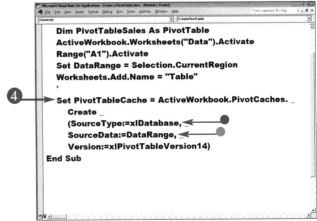

5 Create a PivotTable.

- Where you want to place the PivotTable.

- The name you want to give the PivotTable.

6 Press Alt+F11 to switch from the VBE to Excel, and run the macro.

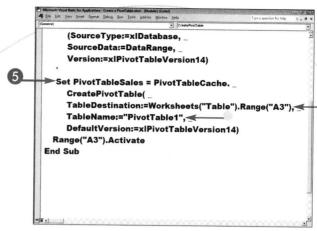

```
      (SourceType:=xlDatabase, _
      SourceData:=DataRange, _
      Version:=xlPivotTableVersion14)

Set PivotTableSales = PivotTableCache. _
      CreatePivotTable( _
      TableDestination:=Worksheets("Table").Range("A3"),
      TableName:="PivotTable1", _
      DefaultVersion:=xlPivotTableVersion14)
  Range("A3").Activate
End Sub
```

The macro creates a PivotTable.

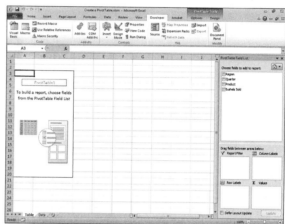

Extra

You can set the `CreatePivotTable` `ReadData` parameter to `True` to create a `PivotTable` cache that holds all of the records from an external database. This, however, can create a large cache. If you set the `ReadData` parameter to `False`, you can set some of the fields to server-based fields.

To construct a PivotTable manually, you choose the fields you want to include in your report and then drag the fields from the PivotTable Field List into the Report Filter, Column Labels, Row Labels, and Σ Values boxes. You can click and drag more than one field into an area.

You can also use the `PivotTables.Add` method to create a PivotTable.

Example:
```
ActiveSheet.PivotTables.Add _
   PivotCache:=PivotTableCache, _
   TableDestination:=Worksheets("Table"). _
      Range("A3"), _
   TableName:="PTSales"
```

Add Fields to a PivotTable

When you manually create a PivotTable, you choose the fields you want to include in your report from the Choose Fields to Add list box and then you drag the fields into the Report Filter, Column Labels, Row Labels, and Σ Values boxes to create report filters, columns, rows, and data fields.

When using VBA, you can create report filters, columns, rows and data fields by using the `PivotFields` object with the `Orientation` property. Use an `XlPivotFieldOrientation` constant to make the assignments. Use `xlColumnField` to add a column label, `xlRowField` to add a row label, `xlPageField` to add a report filter, and `xlDataField` to add a data field. You can refer to each field by using the field name or by using an index value. The first field in the Choose Fields to Add

to Report box has an index value of 1, the next field has an index value of 2, and so on. The following examples are equivalent and use a field name and an index value respectively:

```
With PivotTableSales.PivotFields(2)
    .Orientation = xlColumnField
End With

With PivotTableSales.PivotFields("Quarter")
    .Orientation = xlColumnField
End With
```

When creating a data field, you can use the `Function` property to specify the `XlConsolidationFunction` the field should use. For example, you can specify `xlSum` to sum values.

Add Fields to a PivotTable

① Declare a `PivotTable` object variable.

② Assign a PivotTable to the object variable.

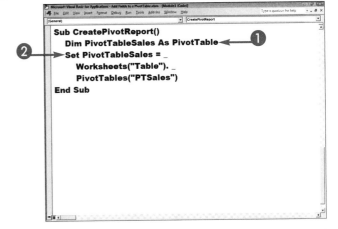

③ Create a column.

④ Create a row.

⑤ Create a filter.

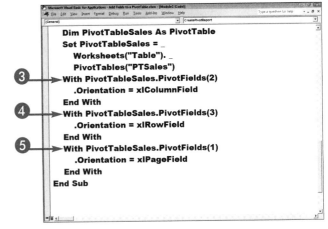

6 Create a data field.

7 Press Alt+F11 to switch from the VBE to Excel, and run the macro.

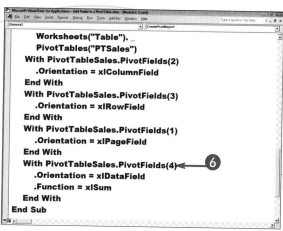

The macro creates a PivotTable report.

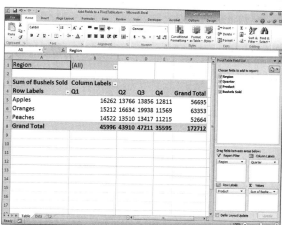

Extra

You can use an `XlConsolidationFunction` to tell Excel which calculation to perform on data fields. The following is a list of `XlConsolidationFunctions`.

CONSTANT	VALUE	DESCRIPTION
xlAverage	–4106	Calculate the average.
xlCount	–4112	Count.
xlCountNums	–4113	Count numerical values.
xlMax	–4136	Display the highest value.
xlMin	–4139	Display the lowest value.
xlProduct	–4149	Multiply.
xlStDev	–4155	Calculate the standard deviation based on a sample.
xlStDevP	–4156	Calculate the standard deviation, based on the whole population.
xlSum	–4157	Calculate the sum.
xlUnknown	1000	No subtotal function specified.
xlVar	–4164	Calculate the variation based on a sample.
xlVarP	–4165	Calculate the variation based on the whole population.

Display Subtotals and Grand Totals

When you create a PivotTable, Excel groups the data for you. Excel groups all items with the same row label together and all items with the same column label together. You can add subtotals to your PivotTable. For example, if you sell apples, oranges, and peaches, in Regions 1, 2, and 3 you can subtotal by product to find the total number of apples, oranges, and peaches sold in each region.

You should structure your data so that Excel groups by product, shows the number of products sold in Region 1, the number of products sold in Region 2, and the number of products sold in Region 3.

Subtotals can be a sum, count, or average, or display some other value. You can use an index value with the `PivotField.Subtotals` property to specify the type of

subtotal you want. See the "Extra" portion of this section for a list of index values.

To add a subtotal to your PivotTable, use the `SubtotalLocation` method. You can place subtotals at the top or the bottom of each group. To place subtotals at the top of each group, assign the `SubtotalLocation` method a constant value of `xlAtTop`. To place subtotals at the bottom of each group, assign a constant value of `xlAtBottom`.

By default, when you create a PivotTable, Excel creates grand totals for both rows and columns. You can create grand totals just for rows, just for columns, or for neither rows nor columns by assigning a Boolean value of either `True` to display a row or column subtotal, or `False` to not display a column or row subtotal, to the `RowGrand` and `ColumnGrand` properties.

Display Subtotals and Grand Totals

① Declare a `PivotTable` object variable.

② Assign a PivotTable to the object variable.

③ Specify the Subtotal location.

④ Do not display a column grand total.

⑤ Display a row grand total.

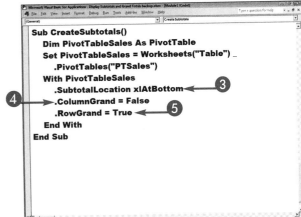

276

6 Create Subtotals.

● Sum.

● Highest value.

7 Press Alt+F11 to switch from the VBE to Excel, and run the macro.

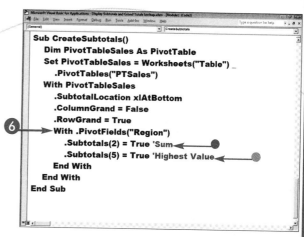

The macro displays subtotals and grand totals.

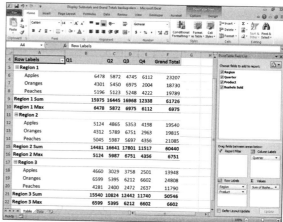

Extra

INDEX VALUE	CALCULATED VALUE
1	Automatic
2	Sum
3	Count
4	Average
5	Highest value
6	Lowest value
7	Product
8	Count Numbers
9	StdDev
10	StdDevp
11	Var
12	Varp

In the example, there are two Row Labels: Region and Product. In VBA, when you create more than one label for a column, row, data, or filter field, you can specify the order in which they appear by using the `PivotFields.Position` property. Assign a value of 1 for the first position, 2 for the second position, and so on.

Example:
```
With PivotTableSales
    .PivotFields("Region").Position = 1
    .PivotFields("Product").Position = 2
End With
```

Filter a PivotTable

You can filter your PivotTable data. Filtering enables you to view only the data relevant to you. For example, if your data consists of Quarters 1 through 4 and you want to focus on Quarter 1, you can filter your PivotTable so only Quarter 1 data appears.

Each field's column label is a pivot item. In VBA, you can use the `PivotItems.Item` method to filter. You simply set the item's visible property to `False`. To make the item visible again, set the property to `True`. You can identify each item by its label or by an index value. The first column or row is column 1 or row 1, the second is column 2 or row 2, and so on.

Filter a PivotTable

① Declare a `PivotTable` object variable.

② Assign a PivotTable to the object variable.

③ Set the `Visible` property to `False` to filter.

④ Press Alt+F11 to switch from the VBE to Excel, and run the macro.

The macro filters Quarters 2, 3, and 4.

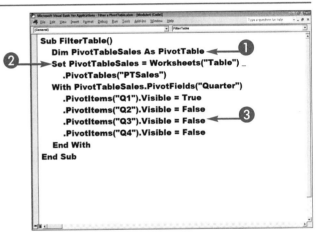

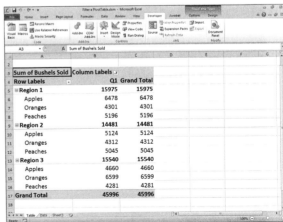

Create Groups

reating groups enables you to compare data. For example, if your PivotTable shows each month as a column, you can group the months so that you can compare quarters. When you group columns or rows, Excel totals the data, creates a field header, and creates a field with an expand/collapse button. If the expand/collapse button displays a plus (+), you can click it to expand the group. If the expand/collapse button displays a minus (–), you can click it to collapse the group.

In VBA, you can use the `Group` method to group. You can use the `Range` property to specify the rows or columns you want to group. For example, if you want to group rows 1 through 3, you can use the syntax `Range("1:3").Group`.

Extra

When you create groups, Excel adds a new column or row label and creates a `PivotItems` collection that contains the groups. You can use the `ShowDetail` property to expand or collapse the groups. You can refer to groups by their index number or their name.

Example:
```
PivotTableSales.PivotFields("Month2")_
    .PivotItems(1)_
    .ShowDetail = True
```

Create Groups

1. Declare a `PivotTable` object variable.

2. Assign a PivotTable to the object variable.

3. Group ranges.

4. Specify whether each group should be expanded or collapsed.

5. Press Alt+F11 to switch from the VBE to Excel, and run the macro.

The macro creates four groups and expands Group 1. It collapses Groups 2, 3, and 4.

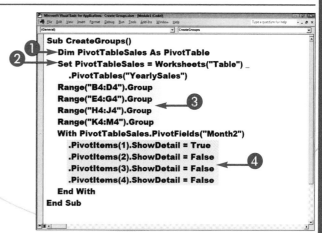

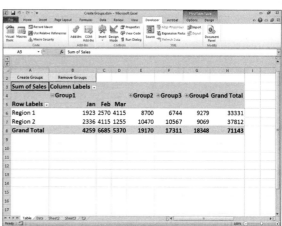

Understanding Excel Events

An *event* occurs in Excel whenever the user performs any type of action. For example, an event occurs when the user closes a workbook. You can use events to trigger the execution of procedures by creating event procedures. Event procedures are exactly what the name describes: procedures that execute when a particular event occurs.

To trap or capture an event with an event procedure, you must place the procedure code in the correct type of module. For example, workbook-related events must be in the `ThisWorkbook` object standard module.

There are several categories of events. Each event category has a set of events associated with it. For example, the `BeforeClose` event is a workbook event that Excel activates when the user chooses to close a workbook, before the workbook closes.

Workbook Events

Excel associates workbook-level events with the workbook in which they reside. You place workbook-level event procedures in the `ThisWorkbook` object module. You create workbook event procedures by naming them `Workbook_event name`. The following table lists the workbook events.

EVENT	WHEN THE EVENT OCCURS
`Activate`	Occurs when Excel activates the workbook, worksheet, chartsheet, or embedded chart sheet.
`AddinInstall`	Occurs when an add-in installs a workbook.
`AddinUninstall`	Occurs when an add-in uninstalls a workbook.
`AfterXmlExportEvent`	Occurs after saves or export of XML data.
`AfterXMLImportEvent`	Occurs after XML data is refreshed or imported.
`BeforeClose`	Occurs before a workbook closes. See the section "Run a Procedure before Closing a Workbook."
`BeforePrint`	Occurs before Excel prints a workbook or a portion of a workbook.
`BeforeSave`	Occurs before Excel saves a workbook. See the section "Run a Procedure before Saving a Workbook."
`BeforeXmlExportEvent`	Occurs before saves or export of XML data.
`BeforeXMLImportEvent`	Occurs before XML data refreshed or imported.
`Deactivate`	Occurs when Excel deactivates a workbook.
`NewSheet`	Occurs when Excel adds a new sheet to a workbook.
`Open`	Occurs when Excel opens a workbook. See the section "Run a Procedure as a Workbook Opens."
`PivotTableCloseConnection`	Occurs after a PivotTable report closes the data source connection.
`PivotTableOpenConnection`	Occurs after a PivotTable report opens the data source connection.
`Rowset Complete`	Occurs when a user drills through a recordset.
`SheetActivate`	Occurs when Excel activates a sheet in the workbook.
`SheetBeforeDoubleClick`	Occurs when a user double-clicks a sheet.
`SheetBeforeRightClick`	Occurs when a user right-clicks.
`SheetCalculate`	Occurs after Excel calculates a sheet.
`SheetChange`	Occurs when cells in a worksheet change.
`SheetDeactivate`	Occurs when Excel deactivates a sheet.
`SheetFollowHyperlink`	Occurs when a user clicks a hyperlink on a sheet.

Workbook Events *(continued)*

EVENT	WHEN THE EVENT OCCURS
SheetPivotTableUpdate	Occurs after Excel updates a sheet of a PivotTable report.
SheetSelectionChange	Occurs when a selection changes in a worksheet.
Sync	Occurs when a local copy of a worksheet is synchronized with a copy on the server.
WindowActivate	Occurs when Excel activates a workbook window.
WindowDeactivate	Occurs when Excel deactivates a workbook window.
WindowResize	Occurs when Excel resizes a workbook window.

Worksheet Events

Excel associates worksheet-level events with the selected worksheet. Event-handling procedures related to a worksheet should be in the standard module for the worksheet object. The following table lists the worksheet events.

EVENT	WHEN THE EVENT OCCURS
Activate	Occurs when Excel activates the worksheet.
BeforeDoubleClick	Occurs when the user double-clicks the worksheet.
BeforeRightClick	Occurs when the user right-clicks the worksheet.
Calculate	Occurs after Excel calculates the worksheet.
Change	Occurs when a user or external link modifies cells on the worksheet.
Deactivate	Occurs when Excel deactivates the worksheet.
FollowHyperlink	Occurs when a user clicks a hyperlink on the worksheet.
PivotTableUpdate	Occurs after a PivotTable report is updated on the worksheet.
SelectionChange	Occurs when a selection changes on the worksheet.

Chart Events

Excel associates chart-level events with the currently selected chart sheet. Event-handling procedures related to a chart should be in the standard module for the chart object. The following table lists the chart events for which you can create event-handling procedures.

EVENT	WHEN THE EVENT OCCURS
Activate	Occurs when Excel activates the chart sheet.
BeforeDoubleClick	Occurs when the user double-clicks a chart element.
BeforeRightClick	Occurs when the user right-clicks a chart element.
Calculate	Occurs after Excel plots the chart.
Deactivate	Occurs when Excel deactivates the chart, worksheet, or workbook.
DragOver	Occurs when the user drags a range of cells over a chart.
DragPlot	Occur when the user drags and drops a range of cells onto the chart.
MouseDown	Occurs when the user presses a mouse button while over a chart.
MouseMove	Occurs when the position of the pointer changes over a chart.
MouseUp	Occurs when the user releases the mouse button over the chart.
Resize	Occurs when the user resizes the chart.
Select	Occurs when the user selects a chart element.
SeriesChange	Occurs when the user changes the value of a chart data point.

continued ➡

Control and Dialog Box Events

Excel associates control and dialog box events with a `UserForm` or the controls that exist on a `UserForm`. Event-handling procedures related to a `UserForm` should be in the standard module for the `UserForm` object. The following table lists the `UserForm` events.

EVENT	WHEN THE EVENT OCCURS
Activate	Occurs when Excel activates a UserForm.
AddControl	Occurs when Excel adds a control at runtime to a UserForm.
BeforeDragOver	Occurs when the user performs a drag-and-drop operation.
BeforeDropOrPaste	Occurs when the user is about to paste the data from the drag-and-drop operation.
BeforeUpdate	Occurs before data in a control is changed.
Change	Occurs when the value property changes.
Click	Occurs when the user clicks a UserForm object.
DblClick	Occurs when the user double-clicks a UserForm object.
Deactivate	Occurs when the user deactivates the UserForm.
Error	Occurs when Excel detects a UserForm control error.
KeyDown	Occurs when the user presses a key.
KeyPress	Occurs when the user presses an ANSI key. ANSI keys produce visible characters.
KeyUp	Occurs when the user releases a key.
MouseDown	Occurs when the user presses a mouse button.
MouseMove	Occurs when the user moves the pointer on the UserForm.
MouseUp	Occurs when the user releases the pointer.
QueryClose	Occurs when Excel closes the UserForm.
RemoveControl	Occurs when Excel removes a control from the UserForm at runtime.
Scroll	Occurs when the user repositions a scroll box on a control.
Terminate	Occurs when Excel terminates the UserForm.
Zoom	Occurs when the user zooms the UserForm.

Application events include all events recognized by the `Application` object. To access an application event, create a class module to contain your application event-handling procedure code. See the section "Run a Procedure When Excel Creates a Workbook" for more information on placing event-handling code in a class module.

The following table lists the application-level events that occur in Excel.

EVENT TYPE	DESCRIPTION
Application	An event that occurs for the application. For example, Excel triggers the NewWorkbook event when it creates a new workbook.
NewWorkbook	Occurs when Excel creates a new workbook. See the section "Run a Procedure When Excel Creates a Workbook."
SheetActivate	Excel activates any sheet in any workbook.
SheetBeforeDoubleClick	Occurs when the user double-clicks any sheet.
SheetBeforeRightClick	Occurs when the user right-clicks any sheet.
SheetCalculate	Excel calculates any worksheet.
SheetChange	Cells on a worksheet are changed by a user or an external link.
SheetFollowHyperlink	A user clicks a hyperlink on a sheet.
SheetPivotTableUpdate	Excel updates a worksheet of a PivotTable report.
SheetSelectionChange	The selection changes on any worksheet.
WindowActivate	Excel activates a worksheet window.
WindowDeactivate	Excel deactivates a worksheet window.
WindowResize	The user resizes a worksheet window.
WorkbookActivate	The user activates a workbook.
WorkbookAddInInstall	An add-in installs a workbook.
WorkbookAddInUninstall	An add-in uninstalls a workbook.
WorkbookBeforePrint	Excel prints an open workbook.
WorkbookBeforeSave	Excel saves an open workbook.
WorkbookDeactivate	Excel deactivates a workbook.
WorkbookNewSheet	Excel adds a new sheet to an open workbook.
WorkbookOpen	Excel opens a workbook.
WorkbookPivotTableCloseConnection	Occurs after a PivotTable report closes the data source connection.
WorkbookPivotTableOpenConnection	Occurs after a PivotTable report opens the data source connection.

Run a Procedure as a Workbook Opens

You can create a procedure that runs automatically each time a workbook opens. Because this type of procedure executes only when a workbook opens, it works well for opening other workbooks, determining if specific conditions are met, and displaying welcome messages.

To have a procedure execute when a workbook opens, create the procedure using the `Workbook_Open` event and add it to the `ThisWorkbook` object standard module. All event-handling procedures for monitoring workbook events must reside in the `ThisWorkbook` object standard module if you want Excel to execute them automatically. If you want a procedure to execute when a workbook opens, you must name the procedure `Workbook_Open`.

Although the procedure resides in the `ThisWorkbook` object standard module, it can access other procedures in

the same workbook. Therefore, you can create a `Workbook_Open` procedure that calls procedures in other modules.

If you want a procedure to execute whenever Excel opens, you can place the procedure in the `ThisWorkbook` object for the Personal Macro Workbook - Personal.xlsb. Because the Personal Macro Workbook always loads as a hidden workbook in Excel, any procedures in this workbook execute when Excel opens. Keep in mind, however, that Excel associates the Personal Macro Workbook with an individual user.

You can keep a `Workbook_Open` procedure from executing for a particular workbook by pressing and holding Shift as the workbook opens. Because workbooks open quickly, make sure you press and hold Shift as you select the workbook.

Run a Procedure as a Workbook Opens

① Open Project Explorer.

② Double-click the `ThisWorkbook` node under the workbook to which you want to add a `Workbook_Open` event.

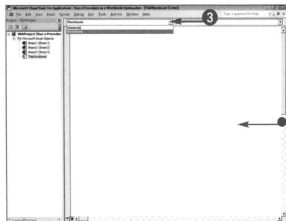

● The standard module for the `ThisWorkbook` object opens.

③ Click the down arrow and then select the Workbook option.

- The Visual Basic Editor creates a `Private Sub` procedure and names it `Workbook_Open`.

4 Type the VBA code to run when the workbook opens.

The example displays the user's name.

5 Press Ctrl+S to save your workbook.

6 Close your workbook.

7 Open the workbook you just closed.

The `Workbook_Open` procedure executes.

In this example, a welcome message appears.

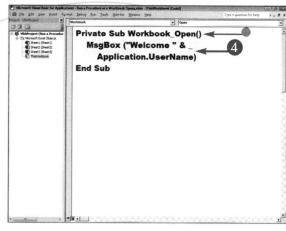

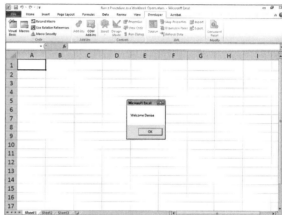

Extra

You can use the `Workbooks` collection object `Open` method to specify the workbook that Excel should open along with the current workbook. For example, if your workbook relies on data values in another workbook, you can open the workbook your workbook relies on, whenever your workbook opens. See Chapter 9 for more information on using the `Open` method.

You can use the Object drop-down list in the Code window to create your `Workbook_Open` Sub procedure. The Object drop-down list contains the objects for which you can create `Sub` procedures in the current standard module. If you access the `ThisWorkbook` standard module, the only available object is `Workbook`.

When you select the `Workbook` object from the Objects drop-down list, the VBE automatically creates a `Private Sub` procedure called `Workbook_Open` because the default event for the `Workbook` object is the `Open` event.

Run a Procedure before Closing a Workbook

You can create a `BeforeClose` event procedure that runs automatically before a particular workbook closes. If the user has made changes to the workbook, the event executes before Excel asks users if they want to save their changes. Because this type of procedure executes only as the workbook closes, it works well for recalculating, resetting the workbook back to default values, and even automatically saving the workbook. The procedure executes when the workbook closes by executing the `BeforeClose` event, which is triggered by the closing workbook.

To produce a procedure that executes when a workbook closes, create a new procedure and add it to the `ThisWorkbook` object standard module for the particular workbook. All event-handling procedures that you create for monitoring workbook events must reside in the `ThisWorkbook` object for Excel to execute them automatically. You must name the procedure `Workbook_BeforeClose`.

Although the procedure resides in the `ThisWorkbook` object standard module, it can access other procedures in the same workbook. Therefore, you can create a `Workbook_BeforeClose` procedure that calls procedures in another module.

The `BeforeClose` event takes one argument, `Cancel`. You can use the `Cancel` argument to change what Excel does after the `BeforeClose` event completes. If the `Cancel` argument has a value of `False`, which is the default, the workbook closes normally. If your procedure sets the value to `True`, Excel cancels the closing process and does not close the workbook. You can set the `Cancel` argument to `True` and then prompt the user for additional information before closing.

Run a Procedure before Closing a Workbook

① Open Project Explorer.

② Double-click the `ThisWorkbook` node under the workbook to which you want to add a `Workbook_Open` event.

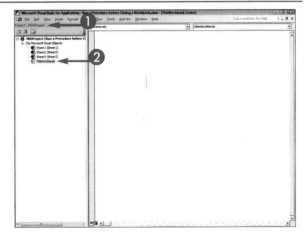

● The standard module for the `ThisWorkbook` object opens.

③ Click the down arrow and then select Workbook.

④ Click the down arrow and then select BeforeClose.

● The Visual Basic Editor creates a new `Private Sub` procedure named `Workbook_BeforeClose`.

Delete the `Workbook_Open Sub` procedure if it appears.

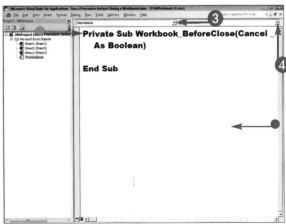

5 Type the VBA code that will run before the workbook closes.

6 Press Ctrl+S to save the workbook.

7 Close the workbook.

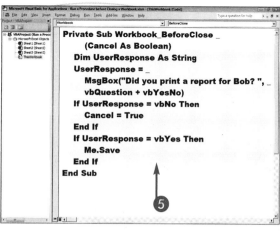

The `Workbook_BeforeClose` procedure executes.

In this example, Excel asks if you printed a report.

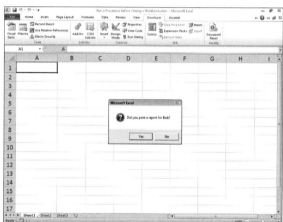

You can use the `Me` keyword in standard modules for Excel objects. The `Me` keyword references the object associated with the module. For example, code created in the `ThisWorkbook` object module links to the workbook object. When you use the `Me` keyword, you reference the workbook object. Therefore, when you add the code `Me.Close` to a module, Excel closes the workbook. The code `Me.Close` is equivalent to using the `ThisWorkbook` object reference. You can use the `Me` keyword when working with `UserForm` modules. When used with a user form, the `Me` keyword references the corresponding `UserForm` and not the controls that you have added to the `UserForm`.

If your procedure has made a change that affects all workbooks, you can use a `BeforeClose` event procedure to undo the change before the workbook closes. For example, if you have a procedure that loads and add-in, you can use the `BeforeClose` event procedure to unload the add-in before the workbook closes.

Run a Procedure before Saving a Workbook

Y ou can create a `BeforeSave` event procedure that runs automatically before Excel saves a workbook. By creating a `BeforeSave` procedure, you can customize the save process. For example, when users select the Save or Save As option, you may want to ask if they have performed all required tasks.

To create a procedure that executes before saving a workbook, create a new procedure using the `BeforeSave` event and add it to the `ThisWorkbook` object standard module for the workbook. All event-handling procedures that you create for monitoring workbook events must reside in the `ThisWorkbook` object. To create a procedure that executes before Excel saves the workbook, you must name the procedure `Workbook_BeforeSave`.

Although the procedure resides in the `ThisWorkbook` object standard module, it can access other procedures in the same workbook. Therefore, you can create a

`Workbook_BeforeSave` procedure that calls procedures in another module in the same workbook.

The `BeforeSave` event takes two arguments that VBA passes to your procedure when the event triggers — `SaveAsUI` and `Cancel`. Use the `SaveAsUI` argument to indicate whether the Save As dialog box appears during the Save command. Set the value of the `SaveUI` argument to `True` to always display the Save As dialog box.

Use the `Cancel` argument to indicate whether the workbook should save. If the `Cancel` argument has a value of `False`, Excel saves the workbook. The default value is `False`. If the `Cancel` argument has a value of `True`, Excel does not save the workbook. From within the `Workbook_BeforeSave` procedure, you can set the value of the `Cancel` argument to specify whether the workbook actually saves.

Run a Procedure before Saving a Workbook

① Open Project Explorer.

② Double-click the `ThisWorkbook` node under the workbook to which you want to add a `Workbook_BeforeSave` event.

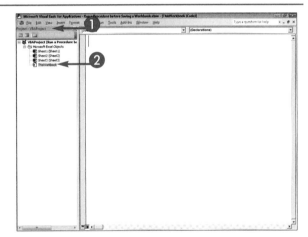

The module for the `ThisWorkbook` object opens.

③ Click the down arrow and select Workbook.

④ Click the down arrow and select BeforeSave.

● The Visual Basic Editor creates a new `Private Sub` procedure named `Workbook_BeforeSave`.

Delete the `Workbook_Open Sub` procedure if it appears.

⑤ Click the Close button to close Project Explorer.

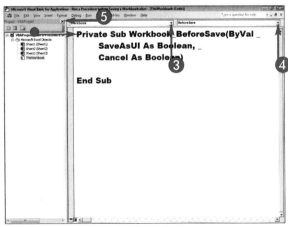

(6) Type the VBA code that will run when the workbook saves.

(7) Press Alt+F11 to switch from the VBE to Excel.

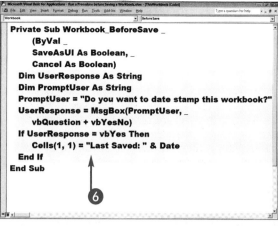

(8) Click the Save button to save the workbook.

The Workbook_BeforeSave procedure executes.

● In this example, the procedure prompts you, "Do you want to date stamp this workbook?"

● Click Yes if you want to date-stamp your file.

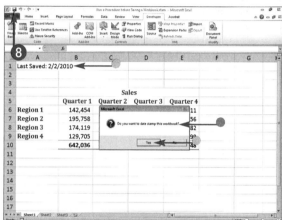

Extra

When you want to make sure that a variable in a procedure does not change the value of variables in other procedures, use the ByVal keyword. For example, the Workbook_BeforeSave Sub procedure includes a ByVal, SaveAsUI argument. To aid in your understanding of ByVal, consider the following example, where the message box displays a value of 10 because the value of TestVal in the Test2 Sub procedure is ByVal. Any changes made to TestVal in the Test2 Sub procedure do not pass back to Test1.

Example:
```
Sub Test1()
   Dim TestVal As Integer
   TestVal = 10
   Call Test2(TestVal)
   MsgBox TestVal
End Sub

Sub Test2(ByVal TestVal)
   TestVal = 55555
End Sub
```

Run a Procedure When Excel Creates a Workbook

If you have settings you apply to every workbook, you can use the NewWorkbook application event to set those settings every time you open a workbook. For example, when you open an Excel workbook, by default it contains three worksheets. If you always need five worksheets, you can create a NewWorkbook application event to create two additional worksheets.

The NewWorkbook application event executes whenever Excel opens a new workbook. Because the event comes from the application and not from an individual object such as a workbook or chart, the process for creating an application event is complex.

When working with application events, first create a class module. Excel only makes code in a standard module available to other modules in the same project or

workbook. When you create a procedure for an application event, you want all open projects to be able to access the code; therefore, you use a class module.

Because Excel does not recognize your application event code until the workbook containing the code opens, open the workbook containing the code first. You may want to add the code to the Personal.xlsb workbook. The Personal.xlsb workbook opens whenever you open Excel, and application event code activates as a workbook opens. See Chapter 1 for more information about the Personal.xlsb workbook.

In the class module, use the WithEvents keyword to declare a public Application object variable. Make the variable public because you want all open projects to access this object variable. See Chapter 3 for more information on public variables.

Run a Procedure When Excel Creates a Workbook

① Click the workbook to which you want to add a NewWorkbook event.

② Click Insert → Class Module.

VBA creates a blank class module.

③ Press F4.

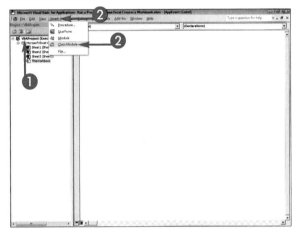

The Properties window opens.

④ Type a name for your class module in the Name field.

⑤ Declare a public Application object using the WithEvents keyword.

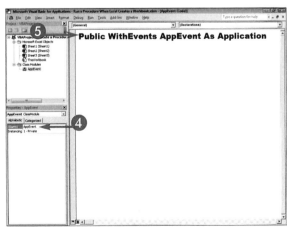

6 Click the down arrow and then select the name you typed in Step 5.

● VBA creates a `Private AppEvent_ NewWorkbook Sub` procedure.

7 Type the code you want to execute when a new workbook opens.

8 In Project Explorer, double-click the `ThisWorkbook` node.

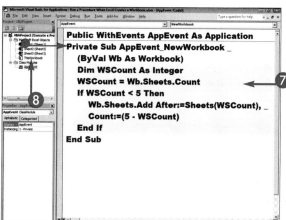

---

continued ➡

After you declare a public `Application` object variable by using the `WithEvents` keyword, use the `NewWorkbook` event to specify that the event executes when Excel creates a new workbook. The `NewWorkbook` event has one argument, `Wb`, which passes to the `Sub` procedure. The `Wb` argument contains the newly created workbook. You can access any of the methods and properties of the new workbook by using the `Wb` argument. For example, you can use the `Name` property to return the name of the new workbook. See Chapter 9 for more information on working with the `Workbook` object.

Creating the `NewWorkbook` Sub procedure in the class module defines the code to run for the event but does not activate the `Sub` procedure. To activate the `Sub` procedure, add code to a `Workbook_Open` procedure that activates the `Application` event procedure. Because the `Application` event code is meant to work with all events generated by the application, you want to add a class module and the activation code to a workbook you open frequently, such as the Personal Macro Workbook. See Chapter 1 to learn more about the Personal Macro Workbook.

To activate the class module code, the module containing the activation procedure must contain a `Dim` statement, which declares an object of the type defined in the class module. Place the `Dim` statement at the top of the standard module. For example, `Dim NewSheets As New AppEvent` creates a new object variable of the type created in the class module. In a procedure, a `Set` statement actually activates the event. To make the `Set` statement execute automatically, place the `Set` statement in the `Workbook_Open` procedure.

Run a Procedure When Excel Creates a Workbook (continued)

The standard module opens for the `ThisWorkbook` object.

⑨ Declare an object variable using the `Application` object you created.

⑩ Create a `Private Workbook_Open Sub` procedure.

⑪ Use a `Set` statement to activate your event.

⑫ Save, close, and reopen Excel.

⑬ Open the workbook containing the `Workbook_open` Sub procedure.

⑭ Click the File tab and then click New.

⑮ Click Create.

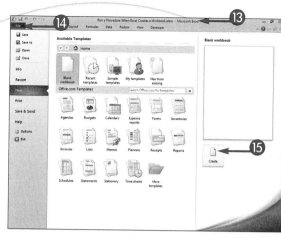

The event-handling procedure executes the code.

● In this example, the procedure adds two sheets to the new workbook.

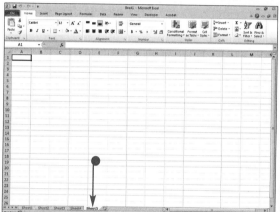

Apply It

When you open the workbook containing the code that activates an application event, the code executes each time you trigger the event. There may be times when you need to deactivate an event so that it no longer triggers. You can create a separate `Sub` procedure that you can call from within Excel at any point to cancel an event. Essentially, you set the property of the `Application` object to `Nothing`, as shown in the following example:

TYPE THIS:

```
Sub CancelEvent()
   Set OpenAppEvent.AppEvent = Nothing
End Sub
```

→

RESULT:

The code cancels the event for the current session of Excel. The next time you start Excel, the event is reactivated.

Creating this type of `Sub` procedure so you can disable an event-handling procedure at any time is a good idea. You can also set the `EnableEvents` property to `False` for the `Application` object, as shown in this code:

TYPE THIS:

```
Sub CancelEvents()
   Application.EnableEvents = False
End Sub
```

→

RESULT:

This code disables all event-handling procedures for the current session of Excel. The next time you start Excel, the event-handling procedures are reactivated.

Execute a Procedure at a Specific Time

You can create a procedure that executes at a specific time by using the OnTime event. For example, you can create a MsgBox that reminds the user of an event 5 minutes before the event starts.

Unlike most other events, the OnTime event is not associated with a specific object. You must access this event by using the OnTime method with the Application object.

The OnTime method has four parameters; only the first two are required: EarliestTime, Procedure, LatestTime, and Schedule. Use the EarliestTime parameter to specify the time at which the procedure executes. Use the Procedure parameter to indicate the procedure to execute at the specified time. Enclose the procedure name in quotes.

Use the optional LatestTime parameter to indicate the latest time when the procedure can run. If the procedure

has not run by the time specified by this parameter, it does not run. The other optional parameter, Schedule, has a default value of True to schedule the OnTime procedure to run again at the specified time or False to clear a previously set procedure.

Because the OnTime event is not associated with a specific object, you can place a procedure containing the method for accessing the event in any standard module. If you place the OnTime method procedure in a standard module, you must run that module to activate the OnTime event code. You can also place the OnTime method in the Workbook_Open procedure so that it loads the event code as the workbook opens. See the section "Run a Procedure as a Workbook Opens" for more information.

When using the OnTime event, you can use Excel's time-numbering system or you can use VBA's TimeValue function. Using VBA's TimeValue function simplifies the process.

Execute a Procedure at a Specific Time

Create an OnTime Event Using Excel's Time-Numbering System

① Name your procedure.

② Create an OnTime event.

● This is the time the procedure will execute.

This will execute a procedure at 11:25 AM.

See the next screenshot for an alternative way to set the time.

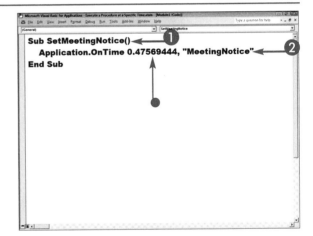

Create an OnTime Event Using VBA's TimeValue Function

① Name your procedure.

② Create an OnTime event.

● This is the time the procedure will execute.

This will execute a procedure at 11:25 AM.

● This is the procedure that will execute.

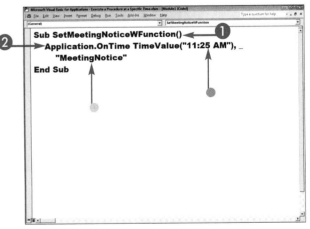

Create a Procedure

① Name your procedure.

② Type the code that you want to execute.

  This causes the computer to beep.

● This displays a message box.

③ Press Alt+F11 to switch from the VBE to Excel, and run the macro.

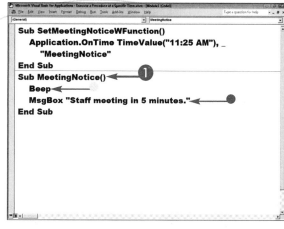

```
Sub SetMeetingNoticeWFunction()
    Application.OnTime TimeValue("11:25 AM"), _
        "MeetingNotice"
End Sub
Sub MeetingNotice()          ①
    Beep
    MsgBox "Staff meeting in 5 minutes."
End Sub
```

Excel executes the procedure at the designated time.

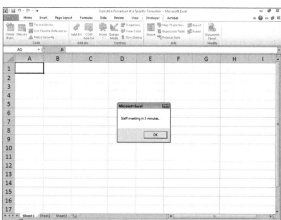

Extra

The `EarliestTime` and `LatestTime` parameters expect time values based on Excel's time-numbering system, which stores all times as decimal values ranging from 0.0 to 0.99999999. For example, Excel stores 12:00 noon as 0.5 and 6:00 PM as 0.75. Because fractional times can be mind-boggling, VBA provides the `TimeValue` function with which you can convert a standard time into the decimal equivalent required. To use the `TimeValue` function, enclose the time you want to convert in quotes. For example, `TimeValue("5:45 PM")` converts 5:45 PM to the appropriate decimal value.

Another useful VBA time function is the `Now` function, which returns the current date and time. When you use the `Now` function in combination with a `TimeValue` function, you can specify how long before an event occurs. For example, to have an event take place in 30 minutes, express the time as follows:

Example:
```
Now + TimeValue("00:30:00")
```

Execute a Procedure When You Press Keys

You can use the `OnKey` event to create a procedure that executes when you press a specific key or combination of keys. For example, you can press Alt+S to sign and date a worksheet. You define the keys you want to use to execute a procedure. If you specify a key combination that Excel already uses, your new definition overrides the Excel combination.

Unlike most other events, the `OnKey` event is not associated with a specific object. For that reason, you access this event by using the `OnKey` method with the `Application` object.

The `OnKey` method has two parameters, `Key` and `Procedure`. Use the `Key` parameter to specify the key combination, which you express as a string consisting of the combined keys you capture. Represent standard keys,

such as *a* and *5*, by simply typing the character for the key. Specify nonstandard keys, such as *Delete* and *Insert*, by placing the key name in curly braces: `{DELETE}` or `{INSERT}`.

Use the `Procedure` parameter to indicate the name of the procedure to execute. Enclose the procedure name in quotes.

Because the `OnKey` event is not associated with a specific object, you can place the procedure containing the method for accessing the event in any standard module. However, if you place the `OnKey` method procedure in a standard module, you need to run the macro to activate the code. You can place the `OnKey` method in the `Workbook_Open` procedure so that it loads as the workbook opens. See the section "Run a Procedure as a Workbook Opens" for more information.

Execute a Procedure When You Press Keys

① Double-click the `ThisWorkbook` node under the workbook to which you want to add a `Workbook_Open` event.

● The module for the `ThisWorkbook` object opens.

② Click the down arrow and then select the Workbook option.

● The Visual Basic Editor creates a `Private Sub` procedure and names it `Workbook_Open`.

Note: See the section "Run a Procedure as a Workbook Opens" for information on the `Workbook_Open` procedure.

③ Create your `OnKey` command.

○ This is the Alt key.

See the Extra section for more information.

○ This is the name of the procedure you want to run.

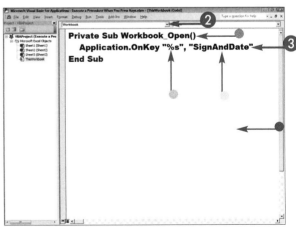

④ Create a `Sub` procedure with the same name you specified in Step 3.

⑤ Type the code that you want to execute.

⑥ Press Alt+F11 to switch from the VBE to Excel, and run the macro.

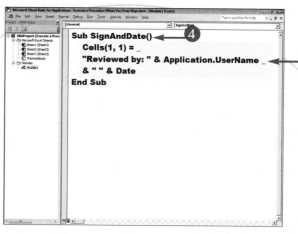

```
Sub SignAndDate()
    Cells(1, 1) = _
        "Reviewed by: " & Application.UserName _
        & " " & Date
End Sub
```

When you press the designated keys. Excel executes the macro.

● In this example, Excel places the username and the date in cell A1 when you press Alt+S.

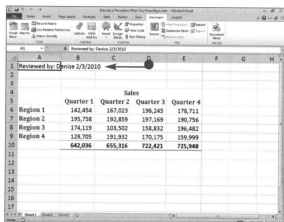

When specifying keys that do not create a character, such as Delete or Down Arrow, enclose the name of the key in curly braces: `{Delete}` or `{Down}`. For some keys, Excel provides special characters to represent the key when you combine it with other characters:

Character	Represents
+	Shift
^	Ctrl
%	Alt
~	Enter

To reassign a particular key combination to its original meaning, omit the `Procedure` parameter:

TYPE THIS:
```
Application.OnKey "+^{LEFT}"
```

RESULT:
The custom key combination assignment is removed, and Excel executes the default command for that key combination, if one exists.

To use one of the special characters in your key combination, enclose the character in braces. For example, to specify a procedure to execute when you press the percent sign, type the following code:

TYPE THIS:
```
Application.OnKey "{%}", _
    "ExecutePercent"
```

RESULT:
Whenever the user presses %, the `ExecutePercent` procedure executes.

Monitor a Range of Cells for Changes

By using the Change event, you can create a procedure that monitors a range of cells and notifies you when a change occurs. Excel triggers this event when the user or an external link changes a value in the selected worksheet. When Excel triggers the event, it sends your event-handling function a Range object containing the cells that changed. You design your procedure to check the range of cells returned and determine if they are in the range of cells you are monitoring.

Because the monitored event relates to an individual worksheet, place the event-handling procedure in the object module that corresponds to that worksheet. For example, to monitor changes to Sheet1, place the code in the standard module for Sheet1. To capture the Change event, name the procedure Worksheet_Change.

The Change event has one argument, Target, whose value Excel passes when it triggers the Change event. The Target argument receives the range of cells that changed. This value passes to your procedure by value and as a result, your procedure cannot change the value of the Target argument.

Although the Worksheet_Change procedure resides in a sheet object standard module, it can access other procedures in the same workbook. Therefore, you can create a Worksheet_Change procedure that calls procedures in another module.

Excel triggers this event only when cell values change due to modifications made by the user or an external link. It does not trigger if a formula or procedure performs a calculation that changes the value or if you add an object.

Monitor a Range of Cells for Changes

① Double-click the sheet you want to monitor for change.

The code module for the sheet opens.

● You can click the Close button to close Project Explorer.

② Click the down arrow and then select Worksheet.

③ Click the down arrow and then select Change.

● The VBE creates a new Private Sub procedure named Worksheet_Change.

④ Type the VBA code that will run when the worksheet changes.

The `Intersect` method determines where ranges overlap. In this example, it determines if the `Target` is in the `WatchRange`.

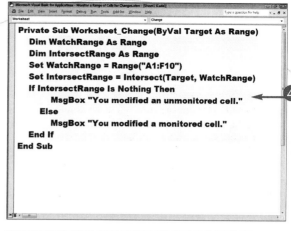

```
Private Sub Worksheet_Change(ByVal Target As Range)
    Dim WatchRange As Range
    Dim IntersectRange As Range
    Set WatchRange = Range("A1:F10")
    Set IntersectRange = Intersect(Target, WatchRange)
    If IntersectRange Is Nothing Then
        MsgBox "You modified an unmonitored cell."
    Else
        MsgBox "You modified a monitored cell."
    End If
End Sub
```

④

⑤ Press Alt+F11 to switch from the VBE to Excel and run the macro.

Each time you make a change the procedure tells you if you are in range or out of range.

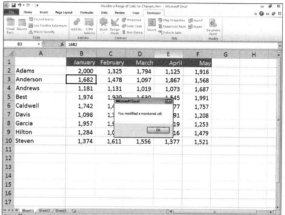

Extra

Because Excel triggers the Change event only when a user or external link changes a value in a cell, there may be instances where Excel does not trigger a Change event when you expect it to. The following table lists instances when Excel triggers a Change event and instances when it does not.

Triggers Change Event

Typing values in cells
Clearing formats
Pressing Delete
Using the Ribbon to delete
Making changes with spell-check
Using Find and Replace

Does Not Trigger Change Event

Calculating new formula values
Changing cell formatting
Using a form
Performing a sort
Making changes from a procedure (macro)
Inserting a comment

Create an Add-In

With add-ins, you can integrate additional functionality into Microsoft Excel. You can create an add-in and use it to add user defined functions, custom dialog boxes, Sub procedures, and custom Ribbon tabs to workbooks. Add-ins are a great way to integrate your procedures into any Excel workbook.

You create an add-in by saving a workbook in the add-in format. By default, Excel places add-ins in a special AddIns folder.

After you save a workbook in the add-in format, the worksheets in the workbook are no longer visible and you cannot make them visible by using the Unhide command. You cannot see or edit the sheets in an add-in workbook. In addition, an add-in workbook does not become a part of the Workbooks collection. You create an add-in when you want to use defined functions, custom dialog boxes, Sub procedures, or custom Ribbon tabs in

multiple workbooks. You cannot use an add-in to share worksheets.

You must install an add-in or open another workbook while the add-in workbook is open to access an add-in's features. See the section "Install Add-Ins" to learn how to install an add-in. If functions created by an add-in are available, when you open the Insert Function dialog box, they appear in the User Defined category. You can select and use them just as you would any other functions. See Chapter 3 to learn more about user-defined functions. When you install an add-in, any key combinations you assign to a Sub procedure become available to the user.

Before you convert a workbook to add-in format, you should thoroughly test it. You can simulate how the macros will function by opening another workbook while the workbook you want to install as an add-in (the XLAM file) is open and executing the procedures.

Create an Add-In

1 Create the workbook you want to use as an add-in.

Make sure it is completely debugged.

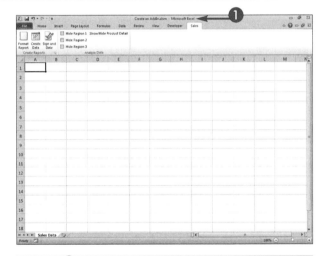

2 Click the File tab.

3 Click Save As.

The Save As dialog box appears.

④ Click the down arrow and then select Excel Add-In (*.xlam) in the Save As Type field.

⑤ Type a name for your file.

⑥ Click Save.

● Note the folder in which Excel is saving the file.

Excel creates the add-in file.

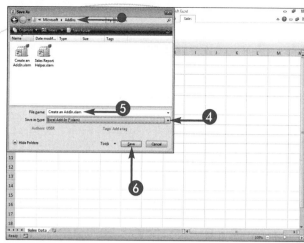

⑦ Open the add-in file.

When you open the add-in file, no worksheets appear.

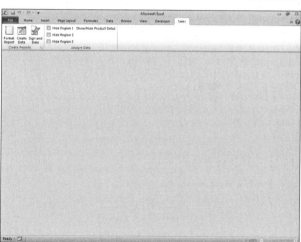

Extra

To distribute your add-in to others, give them a copy of your XLAM file and tell them the proper directory in which to install it. You should password-protect your file. See the section "Set Add-In Properties" to learn how to password-protect an add-in file. You do not need to distribute copies of your XLSM macro file.

You can open an add-in file by clicking the File tab, clicking Open, locating the add-in, and then clicking Open. The add-in opens; however, the name of the file does not appear on the title bar and no worksheet appears. You can open another workbook and use the add-in. This is a great way to test your macro before making it available to the Add-Ins manager. When you save your add-in to the Office library or to a user's AddIns directory, the add-in becomes available in the Add-ins section of the Excel Options dialog box for you to load.

Set Add-In Properties

When you create an add-in, the sheets included in the add-in file are not visible to users; however, if users click the Visual Basic button on the Developer tab of the Ribbon, they move to the VBE where they can view and modify your code. If you do not want users to modify your code, you must use the Project Properties dialog box to password-protect it. Although password-protecting provides some level of security, you should be aware that there are products on the market that can recover your password.

Use the General tab in the Project Properties dialog box to name and describe your add-in. The project name and description appear at the bottom of the View and Manage Microsoft Office add-ins pane and provide the user with a brief introduction to your add-in before installing.

The sheets associated with an add-in workbook are not visible. If you want to view the sheets, open the Properties window in the VBE by pressing F4. If you then click ThisWorkbook in the Project Explorer, the properties for the workbook become available. If you set the `IsAddin` property to `False`, the sheets in your workbook become available.

All functions you create in an add-in file are normally available to users through the Insert Function dialog box whenever the add-in is available. If you create functions you intend to be available only to other functions or procedures, use the `Private` keyword when you create them. To learn more about the `Private` keyword, see Chapter 2.

Set Add-In Properties

Name and Password Protect

① Click Tools → VBAProject Properties.

The VBAProject Properties dialog box appears.

② Click the General tab.

③ Type a project name.

④ Type a project description.

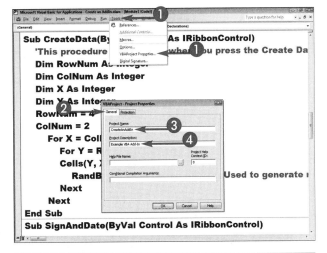

⑤ Click the Protection tab.

⑥ Select the Lock Project for Viewing option (☐ changes to ☑).

⑦ Type a password.

⑧ Type the password again.

⑨ Click OK.

VBA password-protects and adds a name and description to your project.

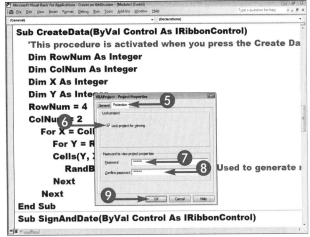

Set IsAddin to False

1 Press F4.

Alternatively, click View ➔ Properties Window.

The Properties window appears.

2 Press Ctrl+R

Alternatively, click View ➔ Project Explorer.

The Project Explorer appears.

3 Click ThisWorkbook.

The workbook properties appear.

4 Set IsAddin to False.

5 Press Alt+F11 to switch from the VBE to Excel.

● The worksheets appear in the add-in.

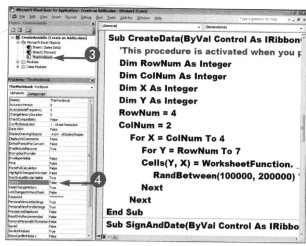

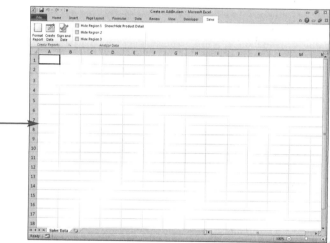

Extra

Before creating your add-in, it is a good idea to add information to the Properties pane. Click the File tab, click Info, and then click Properties. A menu appears. Click Show Document Panel. The Properties pane appears. Type a title in the Title field, type a description in the Comments field, and then close the Properties pane.

In addition to the add-ins you create, you can obtain add-ins from third parties. To learn about special-purpose Excel add-ins in your field, perform a Google search by going to www.google.com. Your search terms should include Excel; the field of knowledge — for example, chemistry; and other information you might have, such as vendor name. Third-party vendors are responsible for supporting their own products.

As with macros, add-ins can spread viruses. For Excel to consider an add-in safe, the add-in must have a current valid digital signature issued by a certificate authority, and the developer of the add-in must be a trusted publisher. If the Excel Trust Center considers an add-in unsafe, it disables the add-in and displays a message bar to alert you to the potentially unsafe add-in. You can click the Options button on the message bar to enable the add-in.

Install Add-Ins

Bundled add-in software is included with Excel, but Excel does not automatically install the software when you install Excel. The following are among the add-ins that come standard with Excel: The Conditional Sum Wizard enables you to create a formula that sums only the values that meet the criteria you specify. The Euro Currency Tools add-in enables you to calculate exchange rates between the Euro and other currencies. The Data Analysis Toolpak provides a number of tools you can use for statistical analysis. Solver enables you to produce the formula result you want by directly or indirectly adjusting cells related to the cell that contains the formula.

You install bundled add-ins and the add-ins you create by using the Excel Options dialog box. You can find all add-ins in the Add-Ins section. When you save an add-in to the Microsoft AddIns folder or to the Library folder

under the Office program, it becomes available for installation in the Excel Options dialog box. Once installed, the add-in is available right away. You can download additional Excel add-ins from the Microsoft download site. For example, for Excel 2010, you can download the Microsoft SQL Server PowerPivot add-in. The add-in is useful if you use PivotTables with large amounts of data from multiple data sources. This add-in produces a fast response time even if you are working with millions of rows of data.

You can also take advantage of third-party add-ins. This type of software adds functionality in support of advanced work in chemistry, risk analysis, modeling, project management, statistics, and other fields. Third-party add-ins usually have their own installation and usage procedures. Consult the developer of these programs for documentation.

Install Add-Ins

1 Click the File tab.

A menu appears.

2 Click Options.

The Excel Options dialog box appears.

3 Click Add-Ins.

● The View and Manage Microsoft Office Add-ins screen appears.

4 Click an add-in.

The example uses the Create an Add-In add-in created earlier in this chapter.

5 Click Go.

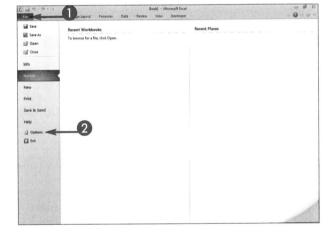

The Add-Ins dialog box appears and provides access to several options.

⑥ Click to select the add-in you want to install (☐ changes to ☑).

⑦ Click OK.

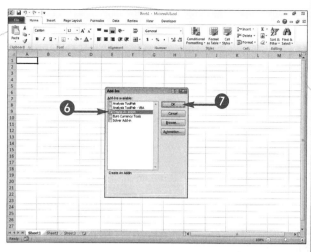

Excel installs the add-in.

● In this example, you know Excel installed the add-in because you can see the custom Ribbon tab.

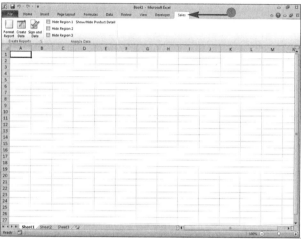

Extra

Removing an add-in from Excel is easy. Click the File tab, click Options, click Add-ins, click the add-in you want to remove, and then click Go. The Add-Ins dialog box appears. Click to deselect the add-in you want to remove and then click OK. Excel removes the add-in.

The only way to remove an add-in from the Add-Ins section of the Excel Options dialog box is to delete the file from the folder in which it is stored.

In Excel 2003, you could click a data point in a column chart twice and you would then be able to resize the columns. This feature was deprecated in Excel 2007. However, Microsoft received a lot of feedback indicating that people liked the feature, so they developed an add-in that can be used with Excel 2007 and Excel 2010. The add-in is called Manipulate Point on Chart. You can download it from the Microsoft download site.

Using VBA to Load Add-Ins

I f you want to add an add-in by using a procedure, use the Add method with an AddIn object. The Add method adds an add-in to the Excel Options dialog box. The following is the syntax for the Add method:

expression.Add(*Filename*, *Open*)

Use the expression to identify the add-in or a variable that represents the add-in. Use the Filename parameter to specify the location of the add-in you want to add. If the file is located in the current folder, type the filename, enclosed in quotes. If the file is located in another folder, type the path to the file enclosed in quotes. If your add-in is located on a removable disk such as a compact disc and you want to move the file from the removable disk to the Library folder under the Office program, set the Open parameter to True. If you want the file to remain on the removable disk, set the Open parameter to False. If you do not include this parameter and your add-in is located on a removable disk, Excel displays a prompt asking the user if he or she wants to move the file to the hard drive. If your add-in is not located on a removable disk, VBA ignores the Open parameter.

The Add method does not install an add-in. To install an add-in, you must set the Install property to True. You can add an add-in and install it in a single step by using the following syntax:

AddIns.Add("Sample.xlam").Installed = True

Using VBA to Load Add-Ins

① Name your procedure.

② Declare a variable as an AddIn object.

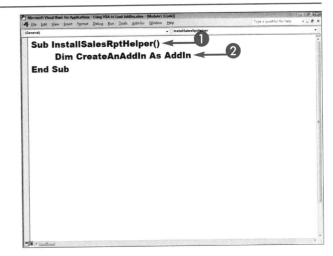

③ Add the add-in.

● This is the add-in file you want to add.

④ Install the add-in.

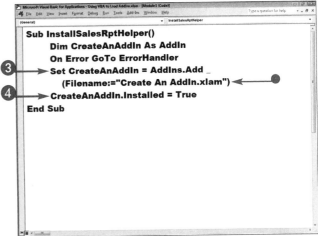

5 Display a `MsgBox` letting you know the add-in has been installed.

6 Handle Errors.

7 Press Alt+F11 to switch from the VBE to Excel, and run the macro.

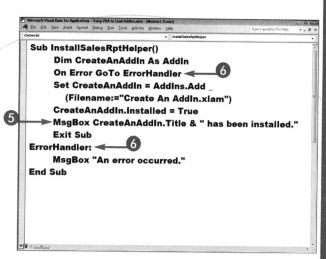

```
Sub InstallSalesRptHelper()
    Dim CreateAnAddIn As AddIn
    On Error GoTo ErrorHandler          ◄─── 6
    Set CreateAnAddIn = AddIns.Add _
        (Filename:="Create An AddIn.xlam")
    CreateAnAddIn.Installed = True
    MsgBox CreateAnAddIn.Title & " has been installed."
    Exit Sub
ErrorHandler:          ◄─── 6
    MsgBox "An error occurred."
End Sub
```

● The macro installs the add-in and displays a message box.

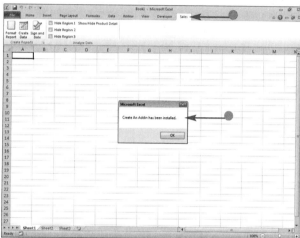

Extra

The Add-Ins dialog box tells you a lot about add-ins. To open the Add-Ins dialog box, click the File tab, click Options, click Add-Ins, and then click Go. The Add-Ins dialog box appears. All of the add-ins available in Excel appear in the Add-Ins dialog box. Each add-in listed is part of the `AddIns` collection. You can reference Add-ins in the `AddIns` collection by their title or by their index value. You determine the index value by the order in which Excel lists the add-ins in the Add-Ins dialog box. The first add-in has an index value of 1, the second 2, and so on. The title of an add-in is the name listed in the Add-Ins dialog box.

You can reference the index value of an add-in or its title to uninstall the add-in. To uninstall an add-in, set the `Installed` property to `False`. The following example uninstalls an add-in.

Example:
```
Addins.("Sample").Installed = False
```

Introducing XML

The default file format for Office 2007 and Office 2010 is EXtensible Markup Language (XML). For this reason, as a VBA programmer, you should have a basic understanding of XML.

The appeal of XML is that it makes exchanging data between different software applications and different computer systems easier. After you mark up your data using XML, it is available to be processed by a variety of different systems, without regard to hardware or operating system. You can use the same XML data in Word, Excel, and Access, and other programs. Prior to Office 2007, Office files were in a proprietary format. Manipulating and sharing the data with other applications and systems was difficult.

XML is similar to HyperText Markup Language (HTML), the language used to format data displayed in a Web page. If you are familiar with HTML, learning XML will be easy. Both HTML and XML are markup languages

and, as such, they both use tags. In HTML, the tags are predefined; in XML, you define the tags.

XML and HTML have different purposes. You use HTML to format data so you can display your data in a Web page. You use XML to describe your data. Your XML tags can be anything you want them to be, but they should describe your data. Each XML tag describes the data contained in the tag.

You do not need to purchase any software to create an XML file; you can create XML in any text editor. For example, you can use Notepad to create an XML file. However, you must give your XML files an .xml file extension.

A complete explanation of XML is beyond the scope of this book. However, the brief overview of XML that follows provides a basic understanding of the examples provided in this book.

Declaration Statement

You start each XML file with a declaration. The declaration lets the program processing your file know that your file is an XML file. The following is an example of a declaration statement:

```
<?xml version="1.0" encoding="UTF-8
   "standalone="yes" ?>
```

Xml identifies the file as an XML file, 1.0 is the version of XML used, UTF-8 is the character set used to encode the data, and standalone tells the processing program whether the document contains references to other documents.

Tags

In XML, you call a unit of data an *element*. You use tags to describe each element. Angle brackets surround tags: < and >. In the following example, `<CustomerName>Royal Inc.</CustomerName>`, `<CustomerName>`, and `</CustomerName>` are the opening and closing tags for the element. They tell you that Royal Inc. is the name of the customer. The opening tag marks the beginning of the element. The closing tag marks the end of the element. The closing tag always includes a forward slash. And be aware that XML is case-sensitive. The tag `<UnitPrice>` is not the same as `<unitprice>`. Your opening tag and closing tag must be in the same case. You place your data between the opening tag and the closing tag. Every tag must include a closing tag.

Empty Tags

Empty tags are tags that do not have any content. Empty tags do not require a closing tag. However, empty tags must include a forward slash as part of the tag. The following is an example of an empty tag.

```
<button id="Button1"
   imageMso="AccessFormWizard"
size="large" label = "Report Format"
onAction= "ThisWorkbook.SignAndDate" />
```

In the example, the element has attributes but no content. You use the element to pass information to the reading program.

Attributes

You can include attributes within an XML tag. Attributes provide information to the program that is manipulating the data. The following is an example of a tag that includes a FileType attribute.

```
<CustomerName FileType ="J5793" > Royal Inc.</
   CustomerName>
```

You must enclose attributes in quotes. You can use single quotes or double quotes. An element can have multiple attributes.

Element Names

You can name elements anything you want; however, element names should describe your data. Also, element names must conform to the following rules:

- Names can contain letters, numbers, and other characters.
- Names cannot contain spaces.
- Names cannot start with the letters XML, a number, or a punctuation character.
- You can use an underscore to separate the words in a name, as in Customer_Information.

You should try to keep your element names short and, although it is allowed, avoid using the "-" and the "." in your element names. If you create an element name such as Customer-Info, the reading program may try to subtract Customer from Info; if you create a name such as Customer.Info, the reading program may think Info is a property of Customer.

Schemas

Schemas are another important component of XML. Schemas contain the rules that help the processing program validate your data. For example, a schema tells the processing program whether a tag should contain text or a number. In that way, the schema prevents the entry of invalid data. For example, if data between your LastName tags should always be a string, a schema prevents the entry of numbers.

If you are importing an XML file into Excel, and your XML file does not have a schema, Excel creates one. Excel maps the items in the schema. Mapping allows you to display in your worksheet only the data you want to see. It also allows you to refresh your data and save your data in XML format.

Structure

You structure XML hierarchically. Consider the following example:

```
<CustomerInfo>
    <CustId>C001</CustId>
        <CustomerName>Royal Inc.</CustomerName>
        <TransDate>2011-06-01</TransDate>
            <PurchaseInfo>
                <Quantity>12</Quantity>
                <ItemNo>OS-001</ItemNo>
                <Description>Pencils</Description>
                <UnitPrice>3.99</UnitPrice>
            </PurchaseInfo>
            <PurchaseInfo>
                <Quantity>6</Quantity>
                <ItemNo>OS-004</ItemNo>
                <Description>Paper</Description>
                <UnitPrice>25.98</UnitPrice>
            </PurchaseInfo>
</CustomerInfo>
```

The data between the CustomerInfo tags contains information about a single customer. The file can contain multiple customers. The information between the PurchaseInfo tags contains information about an individual purchase. In the example, a single customer made two purchases, so the PurchaseInfo tags are inside the CustomerInfo tags. Shown graphically, you can structure data as follows:

```
CustInfo
    Customer 1
        Purchase 1
        Purchase 2
    Customer 2
        Purchase 1
CustInfo
```

Every XML file must have a set of root tags. The root tags describe the document and surround the child tags. Every document ends with a root tag. In the example, <CustomerInfo> and </CustomerInfo> are root tags. All of the tags between the <CustomerInfo> tags are child tags.

When structuring your XML file, you must properly nest your tags. In the example, you must close each purchase before you start a new purchase, and you must close each customer before you start a new customer.

If you want to exchange your data with other systems, your XML file must be well-formed. If your data is not well-formed, your XML file will not work. Well-formed XML files comply with the following rules:

- They begin with a declaration.
- They contain a root tag.
- Every tag either has a closing tag or is an empty tag.
- Opening and closing tags use the same case.
- Tags are properly nested.
- Attributes are enclosed in either single or double quotes.

Understanding Excel XML Files

Prior to Office 2007, by default, Office files were saved as binary files in a proprietary format. You can still save your files in binary format by saving them as Excel 97-2003 files if you need to share files with users who do not have Office 2007 or higher. However, the binary file type is no longer the default. Moreover, when you save your file as an Excel 97-2003 file, Office 2007 or higher features that are not supported in earlier versions are lost.

Starting with Office 2007, the default file type is based on XML. The XML file format has several advantages:

- XML files are smaller. The XML file format uses Zip technology, which compresses the files. As a result, when you compare XML files to binary files, the XML files can be up to 75 percent smaller. This

means they take up less space and are easier to transfer via mechanisms such as e-mail.

- XML files are more secure. In the default XLSX format, you cannot include macros. This gives you assurance that your XLSX files do not include any malicious macro viruses. If you want to save macros in your Excel file, you must save the file with an .xlsm extension. Excel places the macros in a separate part of the file that is more secure.

- Data is easier to recover in XML files. XML files are human-readable. You can open the files and read the contents by using a text editor such as Notepad. If part of the file becomes corrupted, you can open the file and recover the uncorrupted part.

Understanding Excel XML Files

Create and Save an Excel File

1. Create an Excel file.

- Include an image.

- Include a comment.

- Include data.

- Include properties.

2. Click the Save button and then close the file.

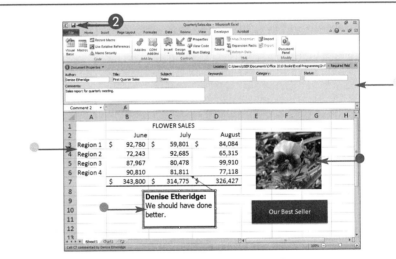

Open an Excel File

1. In Windows Explorer, move to the folder where you saved your file.

2. Right-click the filename.

   A menu appears.

3. Click Rename.

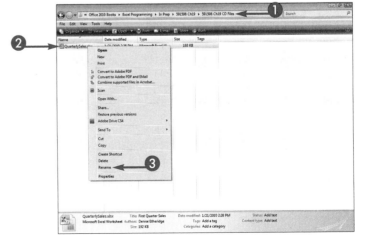

④ Change the file extension to .zip.

Windows asks if you are sure you want to change the file extension. Click Yes.

⑤ Double-click the file.

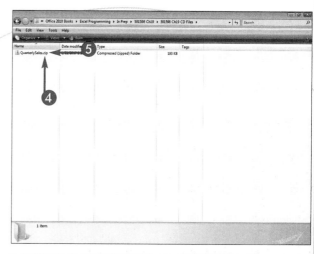

The file opens.

● The _rels folder stores information about relationships.

● The [Content_Types].xml part stores information about what is in the package.

● The xl folder stores the workbook component files.

● The docProps folder stores information about the document properties.

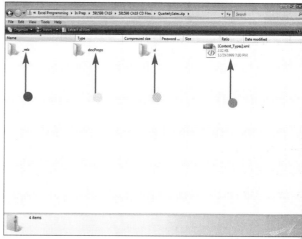

Extra

To assign properties to a file, click the File tab, click Info, and then click Properties. A menu appears. Click Show Document Panel. The Document Properties pane appears in your workbook. Enter the properties you want to enter. In the upper left corner of the Properties pane, click Document Properties, and then click Advanced Properties. The Properties dialog box appears. You can use the Properties dialog box to review properties and add custom properties.

If you have a computer with Excel 97-2003 installed, you can go to the Office Update Web site and download the Microsoft Office system Compatibility Pack for Excel. After you install the Compatibility Pack, you can open Excel 2007 and 2010 files in Excel 97-2003. Excel 2007 or Excel 2010 features and formatting may not appear in the earlier version, but they are still available when you open the file again in Excel 2007 or 2010.

To view the contents of an Excel workbook file, change the file extension to .zip and then double-click the file. To use the file again, change the extension back to the extension the file originally had.

continued →

Understanding Excel
XML Files (continued)

I f you want to see the XML layout for an Excel 2007 or 2010 file, change the file extension on the Excel file to .zip and then double-click the file. The file opens and several folders and files appear.

Office 2007 and 2010 files are in a compressed Zip format; each Zip file is called a *package*. A package has three major components: Part Items, Content Type Items, and Relationship Items.

Each file inside a package is called a *part*. When you open an Excel file, a workbook.xlm file is in the xl folder. You may also find a styles.xlm file. These files are "parts" of the package. Most parts are XML files that describe the data contained in the Excel workbook.

Relationships define how the parts of a document come together to form a document. The relationships are stored in the /_rels folders in .rels files in the root and in subdirectories of the file.

Excel divides a workbook package into several parts. Some of the parts you may see in a package are charts, comments, themes, styles, and workbook drawings. You can manually modify and replace document parts, and you can write programs to modify and replace document parts.

If your document includes images, the actual images are stored in the file. For security proposes, the images are named image1, image2, and so on.

Understanding Excel XML Files *(continued)*

Content Type.xml

① Double-click Content_ Type.xml.

The file opens in your default XML editor.

_rels

① Double-click the _rels folder to open it.

The .rels file appears.

② Double-click the .rels file to open it.

The file sets relationships.

xl

1 Double-click the xl folder to open it.

A number of files and folders appear.

2 Double-click each part and examine it.

This example opens the media folder and then opens the image file.

docProps

1 Double-click the docProps folder.

2 Double-click the parts and examine them.

The document properties appear.

This example opens the core.xml file.

Extra

For a detailed explanation of the concepts presented in this section, download "Introducing the Office (2007) Open XML File Formats" (http://msdn2.microsoft.com/en-us/library/aa338205.aspx) from the Microsoft Web site.

You can modify the contents of an Excel package. In the example, you opened the media folder and viewed the image in your Excel document. If you want to change the image, you can take out the image that is in the file and replace it with a new image, manually or by using a program. You can also change the text in the document manually or by using a program. For example, if you open a comment file, you see comments. If you change a comment, the new comment appears when you open your workbook in Excel again.

As you can see, the XML file format gives you a great deal of flexibility by making your files easy to modify.

Open an XML File in Excel as a Table

I f your Excel data consists of columns and rows, you can convert your data to a table. In Excel, tables allow you to manipulate your data easily. Each column heading in a table contains a down arrow. You can use the down arrow to sort, filter, and otherwise manipulate your data. Having your data in an Excel table greatly enhances your ability to work with your data.

If you have data that is in well-formed XML format, you can easily open the XML file in Excel as a table and then use Excel to manipulate the data. To find out more about well-formed XML format, see the section "Introducing XML."

Excel needs a schema to import your XML data. Schemas enable processing programs such as Excel to validate your data. For example, a schema tells the processing

program whether a particular element should contain text or a number. When you open an XML file, if your data does not have a schema, Excel creates one. Excel infers the schema from the data that is contained in the XML file.

When you open an XML file as a table, Excel also creates an XML map. Excel uses the map to relate the schema to the data in the worksheet. A single workbook can contain several XML maps, and several maps can refer to the same schema.

Excel creates a graphical hierarchical representation of your data in the XML Source pane when it opens your XML file as a table. Open the Source pane to see the representation.

Open an XML File in Excel as a Table

① Click the File tab.

② Click Open.

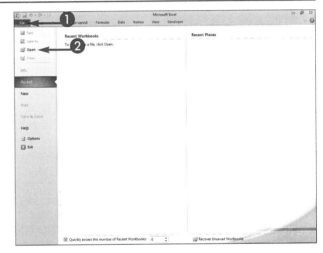

The Open dialog box appears.

③ Locate the folder that contains your XML file.

④ Click the file.

⑤ Click Open.

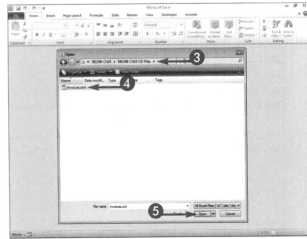

The Open XML
dialog box appears.

6 Click As an XML
Table (○ changes
to ◉).

7 Click OK.

If Excel asks if you
want to create a
schema, click OK.

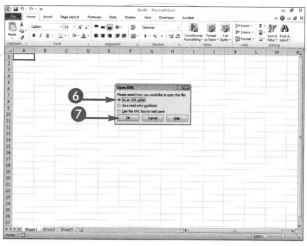

The file appears in
Excel as an Excel
table.

8 Click the Developer
tab.

9 Click Source.

● The map to your
data appears.

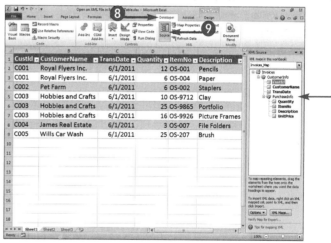

Extra

The Open XML dialog box presents three choices. You can open the file as an XML table or as a read-only file, or you can use the XML Source task pane. The As an XML Table option is explained in this section. The As a Read-Only Workbook option opens the file as read-only and does not create a map to your data. The Use the XML Source Task Pane option creates a map but does not place any elements in your worksheet. For details on how to work with an XML map, see the section "Create an XML Map."

When you import or open an XML file, if the file does not have a schema, Excel creates one for you. To view the schema, click the Developer tab and then click Visual Basic to open the VBE. Once in the VBE, press Ctrl+G to open the Immediate window. In the Immediate window, type `Print activeworkbook.XmlMaps(1).Schemas(1).xml`. VBA prints the schema to the Immediate window. You can copy and paste it into a text or XML editor.

Create an XML Map

When you open your XML file as an Excel table, Excel places all of your data in your worksheet, and you can use the table features in Excel to manipulate your data. Alternatively, you can create a map and place just the elements you want to use in your worksheet. You complete the process in three steps: create a map, move the elements you want to use to your worksheet, and then refresh your data.

When you use the mapping method, you choose what elements you want to appear in your worksheet. This method is useful when your XML file has a large number of elements and you only want to work with a subset of those elements. Click on an element in the XML Source pane and then drag the element onto your worksheet.

Excel calls the list of data elements in the XML Source pane a *map*, and the process of clicking and dragging elements to your worksheet *mapping*. Excel creates a connection between the element in the Source pane and your data. If you want to see the connection, after you place an element in your worksheet, click the element in the XML Source pane and Excel highlights the data in your worksheet. Or, click data in your worksheet, and Excel highlights the element name in the XML Source pane.

When you create a map and then bring your data into Excel, you gain the same benefits as when you open a file in XML format. You can use all of Excel's table features to sort and filter your data.

Create an XML Map

① Click the Developer tab.

② Click Source.

The XML Source pane appears.

③ Click XML Maps.

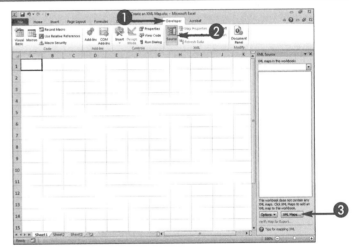

The XML Maps dialog box appears.

④ Click Add.

The Select XML Source dialog box appears.

⑤ Locate the folder that contains the file you want to map.

⑥ Click the file.

⑦ Click Open.

If Excel asks if you want to create a schema, click Yes.

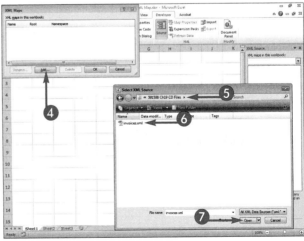

- Excel creates your map.

8 Click OK.

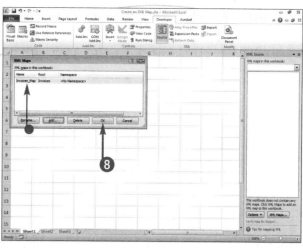

- Excel adds a map to the XML Source pane.

9 Click and drag elements from the XML Source pane to your worksheet.

10 Click the Developer tab.

11 Click Refresh Data.

- Excel adds the data in your XML file to your worksheet.

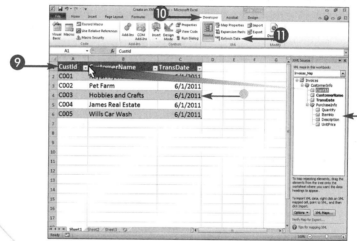

Import and Export XML Files Using Excel

When working with XML data, the data in the XML file may change or you may want to import the additional data. Conversely, you may make changes to the data and want to export the changes to an XML file. If you want to import and export XML data into and out of Excel, use the Import and Export features on the Developer tab. The Import feature opens the Import dialog box, where you can choose the file you want to import. The Export feature opens the Export dialog box, where you can name the file you are exporting.

Importing data enables you to either overwrite your current data or append data to your table. You can use the XML Map Properties dialog box to specify which you want to do. The default is to overwrite existing data with

new data. If the system outputting the data has corrected the data or if your old data is no longer relevant, overwriting your data is the better choice. If the system outputting the data outputs data periodically, appending data is the better choice. Appending data enables you to keep your database up-to-date.

You can export data in XML format by using the Export feature on the Developer tab. When you export data, all of the data must be from a single node in your XML map. If you want to verify that Excel can export your data, click Verify Map for Export on the XML Source pane before exporting. Excel exports your data as a well-formed XML file. A well-formed XML file adheres to all the rules for creating XML files. For more information about well-formed files, see the section "Introducing XML."

Import and Export XML Files Using Excel

Import an XML File

1 Click the Developer tab.

2 Click Import.

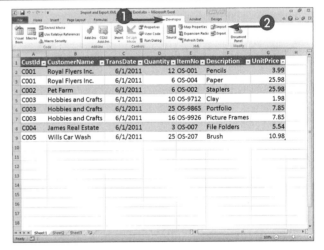

The Import XML dialog box appears.

3 Locate the folder where the file you want to import is located.

4 Click the file you want to import.

5 Click Import.

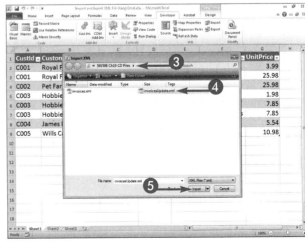

Excel imports the XML data.

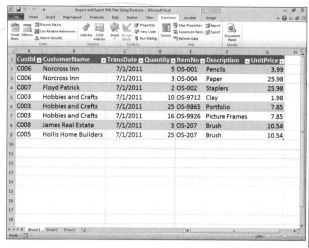

Export an XML File

① Click the Developer tab.

② Click Export.

The Export XML dialog box appears.

③ Locate the folder where you want to save the file.

④ Type a filename.

⑤ Click Export.

Excel exports the file.

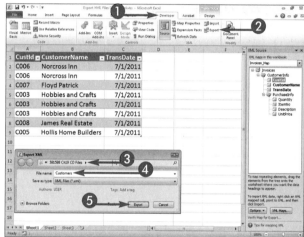

Extra

When you import or refresh data, you can either overwrite your current data or append data. Use the XML Map properties dialog box to specify which you want to do. To open the XML Map properties dialog box, click the Developer tab, and then click Map Properties in the XML group. The overwrite and append options are at the bottom of the dialog box.

The XML Source task pane has several options you can set by clicking the Options button in the lower left corner. Select the Preview Data in Task Pane option to see a sample of the data elements in your XML file in the task pane. Select the Hide Help Text in the Task Pane option to prevent help from appearing at the bottom of the task pane. Select Automatically Merge Elements When Mapping to create a single table when you place elements side by side in a single row in the worksheet.

Load XML Files Using VBA

If you want to automate the process of loading XML data, use the OpenXML method. OpenXML is the VBA equivalent to opening an XML file as a table. As when you open an XML file as a table, OpenXML provides several choices. Make your choice by specifying one of the following XlXmlLoadOption options: xlXmlLoadImportToList, xlXmlLoadMapXml, or xlXmlLoadPromptUser.

If you select the xlXmlLoadImportToList option, VBA creates a map of your data, places the map in the XML Source pane, and then places all of your XML data in a worksheet formatted as a table.

If you select the xlXmlLoadMapXml option, VBA creates a map of your data and places the map in the XML Source pane. Excel does not place any data in a worksheet.

If you select the xlXmlLoadPromptUser option, VBA displays the Open XML dialog box. The user can choose to open the XML file as a table or as a read-only workbook, or use the XML Source task pane. Opening the file as a table is equivalent to the xlXmlLoadImportToList option. Using the XML Source task pane is equivalent to the xlXmlLoadMapXml option.

The following is an example of the OpenXML method:

```
Sub OpenXMLPromptUser()
    Application.Workbooks.OpenXML _
        Filename:"invoices.xml", _
        LoadOption:=xlXmlLoadPromptUser
End Sub
```

Use the FileName parameter to specify the name of the file you want to load. If the file is not located in the current folder, specify the path to the folder.

Load XML Files Using VBA

1 Name your procedure.

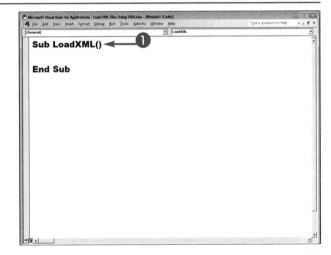

2 Create your OpenXML command.

- This is the file you want to load.

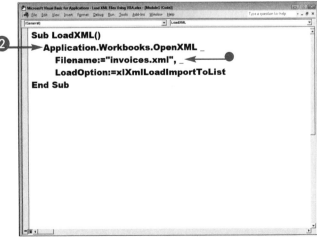

● This is the load option you want to use.

③ Press Alt+F11 to switch from the VBE to Excel, and run the macro.

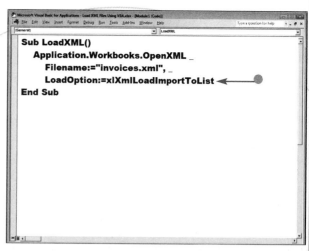

The macro loads the XML file.

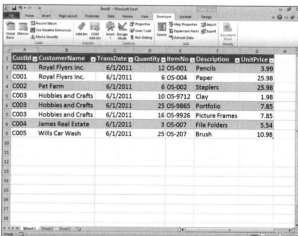

Import XML Files Using VBA

You can use the `XmlImport` method to load data into a map that already exists. This process is similar to clicking the Import button on the Developer tab. You can refresh your data or import new data into your worksheet. The `XmlImport` method has the following parameters: `Url`, `ImportMap`, `Overwrite`, and `Destination`.

The `Url` parameter is required. Use this parameter to target a URL as a data source. Insert the URL as a string enclosed in double quotes. You can also use this parameter to target a file on your local computer. If the file is located in the current directory, type the filename; otherwise, type the path.

The `ImportMap` parameter is also required. For this parameter, supply the schema map you want VBA to use.

You can identify the map by name. When you create a map, Excel assigns it a name. The name appears in the drop-down list at the top of the XML Source pane. You can also view the list of XML maps in your workbook by clicking the XML Maps button in the XML Source pane. If you want Excel to create the map, assign `Nothing` to the parameter, as in `ImportMap:=Nothing`.

Use the `Overwrite` parameter to specify whether you want to overwrite the existing data. Set the parameter to `True` if you want to overwrite the data. Set the parameter to `False` if you want to append to the existing data. `True` is the default value.

Use the `Destination` parameter to specify the top left corner of the range where you want to create the table. If you are importing data into a map that already exists, do not set this parameter.

Import XML Files Using VBA

① Create a map and place the elements in your worksheet.

Note: To learn how to create a map, see the section "Create an XML Map."

● This is the name of your map.

② Press Alt+F11.

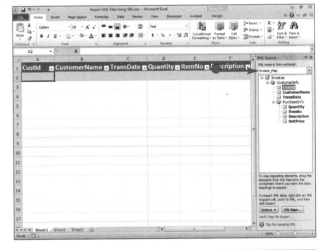

Excel moves you to the VBE.

③ Name your procedure.

④ Declare a variable as an `XmlMap` object.

⑤ Assign your map the `XmlMap` object variable.

● This is the map name.

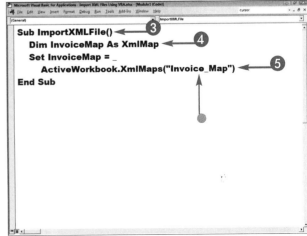

6 Create your `XmlImport` command.

7 Press Alt+F11 to switch from the VBE to Excel, and run the macro.

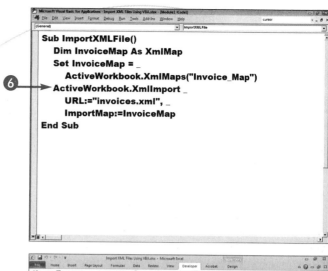

VBA imports your data.

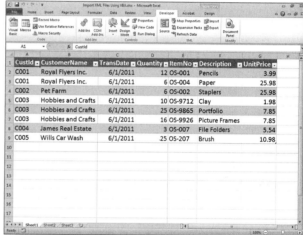

Extra

As an alternative to the syntax in the example, you can use the following syntax to import an XML file. This syntax uses the `XMLMap.Import` method. The first parameter is `Url`. Use this parameter to specify the path to the data. The second parameter is `Overwrite`. Setting the `Overwrite` parameter to `False` causes the command to append instead of overwriting data.

Example:
```
Sub ImportXMLFile()
    ActiveWorkbook _
        .XmlMaps("Invoice_Map") _
        .Import URL:="invoices.xml", _
        Overwrite:=False
End Sub
```

VBA and Excel Object Model Quick Reference

Legend:

Plain courier text = required   [] = optional | = or

Italics = user-defined   . . . = list of items

File and Folder Handling

STATEMENT	DESCRIPTION
ChDir *path*	Changes to the specified folder location.
ChDrive *drive*	Changes to the specified drive.
Close [*filenumber*]	Closes a file opened by using an Open statement.
FileCopy *source, destination*	Copies a file from the source to the specified destination.
FreeFile[(*rangenumber*)]	Each open file is represented by an integer value. Returns the next available integer value for use by the Open statement.
Kill *pathname*	Deletes files from a disk. Use wildcards (*) for multiple characters and (?) for single characters.
Lock [#]*filenumber*[, *recordrange*]	Locks all or a portion of an open file to prevent access by other processes.
MkDir *path*	Creates a new directory or folder.
Open pathname For mode [Access *access*] [*lock*] As [#]*filenumber* [Len=*reclength*]	Opens the specified file to allow input/output operations.
Print #*filenumber*[, *outputlist*]	Writes display-formatted data sequentially to a file.
Put [#]*filenumber*, [*recnumber*,] *varname*	Writes data contained in a variable to a disk file.
Reset	Closes all files opened using the Open statement.
RmDir *path*	Removes the specified folder.
SetAttr *pathname, attributes*	Sets the attribute information for the specified file.
Unlock [#]*filenumber*[, *recordrange*]	Unlocks a file to allow access by other processes.
Width #*filenumber*, *width*	Assigns the output line width for a file opened using the Open statement.
Write #*filenumber*[, *outputlist*]	Writes data to a sequential text file.

Interaction

STATEMENT	DESCRIPTION
AppActivate *title*[, *wait*]	Activates an application window.
DeleteSetting *appname, section*[, *key*]	Deletes a section or key setting from an application's entry in the Windows Registry.
SaveSetting *appname, section, key, setting*	Saves an application entry in the application's entry in the Windows Registry.
SendKeys *string*[, *wait*]	Sends one or more keystrokes to the active window as if they were typed on the keyboard.

Program Flow

STATEMENT	DESCRIPTION
[Public | Private] Declare Sub *name* Lib "*libname*" [Alias "*aliasname*"] [([*arglist*])]	Declares a reference to an external DLL library function.
Do [{While | Until} *condition*] [*statements*] Loop	Repeats a block of statements while or until a condition is true. The condition is checked at the beginning of the loop.
Do [*statements*] Loop [{While | Until} *condition*]	Repeats a block of statements while or until a condition is true. Because the condition is checked at the end of the loop, the block of statements always executes at least once.
Exit Do | For | Function | Property | Sub	Exits the specified Do Loop, For Next, Function, Sub, or Property code.
For Each *element* In *group* [*statements*] Next [*element*]	Repeats a block of statements for each element in an array or collection.
For *counter* = *start* To *end* [Step *step*] [*statements*] Next [*counter*]	Repeats a section of code the specified number of times.
[Public | Private | Friend] [Static] Function *name* [(*arglist*)] [As *type*] [*statements*] [*name* = *expression*] End Function	Defines a procedure that returns a value.
If *condition* Then [statements] [ElseIf *condition-n* Then] [*elseifstatements*]] [Else [*elsestatements*]] End If	Conditionally executes a block of statements based upon the value of an expression.
[Public | Private | Friend] [Static] Property Get *name* [(*arglist*)] [As *type*] [*statements*] [*name* = *expression*] End Property	Declares the name and arguments associated with a procedure.
[Public | Private | Friend] [Static] Property Let *name* ([*arglist*,] *value*) [*statements*] End Property	Declares the name and arguments of a procedure that assigns a value to a property.
[Public | Private | Friend] [Static] Property Set *name* ([*arglist*,] *reference*) [*statements*] End Property	Declares the name and arguments of a procedure that sets a reference to an object.
Select Case *testexpression* [Case *expressionlist-n* [*statements-n*]] [Case Else [*elsestatements*]] End Select	Executes one block out of a series of statement blocks depending upon the value of an expression.
[Private | Public | Friend] [Static] Sub *name* [(*arglist*)] [*statements*] End Sub	Declares the name, arguments, and code that form a Sub procedure.
While *condition* [*statements*] Wend	Executes a block of statements as long as the specified condition is true.
With *object* [*statements*] End With	Executes a block of statements on a single object or on a user-defined data type.

continued ➡

VBA Statements Quick Reference *(continued)*

Variable Declaration

STATEMENT	DESCRIPTION
[Public | Private] Const *constname* [As type] = *expression*	Declares a constant value.
Dim [WithEvents] *varname*[([*subscripts*])] [As [New] *type*]	Declares variables and allocates the appropriate storage space.
Friend [WithEvents] *varname*[([*subscripts*])] [As [New] *type*]	Declares a procedure or variable to only have scope in the project where it is defined.
Option Compare {Binary | Text | Database}	Specifies the default comparison method to use when comparing strings.
Option Explicit	Forces declaration of all variables within the module.
Option Private	Indicates that all code within the entire module is Private. VBA uses this option by default. You can overwrite the effects of this option by declaring a specific procedure Public.
Private [WithEvents] *varname*[([*subscripts*])] [As [New] *type*]	Declares variables and procedures to only have scope within the current module.
Public [WithEvents] *varname*[([*subscripts*])] [As [New] *type*]	Declares variables and procedures to have scope within the entire project.
ReDim [Preserve] *varname*(*subscripts*) [As *type*]	Changes the dimensions of a dynamic array.
[Private | Public] Type *varname* *elementname* [([*subscripts*])] As *type* [*elementname* [([*subscripts*])] As *type*] ... End Type	Defines a custom data type.

VBA Function Quick Reference

Legend:

Plain courier text = required   [] = optional | = or

Italics = user-defined   . . . = list of items

Array Functions

FUNCTION	DESCRIPTION	RETURNS
Array(*arg1*,*arg2*, *arg3*, ...)	Creates a variant array containing the specified elements.	Variant
LBound(*arrayname*[, *dimension*])	Returns the smallest subscript for the specified array.	Long
UBound(*arrayname*[, *dimension*])	Returns the largest subscript for the specified array.	Long

Data Type Conversion Functions

FUNCTION	DESCRIPTION	RETURNS
Asc(*string*)	Returns the character code of the first letter in a string.	Integer
CBool(*expression*)	Converts an expression to Boolean data type (True or False).	Boolean
CByte(*expression*)	Converts an expression to Byte data type.	Byte
CCur(*expression*)	Converts an expression to Currency data type.	Currency
CDate(*expression*)	Converts an expression to a Date data type.	Date
CDbl(*expression*)	Converts an expression to Double data type.	Double
CDec(*expression*)	Converts an expression to a decimal value.	Variant (Decimal)
Chr(*charactercode*)	Converts the character code to the corresponding character. Chr(9) returns a tab, Chr(34) returns quotation marks, and so on.	Variant
CInt(*expression*)	Converts an expression to Integer data type, rounding any fractional parts.	Integer
CLng(*expression*)	Converts an expression to Long data type.	Long
CSng(*expression*)	Converts an expression to Single data type.	Single
CStr(*expression*)	Returns a string containing the specified expression.	String
CVar(*expression*)	Converts any data type to Variant data type. All numeric values are treated as Double data types and string expressions are treated as String data types.	Variant
Format(*expression*[, *format*[, *firstdayofweek*[, *firstweekofyear*]]])	Formats the expression using either predefined or user-defined formats.	Variant
FormatCurrency(*Expression*[, *NumDigitsAfterDecimal* [, *IncludeLeadingDigit* [,*UseParensForNegativeNumbers* [, *GroupDigits*]]]])	Formats the expression as a currency value using the system-defined currency symbol.	Currency
FormatDateTime(*Date*[, *NamedFormat*])	Formats an expression as a date and time.	Date
FormatNumber(*Expression* [, *NumDigitsAfterDecimal* [, *IncludeLeadingDigit* [, *UseParensForNegativeNumbers* [, *GroupDigits*]]]])	Formats the expression as a number.	Mixed
FormatPercent(*Expression* [,*NumDigitsAfterDecimal* [,*IncludeLeadingDigit* [,*UseParensForNegativeNumbers* [,*GroupDigits*]]]])	Returns the expression formatted as a percentage with a trailing % character.	String
Hex(*number*)	Converts a number to a hexadecimal value. Rounds numbers to nearest whole number before converting.	String

continued

continued ➡

Data Type Conversion Functions (continued)

FUNCTION	DESCRIPTION	RETURNS
Oct(*number*)	Converts a number to an octal value. Rounds numbers to nearest whole number before converting.	Variant (String)
Str(*number*)	Converts a number to a string using Variant data type.	Variant (String)
Val(*string*)	Returns the numeric portion of a string formatted as a number of the appropriate data type.	Mixed

Date and Time Functions

FUNCTION	DESCRIPTION	RETURNS
Date	Returns the current system date.	Date
DateAdd(*interval, number, date*)	Returns a date that is the specified interval of time from the original date.	Date
DateDiff(*interval, date1, date2*[, *Long firstdayofweek*[, *firstweekofyear*]])	Determines the time interval between two dates.	Long
DatePart(*interval, date*[, *firstdayofweek*[, *firstweekofyear*]])	Returns the specified part of a date.	Integer
DateSerial(*year, month, day*)	Converts the specified date to a serial number.	Date
DateValue(*date*)	Converts a string to a date.	Date
Day(*date*)	Returns a whole number between 1 and 31 representing the day of the month.	Integer
Hour(*time*)	Returns a whole number between 0 and 23 representing the hour of the day.	Integer
Minute(*time*)	Returns a whole number between 0 and 59 representing the minute of the hour.	Integer
Month(*date*)	Returns a whole number between 1 and 12 representing the month of the year.	Integer
Now	Returns the current system date and time.	Date
Second(*time*)	Returns a whole number between 0 and 59 representing the second of the minute.	Integer
Time	Returns the current system time.	Date
Timer	Indicates the number of seconds that have elapsed since midnight.	Single
TimeSerial(*hour, minute, second*)	Creates a time using the specified hour, minute, and second values.	Date
TimeValue(*time*)	Converts a time to the serial number used to store time.	Date
WeekDay(*date,* [*firstdayofweek*])	Returns a whole number representing the first day of the week.	Integer
Year(*date*)	Returns a whole number representing the year portion of a date.	Integer

File and Folder Handling Functions

FUNCTION	DESCRIPTION	RETURNS
CurDir(*drive*)	Returns the current path.	String
Dir[(*pathname*[, *attributes*])]	Returns the name of the file, directory, or folder that matches the specified pattern.	String
EOF(*filenumber*)	Returns –1 when the end of a file has been reached.	Integer
FileAttr(*filenumber*, *returntype*)	Indicates the file mode used for files opened with the Open statement.	Long
FileDateTime(*pathname*)	Indicates the date and time when a file was last modified.	Date
FileLen(*pathname*)	Indicates the length of a file in bytes.	Long
FreeFile(*rangenumber*)	Returns the next file number available for use by the Open statement.	Integer
GetAttr(*pathname*)	Returns a whole number representing the attributes of a file, directory, or folder.	Integer
Input(*number*, [#]*filenumber*)	Returns a string containing the indicated number of characters from the specified file.	String
Loc(*filenumber*)	Indicates the current read/write position in an open file.	Long
LOF(*filenumber*)	Returns the size in bytes of a file opened using the Long Open statement.	Long
Seek(*filenumber*)	Specifies the current read/write position with a file opened with the Open statement.	Long

Financial Functions

FUNCTION	DESCRIPTION	RETURNS
DDB(*cost*, *salvage*, *life*, *period*[, *factor*])	Specifies the depreciation value for an asset during a specific time frame.	Double
FV(*rate*, *nper*, *pmt*[, *pv*[, *type*]])	Determines the future value of an annuity based on periodic fixed payments.	Double
IPmt(*rate*, *per*, *nper*, *pv*[, *fv*[, *type*]])	Determines the interest payment on an annuity for a specific period of time.	Double
IRR(*values*(), [, *guess*])	Determines the internal rate of returns for a series of cash flows.	Double
MIRR(*values*(), *finance_rate*, *reinvest_rate*)	Returns the modified interest rate of returns for a series of periodic cash flows.	Double
NPer(*rate*, *pmt*, *pv*[, *fv*[, *type*]])	Returns the number of periods for an annuity.	Double
NPV(*rate*, *values*())	Returns the net present value of an investment.	Double
Pmt(*rate*, *nper*, *pv*[, *fv*[, *type*]])	Returns the payment amount for an annuity based on fixed payments.	Double
PPmt(*rate*, *per*, *nper*, *pv*[, *fv*[, *type*]])	Returns the principal payment amount for an annuity.	Double
PV(*rate*, *nper*, *pmt*[, *fv*[, *type*]])	Returns the present value of an annuity.	Double

continued

continued ➡

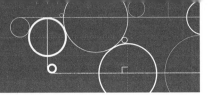

Financial Functions (continued)

FUNCTION	DESCRIPTION	RETURNS
Rate(*nper, pmt, pv*[, *fv*[, *type*[, *guess*]]])	Returns the interest rate per period for an annuity.	Double
SLN(*cost, salvage, life*)	Determines the straight-line depreciation of an asset for a single period.	Double
SYD(*cost, salvage, life, period*)	Determines the sum-of-years' digits depreciation of an asset for a specified period.	Double

Information Functions

FUNCTION	DESCRIPTION	RETURNS
CVErr(*errornumber*)	Returns a user-defined error number.	Variant
Error[(*errornumber*)]	Returns the error message for the specified error number.	String
IsArray(*varname*)	Indicates whether a variable contains an array.	Boolean
IsDate(*expression*)	Indicates whether an expression contains a date.	Boolean
IsEmpty(*expression*)	Indicates whether a variable has been initialized.	Boolean
IsError(*expression*)	Indicates whether an expression is an error value.	Boolean
IsMissing(*argname*)	Indicates whether an optional argument was passed to a procedure.	Boolean
IsNull(*expression*)	Indicates whether an expression contains no valid data.	Boolean
IsNumeric(*expression*)	Indicates whether an expression is a number.	Boolean
IsObject(*identifier*)	Indicates whether a variable references an object.	Boolean
TypeName(*varname*)	Returns the variable type.	String
VarType(*varname*)	Returns the subtype of a variable.	Integer

Interaction Functions

FUNCTION	DESCRIPTION	RETURNS
Choose(*index*, *choice-1*, [*choice-2*, ...])	Selects and returns a value from a list of choices.	Mixed
DoEvents()	Passes control to the operating system so the operation system can process other events.	Integer
Iif(*expr*, *truepart*, *falsepart*)	Evaluates the expression and returns either the truepart or falsepart parameter value.	Mixed
InputBox(*prompt*[, *title*] [, *default*] [, *xpos*] [, *ypos*] [, *helpfile*, *context*])	Displays a dialog box prompting the user for input.	String
GetAllSettings(*appname*, *section*)	Returns a list of key settings and their values from the Windows Registry.	Variant
GetObject([*pathname*][, *class*])	Returns a reference to an object provided by an ActiveX component.	Variant
GetSetting(*appname*, *section*, *key*[, *default*])	Returns a key setting value from an application's entry in the Windows Registry.	Variant
MsgBox(*prompt*[, *buttons*] [, *title*] [, *helpfile*, *context*])	Displays a message box and returns a value representing the button pressed by the user.	Integer
Partition(*number*, *start*, *stop*, *interval*)	Indicates where a number occurs within a series of ranges.	String
QBColor(*color*)	Returns the RGB color code for the specified color.	Long
Switch(*expr-1*, *value-1*[, *expr-2*, *value-2* ...])	Evaluates a list of expressions and returns the value associated with the first True expression.	Variant
RGB(*red*, *green*, *blue*)	Returns a number representing the RGB color value.	Long

Mathematical Functions

FUNCTION	DESCRIPTION	RETURNS
Abs(*number*)	Returns the absolute value of a number.	Mixed
Atn(*number*)	Returns the arctangent of a number.	Double
Cos(*number*)	Returns the cosine of an angle.	Double
Exp(*number*)	Returns the base of the natural logarithms raised to a power.	Double

continued

continued ➡

Mathematical Functions (continued)

FUNCTION	DESCRIPTION	RETURNS
Fix(*number*)	Returns the integer portion of a number. With negative values, returns first negative value greater than or a power equal to number.	Integer
Int(*number*)	Returns the integer portion of a number. With negative values, returns the first negative number less than or equal to the number.	Integer
Log(*number*)	Returns the natural logarithm of a number.	Double
Round(*expression* [, *numdecimalplaces*])	Rounds a number to the specified number of decimal places.	Mixed
Rnd[(*number*)]	Returns a random number between 0 and 1.	Single
Sgn(*number*)	Returns 1 for a number greater than 0, 0 for a value of 0, and –1 number less than 0.	Integer
Sin(*number*)	Returns the sine of an angle.	Double
Sqr(*number*)	Returns the square root of a number.	Double
Tan(*number*)	Returns the tangent of an angle.	Double

String Manipulation Functions

FUNCTION	DESCRIPTION	RETURNS
InStr([*start*,]*string1*, *string2* [, *compare*])	Specifies the position of one string within another string.	Long
InStrRev(*stringcheck*, *stringmatch*[, *start*[,*compare*]])	Specifies the position of one string within another starting at the end of the string.	Long
LCase(*string*)	Converts a string to lowercase.	String
Left(*string*, *length*)	Returns the specified number of characters from the left side of a string.	String
Len(*string* | *varname*)	Determines the number of characters in a string.	Long
LTrim(*string*)	Trims spaces from the left side of a string.	String
Mid(*string*, *start*[, *length*])	Returns the specified number of characters from the center of a string.	String
Right(*string*, *length*)	Returns the specified number of characters from the right side of a string.	String
RTrim(*string*)	Trims spaces from the right side of a string.	String
Space(*number*)	Creates a string with the specified number of spaces.	String

String Manipulation Functions (continued)

FUNCTION	DESCRIPTION	RETURNS
Spc(*n*)	Positions output when printing to a file.	String
Str(*number*)	Returns a string representation of a number.	String
StrComp(*string1, string2*[, *compare*])	Returns a value indicating the result of a string comparison.	Integer
StrConv(*string, conversion, LCID*)	Converts a string to the specified format.	String
String(*number, character*)	Creates a string by repeating a character the specified number of times.	String
Tab[(*n*)]	Positions output when printing to a file.	String
Trim(*string*)	Trims spaces from left and right of a string.	String
UCase(*string*)	Converts a string to uppercase.	String

VBA Function Constants and Characters

vbMsgBoxStyle Constants (MsgBox Function)

CONSTANT	VALUE	DESCRIPTION
vbAbortRetryIgnore	2	Displays Abort, Retry, and Ignore buttons.
vbApplicationModal	0	Creates application modal message box.
vbCritical	16	Displays Critical Message icon.
vbDefaultButton1	0	Makes first button default.
vbDefaultButton2	256	Makes second button default.
vbDefaultButton3	512	Makes third button default.
vbDefaultButton4	768	Makes fourth button default.
vbExclamation	48	Displays Warning Message icon.
vbInformation	64	Displays Information Message icon.
vbMsgBoxHelpButton	16384	Adds a Help button.
vbMsgBoxRight	524288	Right-aligns text in the box.
vbMsgBoxRtlReading	1048576	Used only with Hebrew and Arabic systems for right-to-left reading.
vbMsgBoxSetForeground	65536	Makes message box the foreground window.
vbOKCancel	1	Displays OK and Cancel buttons.
vbOKOnly	0	Displays only the OK button.
vbQuestion	32	Displays Warning Query icon.
vbRetryCancel	5	Displays Retry and Cancel buttons.
vbSystemModal	4096	Creates a system modal message box.
vbYesNo	4	Displays Yes and No buttons.
vbYesNoCancel	3	Displays Yes, No, and Cancel buttons.

continued ➡

vbDayOfWeek Constants

CONSTANT	VALUE	DESCRIPTION
vbUseSystemDayofWeek	0	Uses the system-defined first day of week
vbSunday	1	Sunday (default)
vbMonday	2	Monday
vbTuesday	3	Tuesday
vbWednesday	4	Wednesday
vbThursday	5	Thursday
vbFriday	6	Friday
vbSaturday	7	Saturday

vbFirstWeekOfYear Constants

CONSTANT	VALUE	DESCRIPTION
vbUseSystem	0	Uses system-defined first week of year.
vbFirstJan1	1	Starts with week in which January 1 occurs (default).
vbFirstFourDays	2	Starts with the first week that has at least four days in the new year.
vbFirstFullWeek	3	Starts with first full week of the year.

Format Function Characters

DATE/TIME CHARACTERS	DISPLAYS
d	Day with no leading zero.
ddd	Three-letter abbreviation of day (Sun – Sat).
dddd	Full day name (Sunday).
ddddd	Complete date using short date format.
dddddd	Complete date using long date format.
w	Day of week as number (1 for Sunday).
ww	Week of year as number.
m	Month with no leading zero.
mmm	Three-letter abbreviation of month (Jan – Dec).
mmmm	Complete month name.
q	Quarter of year.
y	Day of year as number.
yy	Year as two-digit number.
yyyy	Year as four-digit number.
h	Hour with no leading zero.

Format Function Characters (continued)

DATE/TIME CHARACTERS	DISPLAYS
n	Minutes with no leading zero.
s	Seconds with no leading zero.
ttttt	Complete time using system time format.
c	Date as dddddd and time as ttttt.

Format Function Predefined Formats

FORMAT	DESCRIPTION
General Date	Uses general date format.
Long Date	Uses system-defined long date, such as Tuesday, August 7, 2011.
Medium Date	Uses the medium date format, such as 07-Aug-11.
Short Date	Uses system-defined short date, such as 8/7/2011.
Medium Time	Uses the medium time format, such as 05:45 P.M.
Short Time	Uses the short time format, such as 17:45.
General Number	Uses the general number format.
Currency	Places the appropriate currency symbol in front of the number.
Fixed	Uses a fixed decimal format.
Standard	Uses standard formatting.
Percent	Converts the expression to a percentage.
Scientific	Displays the expression using scientific notation.
Yes/No	Converts the expression to a Yes or No value.
True/False	Converts the expression to a True or False value.
On/Off	Converts the expression to an On or Off value.

Excel Object Model Constants

XIColumnDataType Constants

CONSTANT	VALUE	DESCRIPTION
xlDMYFormat	4	DMY format date.
xlDYMFormat	7	DYM format date.
xlEMDFormat	10	EMD format date.
xlGeneralFormat	1	General format.
xlMDYFormat	3	MDY format date.
xlMYDFormat	6	MYD format date.
xlSkipColumn	9	Skip Column.
xlTextFormat	2	Text format.
xlYDMFormat	8	YDM format date.
xlYMDFormat	5	YMD format date.

continued ➡

Excel Object Model Constants

XlFileFormat Constants

CONSTANT	VALUE	DESCRIPTION
xlAddIn	18	Excel add-in 2007.
xlAddIn8	18	Excel 97-2003 add-in.
xlCSV	6	Comma-separated values format.
xlCSVMac	22	Macintosh comma-separated values format.
xlCSVMSDOS	24	MSDOS comma-separated values format.
xlCSVWindows	23	MS Windows comma-separated values format.
xlCurrentPlatformText	-4158	Text file based on current operating system.
xlDBF2	7	DBase II format.
xlDBF3	8	DBase III format.
xlDBF4	11	DBase IV format.
xlDIF	9	Data interchange format.
xlExcel12	50	Excel 12 format.
xlExcel2	16	Excel 2.
xlExcel2FarEast	27	Excel 2.0 format — Far East version.
xlExcel3	29	Excel 3.0 format.
xlExcel4	33	Excel 4.0 format.
xlExcel4Workbook	35	Excel 4.0 workbook format.
xlExcel5	39	Excel 5.0 format.
xlExcel7	39	Excel 97 format.
xlExcel8	56	Excel 97-2003 format.
xlExcel9795	43	Excel 95-97 format.
xlHtml	44	HTML format.
xlIntlAddIn	26	Excel international add-in.
xlIntlMacro	25	Excel international macro.
xlOpenXMLAddin	55	Open XML add-in.

XlFileFormat Constants (continued)

CONSTANT	VALUE	DESCRIPTION
xlOpenXMLTemplate	54	Open XML Template.
xlOpemXMLTemplateMacroEnabled	53	OpenXML Template Macro Enabled.
xlOpenXMLWorkbook	51	OpenXMLWorkbook.
xlOpenXMLWorkbookMacroEnabled	52	OpenXMLWorkbook Enabled.
xlSYLK	2	Symbolic link format.
xlTemplate	17	Template file format.
xlTemplate8	17	Template.
xlTextMac	19	Macintosh text file format.
xlTextMSDOS	21	MSDOS text file format.
xlTextPrinter	36	Text file created for a printer (.prn).
xlTextWindows	20	MS Window text file format.
xlUnicodeText	42	Unicode text file format.
xlWebArchive	45	Web archive format (.mht).
xlWJ2WD1	14	WJ2WD1.
xlWJ3	40	WJ3.
xlWJ3FM3	41	WJ3FJ3.
xlWK1	5	Lotus 2.x format.
xlWK1ALL	31	Lotus 2.x .all format.
xlWK1FMT	30	Lotus 2.x .fmt format.
xlWK3	15	Lotus 3.x format.
xlWK3FM3	32	Lotus 3.x and Lotus 1-2-3 for Windows format.
xlWK4	38	Lotus 4.0 format.
xlWKS	4	MS Works file format.
xlWorkBookDefault	51	Workbook default.
xlWorkbookNormal	–4143	Excel workbook format.
xlWorks2FarEast	28	MS Works file — Far East format.
xlWQ1	34	Quattro Pro for MSDOS format.
xlXMLSpreadsheet	46	XML format.

continued ➡

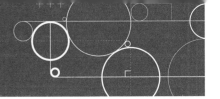
XIChartType Constants

CONSTANT	VALUE	CHART TYPE
xl3DArea	−4098	3D Area.
xl3DAreaStacked	78	3D Stacked Area.
xl3DAreaStacked100	79	100% Stacked Area.
xl3DBarClustered	60	3D Clustered Bar.
xl3DBarStacked	61	3D Stacked Bar.
xl3DBarStacked100	62	3D 100% Stacked Bar.
xl3DColumn	−4100	3D Column.
xl3DColumnClustered	54	3D Clustered Column.
xl3DColumnStacked	55	3D Stacked Column.
xl3DColumnStacked100	56	3D 100% Stacked Column.
xl3DLine	−4101	3D Line.
xl3DPie	−4102	3D Pie.
xl3DPieExploded	70	Exploded 3D Pie.
xlArea	1	Area.
xlAreaStacked	76	Stacked Area.
xlAreaStacked100	77	100% Stacked Area.
xlBarClustered	57	Clustered Bar.
xlBarOfPie	71	Bar of Pie.
xlBarStacked	58	Stacked Bar.
xlBarStacked100	59	100% Stacked Bar.
xlBubble	15	Bubble.
xlBubble3DEffect	87	Bubble with 3D effects.
xlColumnClustered	51	Clustered Column.
xlColumnStacked	52	Stacked Column.
xlColumnStacked100	53	100% Stacked Column.
xlConeBarClustered	102	Clustered Cone Bar.
xlConeBarStacked	103	Stacked Cone Bar.
xlConeBarStacked100	104	100% Stacked Cone Bar.
xlConeCol	105	3D Cone Column.

XlChartType Constants (continued)

CONSTANT	VALUE	CHART TYPE
xlConeColClustered	99	Clustered Cone Column.
xlConeColStacked	100	Stacked Cone Column.
xlConeColStacked100	101	100% Stacked Cone Column.
xlCylinderBarClustered	95	Clustered Cylinder Bar.
xlCylinderBarStacked	96	Stacked Cylinder Bar.
xlCylinderBarStacked100	97	100% Stacked Cylinder Bar.
xlCylinderCol	98	3D Cylinder Column.
xlCylinderColClustered	92	Clustered Cone Column.
xlCylinderColStacked	93	Stacked Cone Column.
xlCylinderColStacked100	94	100% Stacked Cylinder Column.
xlDoughnut	–4120	Doughnut.
xlDoughnutExploded	80	Exploded Doughnut.
xlLine	4	Line.
xlLineMarkers	65	Line with Markers.
xlLineMarkersStacked	66	Stacked Line with Markers.
xlLineMarkersStacked100	67	100% Stacked Line with Markers.
xlLineStacked	63	Stacked Line.
xlLineStacked100	64	100% Stacked Line.
xlPie	5	Pie.
xlPieExploded	69	Exploded Pie.
xlPieOfPie	68	Pie of Pie.
xlPyramidBarClustered	109	Clustered Pyramid Bar.
xlPyramidBarStacked	110	Stacked Pyramid Bar.
xlPyramidBarStacked100	111	100% Stacked Pyramid Bar.
xlPyramidCol	112	3D Pyramid Column.
xlPyramidColClustered	106	Clustered Pyramid Column.
xlPyramidColStacked	107	Stacked Pyramid Column.
xlPyramidColStacked100	108	100% Stacked Pyramid Column.
xlRadar	–4151	Radar.
xlRadarFilled	82	Filled Radar.
xlRadarMarkers	81	Radar with Data Markers.
xlStockHLC	88	High-Low-Close.
xlStockOHLC	89	Open-High-Low-Close.
xlStockVHLC	90	Volume-High-Low-Close.

continued

continued ➡

XlChartType Constants (continued)

CONSTANT	VALUE	CHART TYPE
xlStockVOHLC	91	Volume-Open-High-Low-Close.
xlSurface	83	3D Surface.
xlSurfaceTopView	85	Top View Surface.
xlSurfaceTopViewWireframe	86	Top View Wireframe Surface.
xlSurfaceWireframe	84	3D Surface Wireframe.
xlXYScatter	–4169	Scatter.
xlXYScatterLines	74	Scatter with Lines.
xlXYScatterLinesNoMarkers	75	Scatter with Lines and No Data Markers.
xlXYScatterSmooth	72	Scatter with Smoothed Lines.
xlXYScatterSmoothNoMarkers	73	Scatter with Smoothed Lines and No Data Markers.

XlLineStyle Constants

CONSTANT	VALUE	DESCRIPTION
xlContinuous	1	Continuous solid line.
xlDash	–4155	Dashed line.
xlDashDot	4	Line with the pattern dash dot.
xlDashDotDot	5	Line with the pattern dash dot dot.
xlDot	–4118	Dotted line.
xlDouble	–4119	Double solid line.
xlSlantDashDot	13	Slanted line with the pattern dash dot.
xlLineStyleNone	–4142	No line.

XlBorderWeight Constants

CONSTANT	VALUE	DESCRIPTION
xlHairline	1	Creates a very thin line.
xlMedium	–4138	Creates a medium width line.
xlThick	4	Creates a thick line.
xlThin	2	Creates a thin line.

XlPattern Constants

CONSTANT	VALUE	DESCRIPTION
xlPatternAutomatic	–4105	System default.
xlPatternChecker	9	Checkered pattern.
xlPatternCrissCross	16	Criss-cross pattern.
xlPatternDown	–4121	Downward pattern.
xlPatternGray25	–4124	25% gray pattern.
xlPatternGray50	–4125	50% gray pattern.
xlPatternGray75	–4126	75% gray pattern.
xlPatternGrid	15	Grid pattern.
xlPatternHorizontal	–4128	Horizontal pattern.
xlPatternLightHorizontal	11	Light horizontal pattern.
xlPatternLightVertical	12	Light vertical pattern.
xlPatternLightDown	13	Light downward pattern.
xlPatternLightUp	14	Light upward pattern.
xlPatternNone	–4142	No pattern.
xlPatternSemiGray75	10	75% semi-gray pattern.
xlPatternSolid	1	Solid color, no pattern.
xlPatternUp	–4162	Upward pattern.
xlPatternVertical	–4166	Vertical pattern.

XlYesNoGuess Constants

CONSTANT	VALUE	DESCRIPTION
xlGuess	0	Allows Excel to determine whether data has a header.
xlNo	2	The data does not have a header.
xlYes	1	The data has a header.

XlPasteSpecialOperation Constants

CONSTANT	VALUE	DESCRIPTION
xlPasteSpecialOperationAdd	2	Adds.
xlPasteSpecialOperationDivide	5	Divides.
xlPasteSpecialOperationMultiply	4	Multiplies.
xlPasteSpecialOperationNone	–4142	Does not perform a mathematical operation.
xlPasteSpecialOperationSubtract	3	Subtracts.

INDEX

SYMBOLS

& (ampersand), as concatenation operator, 56
' (apostrophe), 43, 48
* (asterisk) wildcard character, 139
/ (division), as arithmetic operator, 58–59
= (equals) operator, 70–71, 86
^ (exponential), as arithmetic operator, 58–59
> (greater than) operator, 86
>= (greater than or equal to) operator, 86
\ (integer division), as arithmetic operator, 58–59
< (less than) operator, 86
<= (less than or equal to) operator, 86
- (minus sign), as arithmetic operator, 58–59
* (multiplication), as arithmetic operator, 58–59
<> (not equal) operator, 86
+ (plus sign), 56, 58–59, 107
(pound signs) in cells, 197
? (question mark) wildcard character, 139
_ (underscore), 105

A

absolute reference, 9
accessing
  Edit toolbar, 49
  Excel Object Model Reference, 64–65
  Options dialog box, 35
  Visual Basic Editor (VBE), 27
activating
  Visual Basic Editor (VBE), 19, 28–29
  workbooks, 145
Add Watch dialog box, 124–125
adding
  borders, 208–209
  comments to cells, 202–203
  customUI.xml file to workbook, 252–253
  data series to charts, 264–265
  data tables to charts, 270–271
  fields to PivotTables, 274–275
  Form Controls to worksheets, 20–21
  groups to tabs, 249
  macros to Form Controls, 24–25
  modules, 36–37

  options to Ribbon, 254–257
  pages to toolbox, 243
  sheets, 152–153
add-ins
  creating, 300–301
  installing, 304–305
  loading with VBA, 306–307
  removing, 305
  setting properties, 302–303
  third-party, 303
Add-Ins dialog box, 307
ampersand (&), as concatenation operator, 56
And logical operator, 87
apostrophe ('), 43, 48
application events, 283
applying
  Chart Wizard settings to charts, 262–263
  templates to charts, 263
Areas collection, 179
arguments, 45, 72
arrays
  assigning content to cells, 79
  converting lists to, 80–81
  declaring, 76–79
  functions, 80–81, 326–333
  redimensioning, 82–83
  resizing, 81
Assign Macro dialog box, 25
assigning
  array contents to cells, 79
  digital signatures to macros, 10–11
  file properties, 311
  macros
    to buttons, 25
    to pictures, 15
    to Quick Access toolbar, 16–17
    to Ribbon tab, 17
  numbers to cells, 59
  values
    to Form Controls, 22–23
    to user-defined arrays, 84
asterisk (*) wildcard character, 139
attributes
  font, 177
  XML, 308

B

Boolean, 52
borders, adding, 208–209
Break mode (VBE), 123
breakpoints, debugging procedures with inserted, 122–123
Button control, 21
buttons, assigning macros to, 25
ByVal keyword, 289

C

Call keyword, 102–103
calling
  custom dialog boxes from procedures, 234–235
  procedures, 102–103
capturing input from custom dialog boxes, 236–239
case sensitivity (keyboard shortcuts), 14
cell ranges
  combining multiple, 178–179
  copying and pasting, 198–199
  copying to multiple sheets, 206–207
  cutting and pasting, 196–197
  deleting, 182–183
  filling automatically, 204–205
  hiding, 184–185
  inserting, 190–191
  monitoring, 298–299
  referencing, 50–51
  resizing, 188–189
  setting
    column width, 192–193
    row height, 194–195
cells
  adding comments to, 202–203
  assigning
    array contents to, 79
    numbers to, 59
  inserting values in, 191
  linking to controls, 22
  referencing, 50–51
  selecting, 175
  values
    finding, 210–211
    finding and replacing, 212–213

Change Chart Type dialog box, 263
changing
  case of strings, 118–119
  control property values, 233
  object properties, 27, 68–69
  object properties with With statement, 68–69
  project names, 32
chart sheets, 258–259, 261
chart text, formatting, 266–267
Chart Wizard, 262–263
charts
  adding
    data series to, 264–265
    data tables to, 270–271
  applying
    Chart Wizard settings to, 262–263
    templates to, 263
  creating multiple chart type charts, 268–269
  embedding in worksheets, 260–261
  events, 281
  protecting, 168–169
  saving designs as templates, 263
Check Box control, 21
check boxes, 257
clearing print area, 171
closing workbooks, 146–147
code
  commenting, 48–49
  indenting, 97
  labeling, 101
  stepping through, 126–127
Code window (VBE), 26, 31, 34–35
color (font), 69
columns
  converting, 214–215
  setting width, 192–193
combination chart, 268
combining multiple ranges, 178–179
comment lines, 43
commenting (code), 48–49
comments, adding to cells, 202–203
comparisons, creating, 86
concatenation, 56
Conditional Sum Wizard, 304
constants. *See also specific constants*
  creating, 60–61
  defined, 45

INDEX

E

F

INDEX

INDEX

INDEX

INDEX

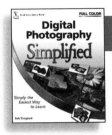

...all designed for visual learners—just like you!

For more professional instruction in a visual format, try these.

All designed for visual learners—just like you!

978-0-470-59161-1

978-0-470-34520-7

978-0-470-55651-1

For a complete listing of *Visual Blueprint*™ titles and other
Visual books, go to wiley.com/go/visual